THE ARCHIVE AND THE REPERTOIRE

A John Hope Franklin Center Book

THE ARCHIVE AND THE REPERTOIRE

Performing Cultural Memory in the Americas *Diana Taylor*

DUKE UNIVERSITY PRESS DURHAM AND LONDON 2003

© 2003 Duke University Press   All rights reserved
Printed in the United States of America on acid-free paper ⊗
Designed by Rebecca M. Giménez   Typeset in Trump Medieval
by Tseng Information Systems   Library of Congress Cataloging-
in-Publication Data appear on the last printed page of this book.
Acknowledgments for the use of copyrighted material appear on
page 328 and constitute an extension of the copyright page.

To Susanita and Halfcito,

one more offering for your altar

And to Marina,

who helps me light the candles

CONTENTS

LIST OF ILLUSTRATIONS

WHO, WHEN, WHAT, WHY

As a child growing up in a small mining town in the north of Mexico, I learned that the Americas were one, that we shared a hemisphere. Many years later, when I arrived in the United States to do my doctorate, I heard that "America" meant the United States. There were two hemispheres, north and south, and although Mexico technically belonged to the northern hemisphere, people usually relegated it to the south—part of "Latin America." Years later, I observed in my daughter's Rand McNally *Picture Atlas of the World* (1993 edition) that the Americas had been divided in three, and Mexico and Central America were called "Middle America," a term that accomplished the linguistic distantiation that the land formation refused to justify. I never accepted this steady attempt at deterritorialization. I claim my identity as an "American" in the hemispheric sense. That means I have lived comfortably, or perhaps uncomfortably, in various overlapping worlds.

My academic career began in a one-room schoolhouse in Parral, Chihuahua, a dusty little town whose only claim to fame was that the great revolutionary leader Pancho Villa had been shot to death there. This was a poor little classroom with a corrugated metal roof reserved for the children of the miners. My father, who ran away from Canada at the age of twenty-one, was a mining engineer. My mother, a student of Northrop Frye whose life's calling was to read who-done-its, would drive me up the crooked dirt road to school. We never knew what grade we were in. Magically, it seemed, we passed from first to second, from second to third. We never got grades; there were no parent-teacher conferences, no progress reports. Just as magically, we graduated. I was nine years old.

I loved my little town. I considered everyone in it my friend. Don Luis owned the pharmacy and lived in the apartment above it with his beautiful wife, who invited me to tea; they were rumored to be rich, owning miles and miles of splendid poppy fields and all sorts of refining machinery that stirred local imaginations. Their assistant, my school friend's father, was found dead one morning, cut up into tiny pieces and hanging in a sack from a tree branch—a message of sorts, though indecipherable to me then. Don Jacinto was the garbage collector who rescued precious items for us kids, like soda bottle caps that hid prizes behind the cork liners. Doña Esperanza, a homeless woman, carried a small metal suitcase full of rocks to throw at her many enemies. She trusted me; we'd sit, legs dangling from the bridge over the dry riverbed, and she'd open her metal case to show me her rocks. In turn, I pulled out the tiny pebbles I saved for her in my pockets. Twice a year, the Tarahumara (the indigenous group Artaud so admired) would come down from the mountains to buy staples. Our worlds didn't touch; I never knew why. We didn't speak their language. We knew little about their way of life. We'd just watch them come and go—another lesson in indecipherability.

If I was going to study, my parents insisted, I had to go away. "You'll go to boarding school in Toronto," my mother said. "You'll like it there. You'll be close to Gramma. But you have to learn English." This meant learning more than the one word I had already perfected, though the way I pronounced it stretched over so many syllables I thought it was a complete sentence: sonofabitché. I remember standing there, in my cowboy boots, my plaid skirt with antigravity suspenders, my brown suede jacket with the fringe, and the pebbles in my pockets. My braids were pulled back so tight I couldn't close my eyes. My little gold scissor earrings that opened and shut dangled from my ears. I promised: "Sí mamá. I learna da inglish." So off I went to Canada, announced back then as my extended home, part of my Américas.

My Gramma stiffened in disapproval. She hated the boots, the jacket, the pigtails, and reminded me that only savages pierced their body. My education, she warned, was about to begin. I tried to change the subject and make polite conversation. "Gramma, how's your cancer?"

During my four years in boarding school, I had to learn new languages—not just the English, French, and Latin that were required. Twice daily, I had to participate in the ritual incantations of High Anglicanism. In response to the demands for weekly offerings, I stuffed buttons in the collection box, holding my skirt and blazer together with safety pins. I hid my plastic Virgen de Guadalupe in a box behind the chest of drawers. I also had to learn a new body language. Off went the Wild West outfit; on came the blazer and tie, the gray skirt, the button-down white shirt, the oxford shoes and knee-highs. I learned to eat sitting up straight, with a book on my head and a newspaper tucked under each arm. They cut my hair; gone forever were my beloved gold scissor earrings that opened and closed. My body, my head, my heart, and my tongue were in training. My small acts of resistance, inspired by my hero Pancho Villa, ran up against the disciplinary machine. My punishments were so regular that they became part of my weekly schedule: I had to run around the school twenty times at 6 A.M. on weekend mornings, while the rest of the girls slept. My teachers smacked me with hairbrushes, made me chew aspirins, and tried teaching me to spin wool so that I'd stop fidgeting. The goal, the headmistress informed me, was that I should become a respectable Anglo gentlewoman, a worthy companion for Canada's brightest and best.

I am delighted to report that, for me at least, the training failed miserably. Yet, when I returned home—now Mexico City—at fourteen, I knew I wasn't Canadian, but I no longer felt completely Mexican. While a citizen of the Américas, I was/am not a happy NAFTA subject, a product of "free" markets and cultural zones. In a world set up in terms of "First World" and "Third World," "white" and "brown," "us" and "them," I wasn't them but I wasn't us either. I wasn't Anglican, but I wasn't Catholic. Ironically, perhaps, that led me to identify with everything, rather than nothing. Identifying with everything rather than nothing may amount to the same thing, but the spirit behind it was far from nihilistic: I overflowed with identifications, white and brown, English- and Spanish-speaking, Anglican and Catholic, us and them. Mine felt like an entangled surplus subjectivity, full of tugs, pressures, and pleasures. I continue to embody these tugs through a series of conflicting practices and tensions.

Because it's been impossible for me to separate my scholarly and political commitments and conundrums from who I am, the essays in this book reflect a range of tone and personal intervention in the discussions. The first three chapters particularly map out the theoretical questions that inform the chapters that follow: How does expressive behavior (performance) transmit cultural memory and identity? Would a hemispheric perspective expand the restrictive scenarios and paradigms set in motion by centuries of colonialism? Although the theoretical implications are no less pressing, the tone in the remaining chapters becomes increasingly personal. As my reflections come out of my own role as participant in or witness to the events I describe, I feel compelled to acknowledge my own involvement and sense of urgency. And, as I argue throughout, we learn and transmit knowledge through embodied action, through cultural agency, and by making choices. Performance, for me, functions as an episteme, a way of knowing, not simply an object of analysis. By situating myself as one more social actor in the scenarios I analyze, I hope to position my personal and theoretical investment in the arguments. I chose not to smooth out the differences in tone, but rather let them speak to the tensions between who I am and what I do.

I wrote this book during the five years that I served as chair of performance studies at NYU, and it reflects many of the conversations that we had around the department's odd, wobbly, crescent-shaped table in the room composed of windows we call the fish bowl. How would we define performance? What would we include in an Introduction to Performance Studies course? Should performance studies—defined by some of us as postdisciplinary, others as interdisciplinary, others as antidisciplinary, others as predisciplinary—have a canon? Who would define it? How can we think about performance in historical terms, when the archive cannot capture and store the live event? I still hear those voices and debates: Fred Moten resisting canons of all kinds, while Barbara Kirshenblatt-Gimblett tried to organize the area exam lists. Richard Schechner and Peggy Phelan would debate whether we could even speak of an "ontology" of performance, while Barbara Browning, José Muñoz, and André Lepecki joined the fray on different sides of the lines. Ngugi wa Thiong'o, always a calming presence, and I spoke of teaching a course on the politics of public space, or perhaps on language rights. All of us sitting there, faculty and often students, came from different academic and personal backgrounds and brought different takes on each issue. One of the things I like most about our conversations is that we never really agreed, and we still haven't succeeded in formulating a clear party, or even departmental, line. The open-endedness and multivocality of performance studies is an administrative challenge (How to devise a meaningful curriculum, or reading exam lists?), but they prove, I believe, the field's greatest promise. However we position ourselves in relation to other disciplines, we have been wary of disciplinary boundaries that preclude certain connections and areas of analysis. So we've kept talking, and even as the individuals around the table change, the conversations keep going. Inevitably, these debates linger throughout the book, not because my colleagues and students are my ideal audience, but because they have been close interlocutors as I wrote.

Some of the questions took on a special urgency for me as a "Latin/o Americanist." Is performance that which disappears, or that which persists, transmitted through a nonarchival system of transfer that I came to call the *repertoire*? My book *Disappearing Acts* had already engaged with the politics of disappearance: the forced absenting of individuals by Argentina's military forces and the paradoxical omnipresence of the disappeared. My scholarly and political commitment to these issues continued through the Hemispheric Institute of Performance and Politics, a consortium that I organized and directed during this same period (http://hemi.nyu.edu). Scholars, artists, and activists throughout the Americas work together in annual *encuentros* (two-week festivals/work groups) through graduate-level, interdisciplinary courses and online work groups to explore how performance transmits memories, makes political claims, and manifests a group's sense of identity. For all of us, the political implications of the project were clear. If performance did not transmit knowledge, only the literate and powerful could claim social memory and identity.

This book, then, constitutes my personal intervention in two fields: performance studies and Latin/o American (hemispheric) studies. Here, I try to put these fields in conversation. How does each expand what we can think in the other? How can performance studies' nervousness about disciplinary boundaries help us destabilize the ways in which the field of "Latin American" studies has been constituted in the United States? Like other area studies, Latin American studies emerged as a result of cold war efforts by the U.S. government to advance "intelligence," language competence, and influence in countries to the south. Consequently, it tends to maintain a unidirectional north-to-south focus, with the U.S. analyst posited as the unseen, unexamined see-er. Hemispheric studies could potentially counter the Latin

American studies of the mid-twentieth century and the NAFTAism of the late twentieth century by exploring histories of the north and south as profoundly intertwined. It allows us to connect histories of conquest, colonialism, slavery, indigenous rights, imperialism, migration, and globalization (to name some issues) throughout the Americas. Circulation in the Americas includes the military traffic in peoples, weapons, drugs, "intelligence," and expertise. It includes the culture industries: television, film, music. It includes practices associated with languages, religious practices, food, style, and embodied performances. If, however, we were to reorient the ways social memory and cultural identity in the Americas have traditionally been studied, with the disciplinary emphasis on literary and historical documents, and look through the lens of performed, embodied behaviors, what would we know that we do not know now? Whose stories, memories, and struggles might become visible? What tensions might performance behaviors show that would not be recognized in texts and documents?

Conversely, "Latin American" studies (like other area studies) has much to offer performance studies. The historical debates concerning the nature and role of performance in the transmission of social knowledge and memory, which I trace to sixteenth-century Mesoamerica, allow us to think about embodied practice in a broader framework that complicates prevalent understandings. Performance studies, due to its historical development, reflects the 1960s conjunction of anthropology, theatre studies, and the visual arts. It also reflects a predominantly English-speaking, First World positioning; most of the scholarship in the field has been produced in the United States, Great Britain, and Australia. But there is nothing inherently "Western" or necessarily avant-garde about the field. The methodology we associate with performance studies can and should be revised constantly through engagement with other regional, political, and linguistic realities. So, although I contest the parochialism of some performance studies scholarship, I am not suggesting that we merely *extend* our analytic practice to other "non-Western" areas. Rather, what I propose here is a real engagement between two fields that helps us rethink both.

Embodied performances have always played a central role in conserving memory and consolidating identities in literate, semiliterate, and digital societies. Not everyone comes to "culture" or modernity through writing. I believe it is imperative to keep reexamining the relationships between embodied performance and the production of knowledge. We might look to past practices considered by some to have disappeared. We might look to contemporary practices by populations usually dismissed as "backward" (indigenous and marginalized communities). Or we might explore the relationship of embodied practice to knowledge by studying how young people today learn through digital technologies. If people without writing are said to have vanished without a trace, how can we think about the invisibilized body online? It is difficult to think about embodied practice within the epistemic systems developed in Western thought, where writing has become the guarantor of existence itself.

The book is intensely personal in another way as well. On January 27, 2001, my closest friends, Susana and Half Zantop, were brutally murdered by two teenage boys in their home in New Hampshire. It was a Saturday afternoon; Susana was making lunch, Half was puttering around, doing chores. Out of the blue . . . Later that year, as I was walking out of the gym, I saw the World Trade Center down the street, on fire. A plane had hit it, someone on the street told me, out of the blue. The terror of those events affected us profoundly. The world has changed for me and for those I love during the time I wrote this book. I dedicate this book to Susana and Half, who did not survive the horror. But I also dedicate it to those who did: their daughters, Veronika and Mariana, my husband, Eric Manheimer, and our children, Alexei and Marina, and my sister, Susan. We are still struggling to learn how to live in this very strange new world.

I want to thank the close friends who have sustained me with their love and conversations during this period and over the past few years. Some are my daily interlocutors, whether in the steam room, the gym, the sushi bar, or the coffee shop. I feel their presence throughout this work: Marianne Hirsch, Richard Schechner, Barbara Kirshenblatt-Gimblett, Leo Spitzer, Sylvia Molloy, Lorie Novak, Faye Ginsburg, José Muñoz, Una Chaudhuri, Mary Louise Pratt, and Fred Myers. Others I see less often, but they remain such a close presence that I can hear their comments before I speak with them: Doris Sommer, Agnes Lugo-Ortíz, Mary C. Kelley, Silvia Spitta, Rebecca Schneider, Jill Lane, Leda Martins, Diana Raznovich, Luis Peirano, Annelise Orleck, Alexis Jetter, and Roxana Verona. What would I do without my family and friends? That's one question I never want to explore.

I also want to thank those who have helped me in other ways. David

Román encouraged me to write a short commentary on tragedy for a special volume he was editing for *Theatre Journal*, an invitation that got me writing again after September 11 and inspired the final chapter of this book. Thanks to my wonderful graduate students and assistants at NYU, all fellow hauntologists, especially Alyshia Galvez, Marcela Fuentes, Shanna Lorenz, Karen Jaime, and Fernando Calzadilla. Karen Young and Ayanna Lee of the Hemispheric Institute of Performance and Politics help make my life easier on a daily basis. Ken Wissoker, Christine Dahlin, and Pam Morrison of Duke University Press have offered steady support.

As figure 2 of this study indicates, the production of knowledge is always a collective effort, a series of back-and-forth conversations that produce multiple results. The Náhuatl-speaking informant tells his story to the Náhuatl-speaking scribe, who in turn passes it to the translator, who transmits it to the Spanish-speaking scribe, who tells the Spanish friar, the official recipient, organizer, and transmitter of the written document. He in turn gives his version, which will make its way back to the Nahua informant. The document also finds its way into the public arena, where it is met with debates ranging from censorious disapproval to profound gratitude. Back and forth. The versions change with each transmission, and each creates slips, misses, and new interpretations that result in a somewhat new original. In this study too, I build on what I have received from others and attempt to contribute to the debate and pass it back into the public arena for more discussion. The slips and misses are, of course, my own.

ACTS OF TRANSFER

From June 14 to 23, 2001, the Hemispheric Institute of Performance and Politics convened artists, activists, and scholars from the Americas for its second annual Encuentro (encounter) to share the ways our work uses performance to intervene in the political scenarios we care about.[1] Everyone understood the "politics," but "performance" was more difficult. For some artists, *performance* (as it is called in Latin America) referred to performance art. Others played with the term. Jesusa Rodríguez, Mexico's most outrageous and powerful cabaret/performance artist, referred to the three hundred participants as *performenzos* (*menzos* means idiots).[2] *Performnuts* might be the best translation, and most of her spectators would agree that you have to be crazy to do what she does, confronting the Mexican state and the Catholic Church head-on. Tito Vasconcelos, one of the first out gay performers from the early 1980s in Mexico, came onstage as Marta Sahagún, then lover, now wife of Mexico's president, Vicente Fox. In her white suit and matching pumps, she welcomed the audience to the conference of *perfumance*. Smiling, she admitted that she didn't understand what it was about, and acknowledged that nobody gave a damn about what we did, but she welcomed us to do it anyway. *PerFORwhat?* the confused woman in Diana Raznovich's cartoon asks. The jokes and puns, though good humored, revealed

1. "PerForwhat Studies?"
Cartoon by Diana Raznovich, 2000.
Reproduced by permission.

both an anxiety of definition and the promise of a new arena for further interventions.

PERFoRWHAT STUDIES?

This study, like the Hemispheric Institute, proposes that performance studies can contribute to our understanding of Latin American—and hemispheric—performance traditions by rethinking nineteenth-century disciplinary and national boundaries and by focusing on embodied behaviors. Conversely, the debates dating back to the sixteenth century about the nature and function of performance practices in the Americas can expand the theoretical scope of a postdiscipline-come-lately that has, due to its context, focused more on the future and ends of performance than on its historical practice. Finally, it is urgent to focus on the specific characteristics of performance in a cultural environment in which corporations promote "world" music and international organizations (such as UNESCO) and funding organizations make decisions about "world" cultural rights and "intangible heritage."

Performances function as vital acts of transfer, transmitting social knowledge, memory, and a sense of identity through reiterated, or what Richard

Schechner has called "twice-behaved behavior."[3] "Performance," on one level, constitutes the object/process of analysis in performance studies, that is, the many practices and events—dance, theatre, ritual, political rallies, funerals—that involve theatrical, rehearsed, or conventional/event-appropriate behaviors. These practices are usually bracketed off from those around them to constitute discrete foci of analysis. Sometimes, that framing is part of the event itself—a particular dance or a rally has a beginning and an end; it does not run continuously or seamlessly into other forms of cultural expression. To say something *is* a performance amounts to an ontological affirmation, though a thoroughly localized one. What one society considers a performance might be a nonevent elsewhere.

On another level, performance also constitutes the methodological lens that enables scholars to analyze events *as* performance.[4] Civic obedience, resistance, citizenship, gender, ethnicity, and sexual identity, for example, are rehearsed and performed daily in the public sphere. To understand these *as* performance suggests that performance also functions as an epistemology. Embodied practice, along with and bound up with other cultural practices, offers a way of knowing. The bracketing for these performances comes from outside, from the methodological lens that organizes them into an analyzable "whole." Performance and aesthetics of everyday life vary from community to community, reflecting cultural and historical specificity as much in the enactment as in the viewing/reception. (Whereas reception changes in both the live and the media performance, only in the live does the act itself change.) Performances travel, challenging and influencing other performances. Yet they are, in a sense, always in situ: intelligible in the framework of the immediate environment and issues surrounding them. The *is/as* underlines the understanding of performance as simultaneously "real" and "constructed," as practices that bring together what have historically been kept separate as discrete, supposedly free-standing, ontological and epistemological discourses.

The many uses of the word performance point to the complex, seemingly contradictory, and at times mutually sustaining or complicated layers of referentiality. Victor Turner bases his understanding on the French etymological root, *parfournir*, "to furnish forth," " 'to complete' or 'carry out thoroughly.' "[5] From French, the term moved into English as *performance* in the 1500s, and since the sixteenth and seventeenth centuries has been used much as it is today.[6] For Turner, writing in the 1960s and 1970s, performances revealed culture's deepest, truest, and most individual character. Guided by a belief in their universality and relative transparency, he claimed that populations could grow to understand each other through their performances.[7] For others, of course, performance means just the opposite: the constructedness of performance signals its artificiality—it is "put on," antithetical to the "real" and "true." In some cases, the emphasis on the constructedness of performance reveals an antitheatrical prejudice; in more complex readings, the constructed is recognized as coterminous with the real. Although a dance, a ritual, or a manifestation requires bracketing or framing that differentiate it from other social practices surrounding it, this does not imply that the performance is not real or true. On the contrary, the idea that performance distills a "truer" truth than life itself runs from Aristotle through Shakespeare and Calderón de la Barca, through Artaud and Grotowski and into the present. People in business fields seem to use the term more than anyone else, though usually to mean that a person, or more often a thing, acts up to one's potential. Supervisors evaluate workers' efficacy on the job, their performance, just as cars and computers and the markets supposedly vie to outperform their rivals. *Perform or Else*, Jon McKenzie's title, aptly captures the imperative to reach required business (and cultural) standards. Political consultants understand that performance as *style* rather than as *carrying through* or *accomplishment* often determines political outcome. Science too has begun exploration into reiterated human behavior and expressive culture through memes: "Memes are stories, songs, habits, skills, inventions, and ways of doing things that we copy from person to person by imitation"—in short, the reiterative acts that I have been calling performance, though clearly performance does not necessarily involve mimetic behaviors.[8]

In performance studies thus, notions about the definition, role, and function of performance vary widely. Is performance always and only about embodiment? Or does it call into question the very contours of the body, challenging traditional notions of embodiment? Since ancient times, performance has manipulated, extended, and played with embodiment—this intense experimentation did not begin with Laurie Anderson. Digital technologies will further ask us to reformulate our understanding of "presence," site (now the unlocalizable online "site"), the ephemeral, and embodiment. The debates proliferate.

One example of the spectrum of understanding is the debate over performance's staying power. Coming from a Lacanian position, Peggy Phelan delimits the life of performance to the present: "Performance cannot be saved, recorded, documented, or otherwise participate in the circulation of representations of representation. . . . Performance's being, like the ontology of subjectivity proposed here, becomes itself through disappearance."[9] Joseph Roach, on the other hand, extends the understanding of performance by making it coterminous with memory and history. As such, it participates in the transfer and continuity of knowledge: "Performance genealogies draw on the idea of expressive movements as mnemonic reserves, including patterned movements made and remembered by bodies, residual movements retained implicitly in images or words (or in the silences between them), and imaginary movements dreamed in minds not prior to language but constitutive of it."[10] Debates about the "ephemerality" of performance are, of course, profoundly political. Whose memories, traditions, and claims to history disappear if performance practices lack the staying power to transmit vital knowledge?

Scholars coming from philosophy and rhetoric (such as J. L. Austin, Jacques Derrida, and Judith Butler) have coined terms such as *performative* and *performativity*. A performative, for Austin, refers to cases in which "the issuing of the utterance is the performing of an action."[11] In some cases, the reiteration and bracketing I associated with performance earlier is clear: it is within the conventional framework of a marriage ceremony that the words "I do" carry legal weight.[12] Others have continued to develop Austin's notion of the performative in many diverse ways. Derrida, for example, goes further in underlining the importance of the citationality and iterability in the "event of speech," questioning whether "a performative statement [could] succeed if its formulation did not repeat a 'coded' or iterable statement."[13] However, the framing that sustains Butler's use of *performativity*— the process of socialization whereby gender and sexuality identities (for example) are produced through regulating and citational practices—is harder to identify because normalization has rendered it invisible. Whereas in Austin, performative points to language that acts, in Butler it goes in the opposite direction, subsuming subjectivity and cultural agency into normative discursive practice. In this trajectory, the performative becomes less a quality (or adjective) of "performance" than of discourse. Although it may be too late to reclaim performative for the nondiscursive realm of performance, I suggest that we borrow a word from the contemporary Spanish usage of performance—*performático* or performatic in English—to denote the adjectival form of the nondiscursive realm of performance. Why is this important? Because it is vital to signal the performatic, digital, and visual fields as separate from, though always embroiled with, the discursive one so privileged by Western logocentricism. The fact that we don't have a word to signal that performatic space is a product of that same logocentricism rather than a confirmation that there's no there there.

Thus, one of the problems in using performance, and its misleading cognates performative and performativity, comes from the extraordinarily broad range of behaviors it covers, from the discrete dance, to technologically mediated performance, to conventional cultural behavior. However, this multilayeredness indicates the deep interconnections of all these systems of intelligibility and the productive frictions among them. As the different uses of the term/concept—scholarly, political, scientific, and business-related—rarely engage each other directly, performance also has a history of untranslatability. Ironically, the word itself has been locked into the disciplinary and geographic boxes it defies, denied the universality and transparency that some claim it promises its foci of analysis. Of course, these many points of untranslatability are what make the term and the practices theoretically enabling and culturally revealing. Performances may not, as Turner had hoped, give us access and insight into another culture, but they certainly tell us a great deal about our desire for access, and reflect the politics of our interpretations.

Part of this undefinability characterizes performance studies as a field. When it emerged in the 1970s, a product of the social and disciplinary upheavals of the late 1960s that rocked academe, it sought to bridge the disciplinary divide between anthropology and theatre by looking at social dramas, liminality, and enactment as a way out of structuralist notions of normativity. Performance studies, which, as I indicated above, is certainly no one thing, clearly grew out of these disciplines even as it rejected their boundaries. In doing so, it inherited some of the assumptions and method-ological blind spots of anthropology and theatre studies even as it attempted to transcend their ideological formation. However, it is equally important to keep in mind that anthropology and theatre studies were (and are) composed of various different, often conflicted, streams. Here, then, I can offer only a few quick examples of how some of the disciplinary preoccupations and methodological limitations get transferred in thinking about performance.

From the anthropology of the 1970s, performance studies inherited its radical break with notions of normative behavior promulgated by sociologist Emile Durkheim, who argued that the social condition of humans (rather than individual agency) accounts for behaviors and beliefs.[14] Those who dis-agreed with this structuralist position argued that culture was not a reified given but an arena of social dispute in which social actors came together to struggle for survival. From the wing commonly referred to as the "drama-turgical," anthropologists such as Turner, Milton Singer, Erving Goffman, and Clifford Geertz began to write of individuals as agents in their own dra-mas. Norms, they argued, are contested, not merely applied. Analyzing en-actment became crucial in establishing claims to cultural agency. Humans do not simply adapt to systems. They shape them. How do we recognize ele-ments such as choice, timing, and self-presentation except through the ways in which individuals and groups perform them? The dramaturgical model also highlighted aesthetic and ludic components of social events as well as the in-betweenness of liminality and symbolic reversal.

Part of the linguistic stream, anthropologists such as Dell Hymes, Richard Bauman, Charles Briggs, Gregory Bateson, and Michele Rosaldo were influ-enced by thinkers such as J. L. Austin, John Searle, and Ferdinand de Saus-sure, who focused on the performative function of communication—*parole*, in Saussure's term.[15] Again, as with the dramaturgical model, the linguis-tic emphasized the cultural agency at work in the use of language: How, to play on Austin's title, did people do things with words? Like the dramatur-gical model, this too stressed the creativity at play in the use of language, as speakers and their audiences worked together to produce successful ver-bal performances. The linguistic stream was also invested in recognizing the creativity in the everyday life of other people, ways of using language that were resourceful, specific, and "authentic."

While performance scholars readily adopted the project of taking embodied enactments seriously as a way of understanding how people manage their lives, they also absorbed the Western positioning of anthropology that continued to wrestle with its colonial heritage. The "us" studying and writing about "them" was, of course, a part of a colonialist project that anthropology had come out of, though the scholars working in the 1970s were trying to break away from the paradigm that fetishized the local, denied agency to the peoples they studied, and excluded them from the circulation of knowledge created about them. Yet communication, for the most part, continued to be unidirectional. "They" did not have access to "our" writing. This one-way writing practice revealed the ongoing ambivalence as to whether "they" occupied a different world—in space and time, whether we are interrelated and coeval. The unidirectionality of meaning making and communication also stemmed from and reflected the centuries-old privileging of written over embodied knowledge. Moreover, little thought was given to the many ways in which contact with the "non-Western" had, for centuries, shaped the very notion of "Western" identity. Some anthropologists and theatre scholars were heavily influenced by the modernist impulse to seek the authentic, "primitive," and somehow purer expression of the human condition in non-Western societies. Attempts in the literature of the 1970s to illustrate that these "others" were in fact fully human, with performance practices as meaningful as "our" own, betray the anxiety produced by colonialism about the status of non-Western subjects.

In spite of the decolonizing sentiments of many anthropologists in the 1970s, the explanatory frameworks they used were decidedly Western. To return to Turner, the most direct influence on performance studies due to his productive association with Richard Schechner, it is clear that whereas the concept of social drama has been foundational to performance studies, the universalist claims he makes for its ubiquity strain against the rather narrow filter he has for understanding it: Aristotelian drama. "No one," Turner asserts, "could fail to note the analogy, indeed the homology, between those sequences of supposedly 'spontaneous' events which make fully evident the tensions existing in those villages, and the characteristic 'processual form' of Western drama, from Aristotle onwards, or Western epic and saga, albeit on a limited or miniature scale." No one, that is, except for those who participated in the events without the slightest notion of these paradigms.[16] Preempting a perceived accusation of Eurocentrism, Turner writes, "The fact that a so-cial drama . . . closely corresponds to Aristotle's description of tragedy in the *Poetics*, in that it is 'complete, and whole, and of a certain magnitude . . . having a beginning, a middle, and an end,' is not, I repeat, because I have tried inappropriately to impose an 'etic' Western model of stage action upon the conduct of an African village society, but because there is an interdependent, perhaps dialectic, relationship between social dramas and genres of cultural performance in all societies" (72). Again, Turner's theories about events structured with a recognizable beginning, middle, and end may have less to do with the "supposedly 'spontaneous'" events than with his analytical lens. The lens, for him as for everyone else, reveals his (our) desires and interests. He may be correct in noting the interdependency of social and cultural performances *within* a specific society, yet it might be important to question whether and how this interdependency would work cross-culturally. Moreover, his position as an "objective" observer looking down on the "object" of analysis sets up the unequal, and distorting, perspective that results in the double gesture that characterizes much of the writing about performance practices in contexts other than our own. First, the observer claims to recognize what is happening in the performance of/by the Other. Somehow, this event is reified and interpreted by means of a preexisting Western paradigm. Second, the recognition is followed by a subtle (or not so subtle) put-down: this performance proves a "miniature" or diminished version of the "original."

From theatre studies—the "maternal" partner, according to Turner (9) —performance studies inherits another form of radicalism: its proclivity toward the avant-garde that values originality, the transgressive, and, again, the "authentic." This is a different but complementary operation: the non-Western is the raw material to be reworked and made "original" in the West. The presumption, of course, is that performance—now understood as drawing heavily from the visual arts and nonconventional theatrical representations, happenings, installations, body art, and performance art—is an aesthetic practice with its roots in either surrealism, dadaism, or earlier performance traditions such as cabaret, the living newspaper, and rituals of healing and possession. The avant-garde's emphasis on originality, ephemerality, and newness hides multiple rich and long traditions of performance practice. In 1969, for example, Michael Kirby, a founding member of the soon-to-be-created Department of Performance Studies at NYU, asserted that "environmental theatre is a recent development" associated with the avant-garde, even though he admits examples from the Greek theatre onward that could well be labeled by the same term. It's the "specific aesthetic element" that, for Kirby, differentiates it from earlier forms.[17] His emphasis on aesthetics, however, does not in fact set recent examples apart from earlier ones. Friar Motolinía, one of the first twelve Franciscans to reach the Americas in the sixteenth century, describes a Corpus Christi celebration in 1538 during which native participants from Tlaxcala created elaborate outdoor platforms "all of gold and feather work" as well as entire mountains and forests populated with both artificial and live animals that were "a marvellous thing to see" and through which spectators/participants walked to gain a "natural" effect.[18] Claims such as the one put forth by Kirby in the late 1960s epitomize the period's self-conscious obsession with the new, as it forgot or ignored what was already there. These kinds of assertions prompted accusations that the nascent field of performance studies was ahistorical if not antihistorical.

There are many more examples of similar forgettings accompanied by new "discoveries" that once again restage the elisions of ties between Western and non-Western practices: Artaud inspired by the Tarahumara, Brecht's reliance on non-Western forms as a basis for his revolutionary aesthetics, Grotowski's interest in the Huichol, to name just the most obvious. Few theorists and practitioners—with notable exceptions—seriously think about the mutual construction of the Western/non-Western in the Americas. That would require that scholars learn the language of the people with whom they seek to interact and treat them as colleagues rather than as informants or objects of analysis. This, in turn, would mean that these new colleagues would remain in the loop of all the projects that involved them, from production, to distribution, to analysis. It would also entail a methodological shift, a rethinking about what counts as expertise or as valid source. It would demand the recognition of the permanent recycling of cultural materials and processes between the Western and non-Western. This reciprocal contact has been most commonly theorized in Latin America as *transculturation*. Transculturation denotes the transformative process undergone by all societies as they come in contact with and acquire foreign cultural material, whether willingly or unwillingly (see chapter 3). Transculturation has been going on forever.[19] But the cross-cultural discussions remain as strained as ever.

The nervousness surrounding the non-Western continues to haunt much of the writing on performance as an aesthetic practice. One example: Patrice Pavis, in his introductory blurb to the section "Historical Contexts" in *The Intercultural Performance Reader*, puts forward a defensive and somewhat paternalistic-sounding project: "We propose to start by bringing together documents and declarations of intent, without allowing ourselves to be intimidated by the hypocrites and bigots of 'political correctness.' In an area like this, we need to be both patient and calm. We are still in a phase of observing and surveying cultural practices, and our only ambition is to provide readers with a number of statements from an infinitely possible range, without the imposition of a global or universal theory to analyse these examples definitively."[20] Just thinking about how to deal with non-Western practices makes Pavis jittery. Claims of inclusion (the "infinitely possible range") no longer mask the practice of exclusion: not a single essay on Latin American performance, for example. Beleaguered Western critics must maintain the father-knows-best stance of patience and calm. Two or three decades after Turner and Kirby, many scholars have lost the easy assumptions regarding decipherability and newness. Pavis understands that "Western" theorists in the 1990s need to renounce claims of global or universalizing theory, though his emphasis on seemingly disinterested observation and survey reinscribe the dominance of the critical position. The statements and "historical" documents, all written by decidedly First-World theorists—Ericka Fischer-Lichte, Richard Schechner, and Josette Féral—set the stage. In a separate section, "Intercultural Performance from Another Point of View," Pavis includes "non-Western" perspectives, though he notes that most of those writing "either live, or have lived and worked, in the United States" (147). Still, they are "foreign" and "Other" and their views "do differ radically from those of the Euro-American interculturalists, being less self-assured" (147).

The double critical move highlights an area of concern (the non-Western) and negates it in the same move. It distances non-Western cultural production as radically other, and then attempts to encompass it within existing critical systems as diminished or disruptive elements. Performance, as Roach points out, is as much about forgetting as about remembering. The West has forgotten about the many parts of the world that elude its explanatory grasp. Yet, it remembers the need to cement the centrality of its position as the West by creating and freezing the non-West as always other, "foreign," and unknowable. Domination by culture, by "definition," by claims to originality and authenticity have functioned in tandem with military and economic supremacy.

Though ahistorical in some of its practice, there is nothing inherently ahistorical or Western about performance studies. Our methodologies can and should be revised constantly through engagement with other interlocutors as well as other regional, racial, political, and linguistic realities both within and beyond our national boundaries. This does not mean extending our existing paradigms to include other forms of cultural production. Nor does it justify limiting our range of interlocutors to those whose backgrounds and language skills resemble our own. What I am proposing is an active engagement and dialogue, however complicated. Performance has existed as long as people have existed, even though the field of study in its current form is relatively recent. Performance studies emerged on the academic scene with inherited baggage, and it has long tried to overcome and often succeeded in overcoming some of those limitations. The Eurocentrism and aestheticism of some theatre studies, for example, clash against anthropology's traditional focus on non-Western cultural practices as meaning-making systems. The belief by anthropologists such as Geertz that "doing ethnography is like trying to read . . . a manuscript—foreign, faded, full of ellipses" and that culture is an "acted document" runs up against theatre studies' insistence on everyone's active participation and reaction.[21] We are all in the picture, all social actors in our overlapping, coterminous, contentious dramas. Even Brechtian distanciation relies on notions that the spectators are keenly bound up with events happening onstage, not through identification but through participation, and they are often called on to intervene and change the course of the action.

In Latin America, where the term finds no satisfactory equivalent in either Spanish or Portuguese, *performance* has commonly referred to *performance art*. Translated simply but nonetheless ambiguously as *el performance* or *la performance,* a linguistic cross-dressing that invites English speakers to think about the sex/gender of performance, the word is beginning to be used more broadly to talk about social dramas and embodied practices.[22] People quite commonly refer now to *lo performático* as that which is related to performance in the broadest sense. In spite of charges that performance is an Anglo word and that there is no way of making it sound comfortable in either Spanish or Portuguese, scholars and practitioners are beginning to appreciate the multivocal and strategic qualities of the term. Although the word may be foreign and untranslatable, the debates, decrees, and strategies arising from the many traditions of embodied practice and corporeal knowledge are deeply rooted and embattled in the Americas. Yet, the language referring to those corporeal knowledges maintains a firm link to theatrical traditions. Performance includes, but is not reducible to, any of the following terms usually used to replace it: *teatralidad, espectáculo, acción, representación.*

Teatralidad and espectáculo, like theatricality and spectacle in English, capture the constructed, all-encompassing sense of performance. The many ways in which social life and human behavior can be viewed *as* performance come across in these terms, though with a particular valence. Theatricality, for me, sustains a scenario, a paradigmatic setup that relies on supposedly live participants, structured around a schematic plot, with an intended (though adaptable) end. One could say that all the sixteenth-century writing on discovery and conquest restages what Michel de Certeau calls the "inaugural scene: after a moment of stupor, on this threshold dotted with colonnades of trees, the conqueror will write the body of the other and trace there his own history."[23] Theatricality makes that scenario alive and compelling. In other words, scenarios exist as culturally specific imaginaries—sets of possibilities, ways of conceiving conflict, crisis, or resolution—activated with more or less theatricality. Unlike *trope,* which is a figure of speech, theatricality does not rely on language to transmit a set pattern of behavior or action.[24] In chapter 2, I suggest that the colonial "encounter" is a theatrical scenario structured in a predictable, formulaic, hence repeatable fashion. Theatricality (like theatre) flaunts its artifice, its constructedness. No matter who restages the colonial encounter from the West's perspective—the novelist, the playwright, the discoverer, or the government official—it stars the same white male protagonist-subject and the same brown, found "object." Theatricality strives for efficaciousness, not authenticity. It connotes a conscious, controlled, and, thus, always political dimension that performance need not imply. It differs from spectacle in that theatricality highlights the *mechanics* of spectacle. Spectacle, I agree with Guy Debord, is not an image but a series of social relations mediated by images. Thus, as I write elsewhere, it "ties individuals into an economy of looks and looking" that can appear more "invisibly" normalizing, that is, less "theatrical."[25] Both of these terms, however, are nouns with no verb; thus, they do not allow for individual cultural agency in the way that *perform* does. Much is lost, it seems to me, when we give up the potential for direct and active intervention by adopting words such as teatralidad or espectáculo to replace performance.

Words such as acción and representación allow for individual action and intervention. Acción can be defined as an act, an avant-garde happening, a rally or political intervention, such as the street theatre protests staged by the Peruvian theatre collective Yuyachkani (see chapter 7) or the *escraches* or acts of public shaming carried out against torturers by H.I.J.O.S., the human rights organization composed of children of the disappeared in Argentina (see chapter 6). Thus, acción brings together both the aesthetic and the political dimensions of perform. But the economic and social mandates pressuring individuals to perform in certain normative ways fall out—the way we perform our gender or ethnicity and so on. Acción seems more directed and intentional, and thus less socially and politically embroiled than perform, which evokes both the prohibition and the potential for transgression. We may, for example, be performing multiple socially constructed roles at once, even while engaged in one clearly defined antimilitary acción. Representation, even with its verb *to represent*, conjures up notions of mimesis, of a break between the "real" and its representation, that performance and perform have so productively complicated. Although these terms have been proposed instead of the foreign-sounding performance, they too derive from Western languages, cultural histories, and ideologies.

Why, then, not use a term from one of the non-European languages, such as Náhuatl, Maya, Quechua, Aymara, or any of the hundreds of indigenous languages still spoken in the Americas? *Olin*, meaning movement in Náhuatl, seems a possible candidate. Olin is the motor behind everything that happens in life, the repeated movement of the sun, stars, earth, and elements. Olin, also meaning "hule" or rubber, was applied to sacrificial victims to ease the transition from the earthly realm to the divine. Olin, furthermore, is a month in the Mexica calendar and, thus, enables temporal and historical specificity. And Olin also manifests herself/himself as a deity who intervenes in social matters. The term simultaneously captures the broad, all-encompassing nature of performance as reiterative process and carrying through as well as its potential for historical specificity, transition, and individual cultural agency. Or maybe adopt *areito*, the term for song-dance? Areitos, from the Arawack *aririn*, was used by the conquerors to describe a collective act involving singing, dancing, celebration, and worship that claimed aesthetic as well as sociopolitical and religious legitimacy. This term is attractive because it blurs all Aristotelian notions of discretely developed genres, publics, and ends. It clearly reflects the assumption that cultural manifestations exceed compartmentalization either by genre (song-dance), by participant/actors, or by intended effect (religious, sociopolitical, aesthetic) that ground Western cultural thought. It calls into question our taxonomies, even as it points to new interpretive possibilities.

So why not? In this case, I believe, replacing a word with a recognizable, albeit problematic, history—such as performance—with one developed in a different context and to signal a profoundly different worldview would only be an act of wishful thinking, an aspiration to forgetting our shared history of power relations and cultural domination that would not disappear even if we changed our language. Performance, as a theoretical term rather than as an object or a practice, is a newcomer to the field. Although it emerges in the United States at a time of disciplinary shifts to engage areas of analysis that previously exceeded academic boundaries (i.e., "the aesthetics of everyday life"), it is not, like theatre, weighed down by centuries of colonial evangelical or normalizing activity. Its very undefinability and complexity I find reassuring. Performance carries the possibility of challenge, even self-challenge, within it. As a term simultaneously connoting a process, a praxis, an episteme, a mode of transmission, an accomplishment, and a means of intervening in the world, it far exceeds the possibilities of these other words offered in its place. Moreover, the problem of untranslatability, as I see it, is actually a positive one, a necessary stumbling block that reminds us that "we"—whether in our various disciplines, or languages, or geographic locations throughout the Americas—do not simply or unproblematically understand each other. I propose that we proceed from that premise—that we do not understand each other—and recognize that each effort in that direction needs to work against notions of easy access, decipherability, and translatability. This stumbling block stymies not only Spanish and Portuguese speakers faced with a foreign word, but English speakers who thought they knew what *performance* meant.

2. Drawing by Alberto Beltrán. Reproduced by permission.

THE ARCHIVE AND THE REPERTOIRE

My particular investment in performance studies derives less from what it *is* than what it allows us to *do*. By taking performance seriously as a system of learning, storing, and transmitting knowledge, performance studies allows us to expand what we understand by "knowledge." This move, for starters, might prepare us to challenge the preponderance of writing in Western epistemologies. As I suggest in this study, writing has paradoxically come to stand in for and against embodiment. When the friars arrived in the New World in the fifteenth and sixteenth centuries, as I explore, they claimed that the indigenous peoples' past—and the "lives they lived"—had disappeared because they had no writing. Now, on the brink of a digital revolution that both utilizes and threatens to displace writing, the body again seems poised to disappear in a virtual space that eludes embodiment. Embodied expression has participated and will probably continue to participate in the transmission of social knowledge, memory, and identity pre- and postwriting. Without ignoring the pressures to rethink writing and embodiment from the vantage point of the epistemic changes brought on by digital technologies, I will focus my analysis here on some of the methodological implications of revalorizing expressive, embodied culture.

By shifting the focus from written to embodied culture, from the discursive to the performatic, we need to shift our methodologies. Instead of focusing on patterns of cultural expression in terms of texts and narratives, we might think about them as scenarios that do not reduce gestures and embodied practices to narrative description. This shift necessarily alters what academic disciplines regard as appropriate canons, and might extend the traditional disciplinary boundaries to include practices previously outside their purview.

The concept of performance, as an embodied praxis and episteme, for example, would prove vital in redefining Latin American studies because it decenters the historic role of writing introduced by the Conquest. As Angel Rama notes in *The Lettered City*, "The exclusive place of writing in Latin American societies made it so revered as to take on an aura of sacredness. . . . Written documents seemed not to spring from social life but rather be imposed upon it and to force it into a mold not at all made to measure."[26]

Although the Aztecs, Mayas, and Incas practiced writing before the Conquest—either in pictogram form, hieroglyphs, or knotting systems—it never replaced the performed utterance. Writing, though highly valued, was primarily a prompt to performance, a mnemonic aid. More precise information could be stored through writing and it required specialized skills, but it depended on embodied culture for transmission. As in medieval Europe, writing was a privileged form practiced by only the specialized few. Through *in tlilli in tlapalli* ("the red and black ink," as the Nahuas called wisdom associated with writing), Mesoamericans stored their understanding of planetary movement, time, and the calendar. Codices transmitted historical accounts, important dates, regional affairs, cosmic phenomena, and other kinds of knowledge. Writing was censored, and indigenous scribes lived in mortal fear of transgression. Histories were burned and rewritten to suit the memorializing needs of those in power. The space of written culture then, as now, seemed easier to control than embodied culture. But writing was far more dependent on embodied culture for transmission than the other way around. Enrique Florescano, an eminent Mexican historian, notes, "Besides the *tlacuilos*, or specialists who painted the books, there were specialists who read them, interpreted them, memorized them, and expounded on them in detail before audiences of non-specialists."[27]

To my mind, however, Florescano's description of these mutually sustaining systems overemphasizes the role of writing. It would be limiting to understand embodied performance as primarily transmitting those "essential facts" (39) written in the codices or painted books. The codices communicate far more than facts. The images, so visually dense, transmit knowledge of ritualized movement and everyday social practices. Many other kinds of knowledge that involved no written component were also passed on through expressive culture—through dances, rituals, funerals, colors, *huehuehtlah-tolli* ("the ancient word," wisdom handed down through speech), and majestic displays of power and wealth. Scribes were trained in a specialized school or *calmecac,* which also taught dancing, recitation, and other forms of communication essential for social interaction. Education focused primarily on these techniques of the body to ensure indoctrination and continuity.

What changed with the Conquest was not that writing displaced embodied practice (we need only remember that the friars brought their own embodied practices) but the degree of legitimization of writing over other epistemic and mnemonic systems. Writing now assured that Power, with a capital P, as Rama puts it, could be developed and enforced without the input of the great majority of the population, the indigenous and marginal populations of the colonial period without access to systematic writing. Not only did the colonizers burn the ancient codices, they limited the access to writing to a very small group of conquered males who they felt would promote their evangelical efforts. While the conquerors elaborated, rather than transformed, an elite practice and gender-power arrangement, the importance granted writing came at the expense of embodied practices as a way of knowing and making claims. Those who controlled writing, first the friars, then the *letrados* (literally, "lettered"), gained an inordinate amount of power. Writing also allowed European imperial centers—Spain and Portugal—to control their colonial populations from abroad. Writing is about distance, as de Certeau notes: "The power that writing's expansionism leaves intact is colonial in principle. It is extended without being changed. It is tautological, immunized against both any alterity that might transform it and whatever dares to resist it."[28]

The separation that Rama notes between the written and spoken word, echoed in de Certeau, points to only one aspect of the repression of indigenous embodied practice as a form of knowing as well as a system for storing and transmitting knowledge. Nonverbal practices—such as dance, ritual, and cooking, to name a few—that long served to preserve a sense of communal identity and memory, were not considered valid forms of knowledge. Many kinds of performance, deemed idolatrous by religious and civil authorities, were prohibited altogether. Claims manifested through performance, whether the tying of robes to signify marriage or performed land claims, ceased to carry legal weight. Those who had dedicated their lives to mastering cultural practices, such as carving masks or playing music, were not considered "experts," a designation reserved for book-learned scholars. While the Church substituted its own performatic practices, the neophytes could no longer lay claims to expertise or tradition to legitimate their authority. The rift, I submit, does not lie between the written and spoken word, but between the *archive* of supposedly enduring materials (i.e., texts, documents, buildings, bones) and the so-called ephemeral *repertoire* of embodied practice/knowledge (i.e., spoken language, dance, sports, ritual).

"Archival" memory exists as documents, maps, literary texts, letters, archaeological remains, bones, videos, films, CDs, all those items supposedly resistant to change. Archive, from the Greek, etymologically refers to "a public building," "a place where records are kept."[29] From *arkhe,* it also means a beginning, the first place, the government. By shifting the dictionary entries into a syntactical arrangement, we might conclude that the archival, from the beginning, sustains power. Archival memory works across distance, over time and space; investigators can go back to reexamine an ancient manuscript, letters find their addresses through time and place, and computer discs at times cough up lost files with the right software. The fact that archival memory succeeds in separating the source of "knowledge" from the knower—in time and/or space—leads to comments, such as de Certeau's, that it is "expansionist" and "immunized against alterity" (216). What changes over time is the value, relevance, or meaning of the archive, how the items it contains get interpreted, even embodied. Bones might remain the same, even though their story may change, depending on the paleontologist or forensic anthropologist who examines them. *Antigone* might be performed in multiple ways, whereas the unchanging text assures a stable signifier. Written texts allow scholars to trace literary traditions, sources, and influences. Insofar as it constitutes materials that seem to endure, the archive exceeds the live. There are several myths attending the archive. One is that it is unmediated, that objects located there might mean something outside the framing of the archival impetus itself. What makes an object archival is the process whereby it is selected, classified, and presented for analysis. Another myth is that the archive resists change, corruptibility, and political manipulation. Individual things—books, DNA evidence, photo IDs—might mysteriously appear in or disappear from the archive.

The repertoire, on the other hand, enacts embodied memory: performances, gestures, orality, movement, dance, singing—in short, all those acts usually thought of as ephemeral, nonreproducible knowledge. Repertoire, etymologically "a treasury, an inventory," also allows for individual agency, referring also to "the finder, discoverer," and meaning "to find out."[30] The repertoire requires presence: people participate in the production and reproduction of knowledge by "being there," being a part of the transmission. As opposed to the supposedly stable objects in the archive, the actions that are the repertoire do not remain the same. The repertoire both keeps and transforms choreographies of meaning. Sports enthusiasts might claim that soccer has remained unchanged for the past hundred years, even though players and fans from different countries have appropriated the event in diverse ways. Dances change over time, even though generations of dancers (and even individual dancers) swear they're always the same. But even though the embodiment changes, the meaning might very well remain the same.

The repertoire too, then, allows scholars to trace traditions and influences. Many kinds of performances have traveled throughout the Americas, leaving their mark as they move. Scholar Richard Flores, for example, maps out the way *pastorelas* or shepherds' plays moved from Spain, to central Mexico, to Mexico's northwest, and then to what is now the southwest of the United States. The different versions permit him to distinguish among various routes.[31] Max Harris has traced the practice of a specific mock battle, *moros y cristianos*, from pre-Conquest Spain to sixteenth-century Mexico and into the present.[32] The repertoire allows for an alternative perspective on historical processes of transnational contact and invites a remapping of the Americas, this time by following traditions of embodied practice.

Certainly it is true that individual instances of performances disappear from the repertoire. This happens to a lesser degree in the archive. The question of disappearance in relation to the archive and the repertoire differs in kind as well as degree. The live performance can never be captured or transmitted through the archive. A video of a performance is not a performance, though it often comes to replace the performance as a *thing* in itself (the video is part of the archive; what it represents is part of the repertoire). Embodied memory, because it is live, exceeds the archive's ability to capture it. But that does not mean that performance—as ritualized, formalized, or reiterative behavior—disappears.[33] Performances also replicate themselves through their own structures and codes. This means that the repertoire, like the archive, is mediated. The process of selection, memorization or internalization, and transmission takes place within (and in turn helps constitute) specific systems of re-presentation. Multiple forms of embodied acts are always present, though in a constant state of againness. They reconstitute themselves, transmitting communal memories, histories, and values from one group/generation to the next. Embodied and performed acts generate, record, and transmit knowledge.

The archive and the repertoire have always been important sources of information, both exceeding the limitations of the other, in literate and semi-literate societies. They usually work in tandem and they work alongside other systems of transmission—the digital and the visual, to name two. Innumerable practices in the most literate societies require both an archival and an embodied dimension: weddings need both the performative utterance of "I do" and the signed contract; the legality of a court decision lies in the combination of the live trial and the recorded outcome; the performance of a claim contributes to its legality. We have only to think of Columbus planting the Spanish flag in the New World or Neil Armstrong planting the U.S. flag on the moon. Materials from the archive shape embodied practice in innumerable ways, yet never totally dictate embodiment. Jesús Martín-Barbero, a Colombian theorist who works in media studies, illustrates the uses that viewers make of mass media, say, the soap opera.[34] It's not simply that the media impose structures of desire and appropriate behavior. How populations develop ways of viewing, living with, and retelling or recycling the materials allows for a broad range of responses. Mediations, he argues, not the media, provide the key to understanding social behaviors. Those responses and behaviors, in turn, are taken up and appropriated by the mass media in a dialogic, rather than one-way, manner.

Even though the archive and the repertoire exist in a constant state of interaction, the tendency has been to banish the repertoire to the past. Jacques Le Goff, for example, writes of "ethnic memory": "The principal domain in which the collective memory of peoples without writing crystallizes is that which provides an apparently historical foundation for the existence of ethnic groups or families, that is, myths of origin."[35] He suggests, thus, that writing provides historical consciousness and orality provides mythic consciousness. Pierre Nora's distinction between the "lieux" and "'milieux' de mémoire" creates a similar binary, whereby the milieux (which closely resemble the repertoire) belong to the past and lieux are a thing of the present. For Nora, the milieux de mémoire, what he calls the "real environments of memory," enact embodied knowledge: "gestures and habits, in skills passed down by unspoken traditions, in the body's inherent self-knowledge, in unstudied reflexes and ingrained memories."[36] The difference between my thinking and his, however, is that for him the mileux de mémoire constitute the primordial, unmediated, and spontaneous sites of "true memory," and the lieux de mémoire—the archival memory—are their antithesis, modern, fictional, and highly mediated. A "trace," "mediation," and "distance," he argues, has separated the act from the meaning, moving us from the realm of true memory to that of history (285). This paradigm polarizes history and memory as opposite poles of a binary. Nora does not differentiate among forms of transmission (embodied or archival) or among different kinds of publics and communities. His differentiation falls into a temporal before and after, a rift between past (traditional, authentic, now lost) and present (generalized as modern, global, and "mass" culture).

The relationship between the archive and the repertoire, as I see it, is certainly not sequential (the former ascending to prominence after the disappearance of the latter, as Nora would have it).[37] Nor is it true versus false, mediated versus unmediated, primordial versus modern. Nor is it a binary. Other systems of transmission—like the digital—complicate any simple binary formulation. Yet it too readily falls into a binary, with the written and archival constituting hegemonic power and the repertoire providing the anti-hegemonic challenge. Performance belongs to the strong as well as the weak; it underwrites de Certeau's "strategies" as well as "tactics," Bakhtin's "banquet" as well as "carnival." The modes of storing and transmitting knowledge are many and mixed and embodied performances have often contributed to the maintenance of a repressive social order. We need only look to the broad range of political practices in the Americas exercised on human bodies, from pre-Conquest human sacrifices, to Inquisitorial burnings at the stake, to the lynchings of African Americans, to contemporary acts of state-sponsored torture and disappearances. We need not polarize the relationship between these different kinds of knowledge to acknowledge that they have often proved antagonistic in the struggle for cultural survival or supremacy.

The tensions developed historically between the archive and the repertoire continue to play themselves out in discussions about "world" culture and "intangible heritage." This is not the place to rehearse the arguments in any detail, but I would like at least to point to some of the issues that concern my topic.

As laws have increasingly come into place to protect intellectual and artistic property, people have also considered ways to protect "intangible" property. How do we protect the performances, behaviors, and expressions that constitute the repertoire? The United Nations Educational, Scientific, and Cultural Organization (UNESCO) is currently wrestling with how to promote the work "of safeguarding, protecting and revitalizing cultural spaces or forms of cultural expression proclaimed as 'masterpieces of the oral and intangible heritage of humanity.'" These safeguards would protect "traditional and popular forms of cultural expression," such as, using their example, storytelling.[38]

Insofar as the materials in the repertoire participate in the production and transmission of knowledge, I agree that they warrant protection. Yet, it is not clear that UNESCO has been able to conceive of how best to protect this "intangible heritage." Although they recognize that the "methods of preservation applicable to the physical heritage are inappropriate for the intangible heritage," these differences can only be imagined in language and strategies associated with the archive. *Masterpieces* points not only to objects, but to an entire system of valorization that Artaud discarded as outdated in the early twentieth century. *Heritage,* linked etymologically to inheritance, again underlines the material property that passes down to the heirs. *Humanity* might well be considered both the producer and the consumer of these cultural goods, but its abstraction undermines the sense of cultural agency. Moreover, UNESCO's goal seems to protect certain kinds of performances—basically, those produced by the "traditional" and "popular" sectors. This move repeats the salvage ethnography of the first half of the twentieth century, implying that these forms would disappear without official intervention and preservation. Part of UNESCO's project involves moving materials from the repertoire into the archive ("to record their form on tape"). However, UNESCO is also consciously trying to protect embodied transmission ("to facilitate their survival by helping the persons concerned and assisting transmission to future generations"). But how will this be accomplished? The one program they have developed thus far, "Living Human

Treasures," protects the "possessors of traditional cultural skills." To me, this conjures up visions of a fetishized humanoid object that Guillermo Gómez-Peña might dream up for a living diorama in an installation. These solutions seem destined to reproduce the problems of objectifying, isolating, and exoticizing the non-Western that they claim to address. Without understanding the working of the repertoire, the ways peoples produce and transmit knowledge through embodied action, it will be difficult to know how to develop legal claims to ownership. But this differs from the "preservation" argument that, to my mind, barely conceals a deep colonial nostalgia.

The strain between what I call the archive and the repertoire has often been constructed as existing between written and spoken language. The archive includes, but is not limited to, written texts. The repertoire contains verbal performances—songs, prayers, speeches—as well as nonverbal practices. The written/oral divide does, on one level, capture the archive/repertoire difference I am developing in this study insofar as the means of transmission differ, as do the requirements of storage and dissemination. The repertoire, whether in terms of verbal or nonverbal expression, transmits live, embodied actions. As such, traditions are stored in the body, through various mnemonic methods, and transmitted "live" in the here and now to a live audience. Forms handed down from the past are experienced as present. Although this may well describe the mechanics of spoken language, it also describes a dance recital or a religious festival. It is only because Western culture is wedded to the word, whether written or spoken, that language claims such epistemic and explanatory power.

The writing = memory/knowledge equation is central to Western epistemology. "The metaphor of memory as a written surface is so ancient and so persistent in all Western cultures," writes Mary Carruthers, "that it must, I think, be seen as a governing model or 'cognitive archetype.' "[39] That model continues to bring about the disappearance of embodied knowledge that it so frequently announces. During the sixteenth century, de Certeau argues, writing and printing allowed for "an indefinite reproduction of the same products," as "opposed to speech, which neither travels very far nor preserves much of anything. . . . *the signifier cannot be detached from the individual or collective body.*"[40] (Parenthetically, the limitation that de Certeau attributes here to speech—"the signifier cannot be detached from the individual or collective body"—also, of course, contributes to the political, affective, and mnemonic power of the repertoire, as I argue in this study.)

Freud's "A Note upon the 'Mystic Writing-Pad' " bypasses the historically situated human body in his theorizations on memory. By using the admittedly imperfect analogy to the mystic writing pad, Freud attempts to approximate the "unlimited receptive capacity and a retention of permanent traces," which he sees as fundamental properties of "the perceptual apparatus of the mind."[41] A modern computer, of course, serves as a better analogy, though it too fails to generate memories and its exterior body—a see-through shell in the recent Macintosh model—serves only to protect and highlight the marvelous internal apparatus. Neither the mystic writing pad nor the computer allows for a body. So too, Freud's analogy limits itself to the external writing mechanism and the pure disembodied psychic apparatus that "has an unlimited receptive capacity for new perceptions and nevertheless lays down permanent—even though not unalterable—memory-traces on them" (228). The psyche can be imagined only as a writing surface, the permanent trace only as an act of writing. Instead of reinforcing memory or providing an analogy, writing becomes memory itself: "I have only to bear in mind the place where this 'memory' has been deposited and I can then 'reproduce' it at any time I like, with the certainty that it will have remained unaltered" (227).

Derrida, in "Freud and the Scene of Writing," refers to the "metaphor of writing which haunts European discourse" without expanding toward the idea of a repertoire of embodied knowledge.[42] Even when he points to areas for further research, he calls for a "history of writing" (214) without noting that history might disappear in its very coming to light. When he writes "Writing is unthinkable without repression" (226), the repression that comes to my mind is that history of colonial repudiation through documentation that dates back to the sixteenth century Americas. For Derrida, those repressions are "the deletions, blanks, and disguises" (226) of and within writing itself—surely an act of writing that stages its own practice of erasure and foreclosure.

The dominance of language and writing has come to stand for *meaning* itself. Live, embodied practices not based in linguistic or literary codes, we must assume, have no claims on meaning. As Barthes puts it, "The intelligible is reputed antipathetic to lived experience."[43] This suggests that

Barthes disagreed with situating intelligibility as antithetical to lived experience, yet in other essays he asserts that everything that has meaning becomes "a kind of writing."[44]

Part of what performance and performance studies allow us to *do*, then, is take seriously the repertoire of embodied practices as an important system of knowing and transmitting knowledge. The repertoire, on a very practical level, expands the traditional archive used by academic departments in the humanities. Departments of Spanish and Portuguese in the United States, for example, emphasize language and literature, though literature is clearly their focus. In Latin American institutions, *departamentos de letras*, which include literature and cultural studies, belong to the school of *filosofía y letras* (philosophy and literature). Some of these departments do focus on oral literatures, which on the surface at least seem to combine materials from the repertoire and the archive. However, the term oral literature itself tells us that the oral has already been transformed into literature, the repertoire transferred to the archive. The oral was "historically constituted as a category, . . . even fabricated," Barbara Kirshenblatt-Gimblett argues, under the forces of nationalism.[45] The archive, in the case of oral literatures, predates and constitutes the phenomena it purports to document. Nonetheless, many of these departments do combine the workings of the archive and the repertoire in productive ways, although perhaps not in the way that scholars might expect. Departments that actually take the teaching of language seriously, for example, have some experience thinking about reiterated, embodied social practice. Students learn a second language by imagining themselves in a different social setting, by staging scenarios where the acquired language takes on meaning, by imitating, repeating, and rehearsing not just words but cultural attitudes. Theorizing these practices, not just as pedagogical strategies but as the transmission of embodied cultural behavior, would enable scholars to branch out into new critical thinking about the repertoire. A performance studies lens would enrich these disciplines, bridging the schism not only between literary and oral traditions, but between verbal and nonverbal embodied cultural practice.

Similarly, performance studies challenges the disciplinary compartmentalization of the arts—with dance assigned to one department, music to another, dramatic performance to yet another—as though many forms of artistic production have anything to do with those divides. This compartmentalization also reinforces the notion that the arts are separable from the social constructs within which they participate—either for the first or nth time. Performances, even those with almost purely aesthetic pretensions, move in all sorts of circuits, including national and transnational spaces and economies. Every performance enacts a theory, and every theory performs in the public sphere. Because of its interdisciplinary character, performance studies can bring disciplines that had previously been kept separate into direct contact with each other and with their historical, intellectual, and sociopolitical context. This training challenges students to develop their theoretical paradigms by drawing from both textual and embodied practice.[46] They receive training in various methodologies: ethnographic fieldwork, interviewing techniques, movement analysis, digital technologies, sound, textual analysis, and performative writing, among others.

Performance studies, then, offers a way of rethinking the canon and critical methodologies. For even as scholars in the United States and Latin America acknowledge the need to free ourselves from the dominance of the text —as the privileged or even sole object of analysis—our theoretical tools continue to be haunted by the literary legacy. Some scholars turn to cultural studies and no longer limit themselves to the examination of texts, but their training in close readings and textual analysis might well turn everything they view into a text or narrative, whether it's a funeral, an electoral campaign, or a carnival. The tendency in cultural studies to treat all phenomena as textual differentiates it from performance studies. As cultural studies expands the range of materials under consideration, it still leaves all the explanatory power with the letrados while occluding other forms of transmission. Dwight Conquergood carries the point further in a recent essay: "Only middle-class academics could blithely assume that all the world is a text because texts and reading are central to their life-world, and occupational security."[47]

It's imperative now, however overdue, to pay attention to the repertoire. But what would that entail methodologically? It's not simply that we shift to the live as the focus of our analysis, or develop various strategies for garnering information, such as undertaking ethnographic research, interviews, and field notes. Or even alter our hierarchies of legitimation that structure our traditional academic practice (such as book learning, written sources, and documents). We need to rethink our method of analysis.

Here I will focus on one example. Instead of privileging *texts* and *narratives*, we could also look to scenarios as meaning-making paradigms that structure social environments, behaviors, and potential outcomes. Scenarios of discovery, for example, have appeared constantly throughout the past five hundred years in the Americas. Why do they continue to be so compelling? What accounts for their explanatory and affective power? How can they be parodied and subverted? Scenario, "a sketch or outline of the plot of a play, giving particulars of the scenes, situations etc.," like performance, means never for the first time.[48] Like Barthes's mythical speech, it consists of "material which has already been worked on" (*Mythologies*, 110). Its portable framework bears the weight of accumulative repeats. The scenario makes visible, yet again, what is already there: the ghosts, the images, the stereotypes. The discoverer, conqueror, "savage," and native princess, for example, might be staple characters in many Western scenarios. Sometimes they are written down as scripts, but the scenario predates the script and allows for many possible "endings." At times, people may actually undertake adventures to live the glorious fantasy of possession. Others may tune in regularly to television shows along the lines of *Survivor* or *Fantasy Island*. The scenario structures our understanding. It also haunts our present, a form of hauntology (see chapter 5) that resuscitates and reactivates old dramas. We've seen it all before. The framework allows for occlusions; by positioning our perspective, it promotes certain views while helping to disappear others. In the *Fantasy Island* scenario, for example, we might be encouraged to overlook the displacement and disappearance of native peoples, gender exploitation, environmental impact, and so on. This partial blinding is what I have previously called percepticide.[49]

The *scenario* includes features well theorized in literary analysis, such as narrative and plot, but demands that we also pay attention to milieux and corporeal behaviors such as gestures, attitudes, and tones not reducible to language. Simultaneously *setup* and *action*, scenarios frame and activate social dramas. The setup lays out the range of possibilities; all the elements are there: encounter, conflict, resolution, and dénouement, for example. These elements, of course, are themselves the product of economic, political, and social structures that they, in turn, tend to reproduce. All scenarios have localized meaning, though many attempt to pass as universally valid. Actions and behaviors arising from the setup might be predictable, a seemingly natural consequence of the assumptions, values, goals, power relations, presumed audience, and epistemic grids established by the setup itself. But they are, ultimately, flexible and open to change. Social actors may be assigned roles deemed static and inflexible by some. Nonetheless, the irreconcilable friction between the social actors and the roles allows for degrees of critical detachment and cultural agency. The scenario of conquest, restaged in numerous acts of possession as well as in plays, rituals, and mock battles throughout the Americas, can be and often has been subverted from within. Examples range from sixteenth-century mock battles to Guillermo Gómez-Peña and Coco Fusco's 1992 "Two Undiscovered Amerindians," a performance in a cage. Like narrative, as V. Propp proposed in 1928, scenarios are limited to a finite number of variations, with their own classifications, categories, themes, forms, characters, and so on.[50] Here, I will simply point to some of the ways that using *scenario* as a paradigm for understanding social structures and behaviors might allow us to draw from the repertoire as well as the archive.

First, to recall, recount, or reactivate a scenario we need to conjure up the physical location (the "scene" as physical environment, such as a stage or place in English; *escenario,*a false cognate means stage in Spanish). *Scene* denotes intentionality, artistic or otherwise (the scene of the crime), and signals conscious strategies of display. The word appropriately suggests both the material stage as well as the highly codified environment that gives viewers pertinent information, say, class status or historical period. The furnishings, clothing, sounds, and style contribute to the viewer's understanding of what might conceivably transpire there. The two, scene and scenario, stand in metonymic relationship: the place allows us to think about the possibilities of the action.[51] But action also defines place. If, as de Certeau suggests, "space is a practiced place," then there is no such thing as place, for no place is free of history and social practice.[52]

Second, in scenarios, viewers need to deal with the embodiment of the social actors. Thus, in addition to the functions these actors perform, so well charted by Propp in relation to narrative structures, the scenario requires us to wrestle with the social construction of bodies in particular contexts. Propp stresses the importance of visual detail in describing the attributes of the characters: "By attributes we mean the totality of all the external qualities of the characters: their age, sex, status, external appearance, peculiarities of appearance, and so forth" (87). But scenarios by definition introduce the generative critical distance between social actor and character. Whether it's a question of mimetic representation (an actor assuming a role) or of performativity, of social actors assuming socially regulated patterns of appropriate behavior, the scenario more fully allows us to keep both the social actor and the role in view simultaneously, and thus recognize the areas of resistance and tension. The frictions between plot and character (on the level of narrative) and embodiment (social actors) make for some of the most remarkable instances of parody and resistance in performance traditions in the Americas.

Take the mock battles of the Moors and Christians, for example, staged in Mexico in the sixteenth century. The tradition, as the name implies, came from Spain, a transplanting of the theme of the reconquest of Spain after the expulsion of Moors and Jews in 1492. In Mexico, these battles ended predictably with the defeat of the Indians-as-Moors and a mass baptism. On the level of the narrative structure that polarizes groups into definable us/them categories, we must agree with commentators who see in these performances the reiterative humiliation of the native populations.[53] In regard to measurable efficaciousness, we might conclude that these scenarios were highly successful from the Spaniard's perspective, leading as they did to the conversion of thousands of people. The embodied performance, however, permits us to recognize other dimensions as well. For one thing, all the "actors" of the mock battles were indigenous; some dressed up as Spaniards, others as Turks. Rather than cementing cultural and racial difference, as the plot and characterization intend, the enactment might have more to do with cultural masquerading and strategic repositioning. The indigenous performers were neither Moors nor Christians, and their reenactments allowed them to dress up and act out their own versions of the us/them. In one particularly humorous rendition, the character of the doomed Muslim king surprisingly turned into that of the conqueror Cortés. The obligatory defeat of the Moor in the scripted version masked the joyful, unscripted defeat of the Spaniards in the performance. In this mock battle, the conquered staged their longing for their own *reconquista* of Mexico, as Max Harris has argued. The space of ambiguity and maneuver does not lie, however, in the "hidden transcript," the term developed by anthropologist James Scott to mark a strategy that subordinate groups create "that represents a critique of power spoken behind the back of the dominant."[54] Transcripts, normally understood as written copy or documents, transfer archival knowledge within a specific economy of interaction. This mock battle makes clear that it's the embodied nature of the repertoire that grants these social actors the opportunity to rearrange characters in parodic and subversive ways. The parody takes place in front of the Spaniards themselves, one of whom was so struck by the incredible display that he wrote a detailed letter to a fellow friar.[55]

Third, scenarios, by encapsulating both the setup and the action/behaviors, are formulaic structures that predispose certain outcomes and yet allow for reversal, parody, and change. The frame is basically fixed and, as such, repeatable and transferable. Scenarios may consciously reference each other by the way they frame the situation and quote words and gestures. They may often appear stereotypical, with situations and characters frozen within them. The scenario of conquest has been replayed again and again—from Cortés's entrance into Tenochtitlán, to the meeting between Pizarro and Atahualpa, to Oñate's claiming possession of New Mexico.[56] Each repeat adds to its affective and explanatory power until the outcome seems a foregone conclusion. Each new conqueror may expect the natives to fall at his feet just on the strength of the reactivated scenario. In time and with changing circumstances, however, the paradigm may become obsolete and be replaced by another. Early sixteenth-century scenarios of conquest, as Jill Lane notes, became recast as scenarios of conversion by the end of the century in efforts to mitigate the violence of the entangled projects.[57] Conquest, as a term rather than as a project, was out. Thus, as with Bourdieu's *habitus*—"a particular type of environment (e.g. the material conditions of existence characteristic of class condition) produces *habitus*, systems of durable, transposable dispositions"—scenarios are "durable, transposable dispositions."[58] That is, they are passed on and remain remarkably coherent paradigms of seemingly unchanging attitudes and values. Yet, they adapt constantly to reigning conditions. Unlike habitus, which can refer to broad social structures such as class, scenarios refer to more specific repertoires of cultural imaginings.

Fourth, the transmission of a scenario reflects the multifaceted systems at work in the scenario itself: in passing it on, we can draw from various modes that come from the archive and/or the repertoire—writing, telling, reenactment, mime, *gestus*, dance, singing. The multiplicity of forms of transmission reminds us of the multiple systems at work. One is not reducible to another; they have different discursive and performatic structures. A cry or a Brechtian gestus might find no adequate verbal description, for these expressions are not reducible or posterior to language. The challenge is not to "translate" from an embodied expression into a linguistic one or vice versa but to recognize the strengths and limitations of each system.

Fifth, the scenario forces us to situate ourselves in relationship to it; as participants, spectators, or witnesses, we need to "be there," part of the act of transfer. Thus, the scenario precludes a certain kind of distancing. Even the ethnographic writers who cling to the fantasy that they might observe cultures from the margins are part of the scenario, though perhaps not the one the writers strive to describe.[59]

Sixth, a scenario is not necessarily, or even primarily, mimetic. Although the paradigm allows for a continuity of cultural myths and assumptions, it usually works through reactivation rather than duplication. Scenarios conjure up past situations, at times so profoundly internalized by a society that no one remembers the precedence. The "frontier" scenario in the United States, for example, organizes events as diverse as smoking advertisements and the hunt for Osama Bin Laden. Rather than a copy, the scenario constitutes a once-againness.

Thinking about a scenario rather than a narrative, however, does not solve some of the issues inherent in representation in any form. The ethical problems of reproducing violence, whether in writing or in embodied behavior, plague scholars and artists, readers and spectators. Saidiya V. Hartman, in *Scenes of Subjection: Terror, Slavery, and Self-Making in Nineteenth-Century America*, writes, "Only more obscene than the brutality unleashed at the whipping post is the demand that this suffering be materialized and evidenced by the display of the tortured body or endless recitations of the ghastly and the terrible."[60] I agree with Hartman that of interest "are the ways we are called upon to participate in such scenes" (3)—as witnesses, spectators, or voyeurs; however, the scenario, as I posit in chapter 2, physically places the spectator within the frame and can force the ethical question: *the signifier*, we recall, "*cannot be detached from the individual or collective body.*" What is our role "there"?

By considering scenarios as well as narratives, we expand our ability to rigorously analyze the live and the scripted, the citational practices that characterize both, how traditions get constituted and contested, the various trajectories and influences that might appear in one but not in the other. Scenarios, like other forms of transmission, allow commentators to historicize specific practices. In short, as I argue in the chapters that follow, the notion of the scenario allows us to more fully recognize the many ways in which the archive and the repertoire work to constitute and transmit social knowledge. The scenario places spectators within its frame, implicating us in its ethics and politics.

In the section that follows, I give an extended example of what an attempt to historicize performance might look like. Although all the chapters in this study look at contemporary performances in the Americas, throughout I propose that some of the debates I deal with can in fact be traced back to the sixteenth century. Scenarios change and adapt, but they don't seem to go away.

HISTORICIZING PERFORMANCE

In order to provide a truthful and reliable account of the origin of these Indian nations, an origin so doubtful and obscure, we would need some divine revelation or assistance to reveal this origin to us and help us understand it. However, lacking that revelation we can only speculate and conjecture about these beginnings, basing ourselves on the evidence provided by these people, whose strange ways, conduct, and lowly actions are so like those of the Hebrews, and I would not commit a great error if I were to state this as fact, considering their way of life, their ceremonies, their rites and superstitions, their omens and hypocrisies, so akin to and characteristic of those of the Jews; in no way do they seem to differ. The Holy Scriptures bear witness to this, and from them we draw proofs and reasons for holding this opinion to be true. —Fray Diego Durán, *History of the Indies of New Spain*

The inaugural moment of colonialism in the Americas introduces two discursive moves that work to devalue native performance, even while the colonizers were deeply engaged in their own performative project of creating a "new" Spain from an (idealized) image of the "old": (1) the dismissal of indigenous performance traditions as episteme, and (2) the dismissal of "content" (religious belief) as bad objects, idolatry. These discourses simultaneously contradict and sustain each other. The first posits that performances, as ephemeral, nonwritten phenomena, cannot serve to create or transmit knowledge. Thus, all traces of peoples without writing have disappeared. Only divine revelation, according to Durán, can help observers like himself recount the past by fitting it into preexisting accounts (such as the biblical). The second discourse admits that performance does indeed transmit knowledge, but insofar as that knowledge is idolatrous and opaque, performance itself needs to be controlled or eliminated. I would argue that remnants of both of these discourses continue to filter our understanding of contemporary performance practices in the Americas, but my emphasis here is on the initial deployment of these two discourses in the sixteenth century. Although I outline the two discourses separately, as they have been handed down to us, they are of course inseparable and work in tandem.

Part of the colonizing project throughout the Americas consisted in discrediting autochthonous ways of preserving and communicating historical understanding. As a result, the very existence/presence of these populations has come under question. Aztec and Mayan codices, or painted books, were destroyed as idolatrous, bad objects. But the colonizers also tried to destroy embodied memory systems, by both stamping them out and discrediting them. The *Huarochirí Manuscript*, written in Quechua at the end of the sixteenth century by Friar Francisco de Avila, sets the tone: "If the ancestors of the people called Indians had known writing in early times, then the lives they lived would not have faded from view until now."[61] The very "lives they lived" fade into "absence" when writing alone functions as archival evidence, as proof of presence.

Performance studies, we might claim anachronistically, was first articulated in the Americas as "absence studies," disappearing the very populations it pretends to explain. Durán's opening statement in his *History of the Indies of New Spain* (written in the second half of the sixteenth century) insists that we would need "divine revelation or assistance" to "provide a truthful and reliable account of the origin of these Indian nations."[62] From the sixteenth century onward, scholars have complained about the lack of valid sources. Although these claims go unchallenged, the early friars made clear the ideological assumptions/biases of what counts as sources. Durán stressed the value of written texts for his archival project, lamenting, "Some early friars burned ancient books and writings and thus they were lost. Then, too, the old people who could write these books are no longer alive to tell of the settling of this country, and it was they whom I would have consulted for my chronicle" (20). That knowledge, he assumes, must necessarily be lost with the destruction of writing. Why else would he not consult the heirs to the "living memory"? He had no choice, he concludes, but to rely on his own best judgment.

Since before the Conquest, as I noted, writing and embodied performance have often worked together to layer the historical memories that constitute community. Figure 2 illustrates the collaborative production of knowledge led by Fray Bernardino de Sahagún that involved recitation, writing, and a back-and-forth dialogue. The Jesuit friar José de Acosta described how young people were trained in oral traditions: "It should be known that Mexicans had a great curiosity in that young people learn by heart the sayings and compositions, and for that they had schools, like colleges or seminaries, where the old taught the young these and many other things that by tradition they conserve as whole as if they had writing among them."[63] Dance/song (areitos and cantares) functioned as a way of telling history and communicating past glories: "The cantares referred to memorable things and events that took place in times past and present; and they were sung in the areitos and public dances and in them too they told the praises with which they aggrandized their kings and people deserving remembrance; for that they took great care that the verse and language be very polished and dignified."[64]

The sixteenth-century indigenous poet Fernando Alvarado Tezozómoc composed a poem to be recited that depicts memory as grounded both in orality and in writing (pictographs):

Never will it be lost, never will it be forgotten,
that which they came to do,
that which they came to record in their paintings:
their renown, their history, their memory.
. . .
always we will treasure it . . .
we who carry their blood and
          their color,
we will tell it, we will pass it on.[65]

The telling is as important as the writing, the doing as central as the recording, the memory passed down through bodies and mnemonic practices. Memory paths and documented records might retain what the other "forgot." These systems sustain and mutually produce each other; neither is outside or antithetical to the logic of the other.

Local scribes in the Andes have also been keeping written records in Quechua and Spanish since the sixteenth century. Even so, historical and genealogical information has been, and continues to be, performed and transmitted through performed "memory paths," as anthropologist Thomas Abercrombie puts it, the ritualized incantations by inebriated males of names of ancestors and sacred places during which they remember and recite the events associated with them. Through these paths, they access ancestral stories, hearsay, and eye-witness accounts. (As the percentage of literate persons in the Andes has actually decreased since the sixteenth century, the need to recognize cultural transmission through embodied knowledge becomes even more pressing.)[66]

Even though the relationship between the archive and the repertoire is not by definition antagonistic or oppositional, written documents have repeatedly announced the disappearance of the performance practices involved in mnemonic transmission. Writing has served as a strategy for repudiating and foreclosing the very embodiedness it claims to describe. Friar Avila was not alone in prematurely announcing the demise of practices, and peoples, that he could neither understand nor control. Again, parenthetically, it is important to stress that the repudiation of practices under examination cannot be limited to archival documentation. As Barbara Kirshenblatt-Gimblett makes clear in *Destination Culture*, exhibitions, model villages, and other forms of live display often do the same: repudiate the cultures they claim to make visible.[67]

What is at risk politically in thinking about embodied knowledge and performance as ephemeral as that which disappears? Whose memories "disappear" if only archival knowledge is valorized and granted permanence? Should we simply expand our notion of the archive to house the mnemonic and gestural practices and specialized knowledge transmitted live? Or get beyond the confines of the archive? I echo Rebecca Schneider's question in "Archive Performance Remains": "If we consider performance as a process of disappearance . . . are we limiting ourselves to an understanding of performance predetermined by our cultural habituation to the logic of the archive?" (100). On the contrary: as I have tried to establish here, there is an advantage to thinking about a repertoire performed through dance, theatre, song, ritual, witnessing, healing practices, memory paths, and the many other forms of repeatable behaviors as something that cannot be housed or contained in the archive.

Now, I will look at the second discourse that admits that performance generates and transmits knowledge, but rejects that knowledge as idolatrous and indecipherable. The charge against the ephemeral and constructed and visual nature of performance has tied into the discourse on idolatry. As Bruno Latour cautions in his essay "A Few Steps toward an Anthropology of the Iconoclastic Gesture," "A large part of our critical acumen depends on a clear distinction between what is real and what is constructed, what is out there in the nature of things and what is there in the representation we make of them. Something has been lost however for the sake of this clarity and a heavy price has been paid for this dichotomy between ontological questions on the one hand and the epistemological questions on the other."[68] How does this fracture between the ontological and the epistemological (the *is/as*) relate to iconoclasm? By delegitimating the constructed as a fetish or idol, the iconoclast attacks it with the "hammer of truth," that is, God, who has not been made or constructed, is alone capable of creating. As the sixteenth-century friar Bernardino de Sahagún explains in his prologue to book 1 of the *Florentine Codex*, the idolater worships the constructed image, forgetting that God, not humans, is "the Creator." "Unhappy are they, the accursed dead who worshipped as gods carvings of stone, carvings of wood, representations, images, things made of gold or of copper."[69] The "things made," representations and images, were all deemed false, deceptive, pitiful, ephemeral, and dangerous. The "fact" that the indigenous peoples had been "deceived" cost them their humanity: "The people here on earth who know not God are not counted as human" (55). In shattering one idol, Sahagún creates his own false representation: the image of native peoples as "vain," "worthless," "blind," "confused. . . . All their acts, their lives, were all viscous, filthy" (59–60). Latour, fully owning the constructedness of the fetish, argues for the constructedness of the fact as well: "The iconoclast . . . naively believed that the very facts he was using to shatter the idol were themselves produced without the help of any human agency" (69).

Importantly, Sahagún's argument centers on binaries created between the visible and the invisible, between embodied and archival knowledge, between those idolaters who worship that which can be seen and those who know that the true God is the one "who is not seen."[70] Sahagún asks the natives to forgo the image and accept "the word . . . here written" (55). The word encapsulates the power of the sacred and the political, for it is the word of God, which "the King of Spain has sent to you," as well as the Pope, "the Holy Father, who dwelleth in Rome" (55). The natives, he objects, know their gods only through their physical manifestations (the sun, moon, rain, fire, stars, etc.), but do not recognize the (invisible) creator behind these manifestations.

Clearly, the Mexica and other conquered native groups did not endorse the Western true/false, visible/invisible divide. They admitted no ontological distinction between human and nonhuman creation (i.e., ritual/ "nature"). Rather, for the Mexicas, human creation participated in the dynamism of the cosmic order. Nature was ritualized just as ritual was naturalized. Mountains and temples shared the same cosmic function of mediating between *cielo de arriba* (the sky above) and *cielo de abajo* (the sky below). This concept has little to do with the theories of representation, mimesis, and isomorphism that underwrite the Western separation between the "original" and the once-removed. The performances—rituals, ceremonies, sacrifices—were not "just" representations but (among other things) presentations to the Gods as forms of debt payment. They constituted the *is* as well as the *as if.* These performances were, of course, also political: they cemented and made visible a social order, remapping the known universe, with Tenochtitlán as the *ombligo* or center.

The Náhuatl word *ixiptlatl,* usually translated as *imagen,* points to the basic misunderstanding. Imagen belongs to the same etymologic family as *imitar.*[71] But ixiptlatl does not mean imitar but its opposite, the understanding of "spiritual being and physical being as fully integrated."[72] Ixiptlatl constitutes a very flexible category that includes gods, god delegates, god impersonators, priests, sacrificial victims dressed as gods, beggars wearing the flayed skins of captives, and wooden and vegetable seed-dough figures.[73] One of the requirements of the ixiptlatl was that it be made, constructed, and that it be "temporary, concocted for the occasion, made and unmade during the course of the action."[74] Its constructed quality enabled, rather than detracted from, its sacred quality because the *making* was the currency of participation. Rather than a fetish, in which *facere* (to make) comes to mean *feitico* (sorcery, artificiality, idols), the ixiptlatl's constructedness allows for communication, presence, and exchange. *Delegado* (delegate) and *represen-tante* (representative) and *enviado* (envoy) are more precise translations for ixiptlatl, reflecting that "which enables the god to present aspects of him-self."[75] In other words, the ixiptlatl more closely coincided with the Catholic idea of transubstantiation than with an image or idol. The consecrated wafer, though man-made, *was* the body of Christ, not a representation or meta-phor. Though it is an object, Catholics see it as imbued with divine essence, accomplishing the integration of spiritual and physical substance. Needless to say, Catholics' deep anxiety about assuring orthodoxy in the understand-ing of the spiritual/physical relationship in their own practice (especially in the age of the Council of Trent) contributed to their dismissal of Mexica's ixiptlatl as "bad objects" (idols).

The temporary nature of the ixiptlatl should not, as the Spaniards would suggest, connote the ephemeral and disappearing nature of the phenome-non. The constant making and unmaking points to the active role of human beings in promoting the regenerative quality of the universe, of life, of per-formance—all in a constant state of againness. Conversely, we can note in passing that the obsessive dependence on ritual participation also suggests that the Mexica and other groups were trapped in a sociopolitical system defined and maintained by ritually induced crisis, whether the rehearsal of the end of the world every fifty-two years in the New Fire ceremony or in relation to other natural cataclysms such as drought or earthquake. The making/unmaking reflects the defiance and terror associated with disap-pearance: the first four suns had all come to a catastrophic end. The ex-treme reliance on performance constituted the attempts by the Mexica to forestall closure by constantly choreographing the various apparitions, cor-respondences, and interventions (divine and human) that kept the universe in movement.

Interestingly, Sahagún interviewed the "leading elders" of villages for years and worked closely with experts "in all things courtly, military, gov-ernmental, and even idolatrous."[76] One assumes that he would have under-stood the multiple functions and meanings of the ixiptlatl as somewhat more complex than the biblical notion of the graven image. Not so. These are the images that he included to back up his argument about the indigenous peoples' idolatrous practices.

Whether the Mexica performances were effective in maintaining the cos-

3. From Bernardino de Sahagún, *Florentine Codex*, ed. and trans. Arthur J. O. Anderson and Charles E. Dibble (Santa Fe, NM: School of American Research and University of Utah, 1982), vol. 1.

mic order or, instead, a symptom of profound disorder is open to debate.[77] But there was no doubt in the minds of any of the early evangelists that performance practices efficaciously transmitted collective memories, values, and belief systems.

Sahagún clearly recognized how beliefs were transmitted through performance, though he acknowledged that he did not understand the content. The Devil "our enemy planted, in this land, a forest or a thorny thicket filled with very dense brambles, to perform his works therefrom and to hide himself therein in order not to be discovered." The enemy of transparency, the Devil takes advantage of songs and dances and other practices of indigenous people as "hiding places in order to perform his works. . . . Said songs contain so much guile that they say anything and proclaim that which he commands. But only those he addresses understand them."[78] The colonists' claim to access met with the diabolic opaqueness of performance: "And [these songs] are sung to him without its being understood what they are about, other than by those who are natives and versed in this language . . . without being understood by others" (58). Shared performance and linguistic practices constituted the community itself. Others could not decipher the codes. The spiritual conquest, these friars feared, was at best tentative. The Devil awaits the "return to the dominion he has held. . . . And for that time it is good that we have weapons on hand to meet him with. And to this end not only that which is written in this third Book but also that which is written in the first, second, fourth and fifth Books will serve" (59).

Writing served as a recognized weapon in the colonial arsenal. Sahagún maintained that he needed to write down all the indigenous practices to better eradicate them: "It is needful to know how they practiced them in the time of their idolatry, for, through [our] lack of knowledge of this, they perform many idolatrous things in our presence without our understanding it" (book 1, 45). "Preservation" served as a call to erasure. The ethnographic approach to the subject matter offered a safe strategy for handling dangerous materials. It allowed, simultaneously, for documentation and disappearance; the accounts preserved "diabolic" habits as forever alien and unassimilable, transmitting a deep disgust for the behaviors described.[79] The studied, scholarly distancing functioned as repudiation. Yet, even after fifty years of compiling the massive materials on Mexica practices, Sahagún suspected that they had not completely disappeared.

These early colonial writings are all about erasure, either claiming that ancient practices had disappeared or trying to accomplish the disappearance they invoked. Ironically, they reveal a deep admiration for the peoples and cultures targeted for destruction, what Sahagún refers to throughout the *Florentine Codex* as "the degree of perfection of this Mexican people." Even more ironic, these writings have become invaluable archival resources on ancient practices. During Sahagún's lifetime, in fact, the Office of the Holy Inquisition concluded that instead of serving as weapons against idolatry, the books preserved and transmitted what they attempted to eradicate. The prohibition was outright: "With great care and diligence you take measures to get these books without there remaining originals or copies of them. . . . you will be advised not to permit anyone, for any reason, in any language, to write concerning the superstitions and way of life these Indians had" (book 1, 36–37). Sahagún died without knowing that one copy of his work had survived.

For all the ambivalence and prohibitions, these sixteenth-century writers begrudgingly observed something again and again: these practices were not disappearing. They continued to communicate meanings that their nervous observers did not understand. In 1539, a governmental edict took a hammer to the indigenous observance of the sacred, demoting it to a secular distraction. It mandated "that the Indians not have fiestas . . . in which there are *areitos*" and prohibited churches from attracting the native population "by profane means that include areitos, dancers, pole-flyers, that look like things of theatre or spectacle, because these spectacles distract their hearts from the concentration, quiet and devotion that one should have for divine practice."[80] The fiestas, dances, and pole-flyers, integral components of the sacred, were now ordered aside in favor of the quiet behaviors the Spaniards associated with "divine practice." In 1544 an edict lamented the "shame that in front of the Holy Sacrament there go men with masks and wearing women's clothes, dancing and jumping, swaying indecently and lasciviously. . . . And, beside this, there is another greater objection, and that is the custom that these natives [*naturales*] had in their antiquity of solemnizing their fiestas to their idols with dances, music, rejoicing. They will think and accept it as doctrine and law that in this foolishness lies the sanctification of the fiestas" (241–42). A 1555 edict calls attention to the continuing nature of theses practices: "Very inclined are the Indians of these parts to dances, and areitos and other forms of rejoicing that since their heathenism they were in the habit of practicing." It also prohibits the following: "no use of insignia, nor ancient masks, that can cause any suspicion whatever, nor singing the songs of their rituals and ancient histories" (245). I'll skip to 1651: "That in the Easter fiestas no profane comedies be permitted, nor indecent things mixed together." But the prohibitions had widened; now the edicts targeted not just the native peoples but the *religiosos* as well: "Clergy should not dress up as women" (252). The practices, these edicts suggest, were in fact expanding, catching on with nonindigenous peoples. In 1670 the edicts include "not only Indians, but the Spaniards and the clergy" (253). In 1702, the battle against idolatrous performance continued with new prohibitions: "That there be no dances or other ceremonies that make allusion or reference to the superstitions of ancient heathenism" (257). And on and on: 1768, 1769, 1770, 1777, 1780, 1792, 1796, 1808, 1813.

Civil and ecclesiastical powers tried to replace the indigenous peoples' opaque and "idolatrous" practices with other, more "appropriate" behaviors: shows of obedience and acquiescence. This clearly involved the transformation of the relationships among space, time, and cultural practice. The Church tried to impose itself as the sole locus of the sacred and organized religious and secular life both spatially and temporally. All indigenous peoples were ordered to live in town with "a good church, and one only, to which all may come."[81] The litany of prohibitions sought to impose new (segregated) spatial practices and make visible the new social hierarchy: "Indians must not live off in the forests . . . under pain of whipping or prison"; "The caciques shall not hold gatherings, nor go about at night, after the bells are sounded for the souls in purgatory"; "All people must bend the knee before the sacrament"; "No baptized person shall possess idols, sacrifice any animals, draw blood by piercing their ears or noses, nor perform any rite, nor burn incense thereto, or fast in worship of their false idols"; "No dances shall be held except in daytime"; "All bows and arrows are to be burned"; "Towns must be in Spanish fashion, have guest-houses, one for Spaniards and another for Indians"; "No negro, slave or mestizo shall enter any village save with his master, and then stay more than a day and night."

These edicts sought to limit the indigenous peoples' capacity for movement, economic independence, self-expression, and community building, and they attempted to simplify surveillance to control visible behaviors. Changes in the patterns sought to interrupt what Maurice Halbwach called "the social framework of memory."[82] Under attack, of course, is the understanding, as Roach puts it, that "expressive movements [function] as mnemonic reserves, including patterned movements made and remembered by bodies."[83] Anything that recalled past behaviors was to be avoided, as was anything that complicated visible categorization and control. The finely honed racial categories put forward in the sixteenth century through the Inquisition—with its categorization of mestizos, mulattos, moriscos, and zambos, among others—participated in the development of techniques for visual control.[84] The many edicts against all sorts of performance practices, from the danced songs or areitos to the "secret" gatherings, conveyed the recognition that they functioned as an episteme as well as a mnemonic practice.

The performance of the prohibitions seems as ubiquitous and continuous as the outlawed practices themselves. Neither disappeared.

Around the hills there are three or four places where [the Indians] used to make very solemn sacrifices and they came to these places from distant lands. One of these is here in Mexico, where there is a hill called Tepéacac and the Spaniards call it Tepeaquilla, and now it is called Our Lady of Guadalupe; in this place they had a temple dedicated to the mother of the gods, whom they called Tonantzin, which means our Mother; there they made many sacrifices to honor this goddess and came to her from distant lands from more than twenty leagues, from all the regions of Mexico and they brought many offerings; men and women and young men and young women came to those feasts; there was a great gathering of people on those days and they all said let us go to the feast of Tonantzin; and now that the Church of Our Lady of Guadalupe was built there, they also call it Tonantzin. . . . it is something that should be remedied . . . this appears to be a satanic invention to lessen the idolatry under the equivocation of this name Tonantzin and they come now to visit this Tonantzin from far off, as far off as before, which devotion is also suspicious because everywhere there are many churches of Our Lady and they do not go to them.—Bernardino de Sahagún, *Historia general de las cosas de Nueva España,*translation in *Memory, Myth, and Time in Mexico,* by Enrique Florescano, trans. Albert G. Bork

Indigenous performances, paradoxically, seem to be transferred and reproduced within the very symbolic system designed to eliminate them: Roman Catholicism. Religion proved a vital conduit of social (as well as religious) behavior. The transfers occurred not just in the uneasy tensions between religious systems but within the religious systems themselves. It was not long before the very friars who had boasted of early spiritual victory over the conquered suspected that these new converts were in fact worshipping their old gods in a new guise.[85] "Offerings to the idols," Sahagún noted, "are clandestinely practiced under the pretext of the feasts which the Church celebrates to revere God."[86] Instead of replacing pre-Conquest forms of worship, the new rituals allowed for their continuity; satanic "equivocation" permitted those kneeling before Guadalupe to direct their attentions to Tonantzin.

The friars riled against any mixing and overlapping of belief systems, threatening to withhold Christian instruction "until the heathen ceremonies and false cults of their counterfeit deities are extinguished, erased."[87] The equivocal (because multivocal) nature of religious practice led friars to suspect the truthfulness of the native's piety. Insisting on strict orthodoxy, they feared anything in indigenous practice that somehow resembled or overlapped with their own. Durán, in the *Book of the Gods and Rites*, draws some uneasy comparisons between the Nahua's practice of human sacrifice and Christian communion, noting "how cleverly this diabolical rite imitates that of our Holy Church" (95). He concludes that either the native peoples already knew about Christianity (and were thus heathens, not pagans) or "our cursed adversary forced the Indians to imitate the ceremonies of the Christian Catholic religion in his own service" (95). Native peoples came to be seen as perpetual performers, engaged in "idolatrous dissembling," "go[ing] about like monkeys, looking at everything, so as to imitate whatever they see people do."[88] *Dissembling* conveys the deep nervousness experienced by the colonial observer when faced with native performance. The suspicions concerning religious orthodoxy were expressed too, as ambivalence toward mimesis. On the one hand, Europeans from Columbus onward had praised the native peoples' capacity for imitation and used that to argue that they could be taught to be Christians and take the sacraments. On the other hand, the mimicry was inappropriate and bestial, "like monkeys." How could the friars tell if their converts were sincere when they bent their knee before the altar? Did the performance of piety confirm Christian devotion?

The religious practices of the various groups of colonizers—Puritanism and Catholicism—affected the way native practices survived. Even as Catholics like Durán equated "Indians" with Jews because of what he saw as the similarities in their religious rites and ceremonies, Catholicism, with its emphasis on images, *auto sacramentales*, and spectacular ceremonies, was considered by Protestants to border on the idolatrous. Later commentators, such as the nineteenth-century ethnologist Charles de Brosse, claimed that the Catholic reliance on images in fact provided the environment in which native belief systems continued to flourish. W. J. T. Mitchell, in *Iconology*, quotes Willem Bosman's view that Catholicism's "ridiculous ceremonies" linked them to the heathens.[89] And it is clear that the early efforts by evangelists to convert native peoples through the use of religious theatre allowed not only for the creation of a new genre ("missionary theatre"), but for the transmission of native languages, staging techniques, and oppositional practices.

Pre-Conquest performances and images continued to be transmitted through multiple syncretic and transcultured forms such as music, dance, the use of color, pilgrimages, the ritualized marking of place (such as small structures known as *santopan*, place of the saint) that later came to be called *altares* but that dated back to pre-Conquest times.[90] Although performed embodied practice might be limited in its reach because the signified cannot be separated from the signifier, the relationship of signifier to signified is not a straightforward one-to-one. The bent knee might signal devotion to the Catholic saint even as it makes manifest continued reverence to a Mexica deity. The act of transfer, in this case, works through doubling, replication, and proliferation rather than through *surrogation*, the term Joseph Roach has developed to think about the ways that transmission occurs through forgetting and erasure: "Into the cavities created by loss through death or other forms of departure . . . survivors attempt to fit satisfactory alternatives."[91] Roach gives an example of surrogation: The King is dead, long live the King. The model of surrogation forgets its antecedents, Roach reminds us, by emphasizing seemingly uninterrupted stability over what might be read as rupture, the recognizable one over the particularities of the many.

Roach's contribution to our thinking about performance as a form of surrogation has been extremely generative, but it is equally urgent to note the cases in which surrogation as a model for cultural continuity is rejected precisely because, as Roach notes, it allows for the collapse of vital historical links and political moves. The friars might well have wished that the new approved social behaviors they were imposing on their native population functioned as a form of surrogation. The recent converts, however, may just as readily have embraced these ambiguous behaviors as a way of rejecting surrogation and continuing their cultural and religious practices in a less recognizable form. The performance shift and doubling, in this case, preserved rather than erased the antecedents. The proliferations of the signified—the many saints and rituals—tell stories of shaky continuities and even reimagined connections in the face of historical ruptures. The "satanic invention" that Sahagún alludes to in the quotation introducing this section allows one deity to be worshipped not only under the guise of another but at the same time as another—a form of multiplication and simultaneity rather than surrogation and absenting.

The widely spreading cult of the Virgen de Guadalupe from the mid-sixteenth century to the present provides one example. Cortés marched toward Tenochtitlán carrying the banner of the Virgen de Guadalupe de Extremadura. In 1531, the Virgen de Guadalupe is said to have appeared to Juan

4. Miguel Sánchez, Virgin of Guadalupe, cover illustration for *Imagen de la Virgen María* (Mexico, 1648).

Diego, a Mexica recently converted to Christianity, in Tepeyac, the site of the Mesoamerican goddess Tonanztin. The early friars, as I noted, worried that Tonanztin had disappeared only to reappear in the cult of the Virgen de Guadalupe. Had the pre-Conquest goddess been successfully surrogated by the Virgin, or did she in fact live on in the Christian deity? Did the uninterrupted pilgrimage to her shrine signal alliance to the old or to the new? How did she go from being the Virgen of the conquerors to the "dark Virgin" of the conquered, from the patron of the newly developing "Mexican" identity (1737), to the Patroness of all Latin America (1910) and the Philippines (1935), to the Empress of the Americas (1945)?[92]

The images in Figures 4 through 6 illustrate the struggles to identify the Virgen with specific sectors of the population, emphasizing her "Mexican-

EN GUADALUPE MARIA
de la Gran Mexico es GUIA

5. Mena, *Imagen de la Virgen de Guadalupe con las armas mexicanas y vista de la Plaza Mayor de México.* Colección Biblioteca Nacional, Madrid.

ness" by accentuating her proximity to Mexican land (the maguey plant), cityscapes (the Virgen as patron of Mexico City), and peoples (the *indígenas*). If we look closely at Figure 6, we notice that there are four other appearances of the Virgen in this one canvas: in the upper left and upper right corners as well as one on each tip of the eagle's wings. The representational practice of multiplying the images of the Virgen reflects the multiplication of the apparitions themselves. There are innumerable transformations of the Virgen into multiple regionally specific figures.[93] Every area colonized by the Spaniards has a pantheon of Virgenes. And this is in addition to the numerous versions and reported appearances of the Virgin of Guadalupe herself, who is patron of ethnically diverse groups throughout the Americas. This strategy

6. José de Ribera y Argomanis. *Imagen de jura de la Virgen de Guadalupe como patrona de la ciudad de México,* 1778. Colección Museo de la Basílica de Guadalupe, Mexico City.

of doubling and staying the same, of moving and remaining, of multiplying outward in the face of constricting social and religious policies tells a very specific story of oppression, migration, and reinvention that might be lost if the model of substitution, loss, and narrowing down were used to explain the "continuities."

Embodied performance, then, makes visible an entire spectrum of attitudes and values. The multicodedness of these practices transmits as many layers of meaning as there are spectators, participants, and witnesses. Sometimes the performances reveal the convergence of religious practices (e.g., adorning the saints with intricate feather work and flowers in the processional paths of Corpus Christi). Sometimes the performance of acquiescence (kneeling at mass, or participating "appropriately" in a ritual) hides either multiple allegiances (thought by the friars to be irreconcilable) or deep disenfranchisement. At times, the natives performed their idolatry for the audience of suspicious friars, who demanded that the neophytes produce their "idols" and confess on pain of torture to the continuity of pre-Hispanic rites "as they were used and accustomed to do in the time of their heathen past."[94] As protestors at the time pointed out, this demand led the native peoples into the ridiculous task of "combing the ruins of Coba, more than twenty-five leagues distant, searching for idols" to produce the fictitious evidence.[95] At times, the transfer of performances outlasted the memory of their meaning, as populations found themselves faithfully repeating behaviors that they no longer understood. At other times, the make-believe quality so commonly attributed to performance offers opportunities for open parody, for example, a representation in which the actor "who plays the part of Jesus Christ came out of the theatre publicly nude with great indecency and scandal."[96] Many contemporary performances carry on these representational traditions as they continue to form a living chain of memory and contestation. Religious pilgrimages maintain certain kinds of transcultured belief, combining elements from various belief systems. Political performance, for example, might draw from pre-Conquest plots to elucidate contemporary conditions for indigenous populations. Performance artists draw from the repertoire to add historical depth to their political and aesthetic claims. Coatlicue, the mother of Huitzilopochtli, the Nahua's principal deity and god of war, reappears in Astrid Hadad's *Heavy Nopal* to denounce pollution, unequal north/south relations, oppressive gender and sexual relations, and anything else that occurs to Hadad as she sings, dances, and delivers her commentaries onstage.

This study traces some of the issues raised here by focusing on twentieth- and twenty-first-century performances in the Americas: How does performance participate in acts of transfer, transmitting memories and social identity? How does the scenario of discovery continue to haunt the Americas, trapping even those who attempt to dismantle it (chapter 2)? And if cultural memory is an embodied practice, how do gender and race affect it (chapter 3)? How does a radically different archive give rise to a new sense of cultural identity (chapter 4)? How do certain scenarios encourage a "false identifica-

7. Astrid Hadad as Coatlicue, in *Heavy Nopal.* Courtesy of Astrid Hadad, 1999.

tion" that gets used politically (chapter 5)? How do the archive and the repertoire combine to make a political claim (chapter 6)? How does performance
participate in the transmission of traumatic memory (chapter 7)? How can
performance help us address, rather than deny, structures of intercultural indecipherability (chapter 8)? Chapter 9 traces my own positioning as a witness
to the events of September 11. The final chapter advocates that we remap our
existing concepts of the Americas and use embodied performance to trace
trajectories and forms of interconnectedness.

I draw from my own repertoire for some of the material in this book: my
participation in political events and performances and my experience of the
attack on the World Trade Center. As a social actor, I try to be attentive to

my own engagement and investment in the scenarios I describe. Some of the transfers that I've been party to have taken place through live enactments and encounters: those at the Hemispheric Institute's encuentros, in public lectures, in the classroom, in activities I share with colleagues and friends. This book, however, is destined for the archive.

2

SCENARIOS OF DISCOVERY

Reflections on Performance and Ethnography

On September 11, 1995, a small New England newspaper ran an article informing its readers that an "expedition claims to have found new tribe in Amazon rain forest." The expedition leader, Marcelo Santos, an expert from Brazil's Indian Agency, recounts coming upon "two huts" in the Amazon, "surrounded by gardens of corn, bananas, manioc and yams. We made noise to announce ourselves, and after a waiting period, the Indians approached." There were two of them. "The Indians—a man and a woman—wore headdresses and jewelry made in part from bits of plastic apparently taken from mining or logging camps. They carried bows and arrows," Santos said. For two hours, the two groups marveled at each other. "The male Indian became fascinated with my watch," Santos said. He gave the man the watch and two knives. Santos vowed to return to the area, taking either a "language expert or an Indian with a similar dialect with us to establish verbal communication." Though there are more than five hundred indigenous groups in Brazil, according to Santos, including some that might still be "undiscovered," a lawyer for landowners claims the story is a hoax, staged to justify indigenous claims to the land.[1]

This is only one in a long line of scenarios of discovery of wild men and women in the New World. Its banality hides its instrumentality and transitivity: the scenario transports "us" (as expedition leaders or newspaper readers) from here to an exotic "there," transfers the not-ours to the ours, translates the Other's systems of communication into one we claim to understand, transforms past enactments (earlier discovery scenarios) into future outcomes (usually loss of native lands). In doing so, the scenario simultaneously constructs the wild object and the viewing subject—producing a "we" and an "our" as it produces a "them." It normalizes the extraordinary conceit that discovery is still possible, that "undiscovered" peoples still exist, without questioning the obvious: *Undiscovered by whom?* These peoples, newsworthy objects, will almost certainly lose their land and way of life as they become entangled in Brazil's legal and political systems. The scenario activates the new by conjuring up the old—the many other versions of the discovery scenario that endow it with affective and explanatory power. The construction of this marvel of undiscovered Otherness is immediately uncut by the oh-not-againness of it all. What else is there to say about the atrocity of conquest? The very scenario that numbs us with familiarity occludes the atrocious outcome. As a paradigmatic system of visibility, the scenario also assures invisibility. All the more reason to wonder, then, why this scenario continues to be replayed, and why it still wields such power. How does the scenario work as an act of transfer that literally transports the native them into our field of vision, into our economic and legal system of operations? How does it transfer the seemingly past (primitive, pre-) into the present as *new*? Or conversely, make participants and readers of newspapers feel that we are being transferred *back* in time and place? Modernity, as Paul Connerton argues, "denies credence to the thought that the life of an individual or community can or should derive its value from acts of consciously performed recall," such as "celebrations of recurrence."[2] Scenarios such as this one have become so normalized as to transmit values and fantasies without calling attention to itself as a "conscious" performance.

This chapter explores the scenario as an act of transfer, as a paradigm that is formulaic, portable, repeatable, and often banal because it leaves out complexity, reduces conflict to its stock elements, and encourages fantasies of participation. The lack of complexity need not suggest that the scenario cannot provoke an affective reaction or conjure up multiple deep-seated fears and fantasies. The sheer number of versions of the scenario of discovery speaks to the overflow of meanings, levels, and possible perspectives. But the basic framework includes particular elements that viewers recognize despite the variations. Much as V. Propp maintains that there are a limited number of narratives with innumerable variations, scenarios also play out the multiple possibilities of a basic sequence.[3]

Although much has been written about narratives as structures of communication, there is also an advantage to looking at scenarios that are not reducible to narrative because they demand embodiment. Scenarios, like narrative, grab the body and insert it into a frame. The body in the scenario, however, has space to maneuver because it is not scripted. As I argued in chapter 1, scenarios generate an important critical distance between social actor and character. Whether it's a question of mimetic representation (an actor assuming a role) or of performativity, of social actors assuming socially regulated patterns of appropriate behavior, the scenario more fully allows us to keep both the social actor and the role in view simultaneously and thus recognize the uneasy fits and areas of tension. After looking at the inaugural scenario of discovery, I explore what those spaces of critical distance and maneuverability might be in the repertoire (Coco Fusco and Guillermo Gómez-Peña's performance *Two Undiscovered Amerindians Visit*) and the archive (the video of the same performance).

FICTIONS OF ORIGIN

In his first letter from his first voyage (1493), Columbus describes how he "found people without number and very many islands, of which I took possession in Your Highnesses' name by royal proclamation and by unfurling the royal standard and with no contradiction."[4] In 1552, almost sixty years later, Bartolomé de las Casas restaged the scene in his summary of Columbus's journal. This is an especially important account because the original and the copy of the journal disappeared from the archive. This, perhaps, is the first hint that the foundational scenario of discovery, like the initial documentation of it, has no original. It is always in quotations, a copy of a lost copy:

> They reached a small island of the Lucayos, which is called in the language of the Indians "Guanahaní." Immediately they saw naked people, and the admiral went ashore in the armed boat. . . . [He] brought out the royal standard, and the captains went with two banners of the Green

8. "Cólon cuando llegó a la India por primera vez . . ." Theodoro de Bry, *Das Vierdte Buch Von Der Neuwen Welt. Oder Neuwe Und Gründtliche Historien/Von Dem Nidergangischen,*vol. 4 of *Grands Voyages-Americae* (Frankfort, 1594).

Cross, which the admiral flew on all the ships as a flag, with an F and a Y, over each letter of their crown. . . . The admiral called the two captains and the others who had landed . . . and said that they should bear witness and testimony how he, before them all, took possession of the island, as in fact he did, for the King and Queen, his Sovereigns, making the declarations which are required, as is contained more at length in the testimonies which were there made in writing. Soon many people of the island gathered there.[5]

The scenario of discovery is theatrical indeed. The self-proclaimed discoverers perform the claim in public by enacting specific movements (planting the flag) and reciting official declarations in a spectacle backed by visible signs of authority (the royal standard and the banners with letters on it). The performance is attended by the witnesses who will write about it, "recorded at great length in the evidence there set down in writing."[6] Those others who look on—the "many people of the island gathered there" and whom Columbus refers to as "Indians" in his first letter—are the unauthorized spectators. The show is and is not for them. The legitimating audience of Europeans and those who will write the testimonies stand on one side. Offstage but centrally important, the King and Queen of Spain are the addressees and beneficiaries of the act, receiving the transfer of possession. And God, viewing the scene from above, is the ultimate spectator: "Let Christ rejoice on earth, as he rejoices in heaven in the prospect of salvation of the souls of so many nations hitherto lost."[7] Peripheral to the action, seemingly, stand those who through this act of transfer become the dispossessed, potential slaves and servants. Columbus interprets the "no contradiction" as a sign of the indigenous people's acceptance of their new subordinate status.[8] The mute acquiescence of naked, defenseless native peoples is forever plotted into the sequence.

The scenario takes place in the here and now of Columbus's first letter—the Caribbean, 1493—yet with an eye to Spain and the future. The claim is performed to be witnessed and recorded: the moves of the repertoire enacted for the archive. The scenario functions as the frame that enables the transfer from the repertoire to the archive. The here was being staged for the there. The paradigm was established: the surveying of the territory, the reading of the official declaration, the unfurling of the banners, the taking possession of the land (which only incidentally appeared to be inhabited already). The ceremony legitimated the act; Columbus, the main protagonist, embodied the power of the realm. The authorized spectators validated the transfer; the unauthorized spectators were reduced to transferable objects. The King and Queen were praised; God thanked; the transfer accomplished.

Nonetheless, the scenario also looked to the past. While celebrating the "new," the formulaic setup legitimated itself through reference to an existing tradition. One particularly surprising aspect of the Columbus scenario, as Stephen Greenblatt points out, is that while it is a first (and he stresses, along with Todorov, the magnitude of this first European contact with the Caribbean), it has an "odd air of quotations" made up of "formularies and stereotypical gestures."[9] Grounded in past acts of possession, whether in relation to the Canary Islands or the Reconquista, the scenario was choreographed in Spain. Certain things had to be said and done to accomplish the transfer. Reiteration lent the scenario intelligibility and legitimacy. The ceremonious style highlighted the magnitude of the acquisition. Yet the bureaucratic, formulaic structure was familiar, and thus automatically normalized the radical newness of the encounter, overriding possible debates and concerns about legality. Columbus's role in the scenario, like his accounts of it, soon found their way back home, preserved in both the repertoire and the archive. Everywhere the Spanish explorers landed, a variation of the scenario was repeated "live" and recorded in the archive.[10] The act underwrote the deed. It set the model for all the following Spanish acts of possession, yet it did so not only by claiming itself to be foundational, but by simultaneously assuming its place as one more act in a long tradition. The scenario thus bridges past and future as well as the here and there. It's never for the first time, and never for the last, yet it continues to be constantly reactivated in the *now* of performance, explaining why "we" have a right to be there, whether it's expeditions or space films, adventure getaways or land grabs.

The corpus of discovery required a physical *cuerpo* or body. Columbus wrote of the people he "discovered" as unarmed, naked, generous, "the finest people under the sun, without evil or deception."[11] Las Casas quotes from the lost journal:

> What follows are the actual words of the admiral, in his book of his first voyage and discovery of these Indies.
>
> "I," he says, "in order that they might feel great amity towards us, because I knew that they were a people to be delivered and converted to our holy faith rather by love than by force, gave to some among them some red caps and some glass beads, which they hung round their necks, and many other things of little value. At this they were greatly pleased and became so entirely our friends that it was a wonder to see. Afterwards they came swimming to the ships' boats, where we were, and brought us parrots and cotton thread in balls, and spears and many other things, and we exchanged for them other things, such as small glass beads and hawks' bells, which we gave to them. In fact, they took all and gave all, such as they had, with good will, but it seemed to me that they were a people very deficient in everything. They all go naked as their mothers bore them, and the women also, although I saw only one very young girl. And all those whom

I did see were youths, so that I did not see one who was over thirty years of age; they were very well built, with very handsome bodies and very good faces. Their hair is coarse almost like the hairs of a horse's tail and short; they wear their hair down over their eyebrows, except for a few strands behind, which they wear long and never cut. Some of them are painted black, and they are the colour of the people of the Canaries, neither black nor white, and some of them are painted white and some red and some in any colour that they find. Some of them paint their faces, some their whole bodies, some only the eyes, and some only the nose. They do not bear arms or know them, for I showed to them swords and they took them by the blade and cut themselves through ignorance. They have no iron. Their spears are certain reeds, without iron, and some of these have a fish tooth at the end, while others are pointed in various ways. They are all generally fairly tall, good looking and well proportioned. I saw some who bore marks of wounds on their bodies, and I made signs to them to ask how this came about, and they indicated to me that people came from other islands, which are near, and wished to capture them, and they defended themselves. And I believed and still believe that they come here from the mainland to take them for slaves. They should be good servants and of quick intelligence, since I see that they very soon say all that is said to them, and I believe that they would easily be made Christians, for it appeared to me that they had no creed. Our Lord willing, at the time of my departure I will bring back six of them to Your Highnesses, that they may learn to talk.[12]

No clothes, no creed, no iron, and certainly no civilization or writing—in short, "a people very deficient in everything." The network of relations among the many native groups all but disappears, reduced to a simple antagonism of people who "come here from the mainland to take them for slaves." No wonder Columbus, and others after him, assumed these empty vessels would never contest the loss of their lands, would never organize against them, and would easily take to Christianity. Of indeterminate race ("neither black nor white"), they appeared as decorative exteriority ("some of them are painted white and some red and some in any colour that they find"). Their "quick intelligence" makes itself manifest in terms of language acquisition: "they very soon say all that is said to them." Columbus praises the indigenous peoples for being able to imitate words, like the parrots that accompany them. Here begins the debate about mimesis that preoccupied the colonizers. Was it the redeeming aspect of mimesis that Columbus saw as a sign of intelligence? Or the rote, unthinking practice that others equated with the animal-like imitation of monkeys and parrots (see chapter 1)? Language did not facilitate communication, yet Columbus claims the powers of decipherability; though the natives had not yet "learn[ed] to talk" (at least in a manner recognized by the colonizer), Columbus states that he "already understood something of the language and signs made by some Indians."[13] Performed behaviors, apparently, were equally transparent: by signs they tell of wounds inflicted by enemy peoples, by signs they tell that "to the south, either inland or along the coast, there was a king who had large vessels."[14] He felt confident that he could decipher their intentions and meanings: "They became so entirely our friends."

Columbus not only invented himself as munificent and semidivine in his journal and letters, he also invented his interlocutors. In addition to generalizing about widespread practice based on isolated examples (all the women go naked, though he saw only "one very young girl"), he also produced images of "natives" he never saw: the cannibals from Caribo, who "eat human flesh . . . and wear their hair long as the women do"; those from an island he calls Faba, where "everyone is born with a tail"; and people from Jamaica, "where all the people are without hair" (43). The women from the "island of women" (Martinique, presumably) "do not behave like women" (41). They "employ themselves in no labour suitable for their sex, for they use bows and javelins" (15).

The central fiction in this invention of the Other is that communication appears to be reciprocal. If Columbus could not prove that his overtures to the natives were requited, either through gift giving or other signs, then how could he interpolate them as willing (or at least noncontradicting) participants in the act of possession? This was a mere formality, much as the recitation of the Requerimiento was (a document read in Latin to indigenous populations by Spanish conquerors before taking the land), yet politically vital nonetheless. As opposed to narrative that, as Greenblatt argues, can "create the illusion of presences that are in reality absences," the scenario can vacate physical presence.[15] The Amerindians, though physically present, are acknowledged only to be disappeared in this act. They, like the animals

Columbus says they resemble, become part of the landscape, found objects to be transferred (like servants and slaves), not subjects or landowners. Their present, as well as their presence, is deferred by the scenario. Their potential humanity is postponed for some later date, when they will be displayed in the Spanish Court: "I will bring back six of them to Your Highnesses, that they may learn to talk."

The use value of "Indians" was multiple. First, the Indians could facilitate his reconnaissance mission if "they might learn our language, and communicate to us what they knew respecting the country" (9). Second, their physical presence would authenticate his story: "I bring with me individuals of this island and of the others that I have seen, who are proofs of the facts which I state" (15). Third, through the "native," the discoverer promotes his centrality and that of his people. Columbus asserted that the astonished natives believed and propagated notions of his innate superiority: "They continue to entertain the idea that I have descended from heaven; and on our arrival at any new place they published this, crying out immediately with a loud voice to the other Indians, 'Come, come and look upon beings of a celestial race' " (9). When he returned to Spain in 1493, Columbus had several Arawacks with him. One was left on display in the Spanish Court until he died, of sadness apparently, two years later.

The scenario thus situates the discoverer as the one who "sees" and controls the scene, and who never feels obliged to describe or situate himself. It is interesting to compare the extensive descriptions of the Indians by Columbus with Theodoro de Bry's sixteenth-century engraving (Figure 8). Columbus sets himself up as the central protagonist—an authoritative, munificent, almost all-knowing "I"; he assumes the role of unseen seer ("I saw," "I knew," and "I believe"). The natives take on imaginary characteristics or fill in for an ancient enemy.[16] In de Bry's engraving, Columbus and his armed soldiers are greeted by natives as more and more Spaniards spill out of the ships. Other Spaniards, their swords on the ground or by their side, erect the cross in the background. As in the description from the journal, Columbus occupies center stage. The generous, seminaked natives come forward tentatively from the side. More seminaked people dance in the background, and in the far distance they become almost indistinguishable from the trees, seemingly "at one with nature." The Spaniards, on the contrary, control nature, their ships and small boats dominating the water. But the oddest thing, to my mind, is that all the bodily ornamentation that Columbus associated with the natives is applied by de Bry to the Spaniards themselves. The ornate doublets give their bodies a tattooed look. The feathers on Columbus's cap, using his own logic, might place him in the animal kingdom. The shadowed faces of the soldiers behind him and the pinched look on Columbus's face compare negatively with the open and expressive faces of their native interlocutors, depicted as beautiful in the style of ancient Greece. While they reach out with gifts, Columbus has one hand behind his back, an ironic commentary on his insistence on reciprocity. In the other he holds a commanding pole with a blade protruding at the end of it. The formality of the scene, the inequality of exchange, and the feeling of menacing inevitability as more and more Spaniards make it to shore bespeaks the limits of the perspectival vision Columbus offers in his journal.

Transmitting the scenario as a narrative, the way Columbus does, downplays some of the incongruities that necessarily come to light through embodiment. De Bry's image complicates the narrative by showing the tensions around body language and by struggling with issues of embodiment, no matter how idealized. An enactment of this same scene would demand that human bodies wrestle with and against those preexisting images. Where, physically, would the "encounter" be located? Who would embody the Spaniards? Who the natives? What would they look like? What race would they be? What gender? How would they perform their identities? The enactment could transmit much of the same information found in Columbus's description and yet transmit the multiple systems at work in the historical layering of cultural attitudes and interests.

Theatrical encounters, certainly, are captured in these scenarios transmitted both through the repertoire and the archive. The letters and journals by explorers, conquerors, and missionaries were widely published (and censored) during the sixteenth century.[17] Performing the act of possession makes the claim; the witnessing and writing down legitimates it. The letters and journals assure the reputation of the colonizer, not just in the eyes of the King and Queen but for generations to come. Accounts from the New World, furthermore, made for fascinating reading and dramatic entertainment back in Europe. "As stories of sexual and familial encounters," Susanne Zantop writes, "these colonial fantasies could take on any generic form. They were cast as children's books or entertainment for adults, as narratives, poetry, or drama."[18] Those Indians who did not understand the performance were nonetheless interpolated as the indispensable, though backgrounded, guarantors of its efficacy. The act transformed the scenario of force and dispossession into one of love and consent: "They were greatly pleased [by the gifts], and became so entirely our friends that it was a wonder to see." Death to those who failed to go along with this performance. The Requerimiento warned that whoever did not recognize the superiority of Catholicism and the Catholic monarchs would be killed or enslaved.[19] The role of the spectator was central, though at times confusing. Besides those who, as witnesses, legitimated the act, those who benefited from it, and those who consumed it, others were dazed. "Even the eminent Spanish Dominican Bartolomé de las Casas," writes anthropologist Patricia Seed in *Ceremonies of Possession*, "wrote that when he heard the Requirement he did not know whether to laugh or to cry. . . . the way the Requirement was implemented strikes many even today as absurd as the text itself" (71). But the performance did not have to be logical or convincing—it just had to be efficacious. This scene would be replayed time and again throughout the Americas as part of the discovery project, as it would also be replayed in the innumerable accounts and representations of the events.

The drama of discovery and display of native bodies—then and now —serves various functions. The indigenous bodies perform a "truth" factor; they "prove" the material facticity of an Other and authenticate the discoverer/missionary/anthropologist's perspective, in terms of both geographic and ideological positioning. That materiality, of course, confirms no one point. As in the case of the native populations of the Americas and the recently "discovered" tribe in Brazil, the native body serves, not as proof of alterity, but merely as the space on which the battles for truth, value, and power are fought by competing dominant groups. The debates between Gínes de Sepúlveda and Bartolomé de las Casas in the mid-sixteenth century is a case in point. Were the Indians by nature inferior, soulless, as Sepúlveda maintained, and therefore "obliged to submit to Spanish rule, as the less intelligent are ruled by their betters"? Or were Indians human beings with souls and, thus, deserving of humane treatment, as las Casas contended?[20] The stakes were enormous: Could their "superiors" work them to death with moral impunity? The outcome of the controversy affected not only the self-image of the conquerors and the fate of the conquered. The inscription of the native body as weak resulted in the abduction and enslavement of "strong-bodied" Africans, brought to the Americas to continue the backbreaking work. Not for that were the native peoples spared. In the fifty years following European contact, 95 percent of the population died.[21] Concerns with economic value have always been deeply entangled in debates about moral value in regard to native populations, and have fueled or foiled the discussions surrounding the definition, status, and rights of the native body. If these natives exist, the Brazilian landowners want to know, what does that do to their own claim to the land? Are there really "undiscovered tribes" that have somehow failed to enter "our" scopic/legal field? Or is the Brazilian government staging this farce to confiscate the landowners' hard-earned holdings?

Then, insofar as native bodies are invariably presented as not speaking (or not making themselves understood to the defining subject), they give rise to an industry of "experts" needed to approach and interpret them: language experts, scientists, ethicists, ethnographers, and cartographers. Like Columbus, many have felt confident that they can interpret the native's gestures and performances. The colonialist discourse that produces the native as negativity or lack itself silences the very voice it purports to make speak. Santos, the head of the Indian Agency, describes the encounter to the journalist who then passes it on to us, the audience unwittingly forged by the scenario. The "primitive" body as object reaffirms the cultural supremacy and authority of the viewing subject, the one who is free to come and go (while the native stays fixed in place and time), the one who sees, interprets, and records. The native is the show; the civilized observer the privileged spectator. We, those viewers who look through the eyes of the explorer, are (like the explorer) positioned safely outside the frame, free to define, theorize, and debate their (never our) societies. The "encounters" with the native create us as audience just as much as the violence of definition creates them, the primitives. Needless to say, the colonizer suspects that he does not understand everything; not all is transparent. Like Bernardino de Sahagún, he may suspect that the devil hides in the performances taking place before his very eyes. However, domination depends on maintaining a unidirectional gaze and stages the lack of reciprocity and mutual understanding inherent in discovery.

In 1992, Latino performance artists Coco Fusco and Guillermo Gómez-Peña decided to put the viewer back into the frame of discovery. They started their Guatinaui World Tour as a sardonic response to the celebrations of the quincentennial:

> Our plan was to live in a golden cage for three days, presenting ourselves as undiscovered Amerindians from an island in the Gulf of Mexico that had somehow been overlooked by Europeans for five centuries. We called our homeland Guatinau, and ourselves Guatinauis. We performed our "traditional tasks," which ranged from sewing voodoo dolls and lifting weights to watching television and working on a laptop computer. A donation box in front of the cage indicated that, for a small fee, I would dance (rap music), Guillermo would tell authentic Amerindian stories (in a nonsensical language), and we would pose for Polaroids with visitors. Two "zoo guards" would be on hand to speak to visitors (since we could not understand them), take us to the bathroom on leashes, and feed us sandwiches and fruit. At the Whitney Museum in New York we added sex to our spectacle, offering a peek at authentic Guatinaui male genitals for $5. A chronology with highlights from the history of exhibiting non-Western peoples was on one didactic panel and a simulated Encyclopedia Britannica entry with a fake map of the Gulf of Mexico showing our island was on another.[22]

For the next year, the highly controversial *Two Undiscovered Amerindians Visit . . .* traveled around the world, from Plaza Colón in Madrid to the Australian Museum of Natural Science in Sydney, the Smithsonian's National Museum of Natural History, London's Covent Gardens, and Buenos Aires, Argentina. Fusco and Gómez-Peña chose countries deeply implicated in the extermination or abuse of aboriginal peoples. By staging their show in historic sites and institutions, they situated the dehumanizing practice in the very heart of these societies' most revered legitimating structures. The performance (among many other things) repeated the colonialist gesture of producing the "savage" body, and it historicized the practice by highlighting its citational character. As in the fifteenth-century Spanish Court, the natives were once again constructed as exotic, mute Others and given to be seen. Furthermore, the performance activated current controversies about what and how museums display. Since their inception in the nineteenth century, museums have literalized the theatricality of colonialism. Somewhat like a scenario, a museum seems both a place and a practice. Though etymologically it is a place or temple dedicated to the muses and functions as an archive in that it also means a study or library, the museum also signals the cultural practice that converts a *place* into a *space*. Museums have long taken the cultural Other out of context and isolated it, reducing the live to a dead object behind glass. Museums enact the knower-known relationship by separating the transient visitor from the fixed object of display. Like discoverers, the visitors come and go; they see, they know, they believe—only the deracinated, adorned and "empty" object stays in place. Museums preserve (a particular) history, (certain) traditions, and (dominant) values. They stage the encounter with otherness. The monumentality of most museums emphasizes the discrepancy in power between the society that can contain all others and those represented only by remains, the shards and fragments salvaged in miniature displays.

The Guatinaui cage confronts the viewer with the "unnatural" and extremely violent history of representation and exhibition of non-Western human beings. Yet, it also enters into dialogue with another history: the caging of rebellious individuals in Latin America from pre-Hispanic times to the recent public caging in Peru of Abimael Guzmán, leader of Sendero luminoso (Shining Path), and the caging of Taliban fighters by the United States in Guantanamo. These performances of power have different histories. In a cage, in a museum, in a society that segregates and incarcerates its Others, Fusco and Gómez-Peña openly gave themselves up to be classified and labeled. Scantily clad, like exhibits in a diorama, they exposed themselves to public scrutiny. Their performance went along with the museum's fictions of discontinuity, for the unknowing past and the informed present appeared to coexist on either side of the bars. The "exotic," the display teased us to believe, could be safely contained. Like the other exhibits, these two beings offered themselves up as all surface—adorned, painted, empty. There was no more interiority to their performance of the stereotype than in the stereotype itself and nothing to know, it seemed, that was not readily available to the viewing eye. Like the stereotype, the "business" of the performance was monotonous and repetitive. Fusco and Gómez-Peña's

vow of silence, their avoidance of eye contact and any other gestures of recognition stripped their performance of anything that could be mistaken for
a "personal" or individual trait. Colonialism, after all, has attempted to de-
prive its captives of individuality. These bodies were presented as little more
than the generic male and female announced in the didactic panel. The observers, like typical visitors, milled around, at times disturbing the repose of
the objects, who were there to be looked at.

The critique of colonialism was multifaceted. The artistic performance
challenged the cultural performance, the way history and culture are pack-
aged, sold, and consumed within hegemonic structures. Performance as an
object of study (the cage performance, in this case) took on performance as
an episteme, as a culturally produced lens.[23] It called attention to the Western history and practice of collecting and classifying.[24] It recalled the construction and performance of the "exotic" staged in the ethnographic fairs
of the late nineteenth century, in which natives were placed in model habi-
tats much as lifeless specimens were placed in dioramas.[25] And it parodied
the assignation of value that the West has placed on the exotic: $1.00. It
suggested the impossibility of self-representation by the "indigenous" contained through the tyranny of representation. It openly confronted the voy-
euristic desire to see the Other naked (passing, of course, as a legitimate
interest in cultural difference) that animates much current ethnotourism.
The world tour, moreover, highlighted the continued circulation of these
images and desires in the global neocolonial, imperialist economy. Fusco
and Gómez-Peña enacted the various economies of the object I alluded to
earlier: the body as cultural artifact, as sexual object, as threatening alterity,
as scientific specimen, as living proof of radical difference. They were anything the spectator wanted them to be, except human. The way they did their
bodies very consciously linked together a series of what Brecht would have
called "quotable" gestures drawn from the repertoire of native bodies developed through ethnographic world fairs, circus shows, dioramas, films, and
pseudoscientific displays. As "objects," Coco Fusco and Guillermo Gómez-
Peña out-fetished the fetish. Fusco played scientific specimen and exotic
curio with her face painted, her voluptuous torso, her grass skirt, wig, sunglasses, and tennis shoes. Gómez-Peña wore his *enmascarado de plata* mask
(in honor of Mexico's famous masked wrestler), sunglasses, briefcase (with
a snake in it), and black boots; his chest was bare. Silent, impassive, en-

ticing, they performed the subaltern in style. Their self-representation belonged less to the colonial grotesque (of the Hottentot Venus variety) than to a postcolonial chic. Nonetheless, there was also something Latin American, something proud, rebellious, humorous, and contemptuous in the way Fusco and Gómez-Peña approached their audiences. Pure critique, and puro *relajo*, a specifically Mexican mode of debunking hegemonic assumptions through a disruptive acting-out (see chapter 4). Relajo signals an attitude of defiance, or disrespect, as it contests the dominant show—or the show of domination—put forward by those authorized to speak.[26] In a museum, the displayed object engages with and disturbs the logic of display.

The performance critiqued structures of colonialism, but there was less of an attack on prevailing structures of sexism or heterosexism. The performers played the male and female referred to in the explanatory panels. There was something very alluring about Fusco with her beautiful face painted and wearing a grass skirt and skimpy bra, and the frequent sexual overtures by men suggest that perhaps the erotic pleasure of her performance eclipsed its ethos. Gómez-Peña's performance of masculinity was also troubling for some audience members. His macho presentation affirmed and challenged the age-old ambivalence and anxiety surrounding the sexuality of the non-white male. His long, straight, black hair brought back Columbus's description of the effeminate natives with "very handsome bodies" and "coarse" hair, "like the hair of a horse's tail." When, for $5.00, he displayed his genitals at the Whitney Museum, he held his penis tucked between his legs, showing only a "feminine" triangle. Yet there was also something threatening about his macho strutting and his spiked gloves and dog collar. Several times on their tour, women actually touched him. One woman in Irvine, California, Fusco recounts, "asked for plastic gloves to be able to touch the male specimen, [she] began to stroke his legs and soon moved towards his crotch. He stepped back, and the woman stopped."[27] Against the body-as-primitive-scenario, the viewer apparently felt tempted to assume a protagonic, exploratory role. And the assumed normativity of the heterosexual "couple" bothered some commentators. Why was gender construction more difficult to deconstruct than colonialism? The unquestioned naturalness of the couple doing their act in public bespoke a different kind of blindness, and prompted lesbian performance scholar Sue-Ellen Case to suggest that all heterosexuals belong in cages.[28]

But the focus of the performance, according to Fusco, was "less on what we did than on how people interacted with us and interpreted our actions. . . . we intended to create a surprise or 'uncanny' encounter, one in which audiences had to undergo their own process of reflection. . . . caught off guard, their beliefs are more likely to rise to the surface" (40).

The spectator was not only in the frame, but became the main player. However, one of the most interesting and complicated aspects to the cage performance was that several performances were taking place simultaneously, each with a supposedly different protagonist, found object, and intended audience. The cage spectacle was multicoded, one performance taking place inside another, as has happened in the Americas at least as far back as the Conquest. As with the enactment of the claim in Columbus's first voyage, there are many audiences being addressed simultaneously. The cage, too, makes one wonder if the show is and is not for those of us standing there, looking on. While Fusco and Gómez-Peña paced in their cage, objects of the audience's gaze, an "expert" with an "Ask Me" button explained the natives' dress, habits, and origins. Someone with a Polaroid took souvenir photos of audience members posed against the couple in the cage. And, all the while, Fusco and Paula Heredia were making a documentary video of the performances and the audiences. Cuts from old movies representing so-called natives were interjected with routines performed by the artists and interviews of audience members in the many sites hosting the cage. So, while viewers were tourists, consumers, confused citizens, or amused performance buffs in one production, they were actors in another—in which, among other things, they played tourists, consumers, confused citizens, and amused performance buffs. The film of the cage, moreover, makes dupes of viewers who think that they're speaking of the live performance. The video, we might be tempted to believe, transparently documents what happened in the performance. But these are quite different acts of transfer, in part because the two mediums—live performance (repertoire) and film (archive)—affect the nature of the audience response. The intense controversy surrounding the cage is, I believe, in part a product of this double staging.

Trying to resist the temptation to "read" one performance as the other, I now briefly look at the way the audience of the performance is constructed in the video. Though the filmmakers selected the responses, the range of reactions to the show, according to Gómez-Peña, was actually wider than what Fusco and Heredia could possibly include. Gómez-Peña speaks of skinheads trying to get into the cage and both he and Fusco document the incident in Buenos Aires when someone threw acid on his leg.[29] Nonetheless, the video shows a fair range of reactions. Many viewers, much to Fusco and Gómez-Peña's surprise, believed the show was "real" and that the Guatinauis came from that far-off world of National Geographicland.[30] They spotted traces of ritual action and other signs of primitivism that they recognized but didn't exactly understand. Others showed more skepticism. One woman, who looked Mayan in origin and expressed an interest in and knowledge about Guatemala, refused to fall for a simplistic "Is it or isn't it" approach to the issue of native identity. Her somewhat defensive and defiant pose suggested that she knew better than to comment on whether "undiscovered" people exist, saying only that if you're willing to pay people to travel around in a cage, you'll probably find candidates. She also eschewed essentialist notions of cultural authenticity, stating that people go into a society and take what they want. Her notion of societies as constantly in flux, absorbing and resemanticizing "foreign" cultural materials, ran along the lines of Latin American theories of transculturation that explain how aspects of native cultures survived and continue to flourish after five hundred years of conquest, colonization, and imperialism. Other viewers felt deterritorialized through the encounter. One woman, sensing the ground beneath her feet shifting, giggled nervously as she concluded that the spectacle made tourists of its audiences. Several people identified (with) the very "real" message underlying the highly parodic performance; a Spaniard, for example, knew it was about the Conquest and colonization; a Pueblo elder looked in the cage and recognized the face of his grandchildren, and lamented that Native Americans are not much better off today. The video shows an Anglo man staring at the couple with rapt attention. He (much like Santos on his Brazilian expedition) marveled at how "natives" are fascinated by miracles of technology they cannot understand. He kept looking, fascinated, at their fascination.[31]

The responses that the video highlights, however, are those by people who felt deceived or offended by the show. These were people who felt drawn or coerced into the scenario of discovery and either believed or felt that were being asked to believe that "primitives" exist. Why these responses, one wonders, given that there was little illusion of authenticity to the performance? Aside from the authoritative framework provided by the museum, the guides, and the Encyclopedia Britannica, everything that the audience saw was blatantly theatrical. The Guatinauis, a word echoing Columbus's "Guanahaní" that sounds like "What now?" demanded incredulity. The point of the performance was to highlight, rather than normalize, the theatricality of colonialism. Fusco and Gómez-Peña parodied Western stereotypes of what "primitive" people do. Every stereotype was exaggerated and contested—the sunglasses offset the body paint, the "traditional tasks" included working on a computer. When paid to dance, Fusco performed a highly unritualistic rap. So, two questions: How could people either believe the show or feel offended by it, maintaining that they were being "deceived"? And why were they, and subsequent viewers of the film, so angry?

Let me start with the first. The gullibility and deception are flip-sides of the same will to believe. The first accepts "the truth" of the colonial claim; the other sees only the "lie." One stubbornly clings to the official version, no matter how glaring the contradictions; the other feels nothing but outrage: Can't anyone be trusted anymore? Some viewers clearly wanted to believe in the Guatinauis. They longed for authenticity. One dollar was a small price to pay for an encounter with "real" otherness. The reassuring notion of stable, identifiable, real otherness legitimated fantasies of a real, knowable "self." The cage might signal dislocation, placed as it was in the very heart of civilization. But the dislocation, one might choose to believe, resulted from the momentary interruption of the primitive into "our" world. It didn't have anything to do with the diasporas and cultural transformations provoked by colonialism. It was worth a dollar to imagine that the Guatinauis' primitive cage in no way reflected back on the troubles of our post-modern societies, and most emphatically not what Homi Bhabha calls the "unhomeliness" of the colonial and postcolonial condition stretching from 1492 to the present.[32]

The cage promised the security of partial recognition; visitors could marvel at the stereotype of the uprooted natives without worrying about the contemporary reality of displacement and migration. Most, if not all, native peoples of the world today are uprooted, forced to migrate or pushed onto reservations of some sort or another. But one could pretend that the show of displacement was unrelated to that history, or to the current history of political exile and migration in the Americas of artists like U.S.-Cuban Coco Fusco or chilango-mexicano-chicano Gómez-Peña. "Home," for the migrant, "is always somewhere else" as Gómez-Peña puts it.[33] For Fusco, deterritorialized from postrevolutionary Cuba, or for Gómez-Peña, who left Mexico City, there is no *there* there. They, like many others, including myself, really are from nowhere, really are Guatinauis of sorts, though not in the way their spectators were being asked to believe. For all the trappings of difference, the subjects and objects may be more similar than one imagines. For some viewers, then, the bars of the cage actually protected against that realization, marking the radical boundary between the "here" and the "there," the "us" and the "them," allowing for no inter-, no cross-, no transcultural nada. Precolonial subjects, frozen in static essence, didn't experience today's mixed ethnic and racial identities. The native body was believable, then, not because it was "real" but precisely because it wasn't. It served to maintain a distance between the *pre-* and the *post-*: precolonial to postcolonial, premodern to postmodern. Rather than challenging us to more fully acknowledge the racial and cultural heterogeneity of communities in the Latin/o Americas in which very real indígenas continue to live in or alongside industrialized centers, the pre/post hammers in distinct and identifiable boundaries. Suspended *over there*, outside time, beyond civilization, the naked, mute native body lures the destabilized postmodern viewer into dreaming about fixed positions, stable identities, and recognizable difference. The degree to which some of the viewers continued to disavow the marked theatricality of the performance attested to how deeply invested they were in maintaining the colonial scenario. The last thing they wanted, it seems, was to recognize the contemporaneity of the postmodern, postcolonial encounter. Maybe that's what made the spectacle so troubling to many spectators: when they got close to the cage and stared at the "savages," they saw themselves reflected in the artists' dark glasses.

Bringing the spectator into the frame, making people see themselves as implicated in these colonial fantasies, is what the performance and the video were all about. So why are so many people who agree politically with the project so angry? I love the video, and the live performance that I imagine I see in it. Yet I believe the anger in part comes from the "testlike" quality of both. No matter what, we fail. But we fail for different reasons depending on the mode of transmission. Here let me point so some of the key differences involved in the transfer from repertoire to archive.

In the live performance, the "test" had to do with whether audience members would go along with the expert's explanations about the Guatinauis and their island. If the spectators believed the show, they were gullible fools or self-interested colonists. But what if they didn't believe the show, that is, if they understood it to be an artistic performance? Some people recognized it was a performance without recognizing that Fusco and Gómez-Peña were the artists. Coco Fusco complains about an audience member at the Whitney Biennial who was willing to pay $10.00 to feed her a banana. In her essay, she writes, "Even those who saw our performance as art rather than artifact appeared to take great pleasure in engaging in the fiction, by paying money to see us enact completely nonsensical or humiliating acts."[34] Could we argue, conversely, that the man was just willing to play along? I asked Gómez-Peña what his ideal spectator would have done. He stated, "Open the cage and let us out." But, unlike the performance that he and Roberto Sifuentes staged on the Tijuana–San Diego border, in which they crucified themselves and explicitly asked audience members to bring them down from the cross, there is nothing in this performance that calls for intervention. The prohibition against uninvited intervention comes specifically from the piece's artistic nature. People who recognize the conventions of performance, as Cervantes so ferociously demonstrated in *Don Quixote*, don't interrupt the show. And, ironically, the ones who actually tried to open the cage during the world tour were the skinheads who wanted to attack the actors physically. So what do we do? Play along as a "good" audience? And what would that mean, exactly? Participate in the fantasy by posing for a photograph with the "natives"? Would it be appropriate to laugh at the obvious parodic mode? Or would that be highly inappropriate, given the West's violent history of displaying, incarcerating, and exterminating human beings? Should we walk out and cancel our membership to the museum? Like las Casas, we don't know whether to laugh or cry.

The cage, it seems to me, trapped spectators in the *is/as* of performance (see chapter 1). The cage *is* a performance—its ontology determines its ephemeral, bracketed nature. It's an artwork, produced and performed by two artists who went on tour to critique the quincentennial. However, the *as* of performance signals its other dimension as critical lens, as a heuristic system. As a critical commentary on the colonial subjugation and exploitation of native peoples, the cage conjures up the hauntology of performance, the embodied apparition of colonial practices that disallows enjoyment and aesthetic pleasure. The scenario evokes an entire history of presentation and representation that has not disappeared. The quotation from the newspaper that opens this chapter is only one indication that government organizations, corporations, and citizens from all political backgrounds continue to struggle with the scenario of discovery, and that it continues to hold affective and explanatory power. There is no appropriate reaction, no "true" or "false" response to this performance that, as Fusco writes, "falls somewhere between truth and fiction" (37). Some spectators felt offended. Others felt sad and confused.

Provoking this state of confusion, guilty pleasure, and genuine sadness is, I feel, the power and the brilliance of the performance. The scenario of discovery continues to haunt us; though associated with past conquests, it is repeatedly conjured up in the here and now for political, evangelical, and economic gain. Spectators need to position themselves within this scenario, and there is no safe or comfortable place. Participating in the live performance allows viewers to feel both contaminated by the spectacle and responsible for locating themselves in relationship to it.

The video—the performance piece now "caught" and transferred to the archive—further accentuates the spectators' discomfort when suddenly faced with the disturbing spectacle of people locked in cages. Several people I've watched the video with felt angry at the intrusive video camera that "outs" spectators as closet colonists or dupes. Sprung on the viewer with the intention of creating "a surprise or 'uncanny encounter,'" the spectacle would surprise anyone.[35] As Gómez-Peña stated toward the end of the video, sometimes it takes a while for the viewers to understand what they're seeing and their role in it. Most of us know all about imperfect responses, painful pauses, or delayed witticisms. But though it had been the artists' intention to create a pause for reflection in the live performance, this is the space that the video does not allow for. Quite the opposite: it freezes that immediate response. Before the spectator can digest and come to terms with the show in the here and now of the live, that response is transferred to the archive and turned into a show for someone else. As video watchers, our pleasure is somehow tied into the audience members' floundering or, worse, humiliation. I personally feel gloriously Latin American when I watch this video, very empowered knowing I "get it" and "they" don't. That's what relajo is all about. Through a disruptive act, relajo creates a community of resistance, a community, as Mexican theorist Jorge Portilla puts it, of underdogs.[36] Relajo is an *act* with attitude. Maybe that's why I love it. But my own pleasure troubles me. Is this the "appropriate" response to a history of dehumanizing colonial subjects? (Even though I relished its sardonic humor, I knew I'd failed the test.)

Another issue: the performance critiques the West's history of ethnographic practice. But is putting the viewer on the spot automatically a form of critiquing the ethnographic, one-way focus? Whereas the live performance situates us all in the Lacanian field of the gaze, in which we're all in the frame, looking at each other looking, the video shifts the borders. Once again, the video watcher is outside the frame, the unseen see-er. We can laugh at others' reactions. We know; they don't. The hierarchies and epistemologies that the performance attacked are in danger of being reproduced. Our looking becomes unidirectional and invasive. "Their" gullibility reaffirms our superior wisdom; "they" once again serve to stabilize "us." Does reversing the ethnographic lens, albeit sardonically, prove less invasive than the ethnographic practice under critique? Unlike the live performance, which offers the spectators a little room to look, and look again, in their attempts to grapple with the colonialism in the heart and soul of Western cultures (assuming the video makers don't pounce on them), the video "captures" or "cages" the viewer. Like the systems of representation it parodies, the video produces and exposes the Other and unwittingly colludes with the ethnographic pleasures it sets out to deconstruct. So, is that the point? That there is no Other, no noncoercive system of representation? We're all trapped in our performative traditions, mimicking the seemingly endless slate-cleaning, original, and elucidating gestures of those who came before, even as we struggle to do away with the cage? Or does the problem have more to do with the way ethnography and performance come together in staging otherness as they seek to elucidate the drama of cultural encounters?

ETHNOGRAPHY

Ethnography not only studies performance (the rituals and social dramas commentators habitually refer to); it is a kind of performance. Some commentators stress that they *perform* ethnography by recording social dramas, ritual action, and other forms of reiterative behaviors. The ethnologist studies theatrical aspects normally associated with acting (movement, body language, gesture), with staging (backdrop, context) and dramatic emplotment (crisis, conflict, resolution) and cultural meaning. The object of analysis is present, embodied cultural behavior that, as in theatrical performances, takes place live in the here and now. The ethnologist (like a theatre director) mediates between two cultural groups, presenting one group to another in a unidirectional way.[37] The target group that is the object of analysis (the natives) does not usually see or analyze the group that benefits or consumes the ethnographer's accounts (the audience). And it rarely, if ever, gets to respond to the written observations that, in some cases, it might never even see. The live audience present in the ethnographic encounter is not the intended audience.

Moreover, the ethnologist plays a role in the drama that he or she (in theory) is there to simply observe. The encounter is constructed theatrically, staged in the here and now, rather than as a past-tense narrative description, but always with its eye to future readers. The ethnographer brackets the moment (here, the drama of "discovery"), chooses the cast of characters by virtue of framing the event, and endows it with shape and meaning. The ethnographic Other, like the dramatic character played by an actor or like Columbus's "Indian," is part "real," part "fiction"; that is, real bodies come to embody fictional qualities and characteristics created by the ethnographer/dramatist/discoverer. Nonetheless, the ethnographer insists that the spectacle is "real" or, as Turner puts it, quoting Galileo's affirmation of the incontestable order of our solar system: "And yet it moves."[38] The spectacle is "real"; it comes first, he insists, the theoretical framework after.[39] And yet, we would answer, we are the products of our own epistemic systems; we are no more outside the cultural repertoires that produce us than the earth is free from the sun's pulls and tugs. This created, fictional Other, child of the colonial cultural repertoire, is the figure that Coco Fusco and Guillermo Gómez-Peña capture and put behind bars. Their enactment shows the violence of the ethnographic performance that tries to pass as real, violent because its theatrical strings are hidden from the spectator's view. The viewer of "real" ethnography (as opposed to Fusco and Gómez-Peña's parody) is supposed to see it as objective authenticity or proof of radical otherness rather than as fantasy.

However, there is also a way in which performance, or at least *this* performance, is ethnographic—though not perhaps in the way that it intends. Much performance, in a sense, has something in common with the raw material of ethnography, stemming from social behaviors, rituals, and dramas that ethnographers make their focus. Performance, too, explores the use and significance of gesture, movement, and body language to make sense of the world. Twentieth-century artists have actively tried to reconnect to ritual action, as evident in the writing and work by major practitioners such as Artaud, Grotowski, and Barba. However, performance is not just a doing, a form of carrying through. Like ethnography, it has also served as an instrument of cultural analysis, though the society under examination has tended to be the artist's own, rather than the Other's. The subject of analysis in the cage performance is not the couple inside but the audience outside. Certainly, the history and practice of Western ethnography is the target of the parody. But the performance is in itself ethnographic. Like the ethnographer, these performance artists made assumptions about the imagined viewers (a "white audience," as Coco Fusco describes it in the opening paragraph of her essay), formulated their goal ("to create a surprise or 'uncanny' encounter, one in which audiences had to undergo their own process of reflection as to what they were seeing"), defined their methodology (interactive performance), and adjusted their expectations according to information gained in the field ("We did not anticipate that our self-conscious commentary on this practice could be believable").[40] They then decided to measure (collect hard data) the size and range of reactions of the audiences that attended the performance. This analysis led to certain conclusions about deeply held Western cultural stereotypes and anxieties that manifest themselves in certain forms of public behavior on the part of spectators (chagrin, insulting and humiliating speech, etc.), which were then broken down and classified according to age, race, class, gender, and national origin. "We found that young people's reactions have been the most humane," Fusco writes (52). Or, "Several feminist artists and intellectuals at performances in the United States" said this (55); "Artists and cultural bureaucrats, the self-proclaimed elite" did that (52); "People of color who believed, at least initially, that the performance was real" did something else (53); and "Whites outside the U.S. were more ludic in their reactions than American whites" (55). While the performance sardonically mimics the gestures of ethnographic displays and dismantles the "real" they purport to reveal, the video in turn wants to function as a "document" of cultural behavior. So, is this reverse ethnography that sardonically shows up the violence inherent in ethnographic practice, as Gómez-Peña and Fusco intend, or is it ethnography, complete with its own inherent violence? Is the discomfort manifested by the audience simply about the troubling content (the treatment of aboriginal peoples)? In part, I believe, the discomfort is about the disconcerting true/false setup. But it is *also* about the way in which the audience is being constructed. The scrutiny of the audience in the video ends up turning spectators into specimens. Does the encounter give us more information about our own cultural fears and fantasies, "our" referring to both the audience at the performance and those captured on tape? Or are the data being used, classified, and presented to some other audience entirely? Does that audience get to respond *to* the show, rather than *as* the show?

These questions, though directed at the performance and particularly the video of the cage, hold for other forms of performance that move the focus from the stage to the audience in an attempt to gauge its habits and belief systems. As culture becomes less a synonym for performance than its field of work, and as performance complicates our understanding of cultural practice so that we recognize the rehearsed and produced and creative nature of everyday life, perhaps we may be excused for wondering who the artists are, who the ethnographer, the dupe, the closet colonist. Who, ultimately, pulls the theatrical strings? Who is positioned where in this most uncanny, postmodern drama of cultural encounters?

3

MEMORY AS CULTURAL PRACTICE

Mestizaje, Hybridity, Transculturation

Setting: Mexico City. (Harpsichord music. Silence. Darkness. A spotlight comes up on the INTERMEDIARY. She sits in a wicker chair and is dressed like a woman of the "pueblo"—a white blouse and a skirt as dark as the rebozo that covers her head.)

INTERMEDIARY: I listened to my heart beat all afternoon. I finished my tasks early, so I sat here, quietly, looking out with blurry eyes, listening to my heart as it beat gently against my breasts, like a cautious lover knocking to come in, or a chick pecking at the walls of its egg, trying to move out into the light. I began to imagine my heart . . . (She brings her hand to her breast.) . . . a sea anemone . . . intricate, delicately colored, tucked away in its cave, an efficient, highly methodical organism devoted to the task of regulating endless distances of crepuscular canals, some wide enough for royal gondolas, others barely wide enough for rowing vegetables and food to market by the slow stroke of the oars . . . all of them pulsing regularly, in order. Locks open and close to the rhythm of the complicated commands of the ever-powerful flower of the heart. And then I thought . . . What if all the hearts in the world were to beat at once? but more of that later. I thought of the air too. . . . It smelled of smoke and stale food . . . but I was like a fish, sitting in my chair submerged in the air. I could feel it against my skin. I could feel its currents brushing on me, like petals of the anemone—air that beats and circulates. And then I began to think about all I know. I know many things. I know herbs. Some heal, others taste good or smell sweet, some have a powerful effect . . . they reconcile . . . some cause death or madness, and others simply grow heavy with tiny flowers. But I know more. I store within myself part of everything I've seen: faces, crowds, views, the texture of rocks, corners, many corners . . . and gestures! . . . contacts! I also retain memories, memories which once belonged to my grandmother, my mother, or my friends . . . many which they, in turn, heard from their friends and old, old people! I know texts, pages, illusions, I know how to go places. I know roads! But knowledge is like the heart, hidden and beating, glowing imperceptibly, regulating canals that flow back and forth and flow into other canals, torrents and unexpected currents managed by radial complexity of very powerful central ventricles. All manner of news comes to me everyday: events . . . they all take shape. Events sound and flash; they make themselves explicit, oracular. They intertwine and germinate. Things happen, and I hear them. . . . I receive them! I communicate them! I assimilate them! I contemplate them! (She gets up.) NEWS!

(Darkness. We hear the racket and screech of a train derailment, whistles, shouts, iron scraping upon iron, crashes. Silence. Lightning flashes. Darkness. The NEWSBOY enters, running.)[1]

Emilio Carballido's play *Yo, también hablo de la rosa* (*I, Too, Speak of the Rose*, Mexico, 1965) opens with the image of a mestiza woman sitting quietly in the midst of the sounds and bustles that are Mexico D.F., today the world's most populated city. The Intermediary pauses from her work, which, we assume from her name, her statement, and the final "NEWS!" has something to do with assimilating and communicating information and knowledge. She contemplates what she knows and how she knows it. As she describes the workings of her heart—an organ that in Mexica thought houses memory—it becomes clear that her body functions as the site of convergence binding the individual with the collective, the private with the social, the diachronic and the synchronic, memory with knowledge. She embodies the locus and means of communication. The journey through the inner workings of her body

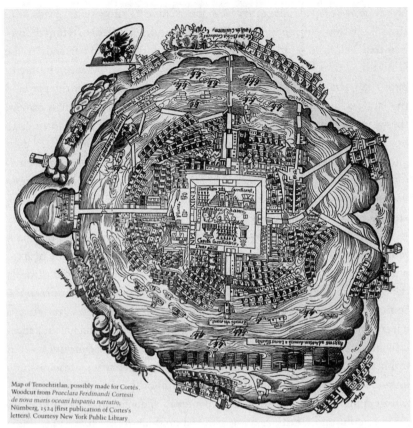

Map of Tenochtitlan, possibly made for Cortés.
Woodcut from *Praeclara Ferdinandi Cortesii*
de nova maris oceani hispania narratio,
Nürnberg, 1524 (first publication of Cortés's
letters). Courtesy New York Public Library

9. Map of Tenochtitlán, a woodcut probably made for Cortés, 1524. Courtesy of New York Public Library.

and its rhythms is also a journey outward through her cityscape, past and present. Her heart, like her memory, acts—pumping the vital fluids through the wide canals and narrow passageways that are her veins and the veins of the ancient city of Tenochtitlán. In the sixteenth century, these canals allowed the *chilampas* (shallow canoes) to transport food through the intricate routes of the city. The royal gondolas of the Mexica *tlatoani* (ruler, literally *speaker*) also passed through the canals in ancient México-Tenochtitlán, the most populated city of its time, a city of canals, man-made channels and bridges, situated on an island in the middle of a lake.[2]

The Intermediary looks to her body as the receptor, storehouse, and transmitter of knowledge that comes from the archive ("I know texts, pages, illusions") and from the repertoire of embodied knowledge ("I also retain memories that belonged to my grandmother, my mother, or my friends"). She knows how to navigate among sources and types of knowledge and facilitates their circulation. Her body is not simply a metonym for the city and the larger social network. Rather, her embeddedness in her environment, the way her consciousness is bound up with the psychic pulse of the city might suggest that each is the product of the other's performance. How does one come to inhabit and envision one's body as coextensive with one's environment and one's past, emphasizing the porous nature of skin rather than its boundedness? How does one construct a city shaped like a heart, with arteries bringing people and goods in and out?

Cultural memory is, among other things, a practice, an act of imagination and interconnection. The Intermediary begins to imagine her heart— her memory. Memory is embodied and sensual, that is, conjured through the senses; it links the deeply private with social, even official, practices. Sometimes memory is difficult to evoke, yet it's highly efficient; it's always operating in conjunction with other memories, "all of them pulsing regularly, in order." Memory, like the heart, beats beyond our capacity to control it, a lifeline between past and future. The Intermediary's consciousness links historical moments: México D.F., capital of the contemporary Mexican Republic, México-Tenochtitlán, center of the ancient Mexica Empire. And her cultural identity as a *mestiza* is a product of that history. There is a continuum between inner and outer, much as there is between the live present and the living past, and a notion (or act of imagination, perhaps) that individuals and groups share commonalities in both the here/now and there/then, made evident through embodied experience. As Connerton puts it in *How Societies Remember*, "Groups provide individuals with frameworks within which their memories are localised and memories are localised by a kind of mapping. We situate what we recollect within the mental spaces provided by the group. But these mental spaces . . . refer back to material spaces that particular social groups occupy."[3] Mexico City certainly functions as the mental and material space providing a framework for individual and collective memory. The buildings and architectural layout remind even the most distracted passerby that this space is a violently practiced place. Mexico City today is a palimpsest of histories and temporalities.

10. View from the ruins of the Templo Mayor. Behind it stands the National Cathedral and in the background is the *torre latinoamericana*. Photo by Diana Taylor, 1999.

The photograph in Figure 10, taken from the ruins of the Templo Mayor, makes evident the colonizers' social practice of annihilation and surrogation. The ancient Aztec *cue* or templo mayor that centered the Nahua world in the sixteenth century was demolished by conquered *indigenas* who were forced to tear down their own world. They were then obliged to use the same stones to build the cathedral that dominates the *zócalo*, Mexico's administrative center. In the background stands the monument to contemporary neocolonialism, the *torre latinoamericana*, the tallest building in Latin America. The landscape, like the culture, like the people themselves (the play suggests) are the product of violent social practices, mutually defining, double and triple coded—traditional and postmodern, rooted, superimposed, and interstitial.

Only after the Intermediary locates herself as a receptor/transmitter within that network of communication does Carballido proceed with the action: "NEWS!" she announces as she stands up to usher in the action. The events are minimal. Throughout the play only one thing happens: two poor children (Polo and Toña), who are playing in a garbage dump, derail a passing freight train. The antecedents are few as well. Polo is not in school because he does not have any shoes. Toña skips because she has not done her homework. They tamper with the public telephones, looking for change; they flip the coins they find with a candy vendor, lose the coins, win them back, buy some candy, and give a few pennies to a passing vagrant. They meet their friend Maximino, who offers them money for school, but they turn it down to play by the dump: "We might find something. You can see the train go by" (49). The children dance around, joke, and pick things up. One of the things they find is a large bucket full of cement, discarded by some builders. On impulse, they roll the pail onto the tracks as the train approaches. The stage lights flash frantically as the audience hears a thundering crash. The lights go out, and in a second we hear the newsboy running through the theatre, crying out the headlines.

The twenty-one scenes of the play pulsate in heartbeats. The title image of the rose works as an organizing epistemological concept; each scene adds one more layer of meaning to the whole. With delicate humor, Carballido presents the various theories regarding the crash, which is restaged four times from different perspectives. A Freudian psychologist speaks of the children's "hidden guilt and desires for self-punishment" and says that we can understand everything by closely examining the individual, the petal of the rose. He compares the dump to human nature: "I don't believe it is necessary to point out that by nature there exists within each and every one of us a veritable garbage dump!" According to the Marxist theorist, we can understand phenomena only by looking at the collective, the whole rose. The children's act reflects the "extreme results" of extreme economic violence: "It is without a doubt a clear expression of class struggle." The newsboy's headlines alternately cast the children as vagrants, as schizophrenics, as criminals, as disenfranchised proletarians. The children's schoolteacher blames the general atmosphere of "idleness," "stupidity," and "lack of civil spirit." The children's mothers blame the absence (through death and alcoholism) of the fathers. Public attention focuses on the "event" as a limit case that epitomizes the sensational and the extreme, but overlooks the crime of poverty, marginalization, and social inequality. An emcee of a quiz show holds up three images of a rose—the close-up of the cell structure, the petal, the whole rose—asking his audience to identify the one, authentic image. All other images must be eliminated as false. Contestants who choose the correct image of the rose will win a prize. For the scavengers who collect the bags of food scattered in the derailment, the accident is a blessing. For the train owners, it is a criminal act of vandalism costing 5 million pesos. Passersby and other assorted characters offer their theories—none really more compelling than the others.

In total, the Intermediary appears four times in the play with books, with warnings, with stories, with enigmatic interpretations. She emphasizes the challenges of interpretation in the story of the "Two Who Dreamed." It is the story of two men (twins? brothers? friends?) who lived in different villages, Chalco and Chalma. In their separate villages and at exactly the same time, both men dreamed of a prodigious figure that appears, instructing him to go to the other's town and, together with him, pray before the sanctuary next to his house. Both men awoke, walked toward the other town, and met halfway. "Each in turn told the other his dream and they were identical . . . like a mirror with two contradictory images." This story, with roots back to the sixteenth century, speaks to both the multiplicity of signs and systems as well as the ensuing problems of decipherability.[4] They do not know how to interpret the dream, or which town to go to. The predicament is ancient, as the Nahua legend attests, yet contemporary and urgent. They flip a coin (much like the children in the play), which falls in a crack: " 'It is a sign,' they said, and so they made camp on the very spot and waited for another sign . . . another dream. . . . The sign never came, and so they decided to fulfill their command right there and then. It was a barren place covered with weeds and rocks" (the dump?), which they cleared and on which they built a "very small church." The men, wearing the garments of their pre-Conquest ancestors, "had a few drinks of mescal and then they danced and prayed. They danced in that complicated rhythm that had been passed down to them from their fathers. They prayed the prayers they had learnt from childhood. Two tired, dirty men decorated with feathers and mirrors danced and prayed in the nocturnal ambiguity of that wilderness without answers. . . . Their time was up and they knew no better way of satisfying the whims of the arbitrary being that had spoken to them in their dreams."

Through stories, the Intermediary sees past and future, and she integrates the many parts into the rhythmic sound of everyone's heart beating at once. The dump is transformed into a magical site of recontextualization and transformation. Her interpretation, that the children become part of everything around them, may not be more convincing than the others, but she plays the vital role of encompassing the many interpretations. In this, her final appearance as the play closes, she it a truly resplendent figure, endowed with spiritual luminosity. Nothing, ultimately, is decided in the play and it offers only a few hints regarding the fate of the characters. At the end, the Intermediary asks us enigmatically, "Do you know how Polo came to own his own garage? And what Toña's marriage was like? . . . that's another story."

ETHNICITY, GENDER, AND CULTURAL MEMORY

The centrality of the Intermediary, combined with her capacity for transformation, challenges the impression that the individual or group is somehow a stable entity, an unchanging conduit for receiving and transmitting the swirl of events around them. The body in embodied cultural memory is specific, pivotal, and subject to change. Why this insistence on the body? Because it is impossible to think about cultural memory and identity as disembodied. The bodies participating in the transmission of knowledge and memory are themselves a product of certain taxonomic, disciplinary, and mnemonic systems. Gender impacts how these bodies participate, as does ethnicity. The techniques of transmission vary from group to group. The mental frameworks—which include images, stories, and behaviors—constitute a specific archive and repertoire. Clearly, the mestiza herself is a product of cultural memory; her body too is mapped by racialized and gendered practices of individual and collective identity. While scholars working across fields in the humanities, social sciences, and sciences are increasingly convinced that race is socially constructed—and I take that as a given here—less work has been done on the way that cultural memory is shaped by ethnicity and gender.[5] Here I suggest the impossibility of separating these three: cultural memory, race, and gender. The Intermediary's opening speech establishes that she is a woman of the pueblo, a mestiza, racially and culturally a mix of indigenous and Spanish stock.[6] *Mestiza* says it all, simultaneously signaling gender, race, ethnic background, and the cultural positioning of liminality: European and indigenous, betwixt and between, central to Mexico's national identity yet politically marginalized. What does mestiza mean, though, in relation to cultural memory? Although the figure of the Intermediary suggests ways in which we might think of mestizo/a memory, it's certainly not

11. *De Español, e India, nace mestizo,* 1774, Museo de América, Madrid.

through the concept of race or blood, as Mexico's foremost theorists of mestizaje argued in the 1920s: "Por mi raza hablará el espíritu" (Through my race my spirit speaks). Race, of course, has historically been equated with blood and skin color. From the sixteenth century onward, the Spanish administration in New Spain established the *casta* or caste system to clearly demarcate bloodlines and racial categories produced by miscegenation. Terms like mestizo, mulatto, morisco, lobo, and coyote sprang up.[7] Though ostensibly grounded in notions of blood, these categories, and the many paintings that depicted them, actually focused more on issues I identify with performance: manner, dress, style, language, religion, and setting.[8] Both the indigenous groups and the Spaniards had a highly codified system of identification grounded in visible social markers.

The caste system, as the illustration in Figure 11 makes clear, marked what got constituted as racial differences by making these immediately discernable to the observer through gradations of skin color, class markers, and performance practices. Visual and performance strategies accompanied discursive ones to produce the newly racialized and gendered subjects they merely claimed to portray. The male is usually depicted as European and the female as indigenous. The image suggests the practice of paternal recognition initially associated with mestizos. The child, dressed like the father, resembles him as a *gente de razón* (a person endowed with reason, as opposed to indigenas, who were denied reason: *gente sin razón*). As such, he is identified with Spaniards and thus warrants the protection of the Spanish father.[9] However, this practice of identifying the children of mixed marriages as Spaniards diminished, according to R. Douglas Cope, after 1570: "Colonials came to regard the terms 'mestizo' and 'illegitimate' as practically synonymous" (18). The children provoked that uncomfortable quandary of definition: neither/nor.[10]

Time complicated the caste system, especially with the accelerated pace of intermarriage. By the nineteenth century, the political exigencies wrought by the independence movements forged new group alliances that further weakened these distinctions. Thinkers in the nineteenth and early twentieth centuries found that they needed to incorporate the indigenous population into their national imaginings, discursively if not politically or economically. The rhetoric about mestizaje as the defining condition of the emergent nation stressed the value of Mexico's pre-Conquest past and the vitality of its racial stock—improved, as theorists put it, by the civilizing influence of the European infusion.[11]

If collective memory relies on social frameworks to enable transmission, then clearly the behavioral practices that define ethnicity participate in that transmission. That is, rather than turn to the language of blood and heredity that theorists such as Vasconcelos used in the 1920s, we would need to think about memory, ethnicity, and gender in terms of the double-codedness of linguistic, epistemic, and embodied practices associated with mestizaje.

The Intermediary, for example, speaks Spanish, but her use of language conveys the poetic accumulation of images and the echoing singsong quality of Náhuatl that relies on mnemonic devices such as repetition and amplification for recalling information. Like the petals of the rose, words and expressions wrap around each other to add more and more nuances about the same thing. One example, taken from the Náhuatl *Huehuehtlahtolli, testimonios de la antigua palabra* might be the terms used by a mother to address her daughter: "Mi niñita, mi tortolita, mujercita, tienes vida, has nacido, has salido, has caído de mi seno, de mi pecho" (My little girl, my little turtledove, little woman, you have life, you've been born, you've fallen from my breast, from my chest).[12] In a continuation of that style, the Intermediary refers to her heart as a cautious lover knocking to come in, or a chick pecking at the walls of its egg, as a sea anemone and an ever-powerful flower. Her particular use of Spanish, then, bespeaks the coexistence of another language alive within it, constituting a linguistic and cultural bilingualism.

Her beliefs and ways of thinking, moreover, signal the confluence of several epistemic systems. Like the ancient Nahua, the Intermediary reveals the logic of accumulation, as the above quotation suggests. One idea links to another, but not in a causal fashion. Rather, she manifests what Mexican anthropologist Alfredo López Austin calls "mythic" thinking, that is, a bent toward taxonomies that connect different social and natural processes "to find equivalences and parallelisms between distinct systems of classification in an attempt to discover . . . absolute congruence and a total order of the universe."[13] The system of equivalences links the human body (the heart) to plants (rose), to animals (sea anemone), to nature (cave), to global harmony (all the hearts in the world beating at once). Linguistic tropes and systems of equivalence (such as metaphor and metonymy) suggest a resemblance, an as-ifness, that hers lacks. Her nonlinear way of thinking, usually associated with the semiliterate realm of the past, ironically resembles the digital concept of networks, circuits, and interconnectivity. Except, of course, her knowledge is embodied and she communicates it in the here and now of performance.

The Intermediary tells stories from the past that continuously unravel into the future. Her presence, as scripted in the play, is both understated and central. She is a vital life force, mediating, interpreting, transmitting. Without her, there is no (his)story. Although a humble woman, she is now a tlatoani of sorts, whose authority stems from speaking. She assumes the pride/authority of the custodian of memory.[14] Her address to the audience is intimate; she speaks both of the past and to the future. She tells stories that date from pre-Conquest times to elucidate the ambiguities of the present. Those stories constitute the frameworks that allow for cultural memory and enable the transmission of particularized knowledge. As she draws both from the repertoire and the archive, the heuristic systems come together in her, and her heart, that potent "central ventricle," commingles them and

12. Flora González as La Intermediaria in *Yo también hablo de la rosa*, directed by Diana Taylor, Teatro Cuatro, New York, 1983. Photo by George Ruben.

pumps new life throughout the individual and social bodies. Though her manner and clothing are simple, befitting a woman from the pueblo, she gradually becomes luminous. Her dark rebozo and skirt of the opening scene become the white, airy, gossamer garments of the end (see Figure 12).

The Intermediary, then, exists in a constant state of transformation. She metamorphoses from the pueblo woman in dark, rustic clothing to a miraculous apparition, one more in the long line of goddess/virgin figures of mixed indigenous and European origins. Here, thinking about race blends with constructs of gender. They prove physically and politically inseparable.

For Mexicans, Mexican Americans, and Chicanas, the feminine gender is always dual, always liminal, always the mirroring of the defied mother (Malinche) and the Virgin.[15] This duality dates back to pre-Conquest times for both the Mexica and the Spaniards. Gender identity, for the Mexica, was not stable.[16] Femininity and masculinity were associated with flux, and some gods were considered to be simultaneously male and female. The feminine part of the duality, however, still occupied the space of negativity, what López Austin maps out as a set of clusters so common to Western thinking. The feminine was "darkness, earth, the low, death, humidity and sexuality, while the masculine was linked to the light, heavens, the high, life, dryness and glory."[17] References to some of the predominantly female goddesses throughout Sahagún's *Florentine Codex* are often ambiguous. Tzaptlan, for example, is said to be "represented as a woman." Chalchiuhtli "was considered a god[dess]. They represented her as a woman." Some descriptions also insist on the goddesses' negativity. Ciuacoatl was "a savage beast and an evil omen. . . . By night she walked weeping, wailing; also was she an omen of war." The goddesses called Ciuapipiltin "were five devils, whose images were of stone."[18] The idea of gender duality sustained the Nahua universe and informed all their social roles and practices, including their militaristic ideology.[19] The cosmic order was predicated on sacrifice (of gods and humans) and was kept in motion through constant warfare, during which the feminine was conquered and literally shattered. Huitziolopochtli, the principal deity of the Mexica and god of war, nightly defeated, and dismembered, his sister, Coyolxauhqui.[20]

In addition to this duality, women were seen as vehicles for transmission, not only of life but also of specific cultural assets such as property rights and social privilege. As Rosemary A. Joyce notes, women were "specifically treated as links to traditions of creation."[21] Because of the basic indeterminacy and liminality associated with gender, Nahua children were disciplined into gendered roles through embodied behaviors: weaving and cooking for girls, war exercises for boys.[22]

The duality and liminality associated with femininity particularly also sustained the ideology of the Spanish conquerors, with the good-evil polarity embodied by the Virgin and Eve. When Cortés arrived in Mesoamerica, he carried the banner of the Virgin of Guadalupe from his region of Extremadura in front of him.

The contact between the Mexica and the Spaniards can be encapsulated through two female images it produced: La Malinche and the brown Virgen de Guadalupe. Malinche, named Malinal or Malintzin at birth, was of a noble family, but, according to Bernal Diaz del Castillo, her mother gave her away to pass on Malintzin's inheritance to a son by a new marriage. Malintzin and nineteen other women were offered as a gift to Cortés in 1519. So begins her history of circulation and substitution which lasts to this day, for, according to the account, her mother gave her away surreptitiously: "To avoid any impediment . . . [they gave her away] by night in order to be unobserved. They then spread the report that the child had died; and as the daugh-

13, 14. From Bernardino de Sahagún, *Florentine Codex*, ed. and trans. J. O. Anderson and Charles E. Dibble (Santa Fe, NM: School of American Research and University of Utah, 1982), vol. 12. Doña Marina negotiates between the indigenous groups and the Spaniards. The bubbles represent the words that go back and forth.

ter of one of the Indian slaves happened to die at this time, they gave it out that this was their daughter."[23] One daughter substituted for another, given to people who would in turn give her as a gift to Hernán Cortés, who in time would give her in marriage to one of his lieutenants.

Malintzin, baptized Marina, was referred to historically as La Malinche, synonymous with (cultural/gender/race) *traitor*. As translator and advisor to Hernán Cortés and mother to their child, she is often named as the mother of the Mexican (mestiza/o) race. She embodies duality (Malintzin/Marina, princess/slave, Náhuatl/Spanish) and occupies the liminal space of the go-between, negotiating and communicating between two peoples. As in Carballido's play, interpretations abound about this figure, but there are few facts.[24] Depicted by her indigenous contemporaries and the Spanish chroniclers as an intermediary, she takes her position between the conquerors and the conquered. Despised by Mexican thinkers, she is seen not as the source of mestizo identity but as the origin of Mexican self-hatred and racial violence.[25] Octavio Paz calls her our Mother, *La chingada* (the fucked one). Mexicans, because of her, are "the fruit of a violation."[26]

Like Malinche, the Intermediary brings the new/s into the world. What she transmits, commingled through her act of transfer, is a new original—

not the European, not the Nahua, but a third, mixed entity, the mestizo/a. The Intermediary, like the Malinche figure, has been humbled and pushed to the margins.

The transformation of Carballido's Intermediary, however, indicates how the despised Malinche is, in fact, inseparable from the Virgin of Guadalupe. Like Malinche, the Virgin has also been called the mother of the mestizo nation. At the end of the nineteenth century, people "asserted that the foundation of Mexico could be dated from the apparition of the Virgin Mary at Tepeyac. . . . they saluted the Virgin as the foundress of the new, mestizo nation."[27] She, like the Intermediary, enfolds the many stories and memories in her encompassing embrace. She too performs the shared consciousness of a people, united only in their devotion to her. In Mexico, these images have historically been doubled, although they are vehemently and violently kept apart. Yet, as Mexican cultural theorist Roger Bartra suggests, we can't understand the Virgin or La Malinche without the other. Malintzin was one of the twenty virgins given by the indigenous people to Cortés, and Cortés gave the Virgin of Guadalupe to the native people, who made her theirs. "In this way," Bartra writes, "the first exchange took place, carnal, symbolic, and material, of virgins for mothers between the Spaniards and the indigenous. . . . Malinche betrayed her people as much as the Virgin betrayed hers, for both gave of themselves. . . . the first gave rise to a stock of mestizos, the second was reborn as the indigenous and brown Virgin."[28]

MESTIZAJE, HYBRIDITY, TRANSCULTURATION

The vital link that the Intermediary performs among embodied knowledge, memory, and history helps us understand the ways that images of racial and cultural "mixing," so embedded in Latin American social imaginaries, also carry histories of transmission. The very notion of racial identity enters the American stage as the product of these complex complicities of archival and embodied systems. From the moment Columbus purported to "observe" and "describe" native bodies, racialized identities sprang from discursive and performance systems of presentation and representation.

Few scholars dispute that the many indigenous cultures of the fifteenth-century Americas were derailed by the arrival of the Europeans. However, more difficulties arise when we try to think through the following: How do populations and culture survive a crash? What happens when the populations themselves undergo change, and become the biological product of the "encounter"? *Mestizaje* (*mestizagem* in Portuguese), the word generally used to denote racial mixing through interracial, heterosexual sex, offers one term for speaking about cultural fusion. *Hybridity*, a botanical term that refers to the engineered (asexual) grafting of two dissimilar entities, offers another. Even though they are often used interchangeably, they are not synonymous. Although both terms revalorize "mixing" (along with terms such as creolization and syncretism), I argue that the unexamined collapse of the two elides different histories of colonization. Significantly, mestizaje has been the preferred term until recently in Latin America, and hybridity dominates postcolonial studies coming out of India and the African diaspora. Finally, is it useful to include the term *transculturation* in this discussion? Coined in 1940 by the Cuban anthropologist Fernando Ortiz, transculturation denotes the transformative process undergone by a society in the acquisition of foreign cultural material—the loss or displacement of a society's culture due to the acquisition or imposition of foreign material, and the fusion of the indigenous and the foreign to create a new, original cultural product. These questions, raised so compellingly in Carballido's *Rosa*, are vital to our understanding of Latin/o American performances of cultural and racialized identity. In what follows, I explore how the theories of mestizaje, hybridity, and transculturation differ because their relationship to embodiment differs. Each model highlights a different facet of colonial history.

Neither hybridity nor mestizaje are new terms. Mestizaje (mestizagem) refers to a concept of biological and/or cultural fusion. As used in the Latin/o Americas, it has a history, it *tells* a history and it *embodies* a history. The primary site of mestizaje is the body, linked as it is to the mestizo/a, the child born of European and indigenous parents. Its root, from *mixtus*, means both the child of racially mixed parents and also cross-breeding of plants and animals. But it stresses the biological over the botanical.[29] Yet, for all the centrality of the body, and though the concepts of mestizo and mestizaje emanate from it, neither term can be reduced to the body. The negotiated subjectivity of the mestizo/a bespeaks alliances far exceeding racial ties, and the intellectual, aesthetic, and political ramifications of the concept of mestizaje shape Latin/o American cultural histories. Along with the birth of the first mestizo comes a whole constellation of stories explaining gender, racial, ethnic, and national formation. Each country in the Americas performs its national identity through the staging and mythification of what it considers to be (usually in the singular) its racial body.[30] Although both terms are used extensively throughout Latin/o America, and have been since the year 1600, in this chapter I focus on the history of their usage in Mexico.[31]

The first mestizo, according to the Mexican legend, as I outlined, was the son born to Cortés and Malintzin/Doña Marina/La Malinche. Whatever the nature of their particular relationship, the term carries with it a history of unequal power relations, racial and sexual domination, and rape: the white male forcing himself on the indigenous woman. The illegitimate, mixed-race child lived the tensions, contradictions, push-pulls, racism, hatred, and self-hatred associated with domination in her or his own flesh. There was little joy at the birth of this "new" race, which was accompanied by political, social, and cultural displacement. Eric Wolf puts it this way: "Disinherited by society, the mestizo was also disinherited culturally. Deprived of a stable place in the social order, he could make only limited use of the heterogeneous cultural heritage left him by his varied ancestors."[32] Although the term mestizo was used proudly by some—el Inca Garcilaso de la Vega being a prime example—the racial category allowed for the cohesive discriminatory caste system to be put in place. There is still deep social prejudice toward the mestizo and mestizaje on the part of the white father, who withholds recognition. The *Diccionario de la Real Academia* (the official dictionary of the Spanish language) waited until 1992 to include mestizaje in its vocabulary, and the *Diccionario del uso del español* (which doesn't include the term at all) defines the act (the verb, *mestizar*) as "adulterating the purity of a race by its cross with others." The father cannot name the child or allow space for her or him in his vocabulary. In fact, if not in theory, the mestizo and mestizaje are inseparable from conquest and colonization.

But there is reprobation on both sides. The offspring blames the mother for his illegitimate status. (I use "his" because, as the following indicates, the attacks on La Malinche come several centuries after the Conquest from Mexican males who, unconsciously perhaps, identify as white.)

During the Mexican period of nation building in the nineteenth century, Malinche was blamed for the downfall of the indigenous world.[33] She betrays through both of her lips, her mouth and her sex, a conflation that stresses the simultaneity of the cultural and sexual penetration of the conqueror.

A history of imperial domination (brought about by native infighting, inferior war-machinery/tactics, and ravaging disease) gets told as one of desire and betrayal. As in other colonial paradigms, the woman "only becomes a productive agent through an act of violation."[34] Malinche also functioned as the hinge in the nation-building discourse of the nineteenth century. In 1886, Ignacio Ramírez compared her to Eve, saying, "It is one of the mysteries of fate that all nations owe their fall and ignominy to a woman."[35] The condemnation of Malinche allowed for the subjugation of the gendered Other (Woman) to rhetorically recuperate the racial Other, the indígena. Both indígenas and mestizos had to be embraced (symbolically, if not in fact) to forge a cohesive, unique sense of national identity after Mexico declared itself independent from Spain. After all, the indigenous past was what most truly differentiated Mexico from Spain and substantiated Mexican claims regarding their unique identity. The price of this highly ambivalent mixed identity, however, meant that racism needed to be displaced and rechanneled as misogyny. Despising La Malinche accomplished the Creole's unspoken racial hatred toward the indígenas, but subsumed under the seemingly justifiable hatred toward women. As Paz revealingly argues in "The Sons of La Malinche," violence against (the indigenous) women surges because *she* is always and inevitably the Malinche. In the mestizo, the biological becomes coterminous with nationalism while gender becomes its opposite. For Paz (again), the Mexican is always male, always mestizo, defined in opposition to the feminine Other. Mestizaje was seen as the cornerstone of the nation-state that sustained an ambivalent, unique, and always negotiated sense of national identity. Mestizaje, as the ideological/political affirmation of the mestizo, involved an equivocal attempt at valorizing a mixed national identity.

The space of mestizaje is also central to this discussion. During the first period following the Conquest, the survivors of the crash spoke of inhabiting *nepantla*, the space between the indigenous and Spanish cultures. Nepantla reflected the cracks, the liminality of a zone that was no longer just indigenous but that was not yet (and never would be) quite Spanish. Thus mestizaje (unlike hybridity) refers to the *both/and* rather than the neither/nor, the double-coded as opposed to the fragmentary sense of subjectivity. The garbage dump, as the site of Carballido's play, captures the geography of the disaster and revalorization of mestizaje. This space that has been dumped on, devalued, that transforms our most intimate objects into abject, dead things is also the space of magical transformation. Things grow in the dump; there is evidence of new life and endless possibilities for reconfiguration. The term nepantla has increasingly explored the glorious possibilities, and concomitant aesthetics, of the terrifying in-between as contemporary theorists and performance artists. Latin Americans and Chicano/as use it to describe their experience of living on the borders: both/and.[36] The aesthetics associated with mestizaje (and to an extent hybridity as well) is what Robert Stam calls "the strategic redemption of the low, the despised, the imperfect, and the 'trashy' as part of a social overturning."[37] The garbage heaps offer ample opportunity for recycling, revalorizing, reaffirming that which dominant culture has thrown away. It is, by definition, a site of the multilayered and incongruous associated with *rasquachismo*, the aesthetic of the underdog. Mestizaje as site and as recuperative practice ushers us into the spectacle of the lost and found in terms of race, gender, and cultural memory; each iteration revalorizes and affirms that which its predecessor denigrated. How to read the codes, the signs, the discarded concepts found in the dump? Carballido depicts a population faced with the never-ending drama of indecipherability, never knowing how to interpret or fulfill the mandates. They continue to act, knowing that they don't know the answer, fully aware that every attempt to make something of the crash is another *historia*, and another attempt at interpretation.

Mestizaje has a history not only as it refers to mixing and cultural doubleness, but also as it has been used in various social projects. In the early twentieth century, mestizaje celebrated the centrality of race and racial intermingling in the national identity of the Americas. José Vasconcelos's famous treatise *La raza cósmica* (1925) sought to offset the eugenics program for "whitening" the Americas of the late nineteenth and early twentieth centuries by arguing that the mestizo was, far from despicable, the model for the "final," "universal," "cosmic race." Because the mestizo/a fused the indigenous, black, Asian, and white races, he/she opened the way for the next fusion that would combine and surpass all preexisting races. Rooted in the concept of race and blood, mestizaje was both essentialist and normalizing. It came to equal national identity, as signified by Mexico's famous motto *Por mi raza hablará el espíritu*. Mestizaje comes into being through visual economies, providing the body and voice of (national) identity. We, Mexicans, *are;* but only insofar as we are *different.* Identity, especially identity as "difference" (original, unique—not Spanish, not indigenous) has to be performed to be seen. Vasconcelos in *Raza cósmica* moved from the biological rootedness of the mestizo to the aesthetic realm of mestizaje. A project that began by accentuating the centrality of the mestizo population of the Americas ended up aspiring to transcend "race" altogether: when all races fuse into one, race itself will prove meaningless. This movement showed the flip side of the eugenics movement, though here disappearance occurred through a politics of inclusion rather than exclusion, through love, desire, and miscegenation rather than racial "cleansing." But the anxiety of disappearance sustains both discourses; the eugenics movement meant to ensure that the white race would not become sullied and disappear even as the raza cósmica aspired to hasten the disappearance of race as an issue. (This ultimate disappearing of race mirrors an earlier "transcendence" of race negotiated by José Martí, Cuba's inspired revolutionary of the late nineteenth century: "There can be no racial hatred because there are no races.")[38] Vasconcelos celebrated mestizaje to combat the growing imperialism of the United States and to offset notions of Anglo-Saxon racial superiority. The mestizo would outgrow the derogatory designation of bastard to become a model for the cosmic race. In his sociopolitical project, Vasconcelos described history as, well, a train: unidirectional, relentless. "There is no going back in History, for it is all transformation and novelty. No race returns" (16). The anxiety surrounding the "wreck" of disappearance gives way to a utopian vision of the "the fusion of peoples and cultures" (18), much in the way that Carballido's play ends with a similar biological/cultural fusion of all hearts beating miraculously as one.

The recuperative project of mestizaje in the early twentieth century has continued, in different ways, to shape its usage today. Behind the current term, the older one remains, transvalued but there. Although mestizaje has been closely linked to projects of the nation-state, Mexico's most particularly, in the examples I've provided, it is not limited to the nation or a fixed sense of national identity. La Malinche again undergoes transformation, this time to become a symbol, rather than a mother, to us all. Tzvetan Todorov, using images from Sahagún's *Florentine Codex*, paints a more positive image of La Malinche as a figure who prefigures nationalism but exceeds it. As a "symbol . . . of the cross-breeding of cultures," she "heralds the modern state of Mexico and beyond that, the present state of us all. . . . La Malinche glorifies mixture to the detriment of purity—Aztec or Spanish—and the role of the intermediary."[39] So too the Virgin's role and significance have expanded beyond national boundaries, The "Mexican Virgin" (the "Mexican Phoenix" of colonial times) was coronated in 1895 and became the patron of the Americas in 1999. Both figures embody the tensions in thinking about identities as local and as hemispheric—Who can claim them? Legitimate them? As one Mexican nationalist put it in the nineteenth century, the Virgin "does not want to be American; she is ours and ours alone." At the occasion of her coronation, some objected that "the image should not be crowned, since God has already crowned it."[40] As with Carballido's Intermediary, La Malinche and the Virgin of Guadalupe signal mestizaje as a biological issue (the mother of the mestizo race), as embodying a living culture, and perhaps most important, as a vital presence that links the past to the present in an embodied way.[41] Though seemingly irreconcilable, the figures form two sides of the same coin, incarnating the consciousness of struggle: you are either with us or against us, our savior or a traitor, the Virgin or Malinche. This double figure, in all cases, is positioned as the link (the intermediary) between the old and the new, the past, present, and future, the European and the indigenous, the local and the hemispheric, the repertoire and the archive. Her body allows the "new" to come into the world, be it the new race, a new belief system, a new sense of national or ethnic identity, or, as in Carballido's play, the face of modernity.

The "newness" extends to new theories of cultural identity among groups. Chicana feminists such as Norma Alarcón, Cherríe Moraga, Chela Sandoval, and Gloria Anzaldúa, for example, draw from La Malinche, from Vasconcelos's la raza, and from theories of mestizaje to define their own feelings of straddling cultures. Anzaldúa, in fact, seems inspired by Carballido's Intermediary, sitting at the busy intersection of the old and the new, when she describes her mestiza: "Like others having or living in more than one culture, we get multiple, often opposing messages. The coming together of two self-consistent but habitually incompatible frames of reference causes un choque, a culture collision."[42] So here we are, back at the scene of the train wreck.

These figures of Malinche and Guadalupe shape the way that Mexican, Mexican American, and Chicana women think about themselves as gendered and racialized subjects. They have been completely internalized. As Moraga notes, "There is hardly a Chicana growing up today who does not suffer under her name even if she never hears directly of the one-time Aztec princess."[43] In a story, Cisneros writes of cutting her hair off for the Virgin and pinning it as a debt payment to her statue.[44] The mental maps, like subjects, change over time. The social frameworks that enable the practice of memory regulate the conflictive ways in which Mexican, Mexican American, and Chicana women inhabit their sexuality and ethnic belonging. Yet we cannot transfer memory outside of these frameworks.

So mestizaje both reveals the marks of its initiating conditions *and* transcends them. It has a history, tells a history, enacts a history through racialized embodiment, and gets retheorized at different historical moments as part of various social projects. Theories of mestizaje migrate from explaining the internal colonialism of Latin America to contemporary Chicano postcolonial struggle.

For all its different deployments—cultural, aesthetic, political—the history of colonial violence, dominance, rape, and desire never quite frees itself of the gendered and racialized bodies that live it. Yet this is never reducible to biology alone. Carballido's Intermediary is more than just a racial mix— she performs the continuity among past, present, and future. She brings the memory of the past into the present even as she makes visible the future. At the same time, she too is a product of the gendered and racial frameworks within which memory acts. The continuum between past and present, between Other and self, between warring opposites characterizes the mestiza consciousness, as Anzaldúa puts it, which entails forsaking the "the split between the two . . . so that we are on both sides of the shore at once" (78). It entails a doubling, a double-codedness, both pre- and post-, both indigenous and Spanish, bilingual, bicultural. This doubleness characterizes nepantla as much as it does Anzaldúa's *Borderlands/La frontera* (which reflects the doubling in the title itself). Instead of either/or, mestizaje entails a both/and. For all its theoretical flexibility, mestizaje tenaciously clings to the body. Néstor García Canclini, the most eminent Latin American theorist to take up the subject recently, in *Culturas híbridas* abandons mestizaje for *hybridization* "because it includes diverse intercultural mixtures—not only the racial ones to which mestizaje tends to be limited."[45] Clearly, there is a new paradigmatic shift afoot in this move. New, but actually not so new. For García Canclini, hybridization offers a more general concept for thinking about tradition and modernity in Latin America. This move, however, replays an earlier history of the shift from mestizaje to hybridity. Etymologically, hybrid, like mestizo, denotes the cross-breeding of people, animals, and plants. Its Latin root, *hibrida*, means *mongrel*; it's not clear whether its other meaning, "insult, wantonness, violation" (the one we now associate with its aesthetic and political edge), is Greek or Latin.[46] More interesting, for me, is that although the word hybrid appears in French in 1596, it does not appear in Spanish until 1817, when it enters the language *from the French*. Interestingly, this period follows the Napoleonic era in Spain. It is indicative that the newly Europeanized Spanish intellectuals, known as the *afrancesados* (Frenchified), would abandon the term mestizo (as perhaps too close to their own history of colonization) and turn to hybrid to further their project of modernization. The choice of different terms, at different historical junctions, adds yet another layer to this discussion. When does one term cease to work, and why?

In spite of the similar etymologies, the current usage of hybrid has a more botanical, scientific, even engineered aspect to it. Generally, it refers to a mixing of species rather than races. This term too has a violent history, but one linked to racial engineering and eugenics. Racist theorists would speak of hybrid people or human "species."[47] Usually, however, the word refers to hybrid plants, in which two species are intentionally grafted together, or to hybrid cultures defined (by Latin Americanists) through "the ways in which forms become separated from the existing practices and recombine with new forms in new practices."[48] Whereas mestizaje tells a *history* of domination, rape, and reaffirmation, hybridity connotes a *process* of social categorization. Instead of the historical head-on of mestizaje (with all its violent and transformative fallout) lived on and through the body of the conquered, hybridity more commonly bespeaks a scientific, conscious project. During the nineteenth century, the heyday of pseudoscientific racist theories, one of the main arguments was that hybrids, constituting different species rather than races, could not reproduce. The products of interbreeding, these "scientists" argued, would degenerate over time. Thus, the model of replication in hybridity consisted of add-ons, accumulation, juxtaposition. So, though there is some overlap between mestizaje and hybridity, the former was a term used by mestizos themselves to describe their experience of an uneasy, at times violent, biculturalism. Hybridity was a derogatory term imposed by those trying to cauterize the biological repercussions of colonialism through discriminatory categorization.

Like mestizaje, the term hybridity currently reaffirms and revalorizes that which had previously been disparaged. The theorists who find the term useful are predominantly the Indian and black cultural theorists writing in the postmodern world of late capitalism, whose history of colonization differs from that in Latin America. Hybridity, in their work, places the poststructuralist, deconstructive theory of subjectivity as decentered, uprooted in conjunction with theories stemming from their postcolonial and diasporic experience. One way to think about the differences in the scenarios of colonization might be in terms of internal versus external colonization. Internal colonization has long and deep roots in Latin America, spanning the late fifteenth to the early nineteenth century. In the fifty years following the Conquest, it is estimated that 95 percent of the native population died. The native populations were thus either eradicated (in the Caribbean) or transformed through interracial reproduction.[49] It is not surprising, then, that theories of cultural mixing should originate in the body itself. External colonization, as in the case of India, started as a commercial venture, with the colonial structure imposed from the top and from afar. Most of the population, as well as the many deep-rooted traditions, survived the arrival of the English. There was less violence, less cohabitation, and far less sexual intermingling. No new race sprang from this encounter, even though there was sexual intermingling, violence, and rape. Unlike the case of Latin America, the offspring born of that "collision" identify with specific ethnic groups rather than as a new race. Therefore, their use of hybridity is both separate and linked to race—separate because it focuses on culture, but linked because the theorists identify themselves as black or people of color. Because of the different history and implementation of colonialism, it seems logical that theorists such as Gayatri Spivak and Homi Bhabha write of hybridity as the effect of colonial power.[50] The "doubleness" produced by hybridity does not refer to people but to signs, systems of power, spaces. Hybridity helps explain how colonial authority gets produced, performed, and sustained. It locates the "native" in the impossible, contradictory in-betweenness of colonial mimeticism. The colonized tried to imitate, or be like, the master. However the "like," was always a "not quite." This "double articulation" resembles nepantla but, to echo Bhabha, I would stress *like*, but not quite.

Nepantla signals the deterritorialization produced by conquest, which included brutal attacks on the native populations, the tearing down of their buildings, the desecration of their gods, the burning of their books. The very ground sustaining the indigenous world, and its cosmology, shifted. It was the same land, but a different space, new because it was unrecognizable. The mestiza, like Carballido's Intermediary, is a product of both the desecrated and the imposed. She occupies the position at the intersection. She receives and transmits the different codes; she contemplates the signs. The double articulation of hybridity does not refer to this mediated space *between*. As Bhabha describes it, it is not rooted but works on the surface through the colonial control of space. Unlike mestizaje, hybridity (for Bhabha) is "not a *problem* of genealogy or identity between two *different* cultures" (114). Hybridity, produced as the effect of colonial power, turns around to threaten or subvert that power. Because the "native" has changed through colonial mimicry to look or act more like the master—becoming like, but not quite—hybridity has also complicated the colonizers' visual control: the master cannot automatically recognize or locate the colonial subject. Hybridity, once imposed by colonial power, now threatens to destabilize it.

We might also think of *I, Too, Speak of the Rose* in terms of hybridity, as different from mestizaje, produced in Mexico. This play brilliantly illustrates the vitality of presence (associated with mestizaje) through the Intermediary. The system in which she operates, however, with its theorists, media personalities, students, and businesspeople, captures the hybridity of the postmodern experience of late capitalism. These interpretations are not organic or rooted in the body (the way the Intermediary's are, or the "two who dreamed"). They are synthetic, add-ons, grafted from "alien" theoretical roots. This does not diminish their validity or persuasive power, but it does place them in a different category. The Intermediary, as an overarching presence, links peoples both horizontally across space—her heart pulses with the city Mexico-Tenochtitlán—and vertically (so to speak), down through the generations. The hybrid, on the other hand, opens outward; more and more variations can be added to the same root. Thus, a plethora of juxtapositions and new configurations are possible. Mestizaje stems from native cultures; its explanatory power lies in elucidating the negotiations involved in adapting to imposed authority. Hybridity, conversely, and Bhabha's colonial mimicry highlight the demands coming from the colonizer. As the play illustrates, both theories elucidate our present, and they are neither mutually exclusive nor identical: they tell us different things about our heterogeneous, multilayered colonial present.

Both theories, mestizaje and hybridity, rely on images of reproduction, whether human or botanical. But there is still another way in which Latin American theorists look at cultural processes that are not predicated on these models. The play also offers another perspective on cultural change, loss, and rejuvenation akin to what Fernando Ortiz, in the 1940s, called "transculturation." Transculturation involves a three-stage process consisting of the acquisition of new cultural material from a foreign culture, the loss or displacement of one's own culture, and the creation of new cultural phenomena. This theory, too, came into being to explain a specific colonial and neocolonial condition. In the 1930s, U.S. anthropologists such as Ralph Linton were advancing theories of acculturation to understand cultural change. Acculturation, however, stressed the losses sustained by native peoples or immigrants when confronted with dominant cultural forces. Politically, this dovetailed with assimilationist thinking in the United States, which proposed a postrace, melting pot vision of the changing population and its cultural practices. For Latin Americans who had no intention of melting into the U.S. pot, acculturation needed to be understood and resisted. Transculturation complicated the model by asserting the creation of new cultural practices. Interestingly, the theory of transculturation, so vital in Latin American scholarship, remains almost unknown in the United States except by Latin Americanists.[51]

Angel Rama, in *Transculturacion narrativa en America Latina*, notes that Ortiz's theory is very Latin American in that "it reveals the resistance to considering one's traditional culture, receiving the impact of the foreign culture that will modify it, as merely a passive or even inferior entity, destined to major losses without the possibility of creative response."[52] For Rama, expanding on the three-step process, Ortiz does not sufficiently emphasize selectivity and inventiveness in transculturation. After all, cultures do not borrow indiscriminately; like the scavenger in Carballido's play, one takes only what one needs. Latin American theatre, Rama notes, did not appropriate the Broadway musical. What it did appropriate were the absurdist, grotesque, and fragmented techniques that reflect a sense of Latin America's chaotic reality as well as more socially oriented dramatic techniques, associated with Piscator and Brecht, to help change local sociopolitical situations. Moreover, when these techniques were borrowed, they were radically altered by their new context. *Rosa* is a fine example of the selectivity and inventiveness that Rama writes of, as well as what he calls the "rediscovery" of "primitive values almost forgotten within one's own cultural system that are capable of standing up to the erosion of transculturation" (39). Rama, then, speaks of four stages in the process—loss, selectivity, rediscovery, and incorporation—all of which take place simultaneously. It is also important to emphasize that transculturation makes room for a reciprocal, two-way exchange through contact. While the Conquest certainly changed performative traditions in the Americas, for example, it also affected the cultural debates and practices back in Europe.

Let's look at *Yo también hablo de la rosa* from the perspective of transculturation. The "borrowings" are obvious, and not just in terms of the Freudian psychology and the Marxist economic theories so prevalent in Mexico around the time the play appeared. There are theatrical borrowings as well. Carballido himself calls the play a *loa,* which is both a short piece (usually one act) presented before a full-length play and a "hymn," a genre that, though common from the Golden Age to the nineteenth century, gradually went out of fashion in the twentieth. The narrator and the episodic structure seem Brechtian; the ritualistic elements, including the final scene, Artaudian. However, looking at the parts separately is misleading. Although *Rosa* has Brechtian elements, this is no Brechtian play, as some commentators claim.[53] Looking at the Intermediary in the light of her own traditions, which include but are not limited to Western theories, we see that her role as narrator stems from her experience in oral culture. We, as audience, experience that tradition in *her* terms. Her speech draws us in, enveloping rather than distancing us, awakening us to the beauty and fluidity of her language. Carballido places us in the same physical position before her that we would assume before a bard; her scenes are intimate, quiet, introspective, or reflective. As Walter Ong states, "The way in which the word is experienced is always momentous. . . . For oral cultures, the cosmos is an ongoing event with man at its center."[54] This experience, then, is profoundly different from that of the audience in Brecht's theatre. Brecht advocates leaving the house lights up to create an informal music hall atmosphere in which people feel comfortable smoking, laughing, and commenting on the action.

The oral tradition also explains the episodic plot in *Rosa*. As in Brecht-ian theatre, some of the twenty-one scenes seem strung together arbitrarily; one could change the order without significantly changing our experience of the play. However, the episodes are not Brechtian if we accept Brecht's own description of episodic plots: "The individual episodes have to be knotted together in such a way that the knots are easily noticed. The episodes must not succeed one another indistinguishably but must give a chance to inter-pose our judgment. . . . To this end it is best to agree to use titles."[55] The episodic structure in *Rosa* is not meant to distance us. Though episodic, the scenes derive their structure from the narrative sequence characteristic of the oral tradition. The Intermediary is telling us the story; from her open-ing monologue, she knows how Toña and Polo's particular story unravels— "but more of that later" (47), she tells us, or "that's another story" (54). The misreading of the episodic plot lies in the insistence on labeling the epi-sodic "Brechtian" rather than recognizing that Brecht's "epic" theatre picks up ("borrows") from the oral tradition. As Ong states, "What made a good epic poet was, among other things of course, first, tacit acceptance of the fact that episodic structure was the only way and the totally natural way of imagining and handling lengthy narrative. . . . Strict plot for lengthy narrative comes with writing" (144). Brecht himself was the first to admit that "stylistically speaking, there is nothing at all new about the epic theatre" (75), that he had used techniques and ideas from Asiatic theatre, medieval mystery plays, Spanish classical theatre, Jesuit theatre, and many more sources. Brecht, in fact, is one of the greatest examples of the vitality, selection, and innovation associated with intercultural exchange. However, what makes him *Brecht-ian* is his particular use of the acquired materials. What makes Carballido *non-Brechtian* is his particular use of *his*.

The seemingly recognizable Western forms hide other logics within them. The double-codedness continues the tradition of hiding one system within another that characterized indigenous resistance to colonialism. Just as image makers might place a pre-Conquest deity behind or inside a Catholic image, the practice of layering multiple systems continues, as *Rosa* shows. As I mentioned in chapter 1, the pre-Conquest worldview was governed by a system of equivalences rather than one based on representation and mimeti-cism. An image, for example, was not a representation of the god, but one more actualization of the god. The human heart, offered in sacrifice, nourished the deities, but in fact, it was only one of many offerings. The heart-shaped fruit from the cactus also served in sacrifice, not because it stood for, or replaced, the human heart but because it was equivalent, one more manifestation of nourishing food. Thus, the Mesoamericans established a whole system of equivalences in which the heart, like the rose, shared a deep correspondence. "Like" refers to this system of multifaceted correspondence rather than a metaphoric substitution or approximation. Understanding the organization of the scenes metaphorically would mean that they pulsate *like* heartbeats, and add to each other *like* petals of a rose. A Mexica, on the other hand, might understand the rose, the heart, the canals of the arteries, the cityspace, knowledge, and memory as elements that are vitally linked, correspondences that flow into each other, contributing to the complex makeup and interconnectedness of the whole. This interpretation of the apparently disconnected elements clearly supports the Intermediary's understanding of interconnectedness expressed throughout the play. Is this pre-Conquest dimension hidden within an apparently Brechtian structure, or is it simply visible to those who understand the codes? As Sahagún suspected in the sixteenth century, performances can occlude even as they make visible. Claims to access dash up against the opaqueness of performance.[56]

The same cross-cultural opaqueness complicates an understanding of the play's ritual elements. The story of "the two who dreamed" and the final scene of the play are not Artaudian because they invoke ritual; rather, Artaud is "ritualistic" because he invokes, even mystifies, Mexican indigenous rites. For Artaud, the non-Western is the "true culture [that] operates exaltation and force. . . . In Mexico, since we were talking about Mexico, there is no art: things are made for use. And the world is in perpetual exaltation."[57] Carballido, on the other hand, does not mystify Mexico's past or, like Artaud, take suicidal risks to recuperate it. Rather, more in the manner we have associated with transculturation, he constantly "rediscovers" (Rama's term) and incorporates the past into the present. The ritual, we noted, does not point toward the past; it relates the experience of two men trying to function appropriately in an inexplicable wilderness devoid of supernatural or divine guidance, drawing from the traditions they have at hand. Moreover, Carballido's ritual dance linking the characters at the end of the play is not an ahistorical or nostalgic return to ritual community. It is a historically accurate depiction of the cultural heterogeneity of Latin America.

So what do these three terms elucidate? What do they obscure? I would argue that all three are products of the train wreck of conquest and colonization. Mestizaje allows us to understand the racial and cultural continuities on the bodily scale—the microcosm in which these conflicts were lived as embodied experience. Memories and survival strategies are transmitted from one generation to another through performative practices that include (among other things) ritual, bodily, and linguistic practices. These practices have histories. Mestizaje, then, takes into account the way culture is transmitted by/through/as embodiment. But clearly, these practices are shaped ideologically as well as genetically; although genetically some mestizos may not differ significantly from indígenas, their sense of themselves made visible through dress, language, and lifestyle is predicated on that separation, that distance.[58] La Intermediary, as a mestiza, is both/and. Hybridity, on the other hand, emphasizes the cultural heterogeneity of places like Mexico City, which the infinite and accelerated rate of the add-ons contribute to and complicate. Hybridity, then, illuminates a highly important aspect of this contemporary, postmodern reality that mestizaje cannot account for. Finally, transculturation, broadly conceived, addresses fundamental issues of transmission found in theories of mestizaje and hybridity but on a grand— trans—scale that notes cultural movements, shifts, reciprocities. It too has a potentially liberatory role because it allows the "minor" culture (in the sense of the positionally marginalized) an impact on the dominant one, although the interactions are not, strictly speaking, "dialogic" or "dialectical." Transculturation suggests a shifting or circulating pattern of cultural transference. The measurable impact of the "minor" on the "major" can be a long time coming. First World commentators often refer to intercultural exchange as if it were a conscious project, a decision to rejuvenate one's exhausted culture by those who, like Brecht, exploit, adopt, or mine other cultures. Latin Americans do not usually allude to such a choice; for them, the concepts of loss and displacement are fundamental (yet noticeably absent from most First World discussion). Many Mexican theorists acutely reflect the sense of displacement of their native cultures while they proudly reaffirm the vitality of their new ones. By stressing the cultural survival and creativity of transculturation, they offset the implication of passivity and reification implied by unequal power. So, should we adopt one term and insist that the other two "be banished from the record," as Carballido's emcee suggests in his televised game show? Or should we try to understand how each contributes to an understanding of cultural transmission?

POSTSCRIPT

In my office at work I have an altar to the Virgen de Guadalupe. There are statues of Virgins in wood, some of metal, some of ceramic, some with roses, and some adorned with the Mexican flag. Some of them are brown Virgins, some black, some white. My mother bequeathed me several. Others I acquired in my wanderings around the Americas. Next to my Virgencitas is a large papier-mâché figure, estilo Posada, of La Soldadera. Because I believe in everything, other cultural icons make it into my altar. I have Ché and Fidel figures, a sampling of Evita memorabilia, and magic powders: Stay Away Law and cans of Success, especially popular among my students. Those who need protection from the evil eye can help themselves to the pink dust a colleague brought from Brazil. My daughter, Marina Malintzin, recently contributed a special offering, a Virgen de Guadalupe whose heart lights up and pulsates when you press the button on the back. She knows I like art that performs. The miracle of reapparition takes place daily—not all the hearts in the world beating at once perhaps, but the continual reactivation of these repertoires that sustain our notions of who we are.

4

LA RAZA COSMÉTICA

Walter Mercado Performs Latino Pyschic Space

We in America shall arrive, before any other part of the world, at the creation of a new race fashioned out of the treasures of all the previous ones: The final race, the cosmic race. —José Vasconcelos, *The Cosmic Race*

What is a "kosmos"? anything ordered or harmonious, but also, by an obvious extension, anything adorned by virtue of arrangement—hence our "cosmetics." —Robert Wardy, *The Birth of Rhetoric: Gorgias, Plato and Their Successors*

They [the native inhabitants of Lucayos] are the colour of the people of the Canaries, neither black nor white, and some of them are painted white and some red and some in any colour that they find. Some of them paint their faces, some their whole bodies, some only the eyes, and some only the nose. —Christopher Columbus, First Letter, in *Four Voyages to the New World*, trans. R. H. Major

I can't wait until 5:45 on weekday evenings, when Walter appears on the Latino TV news program *Primer Impacto* on Univisión to reveal what the stars have in store. By that time of day, I need all the *paz* he has to offer, to say nothing of the "mucho, mucho amor." I wait as the two Latina anchors move us through the program—they wrap up sports, then health, urge us to stay tuned for upcoming natural disasters, then, yes! it's time for Walter.

The rhythmic beating, the strangely disembodied music, and the gyrating graphics of the star-studded cosmos promise to whirl us into the presence of Walter Mercado himself.

THE CAPED CRUSADER

Forget my fortune. I'm not a believer. Or rather, I believe *everything*, which puts a more positive spin on the same thing. What I want to know is: What will Walter wear today? Maybe one of his glamorous capes, reportedly one of thousands stored in an airplane hangar in Miami, which have earned him the nickname "The Caped Crusader." I love them, the gaudier the better, pearl studded, gold trimmed, long and heavy folds of fabulous fabric. Or will he appear more subdued, in his black velvet pantsuit, glittering gold vest, and sumptuous silks? Which of his numerous sets will serve as backdrop? Will he do the Egyptology number—the one where he sits on the gold throne, almost mummified in tulle, surrounded by a Greek column, a glowing sphinx, and hundreds of flickering candles? Or will it be the one I think of as grandma's parlor—equally opulent in a turn-of-the-century style, jammed with over-stuffed brocade sofas (with red lace shawls draped over them), heavy curtains, flowers, and dark wooden carved furniture? Walter sits on the sofa, often holding an oversized, ornamental book or a beautiful rose. Grecian sculptures of beautiful boys grace the surfaces behind him. Once in a while we have the tropical background: Walter on a throne amidst a sea of bright colors and what appear to be real palms swaying in the breeze.

Yet, amid this seemingly endless variety, certain things remain the same. Walter's ash blonde, shoulder-length hair is always swept into a bouncy coiffure. His manicured fingers display oversize dinner rings. His arched brows, large eyes, and full lips are beautifully made up, smiling warmly. How old is he, I wonder. Well over sixty, probably; but he's hard to place. The cosmetic surgery and makeup reveal as much as they conceal. His Spanish, so beautiful, so unlocatable, so artful and artificial signals a pan-Latinoness. One would never know where he's from by his speech, just that he's Latino. He loves his words, he caresses them, rolling them around in his mouth. The staging is the same too. He goes through the horoscope, sign by sign, sometimes drawing or reading from different traditions: tarot, I-Ching, Santería, Catholicism, Hindu mysticism. He claims to have studied them all. He is

15. Walter Mercado.
Photo by Pablo Grosby, 2000.

culto, Puerto Ricans say, or *fino*, as Brazilians put it. Walter, the navigator of infinite sign systems, leads us on a nightly journey to the stars, to the past, to the future, to other traditions and civilizations.

Usually he's playful, a little coquettish, sometimes even naughty—"Now, my little leo," he teases conspiratorially, "listen up, I'm talking to you." Walter knows our secrets, though he cautions us against self-revelation. "Guard your secrets—they're between you and your pillow," he whispers knowingly. Sometimes he's a *comadre,* a friendly next-door neighbor or relative who offers plain, no-nonsense advice on everything from love (which he distinctly distinguishes from marriage) to home décor. Always, he warns us not to judge others: "Don't forget, when you point a finger at someone, three more are pointing back at you," he admonishes, holding up an elegant bejeweled hand by way of illustration. The staging and camera work remain pretty much the same, too. He punctuates each sign by alternating his attention between one of the two stationary cameras. His eyes mist up with a far-away look. Is it the cosmos he's scrutinizing? His makeup? Or the prompt cards? His parting gesture resembles a priest's blessing. In a four-step movement, he raises his hand upward as he wishes us peace, brings it down to his chest, circles his heart, puts his fingers to his lips and extends them toward us as he blows a kiss. He wishes us lots and lots of love. His eyes stay focused, establishing trust and intimacy with the unseen, unknown viewer. He stays looking at us until his image cedes to the original cosmic graphic. A voice-over invites us to write to Walter *directly* at the address on the screen. I know he's talking to me.

Well, sort of. Me and apparently 120 million other people a day, according to his publicity packet. "Walter y las Estrellas" airs on Channel 41 every day. These are different acts of transfer than the ones I've been writing about. Walter, an archival personality, circulates in the postmodern venues of late capitalism. We can pay to hear his voice recorded on his 900-number psychic hotline, "Walter Mercado's Circle of Power." Or we can hear him daily on the radio or read his column. His books, books on tape, and CDs sell by the millions. Walter, a media product, is never and always "live." He offers the illusion that one can reach him or talk to him in person. Walter tells us he's "there" for us, though we never know where. His sites are all sets— we know he has an apartment in New York, a beautiful home in Miami, and a stunning mansion in Puerto Rico, but we never know where he is. Although he travels incessantly, the self-contained sets never give a clue as to what lies outside. The "beyond" is pure simulacrum. But he must exist in person, I suppose. Celebrities such as Bill Clinton, Susan Sarandon, and Madonna have apparently "met" with him. Corporations ask him to look into their (financial) future. Older Latina women, who make up the greatest part of his television audience, believe in him, relying on his judgment for managing daily problems. One of them, featured in one of his promotional videos, claims he always speaks the truth. Some gay Latinos I know also love him, and affectionately call him La Carroca, "porque se echa la casa encima" (he throws everything on). His outlandish style and exuberant flaunting of cultural references put him over the top. How does he get away with this camp performance, I wonder, considering the show targets a broad range of middle- and working-class audiences across the Americas? The extent of his popularity is what I find interesting, especially among Latino and Latin American audiences so commonly held to be conventional on social issues. The sky's the limit, it seems, when it comes to mystical figures.

Oracle workers enjoy a special authority in the Latin/o Americas that is worth noting in relation to the Walter phenomenon. Historical understanding, as the sixteenth-century manuscripts and codices indicate, encompass both past and future events. Moctezuma, for example, relied on *presagios* (foretelling) and soothsayers to foresee the damages wrought by the foreign invaders. In fifteenth- and sixteenth-century Mesoamerica, the soothsayer was "the wise one, in whose hands lay the books, the paintings; who preserved the writings, who possessed the knowledge, the tradition, the wisdom which hath been uttered."[1] The secret lay not only in the books (in the memory bank that I have elsewhere called the archive) but, as important, in the interpretation and performance of the utterances (the repertoire). Nonetheless, soothsayers paid dearly for delivering terrifying interpretations. Moctezuma killed some of his visionaries for predicting the fall of the Mexica Empire and locked others in jail, only to find that they miraculously "disappeared." The authority of soothsayers and later espiritistas and shamans based on their ability to reveal the unforeseen and their capacity to conceal themselves from those in power persisted through the centuries. Charismatic visionary figures surfaced in the seventeenth and eighteenth centuries as resistance leaders, offering oppositional sources of knowledge and cultural practices banned by the Inquisition and the state. Their influence remained in spite of all efforts by the Catholic Church and civil authorities to put an end to their prophetic and personal power.[2] One of the charges against them was their ability to make themselves visible or invisible, as they saw fit. They, unlike regular subjects, seemed to control their embodiment and proved unavailable for scrutiny and surveillance.[3] Their source of power, moreover, rested on visions and practices unavailable to those in positions of secular and religious authority. They sidestepped the hegemonic system of control. One way of understanding how embodied practice transfers social memory and identity through the centuries might entail analyzing the oppositional movements in the Americas organized around these visionary figures.[4]

The ghost of oppositionality continues to empower contemporary Latino/a spiritual performances. They hold out the hope that the marginalized can sidestep dominant power. In the United States, Latino/as often turn to traditional ritual remedies from home to deal with current problems of cultural and physical displacement. Is it magical thinking to hope that a can of "Stay Away Law" will keep the NYPD in check? Can magic powders free modern subjects from scrutiny and surveillance?

Walter, king of the oracle business, is by far the most successful of the many psychics, *curanderos*, and *espiritistas* that compete for the Latino market in the United States. *Botánicas*, *mercados*, Web sites, and specialty shops

16. Poster of El Indio Amazónico in his consultorio in Queens, New York. Photo by Diana Taylor, 1999.

sell many of the products associated with these popular healing practices. Amulets, herbs, candles, soaps, magic powders, charts, scents, incense, and economy-size cans of spray help keep evil forces at bay. Tarot cards, statues of Catholic saints, *eleguas* from Santería, and Vodun dolls rub up against each other on the shelves of these ecumenical botánicas. Like the Latino populations they appeal to, these spiritual practices also share a cultural space more or less peacefully.

Walter's strangely disembodied presence is unusual for espiritistas, many of whom lack access to the media and depend on embodied transmission. The Indio Amazónico, to take another example of a celebrity Latino healer/espiritista, has three *consultorios* in New York as well as one in Los Angeles and a temple in his native Colombia. He offers diagnostic and treatment services—palm reading, tarot, limpias—available in other botánicas. His consultorios, unlike botánicas, resemble a doctor's office more than a pharmacy. He does not sell any products. Rather, a receptionist wearing a lab coat of sorts—a green tunic with stars and symbols on it—attends to the walk-ins, who sit down to wait their turn. Because he's a celebrity, El Indio Amazónico can charge twice as much as other healers do, but it also means that the

17. A poster in El Indio Amazónico's consultorio tells the suppliant what to say: "Jel mi." Photo by Diana Taylor, 1999.

practice depends on his being there, in person. While his assistants take over when El Indio is at his other sites, most clients wait for him to return.

El Indio's consultorio is frankly, and shabbily, theatrical. A four-foot-tall wooden Indian greets visitors at the door. A strategically located donation box invites us to trade dollars for wishes. The large storefront room is partitioned off; the reception area lies to the left. A raised platform, positioned straight ahead, is adorned with electric candles, huge wheels of fortune, cards, a huge palm, and other cosmic paraphernalia. Miraculous spectacles of healing supposedly take place on that stage; we see the props lining the way. Mismatched crutches perch against one wall, apparently ready for the supplicant to grab on the way up to be healed. A poster, like a prompter, tells the suppliant what to say: "Jel mi." A sewing machine to the side attests to the need for last-minute repairs. A large canvas painting of El Indio healing in a native tribe serves to ground this practice in an "authentic" tradition. A wall-size video screen behind the stage shows El Indio in action: a mise-en-abîme.

There are two private areas besides this space. Behind the reception area lies a private interior office where El Indio carries out his individual *consultas*, that is, reads cards, tarot, and palms and prescribes remedies or costly treatments. The inner office, like the large external area, is littered with signs and symbols from every imaginable belief system: horseshoes, Christ figures, Egyptian torsos, and shrunken heads. In the basement, which I was not allowed to visit, El Indio has set up a studio in which he produces the videos that he gives out free to visitors.

The multiple posters, wall paintings, and video images featuring El Indio prepare us for the apparition of El Indio himself. El Indio, who wears handwoven clothes, a feather headdress, a feather through his nose, face paint, beads, and sharks' teeth, both performs and offers a "native" authenticity, an indigenous way of being, knowing, and healing. He explicitly presents himself as *the* repertoire of traditional, embodied knowledge: "testimonio y herencia de una cultura que no ha muerto y se conserva en este personaje" (a testimony and heritage of a culture that has not died and is preserved in this personage), as his promotional video puts it.[5] Although he too pulls from every conceivable tradition, claiming an *espiritismo universal*, El Indio's legitimacy is rooted in his body and his native knowledge. In a self-reflexive act of "rescue ethnography," he objectifies himself, he is all body,

18. El Indio Amazónico's private office. Photo by Diana Taylor, 1999.

a *personaje* who functions as receptacle and conveyor of knowledge. He is living proof of an "authentic" practice that clearly presupposes a "fake." His body serves as the stage for his miraculous power, which he proves by pushing nails through his tongue and lips or slicing his arm with a knife.

However "abnormal" this performance appears, El Indio, like Walter, nonetheless performs a normalizing, regulatory function. He enacts a notion of some pure, authentic tradition still untouched on the margins of modern society. He delivers Latino/as from the postmodern frenzy of Jackson Heights to the tranquility of the premodern through performatic display. El Indio's body transmits the "memory" of the primal bodily integrity he reminds us we have lost and that he alone can reactivate. Dozens of bride-and-groom candles and images of happy heterosexual couples affirm only the most traditional notions of love and happiness. And why, one wonders, would the supplicants have to address El Indio in broken English ("Jel mi") from prompt cards? For all the self-help rhetoric of the video and promotional information, the client still needs El Indio to harness external forces to ensure success. The supplicant, estranged from the authentic practices of a rapidly disappearing Amazon while apparently not yet fluent or incorporated into the dominant culture in the United States, seems doomed to fail. Instead of a both/and, or even an either/or, the spectacle places the client in the space of the neither/nor. One can argue that these performances of subjection follow in the long Latin American tradition of grueling pilgrimages, self-immolation, and other rituals of humiliation. But the client's performance as a distressed, crippled, nonfluent supplicant also reinforces the politically disastrous practice of forcing Latino/as to assume submissive roles. The scenarios enacted on this stage have been conceived by El Indio, who provides the props and the lines. This ritual proves the opposite of confession, the opposite of testifying. It forces clients to enact painful stories that don't belong to them, rather than try to process their own pain or trauma. Sociopolitical subjection thus is rehearsed in the very space in which some Latinos seek empowerment.

El Indio Amazónico's performance illuminates the limitations of embodiment in thinking about Latino/as. This means not simply critiquing the performance of healing staged by El Indio, but what El Indio personifies as well. The specificity of his display—in terms of race, sex, geographical location, ethnic attire, and "primitive" cultural repertoire and performing style—pro-

19. El Indio Amazónico's consultorio. Photo by Diana Taylor, 1999.

voke certain responses. This is the embodiment that must be abandoned, progressives might argue, if we wish to de-essentialize race and ethnicity, the ancestral figure that must be transcended if we continue to endorse the Mexican educator José Vasconcelos's 1925 notion of the cosmic race and mestizaje: "no race returns."[6] Culturally, the Americas have invested heavily in the disappearance of the indigenous presence—our notions of modernity and economic progress depend on it. There is no going back, Vasconcelos reminds us (16), no room for a repertoire of native performance practices in the social process of mestizaje that transcends "difference."

On the opposite end of the representational spectrum, Walter Mercado offers a very different spectacle and practice of Latino-ness. It's not simply that he plays culto to El Indio's primitive in the range of "high–low" aesthetic practices, or that his spectacle appeals to distinct fantasies about class, race, and sexuality. While El Indio Amazónico consciously points to one form of cultural capital rooted in the disappearing past, Walter represents a self-made, endlessly expansive, disembodied identity in the making. His representational options are, of course, a function of his whiteness. El Indio would never be allowed to perform his persona throughout the Americas. Walter assumes his role as the glittery guru who presides over his own version of the "Americas," which includes "countries" such as Miami, Puerto Rico, and many of those Walter-friendly nation-states found on his maps. The Americas he inhabits know each other through their viewing habits—not through shared performance traditions, not through print culture, but united by media conglomerates like Univisión. Walter's performance deals in future(s), those of the up-and-coming Latino/a populations that are rapidly making it as important political and economic forces.

The way these psychics locate the past/future of Latino/a identity is deeply entangled with the embodied and disembodied nature of their performances. El Indio and Walter participate in very different acts of transfer—one legitimated by precarious embodiment, the other spectral, archival, and disembodied. Mercado's character also draws from a wide repertoire of models from various cultural repertoires and archives. These include spiritual leaders of all stripes, clairvoyants, Catholic priests, espiritistas, and show biz celebrities like Liberace and the Latino rock star El Ves. In each case, the divine or occult or celebrity status transcends the pale normativity of secular life. He portrays himself as one more in the long line of child prophets who experienced both personal privation and magical powers at the age of six. He himself recounts how "one day my mother answered the door and there was a whole yard full of people waiting to be touched by 'Walter of the Miracles.' My parents didn't like that at all . . . even though my grandmother was the greatest tarot reader in Spain."[7]

So Walter was chosen, apparently.[8] Instead of presenting himself as the embodiment and culmination of a tradition, the way El Indio does, Walter leaps directly into the superhuman category of the extra-ordinary. I guess it makes sense, then, that his character is out there, beyond convention in terms of sexuality, wealth, style. Like Tiresias, the seer, Mercado is an ambiguous sexual figure: man/woman. His sexual ambiguity, the way he tells it, reflects a touch of the divine: "God is neither man nor woman," Walter writes, tackling the ultimate in Judeo-Christian taxonomies. "The clumsiness of language forces us to describe this supreme being in terms of gender, but its essence extends beyond that, encompassing all" (66). The sexual ambiguity also works well with high-end Catholicism. The Catholic priest is the only man in the Hispanic world allowed to wear skirts. Walter's richly embroidered clothes resemble costly ecclesiastical garb, designed to transcend what it so clearly reveals: the sexual cover-up. The heavy cloth visually suppresses the human body beneath. The richly adorned trim of his cloaks resembles the priest's sash. Walter, like the priest, is supposedly disembodied, all head. The rings recall papal authority. A "prosthetic god," as Freud writes in *Civilization and Its Discontents*, "he is truly magnificent . . . when he puts on all his auxiliary organs."[9] The shrine/set makes visible the power of cultural appropriation. The secluded, walled-off enclosure, filled with candles, scents, heavy fabrics, textures of all kinds, endow the inanimate with the sensuousness denied the flesh.

Interesting, here we are again, disavowing the body.

THE COSMETIC RACE

Astrology, palm reading, tarot, and other healing rituals provide one more entry into a system of signs, one more arena in which psychic subjection gets performed. They too, in their own way, "enact the subject into being," though we know from theorists such as Beauvoir, Foucault, and Butler that the ways the systems are enacted vary considerably.[10] As Walter's warnings and advice make clear, multiple forces pull and push the viewers in his audience. For a bicultural subject, such as Latino/as in the United States, the process of subjection is doubly scripted, doubly complicated—as the external regulatory systems demand different, at times irreconcilable, forms of compliance. Cultural identity is highly performative. Recognition is predicated on embodied behaviors and speech acts: the languages we speak, the way we "do" our gender and sexuality, the ways in which class and race are understood and made visible, the degree of agency displayed by social actors.

But these performances work differently in different cultural systems, as the situation of Latino/as in the United States makes clear. Upper-class Latin Americans may be stunned to find they're automatically considered subalterns in the U.S. popular imagination. Blacks from Puerto Rico, the Dominican Republic, and other parts of the African Americas often get labeled black rather than Hispanic in the United States. Whites, blacks, and Amerindians from Latin America may all be lumped together as "people of color." Visual practices and technologies of identification that have developed in the Americas to fix and catalogue racial categories—from the casta paintings of the sixteenth and seventeenth centuries to nineteenth- and twentieth-century photography—stall before the dilemma: Latino/as are not identifiable by race.[11]

The 2000 census in the United States stumbles before the same realization. The country is now divided in two—not white and black as before, but non-Hispanic (which includes whites, blacks, Asian and Pacific Islanders, multirace, and "others"—groups designated by race) and Hispanics (an ethnic designation that encompasses peoples of any race).[12] "Latinos," or "Hispanics," as the authorities call them, show up the limits of racial classifications and theories.[13] Hispanic, though thoroughly racialized in U.S. dominant culture, is not a racial category. Not a cosmic race, as Vasconcelos argued, that would supersede existing categories ("black, white, Indian, Mongol") by transforming into the fifth mestizo race of the Americas, the "final" "cosmic" race "fashioned out of the treasures of all the previous ones."[14] But a cosmetic race, one in which the outward "look" fails to reveal any ontological stability. What does this mean, exactly? That races have in fact "disappeared," and that the population has fused into a transcendent "cosmic," raceless race, as Vasconcelos envisioned? No, hardly. Politics of racial "difference" continue to control access to power, wealth, education, and health care throughout the hemisphere. The privilege of whiteness has not been superseded anywhere. Now, in the Americas, as in Vasconcelos's writings of 1925, the language of mestizaje attempts to subsume racial categories and racism for specific political ends. But these ends differ. In Mexico, during the 1920s, intellectuals were combating theories of white supremacy coming from the north. There was power in an imagined collective racial identity. Today, in the "north," Latino/as or Hispanics unsettle the U.S. racial imaginary altogether. This is not because Hispanics are considred an ethnicity, not a race. The census itself makes clear that Latino/as "have" a race, but it can be any race. Race, the greatest visible marker in the colonial armory, cannot make visible the nation's largest minority.[15] The cosmetic race, defined by performance practices rather than skin color, destabilizes "race" itself. Genetic research has already debunked the biological underpinnings of racial categories. Now Latino/as have disrupted social and visual systems of identification. Waves of Latino immigration over the past fifty years have blurred all notions of visual identification. Immigrants have come in all colors: "brown" working-class migrations from Puerto Rico and "white" upper- and middle-class antirevolutionaries from Cuba in the 1960s; "white" middle-class Puerto Ricans and the "black" discarded Mariel boatlift people from Cuba in the early 1980s; the recent migrations of political exiles from predominantly "white" countries such as Argentina, Paraguay, Uruguay, and Chile; the constant flow of the politically and economically oppressed indigenous and mestizo peoples from Mexico and Central America. Add these groups to those that have been here before the redrawing of the Mexico-U.S. border in 1848 and it becomes clear why Latino/as seem simultaneously to be everywhere and yet unlocalizable, visible yet unidentifiable. They are all Latino/as, and there is still power in imagined collective ethnic identity.

Latino/as became the largest minority in the United States, though no one seemed to notice. They, like Walter, are depicted as completely invisible, unlocatable, and/or utterly performative. They still drop out of most discussions on race. Few universities have Latino Studies programs, there's no Latino history month or Cesar Chavez civil rights day. Look for the Latino section in the bookstore. Assuming there is something "Hispanic," you will likely find everything from pre-Conquest temples, to Argentine cookbooks, to books on decorating with paper cut-outs. Who knows who Latino/as are or what they have accomplished in the United States? Which archives house their histories, writings, and artistic achievements?

Not surprisingly, as I argued in the opening chapter, this lack of archival presence leads people to question the very existence of these populations. For many, Latino/as have no bodies, it seems. They are shadowy, undocumented laborers who do necessary yet invisible labor. One Latino church on the Lower East Side of New York City that I walk by regularly had a huge mural saying: "Give me their souls—keep the rest." Politicians want votes. The Market wants consumers for midsize cars and long-distance calling cards. Chicano/a playwrights Luis Valdéz and Cherríe Moraga have plays in which their revolutionary protagonists literally have no bodies—just heads.[16] Distorted by oppressive systems of representation, Moraga writes in *Loving in the War Years*, "I became pure spirit—bodiless."[17] When Latino/as do have bodies, they tend to be disarticulated—they are the backs that bend to pick the strawberries, the arms that clean the houses, the hands that push those baby carriages. Or they are the bodies behind bars—among the disproportionate masses of men and women of color incarcerated in the United States.

Who cares for or about the Latino/a body? Most Latino/as have no vote, no right to legal protection, no access to health care or schooling. Embodiment poses political, ethical, and legal problems that many officials and voters in the United States would rather not contemplate.

For others, Latino/as are loud, temperamental, given to excessive affect and self-display. Latino/a identity, then, seems less a question of racial or even geographical origin and more strategies of self-fashioning: language, taste, music, food, and self-identification.[18] Are they, or aren't they?

Cultural imperatives thus crash into each other, at times threatening to break the bicultural subject in two. Instead of the *both/and* of cultural and biological mestizaje, Latino/as in the United States are confronted with an either/or.[19] Walter resists those limitations, exuberantly navigating the both/and: both male and female, both white and Latino, both wealthy and "of the people," both Spanish- and English-speaking, both Puerto Rican and mainlander, both fortune-teller and fortune-seeker. My pleasure in his performance allows me to forget that his ability to navigate those spaces is predicated on his privileged status of wealthy, white male. On one level, then, he simply supports the existing structures of visibility.

On another level, I like to believe (or make-believe), Walter's biculturality still poses a challenge to normativity. As politicians and commentators such as Pat Buchanan and Linda Chavez bemoan, Latino/as often eschew the either/or. Many don't want to be "assimilated." Most choose not to abandon their cultural practices even as they accept new ones. *Bi* is good. Latinos will go to medical doctors if they are sick and have access to Western medicine, but many of them also participate in all sorts of non-Western healing practices. Going to the curandero or espiritista is another example of the both/and. Curanderos, psychics, and espiritistas equate certain kinds of cultural archives and repertoires (herbs, stones, cards, cosmic signs) with cultural competence that involves *knowledge* and *understanding* rather than belief. Participating in a *limpia* (cleansing) is an ontological exercise, another way of being Latino/a. In the United States, these practices highlight the cultural break points, the nodes where conflicting systems come together. Walter and other Latino/a espiritistas make these points visible, charting a sociopolitical, rather than a cosmic, psychic space.

"Can saying make it so?"[20] J. L. Austin, as all performance studies students know, coined the term *performative*, "derived of course from perform" (6), to refer to language that acts. There are cases—wedding ceremonies, christening ships—in which saying something does something (12). Unlike constatives, or declarations of "fact," the performative masquerades: it's a "disguised" form that "apes" statements of fact (4). Yet Austin posits that they work differently: "The constative utterance is true or false and the performative is happy or unhappy" (54). Austin then goes on to develop an elaborate system that identifies infelicitous performatives (things "go wrong on the occasion of such utterances," 14) and points to the many reasons why performatives do not act as anticipated. There are misfires, acts that do not take effect and are declared null and void, either because (1) the procedure used is the wrong one or the person executing it is not the appropriate one ("misinvocation," 17) or (2) the procedure is correct but its performance is bungled ("misexecutions," 17). In this wonderful book, which unravels its argument as it goes along, Austin seems to perform what I would like to underline here. A lot of fun can come from misfires, misinvocations, and misexecutions. Walter, I suggest, is the master of the misfire, an unauthorized person using inappropriate means to disrupt conventional wisdom and to pronounce— and effect—a new social order.

As a performer, Walter specializes in the art of reversal, exaggeration, conflation, contradiction, camp, lo cursi, rasquache, and relajo. He endows the drag queen with papal authority. He reads politics through astrology and comments on the brutality of conquest, slavery, sexism, and other social ills through the movement of the stars. Instead of acting as the intermediary for God's love, he offers us his own. He mixes what claims to pass as high art—his Grecian figurines and great books—with rasquache, the cursi or ridiculous bad taste associated with those who have to make do.[21] He is a ham, a diva, a comadre, a connoisseur, a businessman, and an hombre culto. Mercado, the psychic of the marketplace, is a multizillionaire who sells and endorses products. Super Mercado (supermarket), as one commentator calls him, markets everything from *productos energéticos* to prayer beads he claims have special powers. Mercado is a self-created, self-promoted charismatic spiritual leader who is said to have been a sickly, stuttering child in his native Puerto Rico. He manifests the new Latino/a "destiny," holding up the promise of transformation: from rags to riches, from stuttering to prophetic speech, from Puerto Rico to the world.

Perhaps as interesting, however, is the aesthetic hide and seek going on in Walter's performance, a closeting that lies in the way two practices—the Euro-American camp and the Latin/o American rasquache—come together to conceal what the other reveals. From their initial theoretical articulations (as opposed to practices), neither camp or rasquache are strangers to closeting. Susan Sontag's famous 1964 "Notes on Camp" gave rise to heated debates concerning not only the politics of camp, but the politics of Sontag herself.[22] Although she belatedly associates camp with homosexuals (note 50), she has been accused of downplaying what other commentators see as the vital link between camp and queer performativity.[23] Interestingly, however, that essay also gave rise to the theorization of rasquache. Although rasquachismo has a long history in Mexican and Mexican American popular culture, Tomás Ybarra-Frausto's playful and succinct theoretical articulation of rasquachismo, "Rasquachismo, a Chicano Sensibility," builds from Sontag's essay.[24] The way Ybarra-Frausto models his reflections on Sontag's notes suggests a deep interconnection (as well as a radical divergence) between the two theories that often try to ignore each other's existence.

Like camp, rasquachismo is defined as the "good taste of bad taste."[25] Politically, both are minority discourses that capture the pleasure and fun in oppositionality. Stylistically, both are cursi, translated as "showy, gaudy, pretentious" in the New World Spanish-English Dictionary. Camp, defined by Sontag as a "badge of identity," finds its counterpart in rasquachismo, as "the verbal-visual codes we use to speak to each other among ourselves" (155). Neither camp nor rasquachismo are "elevated" or "serious." Sontag's list of camp items, such as Tiffany lamps and Bellini operas, finds its counterpart in Ybarra-Frausto's list of rasquache items: microwave tamales and "portraits of Emiliano Zapata on velvet" (155). "Camp," according to Sontag, "sees everything in quotation marks. It's not a lamp, but a 'lamp'" (note 10). Rasquache is also citational, recycled, transposed into a context that brings about the reversal from high to low, from reverent to irreverent: Emiliano Zapata, the great revolutionary hero, on shiny cheap velvet. Sontag argues that "the essence of Camp is its love of the unnatural: of artifice and exaggeration" (277). Like camp, rasquache is flamboyant and elaborate, "a rampant decorative sense whose basic axiom might be 'too much is never enough'" (Ybarra-Frausto, 156). Rasquache, like camp, is inseparable from the people who practice it. Thus, Ybarra-Frausto echoes Sontag's fear of "betraying" the sensibility by publicly defining the private code and takes on a nonsolemn, even rasquache, approach to exploring it. Both theories nervously walk the line. Is camp/rasquache about them/it? Or is it about us? Do we become camp/rasquache by talking about it?

Here, then, we have two related "sensibilities" at work. The radical divergence has to do with the agents of these sensibilities and the politics of their practice. Each theory rejects or disavows the subject—in terms of class, race, and sexual orientation—at the center of the other. For Sontag, camp "is by its nature possible only in affluent societies" (note 49), whereas rasquachismo, for Ybarra-Frausto, reflects the taste of the working class: it's "an underdog perspective," "an attitude rooted in resourcefulness and adaptability, yet mindful of stance and style" (156). In the United States, rasquachismo "has evolved as a bicultural sensibility" (156). Sontag's homosexuals also belong to a "minority," but it's a "creative," certainly not ethnic, one (note 51). Conversely, Chicano/as may be down, lively, resilient, and resourceful, but never gay. The Sontag essay links sensibility begrudgingly with sexual practice and class privilege while it assumes racial privilege. Ybarra-Frausto's essay celebrates sensibility as the mark of the working-class MexChicano while strategically assuming heteronormativity. Each essay, it seems, plays hide and seek; each points to what it disavows. Sontag raises the issues of class and race only to dismiss them; camp belongs not to the underclass but to those who experience the "psychopathology of affluence" (note 49). She labels the queer Cuban singer La Lupe as camp—a move that might have opened the discussion to include non–Euro-Americans and people of color as early as 1964—but she only gestures toward possibilities left unexplored. The rasquache essay, too, points away from the queerness at the center of its articulation. Ybarra-Frausto elides the queerness knowingly, perhaps mindful that the Chicano movement of the 1960s, which he argues "reinvigorated the stance and style of rasquachismo" (159), countered racism in part through a machismo that would not tolerate interrogation.

What does it say about Walter the psychic, and about Latino psychic space, that at the end of the twentieth century he performs camp sans sexuality and rasquache sin ethnicity? What fantasies of identification or passing get negotiated in this staging of both/and, neither/nor? Walter the white, oh-so-affluent Latino flamboyantly calls attention to his body and his background, only to emphasize that what he has to offer is not about sexuality or ethnicity, but about the spirit, the soul. Walter the star triumphs as a Latino. Yet, his sense of beauty and order eliminates almost everything that could be "American" in the hemispheric sense of the term. His inspiration flows from antiquity, Egypt, Europe, China—though his appeals to Santería bring him closer to home. Nonetheless, his performance of "civilization" tacitly affirms that civilization comes from "over there" generally and from his Spanish grandmother personally. So too, he closets his sexuality even as he performs it in the most public of spaces. Yet he keeps his secrets and urges us to do the same. Walter is the "don't ask, don't tell" diva of the Latino community, who both practices and preaches a strategic refusal of definition.

Yet, part of his performance includes the rasquache/camp reversal of its very premise. Walter's exuberant display of wealth and success is so transparent it is funny. It makes visible *as fantasy* the aspiration of making it in a country that values whiteness, stardom, and material success. It is not so much a goal as a kind of Freudian "wish-fulfillment."[26] Thus, this performance of affluence and whiteness is not just a disavowal or erasure of the rasquache subject—although it is that—but a participation in the national illusion of "success." Even Latino/as can play. It also makes apparent the ethnically marked desire (however fleeting) for "passing" and transcending the effects of social and racial discrimination. The Walter apparition is so spectral, so disembodied, so virtual that the rasquache reality of disempowerment sustaining it stands out starkly. As Ybarra-Frausto suspected, the rasquache performance makes its viewers and commentators rasquache: this performance is about "us," as participants in this fantasy, not just Walter who stars in it.

The reversal of camp also debunks Walter's sexual closeting. So, although we could argue that Walter tries to hide his sexuality under gaudy priestly attire, I find this aesthetic choice generative. Although he never refers to his own sexual preference, he not only performs it but constantly advocates sexual tolerance, reminding his listeners that love has nothing to do with contractual arrangements. He writes that "we are entering the age of love, and in it the relationships between men and women, between men and other men, between women and other women—even between what we call 'families'—will be altered dramatically and permanently."[27] His closeting also comes with instructions to his audience. Look at me, he seems to say, and think what you will; but don't judge, don't criticize, because remember: when you're pointing at someone, three fingers point back at you. The performance, then, is as much about the audience's role in sexual closeting as about his own.

Walter's unplaceability, in all senses, is key to his popularity. He is everywhere and nowhere, visible yet uncategorizable. He is a crossover artist who exuberantly performs the space of liminality and alternativity, and makes it glamorous. He is the happy performative, the glittery face of the Latino/as' unhappy positioning in the U.S. imaginary, the one who by claiming prominence makes it so. He elevates liminality to a cosmic condition: "We are passing through a portal in time" (2), he writes, and "We are indeed at the time for the total destruction of the old, before the time of rebirth" (57). He occupies the 5:45 P.M. television slot between day and night, between the predominantly female audience for *televnovelas* (soap operas) and the mixed audience for the nightly news. He navigates the liminal zone of speculation that blends fantasy and futures. He takes himself seriously, but we know it's *puro relajo*, just fooling around.

Relajo is a blissfully failed performative, an act that breaks the appropriate system of conventional behaviors and turns its actions null and void. It is liminal mode of action that entails an acting up and an acting out. Relajo, an act of spontaneous disruption, shatters the given configuration of the group or community. In the face of relajo, the conventional procedure cannot go forward. As a form of disruptive or transgressive behavior, relajo manifests both the challenge to and the tacit acknowledgment of a system's limits. It is an act of devalorization, or what the late Mexican intellectual Jorge Portilla calls "desolidarization" with dominant norms in order to create a different, joyously rebellious solidarity—that of the underdog.[28] Relajo is an act of disidentification insofar as it rejects any given categorization without pronouncing or owning another. It is a "negative" form of expression in that it's a declaration *against*, never *for*, a position. Yet, relajo proves nonthreatening, because it is humorous and subversive in ways that allow for critical distancing rather than revolutionary challenge. It is an aside, not a frontal attack. Rasquache (the aesthetic, the attitude), like relajo (the act), is liberating for marginalized communities. Walter's relajo is a performance in that it is always citational, "twice-behaved behavior," and in that it requires repeated externalization. It is a performative in that it brings about the effect it pronounces; it makes visible the attitude of refusal, the moment of interruption or intervention. Walter exalts in his rasquacheness. Through relajo, he flouts conventions, delegitimating normative regulatory systems. He forges a sense of a liberated, bilingual, flamboyant Latino community that is capable of making the rules—not just following them or breaking them. Through relajo, the world becomes divided into those who understand the gesture and those who don't. Relajo reverses the colonialist insider/outsider configuration, embracing those who get the joke and excluding those left wondering what it's all about. Like camp and rasquache, relajo denies easy access. It's a form of minoritarian coding—of revealing and concealing—in order to survive in the public sphere.

This liminality and alternativity of relajo speaks compellingly to the Latino/a experience of social and legal dispossession. Latino/as, for starters, are always in between, marginal to both the Latin American and the U.S. social imaginaries, the victims too often of performative misfires. Law and order in the United States doesn't usually work for Latino/as, part of that population forced to endure ever more aggressive policing. The political space of liminality has, with good reason, usually been associated with anxiety and terror. For Puerto Ricans, national identity has been a space of in-betweenness, often a push-pull between the island and the mainland, between Spanish and English, between a Puerto Rican "identity" and a U.S. passport. Cuban Americans often express their identification with Cuba, though they have no home to go home to. Mexicans in the Southwest were here before the border was, and have been/not been U.S. citizens since the Treaty of Guadalupe Hidalgo offered them their ambiguous status in 1848, a promise that they would be "admitted, at the proper time (to be judged by the Congress of the United States) to the enjoyment of all the rights of citizens of the United States"[29] For them, legal and cultural citizenship has always been a fantasy, a belief in futures perpetually deferred. Newcomers, such as South Americans who cross the U.S. border, face an ever more terrifying liminal zone full of "the Law," coyotes, La Migra, and other dangers. As Alberto Ledesma puts it, they "must learn how to live in the shadows, not knowing the language that is spoken to them, uninformed about any rights they may have, and unable to protest their plight."[30] Even legal residents and citizens are too often treated as cultural aliens and economic pariahs. The psychic toll of subjection makes Latino/as desirous of another Law, another system of signification, an order beyond the law of Church and state.

Walter's performance, I believe, makes visible both the Law and its transgression: that which demands compliance and, at the same time, that which can be deciphered only by those in the know. The Law in Baudrillard's understanding is "part of the world of representation, and is therefore subject to interpretation or decipherment. . . . It is a text, and falls under the influence of meaning and referentiality."[31] Walter provides a parodic challenge to the Law itself by alluding to a higher law that he alone can decipher. He disrupts the traditional archive that has guarded the information of those in power by reading the stars, the tarot, the I-Ching as signs based on a Law deeper, older, more mysterious, and somehow more universally and eternally valid than the Law of the land. He, too, seems to believe in everything (and nothing). He doesn't demand belief. There is no puritanical work ethic to adhere to and nothing to prove. This is not a religion, not an obligation. It is participation, a ganging up, a style, an attitude, an exercise in relajo that enacts the hope that the Law, as a normalizing system, can be safely reversed and transgressed.

Walter, I am convinced, speaks more to a fantasy of "making it" than to spiritual belief—more to make-believe than to belief itself. The Latino psychic reflects, in interesting ways, a Latino psychic space. What is that fantasy of cultural participation, and why is it so compelling, given that it clearly excludes more than it includes? How does Walter's performance of Latinoness tie into other, perhaps more sociological forms of self-imagining, such as the identity formations reflected in the 2000 census? Maybe there are many whys, some having to do with performance, others with gender and sexuality, others with race and ethnicity, others with economics, others with politics, others with spirituality, others with the way they all come together.

Walter's performance of a psychic space, I would argue, is complicated, contradictory, yet overall affirming. He is the symptom of the commodification of identities and the hypertrophy of artifice. Walter makes visible the Latino as Star—on condition that he be white, blonde, male, rich, and entrepreneurial. He is the highly artificial Latino who signals the paradoxical createdness of the Latino as a pan-ethnic category. Latino is itself an accumulation of groups: simultaneously a very real political resource as a collective and "mobilizable" political identity, a media construct, a style, and a consumer market. Consumer society interpolates its subjects through the market, and what is Walter but the paradoxical (dis)embodiment of late capitalism's traffic in identities? Nonetheless, Walter offers a cosmic and cosmetic ordering of the multiple conflicting and chaotic forces tugging at identity. He proposes multiple readings and opens multiple spaces of alternativity. Perhaps what his persona promises Latino/a viewers is a vital psychic space, one with options, with room to maneuver, one that promises access to different kinds of knowledge, different repertoires, different cultural texts, different hermeneutic strategies. There are so many variables for bicultural citizens, so many linguistic, ideological, and sociopolitical factors to negotiate. And every weeknight on Channel 41 Walter assures us, his viewers, that we are in control of the variables, rather than the variables to be controlled.

5

FALSE IDENTIFICATIONS

Minority Populations Mourn Diana

We sat on the sofa—my young daughter, Marina, on my lap—lamenting the death of a woman we didn't know. As the coffin slowly made its way toward Westminster Abbey, the commentators reverentially droned on about the silence, the mood, the dramatic demonstration of public emotion. But there were so many publics, it seemed, participating in what looked like one and the same theatre of mourning. The exclusive, well-behaved public of dignitaries and movie stars inside the Abbey, the charged "popular" audience on the meadows outside, the two billion people watching each other watching around the world. Everywhere the camera rested, people were sobbing silently. The emotion was contagious: the pity for Diana and her boys, the terror of sudden death, the rage at the ungiving queen, the contempt for the unloving husband. As in theatre, emotion gave way to applause. It erupted outside the Abbey following the Earl of Spencer's eulogy and pushed its way inside, back to front, uninvited, disrupting the solemnity and reminding the high and mighty that this was, after all, the public's command performance. Then, as the hearse carrying the remains made its way out of London, the public threw its last bouquets at the departing diva. The incessant repeats of the coverage assured us we were watching "live." What does live mean, I wondered out loud, watching as we were across the Atlantic? "It means we're live and she's dead," Marina explains. Then, "You won't die, will you,

Mummy?" punctuated by crying. "No, darling, no, I promise," suddenly crying too, but embarrassed. Our tears were of a different kind—hers about pity and fear; mine complicated by my determination to resist this kind of identification which I found coercive and humiliating.

What's Diana to me, that I should weep for her? This was an odd mirroring effect—one Diana crying for another.

Once again, I was that awkward, chubby child in Parral, Chihuahua—my hair pulled back in pigtails so tight that my eyes wouldn't shut, my skirt pinned together because I'd popped my button, wearing my cowgirl boots, my fringed suede jacket, and my beloved little gold scissors earrings that opened and closed. My Anglo-Canadian grandmother said I looked like a savage. Princess Anne, she reminded me, didn't wear suede jackets, to say nothing of the scissors earrings. I certainly was not her "little princess" and I would never grow up and marry the Prince if I didn't shape up and act like a good girl. Every holiday brought a new corrective for my savage condition: a royal calendar, a commemorative teacup. Now, there she was, the other Diana, the one who had been tall and blonde and beautiful, the one who would never be caught dead without a button, the one who would sooner have died than be chubby; the one who had married the Prince. And look what happened to her. Here, once more, I was caught in a drama that had unexpectedly become my own. I felt a shudder, sensed the ghost.

DOWNLOADING GRIEF

Whose fantasy was this, I kept wondering during the weeks following the death and funeral of Diana, Princess of Wales? Or, rather, how did so many disparate fantasies come to converge on this rather ordinary human being? The disparity between the accident-as-incident and the spectacularity of the worldwide reaction demanded reflection. Diana's ghost, I suspected, had more to tell us about international relations than did Madeleine Albright. What was the basis of such seemingly widespread identification? Were we watching a hodge-podge of funerary traditions, or was this really a case of multicultural mourning styles coalescing before our eyes? What were the politics of such memorializing energy and the mimetic performances of grief being enacted simultaneously in various parts of the world, the synchronized moments of silence, the condolence book signings, the floral shrines? In Argentina, a magazine ran a drawing of Santa Evita and Santa Diana sitting side by side in heaven. There she was, "the most beloved lady of our time," gracing the stamps of the Togolese Republic. The Trinidadian carnival featured a number, "Paparazzi Is Hell," as a "Tribute to the Queen of Hearts." Memorial walls on the Lower East Side of Manhattan were painted by U.S. artists of color. One mural, by Chico, places her next to other female Latina victims: Selena and Elisa (Figures 20–22), both murdered by people close to them. Was this a conspiracy mural? On another, Diana is a savior, along with Mother Teresa, in "royalty and holiness" (Figure 23). And here, in an admonishing mural by A. Charles that covers a synagogue on Houston Street, Diana's death is depicted as media overkill (Figures 24–26). She's placed next to fallen African American icons Tupac Shakur and Mike Tyson. "Live by the gun, die by the gun." The murals made visible the versions of the saint, victim, and media object circulating in the public sphere. How did these global images get downloaded onto these neighborhood walls? Why would minority populations care about her, when their own icons—from Evita to Selena to Tupac—had fared so poorly in the media? By what mechanism did Diana's popularity get construed as "the popular"? The world willingly suspended its disbelief as this most aristocratic of women, married to a prince and future king, the mother of princes and future kings, who socialized with billionaires and celebrities, was transformed before our eyes into the "people's princess" and "queen of people's hearts."

Diana's life, death, funeral, and afterlife as quasi-sacred relic on display illuminates the way multiple, intersecting social dramas play both globally and locally. All sorts of issues, ranging from eating disorders, to unhappy marriages, to AIDS, to the workings of the media, to neocolonialism, to globalization, seem magically incarnated in her image. The tragic emplotment of the events surrounding Diana and the theatricality of the staging, transmitted internationally, create the illusion of a cohesive, "universal" audience. But is this not perhaps an international spectacle, in the Debordian sense, that "presents itself simultaneously as all of society, as part of society and as an instrument of unification" as it "concentrates all gazing and all consciousness"?[1] There is a difference between playing to a global audience and claiming that the drama has a universal appeal. By looking at the nature and

20, 21, 22. Murals by Chico on East Houston Street in New York City: Diana, Selena, Elisa. Photos by Diana Taylor, 1997.

staging of these social dramas, I explore how globalization gets cast as "universality" and how this "universality" gets downloaded strategically and reconfigured on the local level.

SOCIAL DRAMA

If we follow Victor Turner's model of the "social drama" for a minute, a model he claims to be universally valid, we can easily recognize the four phases he identifies: (1) the breach, or social rupture and flouting of the norm; (2) crisis, in which the breach widens and escalates; (3) redressive action, which seeks to contain the spread of the crisis; and (4) the reintegration, the reordering of social norms.[2] Each of the four stages unfolds in a different dramatic mode, each rivaling the last in pushing the limits of theatricality.

The breach—her divorce from Charles and her estrangement from the Royal family—was pure melodrama. Played in the shrill key of interrogatives, declaratives, and denunciations, the drama unfolded in explosive, sporadic cries and whispers. Almost everyone could (and apparently did) tune in to the latest episodes featuring the insensitive husband, the other woman, the disapproving mother-in-law. The boundaries of the "appropriate" were repeatedly emphasized and transgressed. This private drama so publicly enacted situated protagonists and spectators alike on, and often over, the very brink of the admissible. I, like millions of others, lived the traumas of the infidelities and the self-destructive behaviors, eavesdropped on conversations, and shared the thrill of revelations and denials. When she wasn't struggling to hold back the tears, the captions pointed at the evidence of vulnerability. Her pain became the spectacle, played out in a hide-and-seek mode of strategic self-exposure on her part and unrepentant voyeurism on mine. What made it all so thrilling, of course, was not its originality but its predictability: her story, played out so glamorously in the here and now, was basically the same old story. I, like many, many others, had lived it or seen it all before.

Her death—the crisis—was tragic drama. The fateful crash, which I (like those before me) will replay at length later, moved Diana out of the "same-old" and cast her as the "one." We're alive and she's dead—she's left the anonymity of the "we" to inhabit the singularity of the "she." She crystallized into the original, quintessential, tragic lover, beautiful princess, angel of mercy, and doting mother. Her sudden uniqueness, her tragic magnitude,

23. *(opposite, top)* Mural by Chico, "In Memory of Royalty and Holiness," on 11th Street and Avenue A, New York City. Photo by Diana Taylor, 1997.

24, 25, 26. *(this page and opposite, bottom)* Murals by A. Charles on Houston Street and First Avenue, New York City: Overkill, Diana, Tupac Shakur. Photos by Diana Taylor, 1997.

allowed us to forget for a moment that she was also very much the product of a long history of collective imaginings that have normalized heterosexuality, glorified maternity, fetishized youth and femininity, glamorized whiteness, eroticized imperialism, and promoted a discourse of volunteerism. Live? Or one more repeat of the live?

The redressive action—the funeral—was a theatrical performance. Following in the tradition of other state funerals, this event was one more repetition, only the latest but never the first or the last of such spectacles. Eleanor of Castile, apparently, had a sumptuous send-off in 1290. Evita's funeral in 1952 was a magnificent spectacle, as massive and stately as Diana's. It was a performance, orchestrated with a beginning, middle, and end. The theatricality emanated from the careful choreographing of color, movement, sound, space, and regalia. Theatricality, commonly thought to be an attribute of theatre, clearly precedes and extends beyond it. Communities without theatre (such as non-Western cultures like the Mexica) understood, and were ruled by, theatricality. And issues concerning theatricality lay at the center of many of the tensions between the Queen and the British population. How much or how little theatricality should the country demand in honoring the passing of their Princess?

The theatricality of the event, as state spectacle, claimed visual power through layering, the addition and augmentation of traditional and nontraditional elements. Diana's funeral, weighed down in splendor, outdid those that had come before. But repetition was not simply a mimetic return to former displays of pomp and circumstance. Rather, the pomp associated with the past served to monumentalize the present. Each *re*incarnation gains power through accumulation. Citationality thus was put to the service of originality, enhancing the "new," nontraditional touches, such as Elton John singing his pop hit "Candle in the Wind," in itself recalling an earlier death. Yet, the prescribed, twice-behaved nature of funerals also has another, ritual function. The formal handling of painful or dangerous transitions, or passings, helps regulate the expenditure of emotion. Funerals have long served to channel and control grief. But this televised funeral, with its insistence on participation, seemed to provoke the very emotions it was designed to channel. The spectators, as much as the casket and the visible Royals, became the spectacle for a global audience brought together, perhaps by grief but most certainly by television, newspapers, journals, and the Web. Unlike these earlier events, the media and communications systems performed the identification they claimed to report, assuring us that the loss, like the Princess, was ours.

The phase of reintegration, the period of reordering social norms, played itself out in multiple, less cohesive, less centralized dramas. After the initial phase of virtual participation through frantic memorialization, Diana's ghost became a site of intense renegotiating among various communities. Would the status quo ruptured by the breach be restored? Would the monarchy be reinvigorated, or permanently outmoded? Was Diana the new face of Tony Blair's kinder, gentler, more modern England? Did the burial site constructed by her brother emblematize England's "image in the world [as] a low tech 'theme park of royal pageantry' "?[3] Or had she been transformed into a thoroughly non-British relic in a pay-per-view shrine out of Disney? Are the ruptures and divides made visible by her death overcome in this moment of reintegration, or are the divides more starkly visible than before?

THE HAUNTOLOGY OF PERFORMANCE

Various modalities of expressive culture are made visible through the social drama paradigm outlined by Turner. And he is probably correct in affirming that this four-stage model illuminates all types of social conflict, ranging from office disputes to national conflicts. However, I am less convinced that these dramas play internationally and cross-culturally in any clear-cut way. The "drama" of Diana's death and the "theatricality" of her funeral elide rather than clarify the "trauma" of border crossings as specters traverse ethnic or national boundaries. What counts as a drama in one context gets demoted to a mere incident elsewhere. The Diana specter becomes visible and meaningful as it dances within various scopic, political, and economic repertoires—and vice versa. England's rose occludes Norma Jean as the new candle dancing in the wind. The dance performs more plays of substitution or, in Joseph Roach's term, surrogation: England's rose crowds out Selena, the Rose of Texas; her funeral outdoes Evita's as the most overproduced funeral of the century for a woman.[4] The specter, the spectacle, and the spectator are all dancing at this funeral. Maybe because it's so hard to get a handle on, *spec-ere* (to see) that phantoms, fantasy, and performance have traditionally been placed on the opposite side of the "real" and "historical."

The fantasies in play may be linked to so-called universal and eternal anxieties about a glorious life, an unexpected death, and the fall of the great. The iterative and highly stylized nature of this stately display should not suggest that it is not, at the same time, deeply political and historically specific. What conditions allow these fantasies to become visibly incarnated in a woman no one cares much about? Though the specter may come in and out of time, and though performances make visible the conflicts that otherwise remain diffuse, both specters and performances are very live. "Haunting," Derrida notes, "is historical . . . but not dated."[5] The fantasies converging around the figure of Diana, I suggest, require certain conditions of visibility and bring various histories, ontologies, and hauntologies of performance into focus.

In *Unmarked*, Peggy Phelan outlines the "ontology of performance," stressing the liveness of the performative event, the *now* in which that performance takes place: "Performance's only life is in the present. Performance cannot be saved, recorded, documented, or otherwise participate in the circulation of representations of representation."[6] An event such as Diana's death and funeral, however, also begs us to look at the flip side of performance's ontology, at what Derrida has called its "hauntology." Many cultures are grounded on the notion of a second coming: the Mexica, the Christian, the Jewish, the Marxist, to name a few. The ghost is, by definition, a repetition, Derrida's *revenant*. This is the moment of postdisappearance, rather than the moment preceding it that Phelan points to. The sumptuousness of the ceremony performs the sacralization of the *remains,* theoretically antithetical to performance. The remains, in this spectacle, take on a life of their own—so much so that one tabloid photo montage has Di looking on at her own funeral from the corner with a bittersweet smile, one more witness to an event that has overtaken her. The body we assume lies in the coffin is all that we have to assure us that Diana was real. It provides the authenticating materiality that sustains the performance of resuscitation. In spirit, she was present at her funeral, as perhaps, inversely, we could argue that she was absent from her life. The shrine housing her remains will continue to guarantee the materiality of the global phenomenon that is Diana, the massive reappearance of the revenant. Politically and symbolically, we haven't seen the end of her. The caption of a recent photograph of a London newsstand states that "one might be forgiven for imagining that Diana never died last August. The Princess of Wales still keeps the presses roaring."[7] The February 2, 1998, cover of *People* depicts Diana as active in death as she was in life: "In death as in life, she has raised millions for charity."

My view of performance rests on the notion of ghosting, that visualization that continues to act politically even as it exceeds the live. Like Phelan's definition, it hinges on the relationship between visibility and invisibility, or appearance and disappearance, but comes at it from a different angle. For Phelan, the defining feature of performance—that which separates it from all other phenomena—is that it is live and disappears without a trace. The way I see it, performance makes visible (for an instant, live, now) that which is always already there: the ghosts, the tropes, the scenarios that structure our individual and collective life. These specters, made manifest through performance, alter future phantoms, future fantasies. Diana may have been the product of one way of envisioning royalty, but she has changed the look, style, and scope in which royalty will be performed, and desired, in the future. Her enactment left a trace. Every woman running for political office in Argentina today wears the obligatory dyed blonde bun and Dior suit associated with Evita. In one sense, of course, the live performance eludes the "economy of reproduction," as Phelan puts it.[8] But I would argue that its efficacy, whether as art or as politics, stems from the way performances tap into public fantasies and leave a trace, reproducing and at times altering cultural repertoires. Performance, then, involves more than an object (as in performance art), more than an accomplishment or a carrying through. It constitutes a (quasi-magical) invocational practice. It provokes emotions it claims only to represent, evokes memories and grief that belong to some other body. It conjures up and makes visible not just the live but the powerful army of the always already living. The power of seeing through performance is the recognition that we've seen it all before—the fantasies that shape our sense of self, of community, that organize our scenarios of interaction, conflict, and resolution.

What conditions of visibility are needed to conjure up the ghost? Of all the many potential specters, why do certain ones gain such power? Why Diana and not somebody else? Why, as Michael Taussig asks in *Mimesis and Alterity*, does the spirit (and, I would add, the ghost) need embodiment at all?[9] Evita's corpse, perhaps, can shed some light on the need to give material shape to a political force. The most politically powerful woman in the world in the early 1950s, Evita has the world's most expensive corpse. It cost

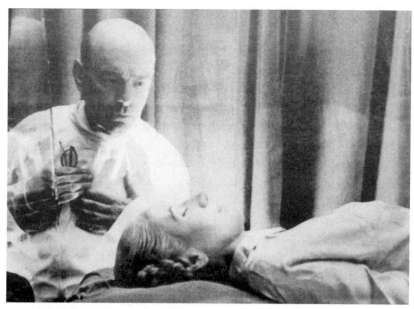

27. Dr. Ara and Evita's corpse. From *Página12*, September 22, 1996. Photo courtesy of Diana Taylor.

$200,000 to embalm her and three wax copies were produced to trick all the would-be body snatchers. The copies were so authentic that Dr. Ara removed the tip of her little finger to distinguish her real body from its replications. The original, here as elsewhere, is never as whole as its representation. Her body, the most politically charged fetish of the twentieth century, is key because it anchors the "other Eva," the more powerful one, the one whose ghost continues to dominate Argentine politics. *Spec-ere*, to see, is possible only through a history of spectacles and ghosts. Performance, be it artistic or political, accomplishes a moment of revisualization. It disappears only to hover; it promises or threatens to reappear, albeit in another shape or form.

Performance becomes visible, meaningful, within the context of a phantasmagoric repertoire of repeats. But there is a double mechanism at work. On the one hand, we see only what we have been conditioned to see: that which we have seen before. So part of the grief we feel surrounding Diana's death is that she is so familiar to us. She represents the most general, undifferentiated version of the death of the beautiful woman, a scenario so powerful, so naturalized that it underwrites the Western imaginary and seems

28. "La Otra Eva,"
Página12, Radar section,
September 22, 1996. Photo
courtesy of Diana Taylor.

always to have been there.[10] On the other hand, the spectacle presents itself as a universal and unifying event. But spectacle, to conjure up Debord for a minute, "is not a collection of images, but a social relation among people, mediated by images."[11] The spectacle, then, is that which we do *not* see, the invisible that "appears" only through mediation. Diana's specter unites the spectators in the fantasy of loving and losing a woman no one really knows even as it hides the social relations among the very people who, theoretically, participate in the fantasy. Diana's death looks more like one more repetition of the same. Her death (singular and sudden) represents both the instant of her passing ("real," not-performatic) *and* the reappearance of another death: Evita, Selena, Marilyn Monroe, Mother Teresa. As Elisabeth Bronfen argues, "The death of a beautiful woman emerges as the requirement for a preservation of existing cultural norms and values. . . . Over her dead body, cultural norms are reconfigured or secured, whether because the sacrifice of the virtuous, innocent woman serves a social critique and transformation or because a sacrifice of the dangerous woman reestablishes an order that was momentarily suspended due to her presence."[12] This seemingly univer-

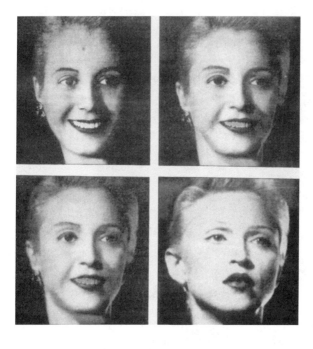

29. Evita fades
into Madonna on
the cover of *La Maga*,
January 31, 1996.
Photo courtesy of
Diana Taylor.

sal scenario elides the politics of cultural transmission. What we don't see, as the world mourns Diana, is that these women (judged innocent or dangerous, and usually both) form part of profoundly different imaginaries, and the borders of these imaginaries are policed. The specter hides the spectacle. The mourning rituals may be similar; they may even encourage fantasies that they are communicable to different populations. But the politics are untranslatable.

POLICING THE IMAGINARY

Chicanas and Chicanos, as well as other Latinos, mourned Selena en masse, covered her coffin with thousands of roses, gathered tens of thousands of signatures in commemorative books, declared an official Selena Day, and attempted to inscribe her name and face on everything from Web sites to memorial walls to Coca-Cola bottles. The similarity of the rituals highlights the lack of empathetic reciprocity; theatricality blinds even as it makes visible. The redressive moment of one social drama (Selena's funeral) signals the moment of breach in another. A few hours before her funeral, Howard

Stern had already shipped her back to Mexico: "Selena? Her music is awful. I don't know what Mexicans are into. If you're going to sing about what's going on in Mexico, what can you say? . . . You can't grow crops, you got a cardboard house, your eleven-year-old daughter is a prostitute. . . . This is music to perform abortions to!"[13] According to Stern, this death proves too lowly to constitute a drama. It's reduced to an incident—no drama, no breach. These nondramas don't travel. How, then, do some ghosts dance over cultural boundaries while others are stopped, strip-searched, and denied entry?

The specter is as visible and powerful as the cultural scenarios surrounding it. Stern's "What can you say?" relegates Selena to the ignominy of particularism: poverty, deviance, genocide. Stern sets himself up as the *migra* of the imaginary, the border police who ensure that certain identifications don't sneak into dominant culture. There are no fictions of the reciprocity that Walter Benjamin ascribes to translation here, no lip service to communication, no invitation to make meaning in this puzzling affair—we don't understand you, what are Mexicans into?[14] Punto. The performance of explicit noncaring performs the breach even as it denies the drama. By refusing to acknowledge a loss, it forecloses the possibility of redressive action and reintegration. The contempt of mourning rite denies the ghost its afterlife: this is about aborting. Diana, on the other hand, is invoked in hushed, reverential terms. She is assured an afterlife either as saint, as mother of the future king, or as a fund-raiser for charities. Guaranteed a visa, her face crosses borders on stamps, calendars, magazines. Her image serves as the occasion for bringing artists together in the service of disenfranchised communities, even as members of those communities are denied the stage. Yet everyone, it seems, is invited to participate and conjecture—to participate by conjecturing. The staging of her death ricochets between twin poles of singularity and universality; Diana's life and death, though utterly unique and one of a kind, nonetheless sheds light on misery, suffering, and stoicism everywhere. The coverage relished each detail, including what she ate for dinner on that fateful night! Yet it shunned particularism, stressing that this death was also about everything and everyone. Immediately, the death was aestheticized as drama and cast in the most powerful and universalizing paradigm available to meaning-making culture: tragedy.

Diana's death and funeral is the clearest example I have ever witnessed of an Aristotelian tragedy of international magnitude, "made sensuously attractive . . . enacted by the persons themselves," provoking pity and fear in millions of spectators. True, Aristotle insists that tragedy is the "imitation" of an action, rather than the real action itself.[15] And in a sense, of course, the distinction between art and life is a vital one. But there is also a way in which life imitates or is constructed through art, and not the other way around, that allows us to think of life as performative in the early Butlerian usage of the term as "a stylized repetition of acts."[16] The "Diana" we knew was a performative construct, the product of stylized acts—royal protocol, fairy tales, designer styles, and Hollywood fantasy—a real princess, a royal model as well as a new model for royalty. Her wedding provided the role and inserted her into a script shaped by tradition. She temporarily fit the bill (a young, aristocratic, malleable, good-looking virgin), the way an actor might be typecast for a role. What, one wonders, is real about this live performance?

Diana's death seemed similarly scripted, not by royal protocol this time but by "fate" and the media. Everything about it was "impossibly tragic." It was significant and of Aristotlean "magnitude" due to the nobility and beauty (heroic stature) of the woman, the struggle to shape her own destiny, the tricks to ward off fate (the real driver leaving the Ritz as decoy). Diana's *hamartia* (tragic flaw) was so simple, so human according to the media/chorus: she merely wanted to be happy. The *peripeteia*, or reversal of fortune, was abrupt. The inevitability of the *catastrophe* was almost a given, considering the persistent mad chase by the paparazzi and the equally mad attempts at flight. The identification, as always in tragedy, was written into the performance. We don't have to know these great figures in order to weep for them.

And the timing couldn't be more tragically ironic. Just as she was starting her new life, which she had attained against all odds, she died on the very night he gave her "the ring." Not only that, she died with her lover—the latest version of the "star-crossed lovers," as one tabloid called them. Even the names played into the tragedy as Dodi, meaning "my beloved" and Di raced off to their "destiny" (as the accident is repeatedly alluded to by the tabloids). It was already written—not just in Aristotle but in the *Song of Songs:*

"Dodí li va-aní lo" (My beloved is mine and I am his). Others find her death already coded in Genesis. The spectacle of the death elicits the specters of the already there. We're moved because we already know the story: the dark tunnel, the frantic chase, Diana the huntress hunted down. The paparazzi, who dedicated their lives to "doing Di," to banging, blitzing, hosing, ripping, smudging, and whacking her (all words, we learn, for taking pictures rapidly), finally got their prey.[17] The pace of the drama was fast, the tunnel tomb-like in its dark enclosure; the plot revolved around sex and love; the reversal from supreme happiness to sudden death was precipitous; the end unexpected, shocking. And there was even a whiff of conspiracy about this end to a life that was otherwise so transparent, so devoid of mystery. Was the thought of Diana marrying an Egyptian playboy with a purportedly mafioso background too much for the royal family? The innocent woman had little by little become the dangerous woman—the woman whose bulimia, suicide attempts, and infidelities threatened the image of the royal body, and now, its ethnic purity and exclusivity. Or was her accident contrived by the royal family to elicit popular support for itself? Project Interflora, an online site warning of royal conspiracy, had also seen it all before and warned its audience, "REMEMBER! Awaken!!!!" It reads the "Di thing" as a way of assuring the "continuance of the Monarchy." The floral tributes are an example of "Flower Power . . . an MI5 mind control program aimed at mass manipulation of the hearts and minds of the people of Britain. . . . These floral tributes are NOT spontaneous!" Even Aristotle could not have envisioned a more perfectly crafted plot. While one tabloid headline screams out "She didn't have to die!" the way that the media "made sense" of her death stressed the tragic inevitability of "the love she died for."[18] Anyone who has grown up with *Romeo and Juliet* or *West Side Story*, not to mention Agatha Christie and the Old Testament, might find something to relate to in this drama.

Diana's death precipitated a process of transformation and resolution on multiple levels. Diana, the dangerous and transgressive woman, "died a lover."[19] However, she was buried a mother, an innocent victim, a model of humanitarianism, a quasi-saintly do-gooder, and a member of the royal family. Once again, her image was transposed from one economy to another: the fairy tale princess in the heavy gown of the wedding photos and the formally attired, motherly wife of the early years had already given way to the casual, lightly clad, jet-setting image of her final years. Her death weighted her down again with the heavy brocade of the royal colors. She was back in the fold, center stage in the state's (polyvalent) self-imaging. After her wedding to Dodi, a sumptuous state funeral would have been unthinkable. Even as it was, the Queen initially demanded that "Diana's body should not be placed in any of the royal palaces and should be taken to a private mortuary."[20] The body, now saturated with the sacred/abject power of the transgressor, had to be kept away from the royal. It was "private" now, exiled to the mundane sphere of the ordinary. But the non-Royals wouldn't have it, not for "their" Princess. It was the Queen's turn to undergo public shaming. The "people" forced her to perform her emotions, whether she felt them or not. "Show Us You Care," demanded *The Express*; "Your People are Suffering: SPEAK TO US MA'AM," *The Mirror* shouted from the stands. "Where is Our Queen? Where is Her Flag?" *The Sun* wanted to know. "Let the Flag Fly at Half Mast," the *Daily Mail* insisted, giving the Queen her own little lesson in protocol.

The funeral was equally dramatic, though in a different way. This was imperial theatre, theoretically brokered by the "people" and elaborately negotiated by all parties. The behind-the-scenes bickering of how much or how little (whether in terms of spectacle, emotion, or viewers) was suspended by the splendor of the affair. The lavishness of the funeral made visible that the feuding, like the body, could be laid to rest; now that Diana was dead, rivalries and contentions could be forgotten. The country was once more united in tragedy, and the overwhelming sensual experience (the smell of the flowers, the echoing sound of the horses' hooves, the trembling bodies of sobbing spectators) rekindled the erotic, though ambivalent, attraction to the state. So the funeral was an act of national conflict and resolution, an act of remembering one Diana by forgetting the others, of celebrating a life and transcending (obscuring) it with claims to a higher purpose and a sanctity it never had. The transgressive, casual Diana was now thoroughly snuffed out, in part, by the very people who claimed to love her.

The funeral as imperial theatre was the opposite of the death as drama. As in theatre, a word that refers both to the physical, institutional frame and the intentional action that takes place within its limits, the theatricality of the funeral elided issues of Diana's relationship to the monarchy by normalizing the rite of passage within the demarcations of historical tradition.

Tensions disappeared behind the sensuousness, the ceremony of it all. The route, the lines of spectators, the choreography of the funeral party: this was a deliberate staging of the restoration of order, carefully modeled on previous, orderly funerals. It was about the "again," "now," and "as always" of royal self-representation. It disappears only to reappear. The achingly slow procession signaled the seemingly eternal and stable quality of a royal order now so openly up for grabs. The monarchy on show was very different from the one that waved at the world during the wedding. But the physical staging was also an act of restoration; it bracketed and emplotted the event, the first and last act of the Princess of Wales. After the abrupt crisis caused by the crash, the funeral provided aesthetic closure and emotional resolution. As in ritual, this final stage promised to be deeply conservative. The restitution of the social order, disrupted but probably not profoundly altered by the crisis, meant that Diana once more returned to the official body she tried so hard to elude. As Charles, the two young Princes, Prince Philip, and Earl Spencer followed the coffin on foot, it was clear that the procession was as much about possession and control as about emotion and empathy.

What do "the people" have to do with this imperial theatre, with the struggles between the Queen and the Prince, the Windsors and the Spencers, the Tories and Tony Blair's Labour Party? Que vela tenemos nosotros en este entierro? How do "the people" get constructed? The "staging of the popular," as Néstor García Canclini argues in *Hybrid Cultures*, "has been a mix of participation and simulacrum."[21] Newspapers around the world ran the same article, extending the reach of the we as it extended its audience. The same picture of Diana would appear, often with the same text, reporting on our reaction to the devastating turn of events. One Web site instructed the user to "send your feelings, condolences, or memorial regarding Princess Diana by *clicking here.*" The "Princess Diana fax poll" (set up by *The Post*) asked people to define what she meant to them.[22]

In England, the event was interpreted as a "revolution" (of sorts) because it showed "the people" their new power. The *New York Times* reported the "remarkable confrontation between the British people and Buckingham Palace and . . . an even more remarkable royal retreat."[23] "The people" won their show-down with the Queen. They had demanded the pomp and ceremony of empire self-fashioning. The ritual, traditional to the extreme, could be read as a subversive reversal, for it was the public, not the Crown, who ordered it.

Now, Tony Blair would have us believe, the old aristocratic ways vanished in one more act of surrogation: The Queen is dead, Long live Diana, the Queen of the people's hearts. Diana was the new face of the new England: stylish, youthful, and compassionate. Hegemony now enjoyed a more casual, photogenic look. Diana, like England, was coming out of a depression. She would be the goodwill ambassador, the kinder, gentler, post-Thatcher face of England. Instead of politics, style. Instead of bitter ideological divides, consensus and national unity. "The people" were featured as actors, rather than spectators, in the national drama.

The drama, then, is not just about Diana's tragic death, her regal funeral, or the current political situation in England. The event, commentators insist, is performative; it is about changing structures of feeling. It changed the way the English performed their emotions: Out with stiff upper lips and mean-spirited politics; in with touching, smiling, and generous public displays of spontaneity. Diana touching AIDS patients, or dying children, signaled a new mode of being (British).

LOSS

Loss. A ghost is about loss, loss made manifest, the vision of that which is no longer there. But what, I wonder, has been lost? Diana's candles, like Evita's and Mother Teresa's, provided the thousand points of light that corporate governments no longer feel compelled to provide. Lost, too, were both a working-class and a feminist agenda. Unlike Evita, who came from a working-class background and wielded unprecedented political power in Argentina, Diana and Mother Teresa had no political aspirations. Evita's popularity, channeled into a formidable populism, exceeded her death to the point that her ghost is still the most politically powerful player in Argentine politics today. This world is not ready for another Evita. The female powerhouse of the 1940s and early 1950s becomes the apolitical, unthreatening sophisticate of the 1990s. Evita too is denied a visa. When she was resuscitated in the movie *Evita*, Madonna was a style, a "look." The passionate public of political actors who maintained Evita in power melted into teary-eyed spectators and consumers. Evita's prophecy of her revenance, "I will return, and I will be millions," seemed ironically fulfilled. For here she was, incarnated by

Madonna, of all people. Even the walls cried out in protest: "Out Madonna, Evita lives." Evita lives, but only in Argentina. In the United States, she is a lipstick, a fascist, a whore, and an oddity. What next, Frank Rich asks? Maybe "Barbie-like Evita dolls laid out in little clear plastic caskets."[24] The conjuring act accomplishes one more disappearance by repetition—one face for another, one name for another, Evita dissolves in Madonna, while Madonna gains visibility through Evita.

So the choices were not, and never could be, between Diana and Evita, but about Diana and Mother Teresa. A 1998 *New Yorker* cartoon by Frank Cotham showed winged inhabitants of heaven moving along Princess Di Way and Mother Teresa Blvd. The way of the Empire and the way of the Church each take their ambassadors on the clearly one-way journey across borders, unsolicited yet living proof that the First World cares. In the language of love rather than power, these women claim to relinquish their enormous political, economic, and symbolic capital to the have-nots. As with all overloaded icons, these women looked so transparent. It's all so simple, this love talk. One could love Diana and love Mother Teresa and still hate politics, as if the naturalized act of charitable giving had nothing to do with the expansionism of imperialism, Catholicism, and late capitalism.

Lost too, perhaps, is the colonial nostalgia for the Royal Love. For viewers in the former colonies, Diana also embodied a love-hate relationship with empire and imperialism, which she simultaneously represented and transcended. Her estrangement from the Royals allowed for the ambiguous positioning, the nepantla of Latin American postcolonialism, or the "ambivalence" stemming from what Homi Bhabha refers to as the "double articulation" (the like, but not quite) of the colonial predicament.[25] What options do colonials have but to juggle the complicated play of identification/disidentification? She was living proof that the Royal Love had failed. Yet the love of the Royal could continue through our love of her. And our love for her led us to the possibility of transcending the racism at the heart of colonialism through her new romantic attachment to Dodi. This dark, sexy, playboy Other, the ultimate consumer, was the antithesis of Charles, the ultimate, old fashioned, nerdy "one of them." It made her, supposedly, "one of us"—one of those left out or betrayed by an atrociously uptight establishment. Okay, Dodi was a billionaire jet-setter, maybe not quite one of us, and in our heart of hearts we wonder if they would have been happy, but the beauty of fairy tales depends precisely on the suddenness and untimeliness of their endings.

In another way, of course, Diana's death was about the loss of another form of materiality. Her image gave a "universal" face to the disembodied globalism facilitated by satellites and the World Wide Web. A product of intercommunication systems, the Diana we saw was never and always live. Never live because, as one publication put it, "No Pix, No Di."[26] Her liveness was a product of mediation. Susan Stewart, in *TV Guide*, writes, "I know for a fact that Diana existed apart from television: I once shook her hand. It was exciting—she was already an international icon—but almost meaningless. All I remember is a blur of blond hair, a purr of a greeting. There are at least a dozen film clips of Diana more vivid in my mind than our actual off-screen meeting."[27] Her physical existence, redundant even in life, served merely to authenticate her more complete, real, and ubiquitous image that continues to defy the limits of space and time.

Thus, she was never (but is always) live and here everywhere, haunting our present. A Virtual Di, her image outlives her death; the signifier has no need of the signified, except as authenticating remains. She existed; that's enough to hang our dramas on. The Web asks us to light a candle for her, expanding the simulacrum of participation. She is a fetish, a sacred image whose meaning emanates not from within but is assigned to it from without. As a fetish (whether in psychoanalytic terms or as commodity fetishism), her success stems both from the facility with which anxieties and fears are displaced onto her and the process of disavowal whereby the public can admire the image while ignoring the violence that contributed to its making. Her vulnerability, unhappiness, and physical distress only contributed to her popularity, for as someone noted, the unhappier she was, the better she looked. After her death, a new (and improved) generation of commodities circulate with her image on them: commemorative stamps, plates, and dolls. The music and books she inspired reached the top of the charts and grossed millions of dollars. Her name is invoked in the war against drunken driving, land mines, AIDS, bulimia, and other assorted social ills. A new army of designers will take charge of dressing and tutoring the ghost. Sightings have been reported. New performances, political, artistic, or entrepreneurial, rise

30. (*left*) "No More Spectacles," graffiti-altered mural by A. Charles, on Houston Street and First Avenue, New York City. Photo by Diana Taylor, 1997.

out of these archival remains. Other women will dance in that space of impossibility made visible by her performance.

NEGOTIATING THE LOCAL

After the orgy of promiscuous identification has passed, do communities feel the abandonment and exploitation of the one-night stand? When we look in that colonial mirror, does her reflection look back at us, or do we see ourselves, complete with pigtails and popped buttons? The murals in Figures 20–26, as spaces of communal, public mourning, show signs of ongoing debate. Rather than simply reiterate the universal show of love and loss, the murals make the events local, bringing them right into the heart of the community. "Why do we care about Diana?" they seem to ask. By honoring her untimely death, the memorial walls situate her squarely in the long, unacknowledged history of untimely deaths in these neighborhoods. They call attention to the gang and police violence in New York City that

31. "No Saints, No Sinners," graffiti on the Diana mural by Chico, on East Houston Street, New York City. Photo by Diana Taylor, 1997.

people prefer to overlook. But the walls also manifest the anger of the un-requited, the "why should we care about her when no one cares about us?" The Latino murals to Princess Di now have "Die" written all over them. Someone has written "NO MORE SPECTACLES AT ALL, LADY DIE" in yellow paint on the admonishing mural that had warned about media overkill (Figure 30). The mural that had declared its love for Diana, announcing that she would be missed worldwide, now has a consciously postcolonial message on it: "We spent years of toil to break from the tyranny of British rule. NO SAINTS, NO SINNERS" (Figure 31). The Holiness and Royalty mural featuring Diana and Mother Teresa not only screams "DIE! DIE! DIE!" but participates in another form of circulation (Figure 32). This mural shows more than the displaced images of transnational globalization. It captures, too, the flip side of that same economy that leaves people out in the cold: the displaced people, poverty, and homelessness that volunteerism does not dissipate on the Lower East Side. The homeless man places himself, like an offering, at this "altar" to holiness.

Diana's ghost keeps dancing, tracing the convergence of preexisting phantoms and the latest crisis—always a rewriting, an updating, a making actual, of something that is already. Because we are all caught in transnational economic and iconographic systems, we have no choice, it seems, but to participate in the circulation of capital, symbolic as well as economic. How we download these images and engage with them, however, reflects the power of the local community in framing the terms of the debates. On one level, of course, Diana's death and funeral constitute a global drama of mass appeal. Here are all the ingredients of a successful tearjerker: the death of a noble, beautiful, and misunderstood princess. Thus, it is both a first and a repetition, a ghosting, a performative reappearance. In this particular staging, "the people" are not only the consumers but also the constructed of this death. The spectacle of the specter makes the spectator. Instead of mourning, the undifferentiated multitudes consume grief—the recipients, not the agents, of an emotion that is not their own. "The people" light imaginary candles for

32. "Die, Die, Die," graffiti on "In Memory of Royalty and Holiness" mural by Chico. Photo by Diana Taylor, 1997.

33. The facade that A. Charles painted on Houston Street undergoes gentrification. Photo by Diana Taylor, 2000.

Diana on the Web in a virtual act of identification. But, on another level, the event has also staged the need for active participation. Is it so strange that we may want to act in a drama we know full well is not our own? If we must engage, as it seems we must, these muralists show that people will establish the terms of conversation. Rather than constitute one more space for a downloading of the global, it opens one more strategic site for the negotiation of the local. Maybe it's not so odd that we, like the artists of the memorial walls, may wish to insert our own version of events by placing her next to our victims, next to other icons of caring, knowing full well that the gesture will never be reciprocated. But as always, there is the ambivalent push-pull of the imperial fantasy. The DI erupts in DIE. These rituals of passing insist that we forget that we don't belong, even as we remember.

We walk around the streets of the Lower East Side, Marina and I, taking photographs. The walls change constantly, reflecting new social interests

34. "Overpopulation Is Killing Us," mural by Chico on East Houston Street. Photo by Diana Taylor, 2000.

and concerns. The synagogue, later converted into a Yiddish musical theatre venue, on which A. Charles painted Tupac, Tyson, and Diana, was boarded up for a year. It recently opened as a posh movie theatre, showing excellent alternative films (Figure 33). After September 11, Chico used the wall on which he painted "In Memory of Royalty and Holiness" to commemorate those lost in the attack (see chapter 9). I had forgotten that he had long since painted over the faces of Diana and Mother Teresa. He had clearly wanted to blot out his bout with false identification. "What was here before?" I asked Marina. She too has forgotten. Later we remember: a huge, banal "Wouldn't it be beautiful?" had been written on an equally banal image of the sun setting over the peaceful sea. It had nothing to do with anything—very unusual for mural art. No wonder we didn't recall. On Houston, the three large walls dedicated to Diana, Elisa, and Selena had also undergone change. Chico had repainted Selena and Elisa, whose faces are still up today. Diana was gone, surrogated by the image of a cat and a dog against the New York skyscape. "Overpopulation is killing us: Please spay or neuter," and below it the name of a clinic. Even Selena had an arrow over her head, pointing to a pharmacy around the corner (Figure 34). Lots of disappearances, lots of forms of forgetting. Soon, we will forget that we have forgotten.

6

"YOU ARE HERE"

H.I.J.O.S. and the DNA of Performance

May 31, 2000, Buenos Aires, Argentina. 6:30 P.M. I'd been given a map and flier. Escrache al Plan Condor, organized by H.I.J.O.S.—the children of the disappeared. When I arrived, it was just getting dark. Young people had begun to converge on the designated street corner. I knew some of them, the members of H.I.J.O.S. who had invited me to participate, and young activists from Grupo Arte Callejero. The noise was revving up. A van, fitted with loudspeakers, started emitting rock music. Activists prepared their signs, placards, photographs, and banners. For all the motion and commotion, I felt a haunting. These young people, with their long hair, beards, Andean ponchos, and nouveau hippy chic, took me back to the 1970s in Latin America. That's what I looked like back then. That's what their parents—the generation of the disappeared—looked like. Now, in the year 2000, a new generation of activists was taking to the streets in Buenos Aires, tonight to protest the hemispheric "Plan Condor," organized by the CIA and implemented by the military dictatorships throughout Latin America. This network assured that persecuted leftists would be caught and "disappeared," even if they were lucky enough to escape their own country. In Argentina, these leftists were tortured in (among many other places) two garages, the Orletti and the Olimpo, which functioned as concentration camps. Today, people take their cars there to be serviced, many of them oblivious to this

history. H.I.J.O.S. members were going to remind all who would listen about this criminal history through the *escrache*. The atmosphere was festive, but serious nonetheless. "Be careful," people warned each other. Infiltrators had been known to join previous escraches and start trouble to provoke police intervention. "Hold hands. Don't let anyone into the circle. Keep your eyes on those next to you." The giant circle inched forward, our trajectory characterized by stops and starts as we moved together, dancing, shouting, singing, down the streets of Buenos Aires. The van, churning out the music and running commentary, slowly led the way. "Neighbors, listen up! Did you know that you live next to a concentration camp? While you were at home, cooking veal cutlets, people were being tortured in those camps." I looked up to see our audience—people on balconies, behind windows, looking down at the massive spectacle. Some waved. Others closed the curtains or retreated inside. Some must have joined the circle because there were more and more of us. We kept going, first to Olimpo, where the police were waiting, lined up in front of the garage. Then, after writing the crimes committed there by the Armed Forces in yellow paint on the pavement in front of the block-long

35, 36, 37. Escrache al Plan Condor, May 31, 2000. Photos by Diana Taylor.

building, the group moved on the Orletti. Again, the police were waiting, and again, H.I.J.O.S. covered the street with yellow paint.

Marking the space was thrilling—members of H.I.J.O.S. and all those accompanying them started dancing and singing again. Individual members began addressing our group, talking about what the event meant to them. The trauma was palpable, the emotional power contagious, and the sense of political empowerment energizing. Even I, a foreigner with little immediate relationship to the context, felt renewed hope and resolve. I had returned to Argentina with a sense of loss—the Madres were getting older. Although they continue their weekly march around the Plaza de Mayo, I wondered how the human rights movement would survive their demise. But here were H.I.J.O.S., young, joyful, and determined to carry on the performatic protest. If performance transmits traumatic memory and political commitment, those of us accompanying them seemed to have caught it.

Why, I wondered, do so few scholars think about the way performance transmits traumatic memory? How do those of us who have not suffered the violence come to understand it? And participate, in our own ways, in further transmitting it? This chapter explores these questions. Although I cannot transfer the impact of the event through the live enactment I experienced, I hope I succeed nonetheless in further transmitting my reflections to the reader through this writing.

Escraches, acts of public shaming, constitute a form of guerrilla performance practiced by Argentina's children of the disappeared to target criminals associated with the Dirty War. Usually escraches are loud, festive, and mobile demonstrations involving three hundred to five hundred people. Instead of the circular, ritualistic movement around the square that we have come to identify with the Mothers of Plaza de Mayo, H.I.J.O.S., the organization of children of the disappeared and political prisoners, organize carnavalesque protests that lead participants directly to a perpetrator's home or office or to a clandestine torture center.[1] Escraches are highly theatrical and well-organized. *Theatrical* because the accusation works only if people take notice. Giant puppets, military pigs-on-wheels, and at times huge placards of photo IDs of the disappeared accompany the protesters as they jump and sing through the streets (Figures 38 and 39). All along the route, vans with loudspeakers remind the community of the crimes committed in that vicinity.

Well-organized because H.I.J.O.S. prepare the community for the acción. For a month or more before the escrache, they canvas the neighborhoods in which perpetrators live and work, showing photographs of them and giving information. Did they know that their neighbor was a torturer? How do they feel about working with him? Or serving him lunch? Or selling him cigarettes? They plaster the photograph in the shops, restaurants, streets and on neighborhood walls. When the time for the escrache arrives, H.I.J.O.S. members find themselves accompanied not just by human rights activists but by those incensed that they continue to live in such proximity to political violence. With the help of activist artists, such as Grupo Arte Callejero, they post street signs that incorporate the photograph to mark the distance to a perpetrator's home (Figure 40). When they reach their destination, H.I.J.O.S. paint the repressor's name and crimes in yellow paint on the sidewalk in front of the building. Even though the police, always forewarned, circle the targeted property, the protesters peacefully and persistently go about their work of making the crime visible. The human rights violations, they remind onlookers, have not been punished nor, in fact, ended. Protesters provide an alternative map of Argentina's sociohistorical space: "You are here"—five hundred meters from a concentration camp (Figure 41).

Though carnavalesque and rowdy, escraches enact collective trauma. These performances not only make visible the crimes committed by the military dictatorships of the 1970s and 1980s, but they also make visible the lasting trauma suffered by families of the disappeared and the country as a whole. However, the interrelated protest movements staged by H.I.J.O.S., by the Mothers, and by the Grandmothers of Plaza de Mayo use trauma to animate their political activism. They have contributed to human rights efforts by successfully transmitting traumatic memory from one generation to another and from the Argentine political context to an international public that did not live the violence firsthand. Those acts of transfer prove vital to an understanding of cultural agency.

How does performance transmit traumatic memory? The individual focus of trauma studies clearly overlaps with the more public and collective focus of performance studies:

1. Performance protest helps survivors cope with individual and collective trauma by using it to animate political denunciation.

38, 39. H.I.J.O.S. and Grupo Arte Callejero participate in an escrache. Escraches are characterized by their rowdy and festive mood. A truckload of protesters exhibit their signs and banners. The banner on the truck exclaims: "If there is not justice, there will be an escrache." Photos courtesy of H.I.J.O.S.

40. Street signs with the photograph of the perpetrator to mark the distance to his home, 2000. Courtesy of Grupo Arte Callejero.

2. Trauma, like performance, is characterized by the nature of its "repeats."

3. Both make themselves felt affectively and viscerally in the present.

4. They're always in situ. Each intervenes in the individual/political/ social body at a particular moment and reflects specific tensions.

5. Traumatic memory often relies on live, interactive performance for transmission. Even studies that emphasize the link between trauma and narrative make evident in the analysis itself that the transmission of traumatic memory from victim to witness involves the shared and participatory act of telling and listening associated with live performance.[2] Bearing witness is a live process, a doing, an event that takes place in real time, in the presence of a listener who "comes to be a participant and a co-owner of the traumatic event."[3]

The possibility for recontextualization and transmission of performance and trauma nonetheless points to important differences. In performance, behaviors and actions can be separated from the social actors performing

41. "You are here": 500 meters from a concentration camp, 2000. Courtesy of Grupo Arte Callejero.

them.[4] These actions can be learned, enacted, and passed on to others. The transmission of traumatic experience more closely resembles "contagion": one "catches" and embodies the burden, pain, and responsibility of past behaviors/events. Traumatic experience may be transmittable, but it's inseparable from the subject who suffers it.

Thus, in understanding performance protests driven by traumatic memory, it's important to bring trauma studies, which focus mainly on personal pathology and one-on-one interactions, into dialogue with performance studies to allow us to explore the public, nonpathological cause and canalization of trauma. By emphasizing the public, rather than private, repercussions of traumatic violence and loss, social actors turn personal pain into the engine for cultural change.

The protest movements I examine here developed along clear generational lines around the disappeared: grandmothers (*las Abuelas*), mothers (*las Madres*), and children of the disappeared, exiled, and political prisoners (H.I.J.O.S.). Just as the generations share genetic materials, which these groups have actively traced through DNA testing, there are performance strategies (DNA of performance) that link their forms of activism. One important feature is that these groups see themselves linked genetically, politically, and performatively. Here I look at various iterations of performance protest involving photography that have taken place over the past twenty-five years. One clear strategy that reveals both the continuation and the transformation of cultural materials becomes recognizable in the use of the photo IDs to bring together the scientific (DNA testing) and performative claims in transmitting traumatic memory. Strategies, like people, have histories. In this case, the strategies work to reappear those who have been erased from history itself.

From 1977, almost at the beginning of the Dirty War, the Abuelas and the Madres started calling public attention to the dictatorship's practice of "disappearing" those who opposed them in any way. Among the thirty thousand disappeared who were tortured and murdered, ten thousand were women, hundreds of them pregnant. They were killed as soon as they gave birth. Their children, born in captivity, were also disappeared—not killed, in this case, but adopted by military families. There are still about five hundred disappeared children, young people born in Argentine concentration camps between 1976 and 1983 who may know little or nothing about the circumstances surrounding their birth. However, the military did not abduct the young children who had already been born to the people they disappeared. These, whom I call "children of the disappeared" (as opposed to the "disappeared children"), were born before their parents were abducted and were raised by their relatives. Like their disappeared siblings, many of these young people grew up knowing little or nothing about their parents. One member of H.I.J.O.S. told me that he grew up believing that his parents had been killed in an automobile accident. His relatives lied because they did not want him to put himself in danger, as his parents had, by becoming involved in issues pertaining to social justice. So there are two sets of children: the disappeared children who usually do not know their history and, hence, the existence of these brothers and sisters, and the children of the disappeared, many of them now informed and active in H.I.J.O.S., who continue to look for their siblings and pursue social justice.

While H.I.J.O.S. members explicitly acknowledge their many debts to the Abuelas and Madres—especially, perhaps, the fact that these women initiated the performance protest associated with the disappeared—their own performances reflect ensuing political and generational changes. What strategies get transmitted? How do these groups use performance to make a claim? Let's look first at how the Madres and Abuelas perform their accusations and demands.

The spectacle of elderly women in white head scarves carrying huge placards with photo IDs of their missing children has become an international icon of the human rights and women's resistance movements. By turning their "interrupted mourning process" into "one of the most visible political discourses of resistance to terror" the Abuelas and Madres introduced a model of trauma-driven performance protest (Figures 42 and 43).[5] Each Thursday afternoon for the past twenty-five years the women have met in Plaza de Mayo to repeat their show of loss and political resolve. At first, at the height of the military violence, fourteen women walked around the Plaza two by two, arm in arm, to avoid prohibitions against public meetings. Though ignored by the dictatorship, the women's idea of meeting in the square caught on throughout the country. Soon hundreds of women from around Argentina converged on the Plaza de Mayo in spite of the increasing military violence directed against them. Ritualistically, they walked around this square in the heart of Argentina's political and financial center. Turning their bodies into billboards, they used them as conduits of memory. They literally wore the photo IDs that had been erased from official archives. Week after week in the Plaza de Mayo, the Madres accused the military of disappearing their children and demanded that they be returned alive ("Aparición con vida"). After the worst moment of military violence passed, the Abuelas and Madres started carrying a huge banner in front of them as they walked around the Plaza. With the return to democracy in 1983, they began to accuse the new government of granting impunity to the criminals (Figure 44).

Using loudspeakers, they continued to make their demands, naming their children and those responsible for abducting them. They claimed the Plaza as their own, painting their emblematic scarves, made of their children's diapers, in white paint around the circle. Even now, they continue their condemnation of the government's inaction in regard to the human rights abuses committed during the Dirty War (Figure 44). *Otro govierno, misma impunidad:* "Different government, same impunity." Each claim has been backed by performative evidence: the placards with the photo IDs, the list of repressors. Much as the Abuelas relied on DNA testing to confirm the lin-

42. Protests by Abuelas and Madres de Plaza de Mayo denounce the government by using banners. They carry the photographs of their disappeared, 1983. Photo by Guillermo Loiácono.

eages broken by the military, they and the Madres used photo IDs of their missing children as yet another way to establish "truth" and lineage.

This representational practice of linking the scientific and performatic claim is what I call the DNA of performance. What does the performatic proof accomplish that the scientific cannot achieve on its own? How does this representational practice lay a foundation for movements that will come after it?

DNA functions as a biological archive of sorts, storing and transmitting the codes that mark the specificity of our existence both as a species and as individuals.[6] Yet it also belongs to the human-made archive, forsenic or otherwise. The archive in this case maintains a particularly grisly core— DNA, dental records, documents, photographs, police files, and bones—supposedly resistant to change and political manipulation. As the forensic specialist Clyde Snow observed, "These people are probably more afraid of the dead than they are of the living. Witnesses may forget throughout the years, but the dead, those skeletons, they don't forget. Their testimony is silent, but it is also very eloquent."[7] The scientific, archival evidence of DNA offered

43. Madres de Plaza de Mayo continue their condemnation of their government's human rights abuses, 2000. Photo by Diana Taylor.

44. *Otro govierno, misma impunidad:* "Different government, same impunity," 2000. Photo by Diana Taylor.

by the Abuelas was clearly central to their strategy of tracing their missing loved ones as they accused the military of their disappearance.

Testimonial transfers and performance protest, on the other hand, are two forms of expressive social behavior that belong to the discursive workings of what I have called the repertoire. The embodied experience and transmission of traumatic memory—the interaction between people in the here and now, whether in giving testimony, in psychoanalysis, at a demonstration, or in a trial—make a difference in the way knowledge is transmitted and incorporated. The performatic dimension of their protests brought attention to the national tragedy in the first place. The Abuelas and Madres performed the evidence by placing it on their bodies as they took to the Plaza. Human rights trials and commissions, such as Argentina's National Commission on the Disappeared (which issued *Nunca Más* to report its findings) and South Africa's Truth and Reconciliation Commission, understand the importance of live hearings in making citizens feel like co-owners of the country's traumatic past.[8]

In between and overlapping systems of knowledge and memory constitute a vast spectrum that might combine the workings of the "permanent" and the "ephemeral" in different ways. Each system of containing and transmitting knowledge exceeds the limitations of the other. The live can never be contained in the archive; the archive endures beyond the limits of the live.

The DNA of performance, then, draws from two heuristic systems, not only the biological and the performative, but the archive and the repertoire. The linkage refutes colonial notions that the archival and biological are more lasting or accurate than embodied performance practice. Both binary systems prove fragile on an individual basis, both susceptible to corruption and decay. Biologist Richard Dawkins makes an important contribution to our thinking about genetic and cultural forms of transmission as well as the repertoire and the archive. The cultural replicators he calls memes (coined to evoke *imitation, memory,* and the French *même* and to sound like *gene*). Examples of memes include many of the same embodied practices and forms of knowledge that I associate with the repertoire: "tunes, ideas, catch-phrases, clothes fashions, ways of making pots or of building arches."[9] Though a scientist, Dawkins challenges prejudices that valorize the permanence of the archive and the scientific over the repertoire. Neither individual genetic nor memetic material usually lasts more than three generations.[10] Books fall apart, songs are forgotten. Longevity alone cannot guarantee transmission. Things disappear, both from the the archive and from the repertoire. Nor can "copy fidelity" account for transmission; this too proves faulty, both with genes and memes, in the archive and in the repertoire. Ideas and evidence change, at times beyond recognition. So cultural materials, Dawkins concludes, survive if they catch on. They need to be "realized physically" (207) in the public arena. The Madres movement, Dawkins would say, was a meme that "caught on": members of human rights movements throughout Latin America, the Middle East, the former Soviet Union, and other areas have started carrying photographs of their disappeared.

The DNA of performance differs somewhat from Joseph Roach's "genealogies of performance." In thinking about the transmission of cultural memory, Roach explores "how culture reproduces and re-creates itself by a process that can best be described by the word *surrogation.* In the life of a community, the process of surrogation does not begin or end but continues as actual or perceived vacancies occur in the network of relations that constitutes the social fabric. Into the cavities created by loss through death or other forms of departure . . . survivors attempt to fit satisfactory alternatives."[11] His example: "The King is dead, long live the King."

Surrogation explains numerous reiterations that involve a narrowing down: instead of the two royal individuals, we have one King. The act of substitution erases the antecedent. "King" is a continuous role that endures regardless of the many individuals who might come to occupy the throne. The model of surrogation stresses seemingly uninterrupted continuity over what might be read as rupture, the recognizable one over the particularities of the many.

Although it is imperative to think of performance as a practice that persists and participates in the transmission of knowledge and identity, it is equally urgent to note the cases in which surrogation as a model for cultural continuity is rejected precisely because, as Roach notes, it allows for the collapse of vital historical links and political moves. Whether one sees cultural memory as continuous because it *relies on* or *rejects* surrogation might well depend on the beholder. There are many examples in the colonial history of the Americas of colonizers and evangelists clinging to their belief of successful substitutions (their values and images supplanting "pagan" ones) when in fact a performatic shift and doubling had occurred that preserved,

45. This photograph, "Anatomy of Terrorism," shows the use of photography as evidence during the Trial of the Generals in 1985. Photo by Daniel Muzio.

rather than erased, the antecedents. A pagan deity might continue to exist within the Catholic image meant to replace it. The strategy of using photographs of the disappeared that links these various movements is also a way of highlighting, rather than filling, those vacancies created by disappearance. Thinking about a DNA of performance helps focus on certain kinds of transmission that refuse surrogation. The use of these images suggests, as does the analysis of DNA, that nothing disappears: every link is there, visible, resistant to surrogation. The Grandmothers, the Mothers, the disappeared, and the children establish a chain in and through presentation and representation.

These claims—the genetic and the performatic—work together. The relationship is not simply metaphoric. Rather, I see them as interrelated heuristic systems. They are linked and mutually sustaining models that humans have developed to think about the transmission of knowledge. Moreover, they work both ways. Forensic specialists have long relied on representation, performance, and live presentation to convey an understanding of their findings. The photograph in Figure 45, "Anatomy of Terrorism," shows the use of photography as evidence during the Trial of the Generals in Argentina in 1985. The room is in darkness; the "audience" sits facing the illuminated screen; a "director" asks people to focus on the photograph of the cracked skull. The scales of justice, engraved on the high-back chair to the left, promise due process. The demonstration effects social change, as those in attendance have the power to pass judgment. Scientific explanations and "proofs," the photograph shows, depend for their validity on the way they are presented and viewed by jury and judge. The theatrical nature of this presentation is not metaphoric; rather, it delivers the claim itself. Facts cannot speak for themselves. The case needs to be convincingly presented. So too, thinking about a DNA of performance means that performance contributes to the proof of the claim itself.

The photographs used by the Abuelas and Madres and later (in a rather different way) by H.I.J.O.S. present a kind of proof, evidence of the existence of the people in them. They played a particularly vital archival and performatic role at the beginning of the movement, in the absence of other social and legal structures that could redress the crimes against humanity committed by the Armed Forces. Like DNA, the photo IDs strive to establish the uniqueness of each individual. Except in the case of identical twins, no two human beings have the same DNA, even though our shared genetic makeup is strong enough to link us all to the prehistoric Lucy. Like DNA testing, photo IDs usually serve to identify strangers in relation to the state.[12] Normally categorized, decontextualized, and filed away in official or police archives, they grant the government power over the marked citizen. Photographed in conditions of absolute sameness—white background, frontal pose, hair back, ears exposed, no jewelry—the individual differences become more easily accessible to scrutiny and "positive identification." The tight framing allows for no background information, no context, no network of relationships. The images appear to be artless and precise. Yet they are highly constructed and ideological, isolating and freezing an individual outside the realms of meaningful social experience. The images tend to be organized in nonaffiliative categories; that is, individuals may be classified as criminals or subversives but not as members of a particular family.

Photography and DNA offer radically different proofs of "presence," of course, each one making visible what is totally inaccessible to the other. We can't test a photograph for DNA any more than we can recognize physiognomies by looking at our genes. But both DNA and the photographs transmit highly coded information. Like DNA, the images and strategies conveyed through these performances build on prior material, replicating and transforming the received "codes." Not all the inherited materials get reused; some are incorporated selectively, others get discarded as "junk DNA." Moreover, DNA does not dictate biological determinism. Recent studies have shown the degree to which it is capable of changing rather than simply transmitting codes in the process of cultural adaptation through "messenger RNA." So too, these performances change the sociopolitical environment even as they develop within it. The information conveyed through the performances, like the genetic information, appears in highly coded and concentrated, yet eminently readable form. The images function as markers, identifying an entire movement.

The performance protest using photographs in itself was an example of adaptation to the political context. In Argentina, the photo ID has played a central role both in the tactics of the Armed Forces and in the protests by relatives of the disappeared. When a whole class of individuals (classified as criminals and subversives) was swept off the streets, their images in the archives disappeared with them. Although the government claimed not to know anything about the missing persons, witnesses testified that they saw officials destroy the photo IDs and other photographic images of prisoners in their control.[13] Families of the disappeared also testified that members of the military or paramilitary task forces raided their homes and stole photographs of their victims even after they had disappeared the victims themselves.[14] The idea, supposedly, was that by disappearing the documentary evidence of a human life, one could erase all traces of the life itself. This strategy works as the negative image of what Roland Barthes has called the "special credibility of the photograph."[15] Destroy the photograph, destroy the credibility or the very existence of a life. Both the Madres and the military enact— in their own ways—the faith in photography as one particular type of evidence.

When the Madres took to the street to make the disappearances visible they activated the photographs, performed them. The need for mobility, combined with the importance of visibility from a distance, determined the oversize yet lightweight placards that the women paraded around the Plaza. This, like all performances, needed to engage the onlooker. Would the national and international spectators respond to their actions, or look away?

By wearing the small photo IDs around their necks, the Madres turned their bodies into archives, preserving and displaying the images that had been targeted for erasure. Instead of the body in the archive associated with surveillance and police strategies, they staged the archive in/on the body, affirming that embodied performance could make visible that which had been purged from the archive.[16] Wearing the images like a second skin highlighted the affiliative relationship that the military tried to annihilate. The Madres created an epidermal, layered image, superimposing the faces of their loved ones on themselves. These bodies, the images made clear, were connected— genetically, affiliatively, and now, of course, politically. This representational tactic of indexibility mirrored the more "scientific" one undertaken by the Abuelas: to establish the genetic link between the surviving family members and the missing children by tracing DNA.

The Abuelas, in turn, picked up the representational strategies used by the Madres to further develop the use of photography in searching for their disappeared grandchildren. While they have continued to use DNA testing to find these children, they have also begun to rely heavily on photography. In a recent exhibit, *Memoria gráfica de Abuelas de Plaza de Mayo* at the Centro Cultural Recoleta in Buenos Aires (April 2001), they exhibited the same photographs that the Madres have long paraded around the Plaza. Here, the photos are set up in family units: the photos of the missing father and the missing mother. Next to these, however, they inserted a mirror in place of the photo of the disappeared child. Spectators under the age of thirty looking into that mirror need to ask themselves: Am I the missing child?

In the photos in Figures 46 and 47, a mother and daughter walk through the exhibit. Although a photography exhibit might seem to belong more to the archive than to the embodied repertoire, this one works like a performance installation that produces shock and, hopefully, on some level, recognition. The museum space itself transforms into a politically haunted yet all too live environment of trauma. The installation demands live participation and identification. A person cannot walk through the exhibit without being caught in the frame. Even the photographer, as these images illustrate, finds herself reflected and implicated in this exhibit that does not allow itself to be viewed or photographed without engagement. The spectator may not be the disappeared child, but five hundred children continue to be disappeared. Not just personal, or even national, issues of memory and identity are at stake. As

46, 47. The placement of mirrors next to images of the disappeared in the photography exhibit *Memoria gráfica de Abuelas de Plaza de Mayo* at the Centro Cultural Recoleta in Buenos Aires (April 2001) forces spectators to ask themselves: Am I their disappeared child? Photos by Gabriella Kessler, courtesy of Paula Siganevich.

the Abuelas put it, "Encontrarlos es encontrarnos" (Finding them is finding ourselves).[17] Memory, as the Abuelas' exhibit makes clear, is an active political practice. "When they ask us what we do, we can respond, we remember." Traumatic memory intervenes, reaches out, catches the spectators unaware, and places them directly within the framework of violent politics. The mirrors remind the onlookers that there are several ways of "being there." The DNA of performance places participants and spectators in the genealogical line, heirs to a continuing struggle for national identity and definition.

Like the Abuelas and Madres, associations that politicize affiliative bonds, H.I.J.O.S. emphasize the group's identity as an organization based on (but not reduced to) biological kinship.[18] Just as the Madres consider themselves sociopolitical mothers of all the disappeared, so too H.I.J.O.S. struggle to ensure justice for all the disappeared by bringing criminals to trial. "Juicio y castigo" (Justice and Punishment) is their motto, and their sights are clearly set on the repressors. For most of these young people who grew up without their parents memory is, on one level, a political project.

Like the Madres, H.I.J.O.S. continue their fight against impunity and forgetting through the highly visible use of public spectacle, using their bodies to humiliate those in power. Like the Madres, H.I.J.O.S. meet at a predetermined time and place to carry out their protest en masse. They move in unison, yelling, singing, dancing, and holding hands to create a protective ring around the protestors even as they deliver their denunciations. Some of the visual features of their activism resemble the Madres': the use of the long horizontal banner with their name on it and the large placard photographs of the disappeared (Figures 48 and 49).

Nonetheless, their performance in fact looks and feels very different. Whereas the Abuelas and Madres have been exposing the military since they began, the staging differed: they chose to focus their claims on the disappeared (and by extension, accused the military) rather than the direct "outing" of individuals and organizations. Setting off into the dark corners of Buenos Aires during the Dirty War would have proved suicidal. The Abuelas and Madres, by necessity, had to stay in the most visible place in Argentina and emphasize the traditional (nonconfrontational) nature of their demands; they presented themselves as harmless mothers looking for their children. Although H.I.J.O.S., like the Abuelas and Madres, admit that their personal loss animates them, they act from a position of joy and hope.[19] Instead of

48. At protests, H.I.J.O.S., like las Madres, use the long horizontal banner with their name on it, 2000. Photo courtesy of H.I.J.O.S.

49. The large placard photographs of the disappeared haunt the protest practice, 2000. Photo by Mariano Tealdi.

the ritualistic protest and mourning of the Madres, confined to the Plaza de Mayo, H.I.J.O.S. organize carnivalesque escraches or acts of public shaming. The word *escrache* is etymologically related to *scracè = expectorar,* meaning roughly "to expose."[20] Members of H.I.J.O.S., now in their twenties, enjoy the physical exertion that characterizes their brand of activism. Because H.I.J.O.S. entered the public arena more than a decade after the fall of the military, they can afford to be more confrontational in their use of techniques and public space. They can directly challenge perpetrators and force Argentina's criminal politics into the open. These range from little-known physicians who assisted in torture sessions, to the CIA, to the infamous Alfredo Astiz, known as the Angel of Death, who infiltrated the Madres group and killed fourteen of them, to the U.S.-run School of the Americas that trained torturers, to the infamous Campo Olimpo and Plan Condor. The escraches aim to heighten public awareness that these unpunished crimes, criminals, and criminal organizations continue to exist in the context of a supposed return to democracy. Current neoliberal economic policies in Latin America, they argue, simply continue the economic policies of the dictatorship in more modern guise.

H.I.J.O.S. also promise to continue: "Si no hay justicia hay escrache" (If there is no justice, there will be escraches). Two can play the waiting game. The aging Abuelas and Madres have spawned the next generation of activists. H.I.J.O.S. also continue the use of photographs in several different ways; they hunt down recent photographs of their military targets to use in their escraches and in their publications. Military repressors, not surprisingly, are now the first to burn their own photographs as they struggle to change their look and reinvent their identity. To paraphrase Barthes yet again: Eliminate the photograph, eliminate the criminal/crime. H.I.J.O.S. follow their prey and secretly photograph them when no recent photographs are available. Some might argue that this is one example of how H.I.J.O.S. inherit strategies used by the military as well as activist materials used by the Madres. H.I.J.O.S., after all, target the perpetrators, follow them to their home, and make sure that they feel watched and unsafe no matter where they are. They orchestrate a public relations war on their enemies, just as the military tried to convince the general population that their victims were dangerous guerrillas. Still, their tactics serve to identify individuals responsible for gross crimes against humanity. The performatic interruption, no matter how unwelcome, does not threaten their life. Like the Madres and Abuelas, H.I.J.O.S. claim institutional justice, not private vengeance.

Another use of photography is far more personal, related to the more individual and private dimension of trauma. Although H.I.J.O.S., like the Madres and Abuelas, do not highlight individual or personal loss and trauma, trauma defines them, not just as individuals haunted by personal loss and pain, but as a group shaped in response to atrocity. Some members of H.I.J.O.S. create collages and installations where they insert their own photograph next to their missing parent(s). These new "family portraits" of course give a sense of physical proximity and intimacy that was denied them in reality.

Some children of the disappeared from Tucumán sat for a series of thirty-three portraits by Julio Pantoja, an important Argentine photographer who took the images as his own act of protest in the face of ongoing political impunity. Asked to represent themselves as they chose, these young people depicted their struggle with their history and situated themselves in relation to their parents and to the violent ruptures created by their disappearance. Of the thirty-three photographs in the collection, twelve of the children posed with a photo of their disappeared parent. The centrality of the photographs, on one level, bespeaks a profound personal truth: these children know their parents only from photographs. Many of them are now the same age as their parents were when they disappeared (Figures 50–52).[21]

These portraits illuminate the political hauntology I sensed at the escrache. In them, the young people hold photographs of the previous generation of young people. The faces in both sets of photographs (Pantoja's and the ones the children are holding) demand a double-take. The photographs of the disappeared, if anything, seem more hopeful than their heirs'. Soon, the children—who will always be known as children of the disappeared— will be older than their parents. The portraits, however, indicate that the children, both genetically and visibly, resist the tugs of surrogation. While many of the children idealize their missing mothers and fathers, they haven't taken up their fight in any straightforward way—except as the fight for justice and human rights. Rather, they assume their place in a line that signals rupture and continuity. The place of the missing member of the family is reserved, made visible, through the photograph. In four of these cases, the children chose the same photos used by the Madres in their demonstrations. The isolated head shots have a recognizable history. In these photos, the par-

50, 51, 52. *(this page and opposite)* These children of the disappeared knew their parents only from photographs. Many of them are now the same age as their parents when they were disappeared. Photo exhibit by Julio Pantoja, "Los Hijos, Tucumán veinte años después," Tucumán, 1999.

ents reappear as *desaparecidos*. By including these particular images in their own portraits, the children acknowledge not just the existence of their parents but the violent history of political struggle surrounding the images of the disappeared. Unlike the familial photographs chosen by the other eight children, these four are oversize, cropped and mounted to be viewed in the public arena. Used formerly as weapons in a war of images, they (like the violent loss) prove impossible to domesticate. Like the Madres, the children struggle to repossess the images and recontextualize them, either by reintroducing them in the domestic space or by holding them against their own bodies. They, like the Madres, have become the paradoxical living archive, the embodied home of the "remains." We see the past reiterated, not in the photographs as much as in the positioning of the children themselves. Like the Madres, the children represent themselves as the conduit of memory.

Of interest here, H.I.J.O.S. at times use the blown-up photo IDs of the dis-

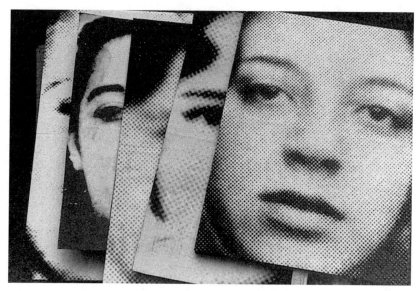

53. H.I.J.O.S. use the blown-up photo IDs of the disappeared in their rallies, 2000. Photo by Mariano Tealdi.

appeared in their rallies (Figure 53). I find the use of the same, recognizable photographs of the disappeared in the H.I.J.O.S. escraches interesting, especially considering that they appear in the demonstrations after the Madres have stopped (for the most part) carrying theirs. The Madres continue to wear the small ID photo, encased in a plastic pocket, around their necks. The large images on placards, however, belong to the past. The Madres' goal now is less to give evidence to the existence of the missing than to denounce the politics of impunity. "We know who the disappeared were," the Madres said when they changed strategy in 1983. "Now let's see who the disappearors are."

H.I.J.O.S., on the other hand, never sought to give evidence in the same way. They entered the political arena long after the Madres had declared "We know who the disappeared are." They never needed to prove, as the Madres once did, that their loved ones were missing. Their use of the photographs reflect the power of the repertoire more than the archive, the point being to mark the performance continuities rather than positive identification. When H.I.J.O.S. carry the photo IDs in their rallies, they index the continuity of a political travesty: the fact that the repressors have not been punished. Some gains have been made by H.I.J.O.S.; for example, the medical doctor targeted by H.I.J.O.S. for his role in torture sessions lost his job. And Astiz, facing extradition charges from several governments, cannot leave the country; at home, the situation has become uncomfortable and his movement restricted. Because he has been the target of repeated escraches (the most notable one in the courtroom itself), he simply cannot find a place to hide. Also, Argentina has recently asked Pinochet to be extradited to answer charges about his role in Plan Condor. The hope of human rights groups is that various international justice systems will form their own hemispheric, and even global, network—based, ironically, on the model of Plan Condor. Torturers and murderers would not be able to evade justice, either at home or abroad. But much remains to be done. And H.I.J.O.S. vow to keep up the escraches until justice has been served.

By carrying the photo IDs during their rallies, however, H.I.J.O.S. members point to the continuity of a representational practice. They are "quoting" the Madres, even as they acknowledge other influences: the carnavalesque images by Goya, among others. They, like the Madres, take the archival photographs and doubly remobilize them: they signal both the archival use of the ID and the performative use associated with the Madres. The archival photos are again performed, but now in a more complicated manner that signals various artistic and representational practices as well as the clearly defined political ones. The photographs, I contend, serve as placeholders in a sense, a way of securing the place of the disappeared in the genealogical chain. They assure that the disappeared are neither forgotten nor "surrogated." No one else will take their place. The photograph in Figure 53 layers the faces, allowing them all to be seen partially, to reinforce the idea that nothing disappears. H.I.J.O.S. continue the genetic line—and, to some degree, the political trajectory of defiance—calling attention to the violence of the breaks.[22] Unlike surrogation in Roach's genealogy of performance, which covers up the vacancy by substituting one figure/person for another (The King is dead, long live the King), the DNA of performance, like this photograph, demonstrates the continuity without surrogation. The specific link—though missing—can and needs to be identified for the genealogy, and the denunciation, to make sense.

Performance, then, works in the transmission of traumatic memory, drawing from and transforming a shared archive and repertoire of cultural images. These performance protests function as a "symptom" of history (i.e.,

54. "Usted Está Aquí,
You Are Here," 2000. Courtesy
of Grupo Arte Callejero.

acting-out), part and parcel of the trauma. They also assert a critical distance
to make a claim, affirming ties and connections while denouncing attacks
on social contracts. And, like trauma, performance protest intrudes, unexpected and unwelcome, on the social body. Its efficacy depends on its ability
to provoke recognition and reaction in the here and now rather than rely on
past recollection. It insists on physical presence: one can participate only by
being there. Its only hope for survival, as Dawkins might put it, is that they
catch on; others will continue the practice.

Finally, these trauma-driven performance protests offer another caution-
ary note. With all the emphasis on collective action organized by survivors—
Abuelas, Madres, and H.I.J.O.S.—these groups are the first to remind spectators not to forget their role in the drama (Figure 54). Most of us addressed or
implicated by these forms of performance protest are not victims, survivors,
or perpetrators—but that is not to say that we have no part to play in the
global drama of human rights violations. The Dirty War, sponsored by the
CIA and School of the Americas and organized through the workings of Plan
Condor, was truly hemispheric. Thus, the DNA of performance, like current

biological research, might expand, rather than limit, our sense of connect-edness: we all share a great deal of genetic, cultural, political, and socioeconomic materials. "You Are Here" marks not only the performance space but also the collective environment of trauma that addresses and affects everyone. We are (all) here.

7

STAGING TRAUMATIC MEMORY

Yuyachkani

In her trance, an Andean peasant woman, Coya, sees two forces collid-
ing, destroying everything. As a traumatized Coya speaks of what she sees,
she transmits her anguish to her sister, Huaco, and their father, Papai. In
her vision, an army tramples the population. The devastation is complete.
The corpses have "disappeared" but, then, so has life itself: "Ningún cuerpo
quedaba sobre la tierra, y ustedes ya no estaban más conmigo" (There were
no bodies left on earth, and you two were no longer near me). Her father re-
minds the women that they need to seek the seeds of life. The task seems
both terrifying and ludicrous: "I've witnessed so much death," states Huaco,
"and you're asking me to go look for the seeds of life!"

Masked dancers from pre- and post-Hispanic performative traditions appear
onstage and fight ferociously for influence over the peasants—dancing devils
and spiteful archangels with trumpets like muskets, transformed into crazed
figures of power. The archangels fight for ownership of the peasants' souls
in the "danza de la diablada" or devil dance from the Fiesta de la Cande-
laria in Puno. These dances, performed annually for hundreds of years, tell
a story as old as the Conquest, as recent as the criminal violence associated
with Sendero luminoso, the Shining Path. The peasants die, but not before
they have found the seeds of life. They throw some into the ground, and en-

trust the rest into the hands of the patient Equeco, the good-luck figure from Andean folklore who ends the play as s/he began: "These seeds were given to me by a woman, who told me a story. . . ."

The play *Contraelviento* (*Against the Wind*) was created by Peru's leading theatre collective, Yuyachkani, in 1989, at the height of the country's most recent civil conflict. It recounts the testimony of an indigenous survivor of the 1986 massacre at Soccos, in Ayacucho. "In Quechua, the expressions 'I am thinking,' 'I am remembering,' 'I am your thought' are translated by just one word: Yuyachkani," the noted Peruvian commentator Hugo Salazar del Alcazar wrote in one of his many newspaper pieces on the Yuyachkani theatre group.[1] The term Yuyachkani signals embodied knowledge and memory and blurs the line between thinking subjects and the subjects of thought. The reciprocity and mutual constructedness that links the "I" and the "you" is not a shared or negotiated identity politics—"I" am not "you," nor claiming to *be* you or act *for* you. "I" and "you" are products of each other's experiences and memories, of historical trauma, of enacted space, of sociopolitical crisis. But what is embodied knowledge/memory, and how is it transmitted? And how does it differ from the archival, usually thought of as a permanent and tangible resource of materials available over time for revision and reinterpretation? What is at stake in differentiating between these systems of organized thought, especially, perhaps, when thinking about trauma? The transitive notion of embodied memory encapsulated in Yuyachkani—the "I am remembering/I am your thought"—entails a relational, nonindividualistic understanding of subjectivity. Coya, the indigenous survivor, recounts a vision of annihilation that is and is not her own. The "I" who remembers is simultaneously active and passive (thinking subject/subject of thought). Yuyachkani, as a collective theatre group, sees itself implicated—both as product and as producer—in various modes of cultural transmission in an ethnically mixed and complex country. For the past thirty-one years, the group has participated in at least three interconnected survival struggles: that of Peru, plagued by centuries of civil conflict; that of the diverse performance practices that have been obscured (and at times "disappeared") in a racially divided, though multiethnic Peruvian culture; and that of Yuyachkani itself, made up of nine artists who have worked together in the face of political, personal, and economic crisis. In adopting the Quechua name,

55. Teresa Ralli in *Contraelviento*, 1989. Photo by Miguel Villafañe. Reproduced by permission.

the group of "white," mestizo, and indigenous artists signals its cultural engagement with indigenous and mestizo populations and with complex, transcultured (Andean-Spanish) ways of knowing, thinking, remembering. Yuyachkani attempts to make visible a multilingual, multiethnic praxis and epistemology in a country that pits nationality against ethnicity, literacy against orality, the archive against the repertoire of embodied knowledge. In Peru, the urban turns its back on the rural, and languages (Spanish, Quechua, and Aymara) serve more to differentiate among groups and silence voices than to enable communication. Yuyachkani, by its very name, introduces itself as a product of a history of ethnic coexistence. Its self-naming is a performative declarative announcing its belief that social memory links and implicates communities in the transitive mode of subject formation.

There is a continuum of ways of storing and transmitting memory that spans from the archival to the embodied, or what I have been calling a repertoire of embodied thought/memory, with all sorts of mediated and mixed modes in between. The archive, as I noted in chapter 6, can contain the grisly record of criminal violence—the documents, photographs, and remains that tell of disappearances. But what happens, Yuyachkani asks, when there are no photographs, no documents, when even the bones lay scattered by the wayside? The repertoire, for them, holds the tales of the survivors, their gestures, the traumatic flashbacks, repeats, and hallucinations—in short, all those acts usually thought of as ephemeral and invalid forms of knowledge and evidence. As I pointed out earlier in this study, there is a politics behind notions of ephemerality, a long tradition, which in the Americas dates back to the Conquest, of thinking of embodied knowledge as that which disappears because it cannot be contained or recuperated through the archive. Nonetheless, multiple forms of embodied acts are always present, reconstituting themselves—transmitting communal memories, histories, and values from one group/generation to the next.

Focusing on Yuyachkani's political performance practices, this chapter teases apart several interconnected questions central to performance studies, Latin American studies, and psychoanalysis: What is at risk politically in thinking about embodied knowledge and performance as that which disappears? How, then, do we think about trauma, anti-archival by definition? Its very nature "precludes its registration," leaving no trace because "a record has yet to be made."[2] Whose memories, whose trauma, "disappear" if only archival knowledge is valorized and granted permanence?

Thinking about the interconnections among atrocity, embodied knowledge, and subjectivity proves urgent for the many populations in the Americas that have experienced centuries of social trauma. Approaches to memory and trauma that privilege the individual subject fail to do justice to the cumulative and collective nature of the trauma suffered by illiterate and literate communities alike, transmitted through embodied performances. But these forms of embodiment may be difficult to decipher. The archive and the repertoire are culturally specific; while the systems may help us understand cultural memory throughout the hemisphere, the content in each will usually not be transferable.

Yuyachkani's work has drawn on Peru's archive and repertoire not only to address the country's many populations but to elucidate the multiply constituted history. Some dance, sing, speak, or otherwise perform historical memory, while others access alternative sources: literary and historical texts, maps, records, statistics, and other kinds of archival documents. Nonetheless, contradictions abound. How can a group, made up predominantly (but certainly not exclusively) of urban, white/mestizo, middle-class, Spanish-speaking professional theatre people think/dance/remember the racial, ethnic, and cultural complexities and divides of the country without minimizing the schisms or misrepresenting those who they are not? Who exactly is thinking whose thought? Thought and remembrance, as the name Yuyachkani makes clear, are inseparable from the "I" and "you" who think them. As a group made up predominantly of Limeños, does Yuyachkani have access to the memories of the Andean communities? Can it celebrate their fiestas or perform their rituals? Can Yuyachkani tell their story of cumulative social trauma? How to avoid charges of cultural impersonation and appropriation?

One obvious response to this danger of cultural trespassing that threatens practitioners lies in simply turning one's back on the rural indigenous and mestizo populations and tacitly accepting that performance is a European practice carried out by and for white urban audiences in the Americas. The indigenous and mestizo practices, one can argue, belong to self-contained, parallel circuits of cultural (and economic) transmission: oral, mythic, calendar-based fiestas, rituals, and festivities. Theatre practitioners, then, might decide to stick to European repertoires and archives. There are all sorts of staging, lighting, and acting traditions and methods and theories of professional training to choose from. By sticking to this pool, practitioners might either want to distance themselves from the "noneducated" elements of the population or signal their fear of appropriating artistic languages that are not their own. Why not do Brecht, still the most honored theatre practitioner in Latin America and, ironically, the world's greatest borrower? After five hundred years of colonialism, many Latin Americans, especially those from middle-class, urban backgrounds and education, are far more familiar with First World cultural materials that are readily available through the media and publishing circuits than those "'nonreproducible" performances from their own countries. Some acts of appropriation are safer, and potentially less offensive, than others. Class, racial, and linguistic affinities often supersede bonds that grow out of geographic and national interconnectedness.

If, conversely, one acknowledges that indigenous and rural mestizo populations also have deep performance traditions that make up part of the rich repertoires of the Americas, then how do artists from all ethnic backgrounds approach their multiethnic, transculturated traditions? Can they draw from these diverse cultural backgrounds with the same ease with which contemporary European practitioners draw from their recent and distant past? Is this, or any, "borrowing" unburdened by the political, historical, or aesthetic baggage of "value" attached to "style"? Do *criollo* (European American) or mestizo performances that include indigenous elements in their work risk turning them into exotic, folkloric add-ons? Performing "Indian" often reveals some kind of romantic notion of authenticity in festivals, pageants, and national spectacles.[3] It's not difficult to see the dangers of separating performance practices from the people who perform them and from the ideological framework that gave them rise. How can a theatre group such as Yuyachkani dream of avoiding all the representational pitfalls?

Thinking about how performance participates in and across these networks of social memory might allow us to consider cultural participation more broadly. Although criollo, middle-class Peruvians share innumerable artistic traditions with Europeans, they also clearly participate in the reality of Peru's social, racial, linguistic, and political cacophony. The very categories—criollo and Indian—are a product of that conflict, not its reason for being.

"The people called Indians" are a product of naming. It is through this performative invocation by the colonist that "Indians" enter the world stage. The archive, like the repertoire, is full of scripted performances: some that disappear, some that evoke, some that invent their object of inquiry. The naming of the "people called Indians" both conjured up and disappeared a people, the many ethnic groups suddenly lumped together as "Indian." The same "scenario of discovery" created the white conquerors. The criollo colonizers proved a mixed group indeed, including converted Jews (*conversos*) and free and enslaved Africans.

These antagonistic positions have been polarized and cemented into the social imaginary as biological fact. This way of thinking of lineage and tradition would certainly insist on keeping the various circuits of memory and transmission separate—to each their own. But there is a competing imaginary, that of the nation-state, conjured into being in Latin America during the nineteenth century. National identity, theoretically, supersedes regional or ethnic difference. This model assumes that Peruvians, for example, are a product of and participants in mutually constituting historical and cultural processes. However, the national imaginary is shaped not only by what it chooses to remember, but also by what it chooses to forget, as Ernest Renan observed over one hundred years ago.[4] Peruvians participate by forgetting, not just by remembering. Therefore, it's not a question of *if* but rather *how* they participate.

Yuyachkani, Peru's internationally acclaimed collective theatre group, actively stages Peru's social memory. It is a product of complicated national, ethnic, linguistic, cultural memory and thought. Actors Teresa Ralli, Rebeca Ralli, Ana Correa, Débora Correa, Augusto Casafranca, Julian Vargas, and Amiel Cayo, the director Miguel Rubio, and the technical director Fidel Melquiades (most of whom have been in the group since it started in 1971) got to know each other as members of Yego, a group of committed theatre practitioners. When they decided to form a group, Teresa Ralli recalls, "the first thing we had was the name. We called ourselves Yuyachkani before we had even worked on a play."[5] Now, they have their own two-hundred-seat theatre and work space, Casa Yuyachkani, and have worked together for over thirty years, a momentous achievement, given the severe economic and political hardships they have faced. Only a few other Latin American collectives— most notably La Candelaria and TEC from Colombia, Galpão from Brazil— boast similar accomplishments.

   This group of nine members has made visible a series of survival struggles culminating in the recent atrocities associated with Sendero luminoso (Shining Path) that left some thirty thousand people dead and eighty thousand homeless. Perhaps as daring, however, Yuyachkani has insistently remembered Peru as one, complex, racially, ethnically, and culturally diverse country. "Perú es un país desmemorizado" (Peru is a de-memorized country), says Teresa Ralli, and the *de* captures the violent refusal at the heart of a country that does not recognize or understand the realities of its many parts. The white, Westernized Lima, built with its back to the Andean highlands (which has been called the *mancha india* or the Indian stain), affords Yuyachkani one of the spaces to stage this re-membering for urban audiences.[6] They perform throughout the city, staging public acts on streets, in schools, on the steps of the national cathedral, in orphanages, cemeteries, and government buildings. They also stage street performances in nontheatrical spaces throughout the country, starting conversations, par-

56. Patio, Casa Yuyachkani. Edmundo Torres, their long-time mask maker, dances the role of the *China diabla,* July 1996. Photo by Diana Taylor.

ticipating in protests and celebrations. Recognizable characters from traditional and popular culture—musicians and masked figures on stilts—parade through the streets inviting spectators to join in. These parades, as Ana Correa describes them, end in a fiesta in which participants start talking and getting to know each other. Drawing from Western models (Brecht's political theatre) and Boal's theatre of the oppressed as well as Quechuan and Aymaran legends, music, songs, dances, and popular fiestas, Yuyachkani asks spectators to become participants in Peru's rich performance traditions. Thus, their work presses spectators to take seriously the coexistence of these diverse ethnic, linguistic, and cultural groups and to bear witness to Peru's history of extermination and resistance, alienation and tenacity, betrayal and remembrance.

When Yuyachkani began working in the early 1970s, the members of the group saw themselves as politically committed popular theatre practitioners. Popular theatre in the late 1960s and early 1970s, with its "*by* the people *for* the people" ethos, challenged the systems that placed Theatre with a capital T and Culture with a capital C in lofty, aesthetic realms, beyond the reach of working-class people and racially marginalized communities. Popular theatre groups in Latin America and the United States (Bread and Puppet, San Francisco Mime, Teatro Campesino, to name just a few) tended to work as collectives. The members of Yuyachkani, for example, meet every morning at their Casa Yuyachkani and work on developing new material and ideas. They have lunch together in their communal kitchen, and meet again in the afternoon to rehearse or warm up for an evening performance. Like all collective theatre, they rejected the playwright- and "star"-driven theatrical models that dominated high-brow and commercial theatre.[7] They took the theatre out of elite spaces, staging free performances that had to do with the real-life economic and political conditions of working people. Political and economic issues took precedence over aesthetic concerns. They toured their shows to rural communities that never really had access to theatre and involved spectators in many aspects of the productions. Working under the Brechtian influence, popular theatre in Latin America was closely linked to strikes and other class/labor struggles.

As I have argued elsewhere, there are some fundamental limitations and built-in contradictions to "popular theatre," no matter how important and laudable the projects have been in general.[8] Popular theatre at times presented an oversimplified and programmatic view of conflict and resolution. In Latin America and elsewhere, popular theatre was often animated by Marxist theories. Progressive, at times militant, university students and intellectuals instructed the disenfranchised on how to improve their economic lot or lead a more productive life. Because Marxism privileged class, anticapitalist, and anti-imperialist struggles at the expense of racial, ethnic, and gender conflict, its implementation in popular theatre groups in Latin America ran the risk of reducing deep-seated cultural differences to class difference. In Peru, and other countries with large indigenous and mestizo communities, the "proletariat" in fact consisted of indigenous and mestizo groups who lived on the margins of a capitalist society for various reasons, including linguistic, epistemic, and religious differences not reducible to (though bound into) economic disenfranchisement. A call for solidarity organized around anticapitalism allowed for rampant, unthinking trespassing on cultural, ethnic, and linguistic domains. Furthermore, the "popular," as understood by some of its activists, became entangled with fantasies of a simple, pure world existing somewhere beyond the grips of capitalism and imperialism. The less the practitioners truly knew the communities they were engaging, the more the discrepancies in power and the lack of reciprocity threatened to place them in positions of moral superiority reminiscent of religious proselytizers.

These problems plagued the initial endeavors of Yuyachkani. The marginalized groups they were addressing in their own country had their own languages, expressive cultures, and performance codes that the group knew nothing about. Miguel Rubio recalls how, during that first play, *Puño de Cobre* (1971), in which they performed for miners, the actors dressed in jeans and played a variety of roles and characters. After the performance, one miner commented, "Compañeros, that's a nice play. Too bad you forgot your costumes."[9] Unlike some of the other popular theatre groups of the period (both in Latin America and the United States) who set about to enlighten an exploited population, Yuyachkani realized that they needed enlightening: "Much later," Rubio continues, "we understood why the miners thought what they did. We had forgotten something much more important than costumes. What they wanted to tell us was that we were forgetting the audience that we were addressing. We were not taking their artistic traditions into consideration. Not only that, we didn't know them! The miners came from rural areas rich in cultural traditions. They were right. How could they imagine a play about them that did not include their songs, or the clothing of the women who so proudly conserve their traditional dress, or the figures who tell stories as they dance?" This became the beginning of the ongoing education of Yuyachkani. Their theatre no longer became "about them" but about a more complex reflection on Peru's ethnic and cultural heterogeneity. They added members from these rural communities to their group; the actors learned Quechua; they trained in indigenous and mestizo performance practices that included singing, playing instruments, dancing, movement, and many other forms of popular expression. They expanded the notion of theatre to include the popular fiesta that emphasizes participation, thus blurring the distinction between actor and spectator. Performance, for Yuyachkani as for other popular theatre groups, provided an arena for learning—but here it was Yuyachkani learning "our first huaylars, pasacalle, and huayno dance steps[;] between beers and warm food, we started to feel and maybe to understand the complexity of the Andean spirit."[10] Performance did indeed offer enlightenment and intergroup understanding, but

Yuyachkani admits to having taken the first steps in learning about rural populations by participating in their cultural practices. According to Hugo Salazar del Alcazar, this was the first phase of Yuyachkani's development, which focused primarily on political issues.[11]

Since those beginnings, Yuyachkani has continued to train in various linguistic and performance traditions to offer a deeper vision of what it means to "be" Peruvian, one that reflects the cultural, temporal, geographical, historical, and ethnic complexity of that articulation. There are many tenses involved in *to be* and various ways of situating the *pre-* and *post-* markers, depending on who is doing the telling. For Yuyachkani, this performance includes the layering and juxtaposition of the diverse traditions, images, languages, and histories found in the country. Poised between a violent past that is never over and a future that seems hopelessly prescribed, their performances re-present images and scenarios that live and circulate in a variety of systems and forms, from the media to children's stories, martial arts, silent movies, and indigenous myths. This second phase of Yuyachkani's development, according to Salazar, focuses more on the cultural debates around *lo nacional*. The group studied José María Arguedas's work on Andean myths and performances to understand the ancient traditions that persist in contemporary cultural practices. A play such as *Los músicos ambulantes* (*The Traveling Musicians*, 1983) draws from the famous folktale "The Musicians of Bremen" and Arguedas's *Todas las sangres* to tell a humorous and beautiful story of homelessness, social injustice, and the importance of working together. In an aesthetically rich performance full of masked figures, music, dance, and comic routines, the little red hen, the mangy dog, the wily cat, and the lame donkey realize that for all their differences and incompatibilities, they're better off together than apart. The play also works on different levels for different audiences. In one sense, the play is an important reflection on Peru's racial makeup. The dog represents the criollo Limeño from the *barrios altos* or poor sectors of the city. The hen stands for the Afro-Peruvian populations. The cat comes from the *selva*, the Peruvian Amazon Valley, and the donkey represents the *cholo serrano*, the mestizo from the Andes. These figures, all of whom have been persecuted, beaten, and exploited, come together to rebel exuberantly against the *patrón*. The negotiation among them requires that they get to know each other, to recognize each other's strengths and what each contributes to the group. But it also requires that the group respect each member's individuality. On this more personal level, the play summed up Yuyachkani's predicament at the time: How, as Miguel Rubio asks, does the group allow each member to flourish individually without threatening the existence of the whole? Yet, even for those who do not get the racial or personal subtext of the performance, the play is enormously appealing—sparkling with humor, energy, music and intelligence. This play rejoices in the fact of transculturation, for the only music these characters can create requires a bringing together of the various distinct elements and traditions. The music from the jungle harmonizes with that from the Andes, the coastal plains, and the Afro-Peruvian communities. The play's national and international popularity enabled Yuyachkani to buy Casa Yuyachkani. Because this play is so well-known, moreover, these characters can intervene in the national drama. When the economic situation in Peru gets particularly critical, the little red hen of the production (Ana Correa) performs an *acto público* by joining the line of retired people waiting for social security monies to complain about being penniless. "Cómo como?" (How am I to eat?), she demands impatiently, as she clucks and struts about (Figure 57). And Teresa Ralli, the mangy dog, visits children at an orphanage (Figure 58).

Yuyachkani has developed more troubled plays to think through the civil violence and the apparent impossibility of respectful coexistence in a country torn apart by injustice and rage. *Encuentro de zorros* (1985) draws from ancient myths of *el zorro de arriba* and *el zorro de abajo* (the fox from the highlands, the fox from the lowlands), preserved in Peru's repertoire and archive.[12] The legend of the two foxes was already considered ancient when it was first written in the sixteenth-century *Huarochirí Manuscript*, and it was reworked in Arguedas's famous "El zorro de arriba y el zorro de abajo" (1968). The foxes, symbols of change, appear in moments of extreme social crisis. In their first appearance, some twenty-five hundred years ago, they met to decry social injustice. Their challenge, as they describe it, is to devour the world and create a new one. Yuyachkani uses the myth to again think through Peru's geographic, ethnic, and linguistic schisms; el zorro de arriba represents the populations from the Andean highlands, while the zorro de abajo typifies those from Lima's coastal region. They meet once again in the violent throes of mass migration due to Peru's civil war of the 1980s and 1990s. Beggars, thieves, and drunken clairvoyants push a Mother Courage–

57. Ana Correa, right, in her costume from *Los músicos ambulantes,* participating in a public protest, 1996. Photo by Miguel Villafañe. Reproduced by permission.

type cart and offer a grim perspective on Peru's urban landscape. Rather than a respectful coexistence, these characters show a world devastated by criminal violence, displacement, and unemployment. The world is turned upside down, "parents against children, children against parents, the living against the dead and the dead against the living." *Retorno* (1996) shows the aftermath of Peru's Dirty War. People have been left stranded and disoriented, the villages destroyed, the harvest lands burnt. A reenvisioning of Beckett's *Waiting for Godot, Retorno* stages the despair and isolation of those who have nowhere to go. There is no going forward, no going back, no home to return to.

Two of Yuyachkani's best-known pieces, *Contraelviento* (1989) and *Adios Ayacucho* (1990), combine moments from Peru's remote and recent past to reflect on the transmission of traumatic social experience. Developed and performed during the conflict between the military and Sendero luminoso, these works specifically engage the questions I posed earlier: How does the repertoire store and transmit social memory? Whose memories/traumas disappear if we privilege the archive over the repertoire of embodied experience/knowledge?

Contraelviento, one of Yuyachkani's largest and most spectacular pieces,

58. Teresa Ralli, left, in her costume from *Los músicos ambulantes*, performs in an orphanage, 1996. Photo by Miguel Villafañe. Reproduced by permission.

reenacts the testimony of an indígena survivor of a massacre in which peasants were forced off a cliff to their deaths. The performance stages one more traumatic repeat: Coya, in a trance, revisits the scene of devastation. Her body shudders as she reexperiences the intrusive image. An entire community has been annihilated by armed forces. The shudder harnesses various political moments: the unsolicited reappearance of a traumatic event situated firmly in the past; the witnessing of an atrocious episode in the here and now. It is the here, now, and always of a violent history of the exploitation and extermination of indigenous peoples; it conjures up the vision of a future catastrophe. The body responds to and communicates a violent occurrence that may be hard to locate temporally or spatially.

Coya's sister and father listen to her testimony. They all understand that a furiously approaching storm will scatter them. Huaco, raging against the violence she sees coming, joins the guerrillas, fighting fire with fire. Papai stays firm to his commitment to find the seeds of life by practicing ancient invocational rites. Coya runs to the courts, hoping to find redress through the justice system. The judges—farcical, aged, bent figures with oversize hats who perform a vaudeville version of the pre-Conquest comic dance of *los viejitos* and speak broken English—pretend not to understand her. Her language, represented as flute music, needs to be translated by Peru's famous sell-out character, the *Felipillo*, translator to the conquerors. "This woman says that she comes from far away to tell us that her ancestors have told her that the Caporal is killing them. . . . She says too that everyone's life is in great danger and that the seeds of life are being destroyed." The judges dismiss her with a good beating: "If that woman can't speak, it's because she has something to hide." This scene elucidates several points in my argument: the courts, an archival, document-producing system that in the Americas serves the interests of the powerful, cannot encompass or "understand" pleas from the poor. (Official documents, records, and figures relating to genocidal practices rarely ever make it into the national archives.) Institutionalized circuits of memory and transmission keep the dominant sectors of the population walled off from the rural mestizo and indigenous populations. Expressions of trauma might just as well be delivered in a foreign tongue.

Contraelviento was performed at the peak of militarized conflict in Peru. "Disappearances" and mass murder had become common political practice in Latin America during the 1970s and 1980s. How, Yuyachkani asked itself, can theatre compete with or elucidate the theatricality of political violence? Miguel Rubio sums up the challenge: "Nothing that you create on stage can compare with what is happening in this country."[13] Furthermore, the heightened spectacularity of political terrorism, as I argue elsewhere, forces potential witnesses to look away.[14] It blinds the very spectators whom theatre calls on "to see." What role do artists have, Adorno asks, when genocide is part of our cultural heritage?[15]

In the most lyrical of forms, *Contraelviento* succeeds in posing the most urgent questions. How can indigenous and mestizo communities address genocidal policies and practices that often are not acknowledged by the national or international community? Through performance—the music, masked dances, and ritual incantations—the play suggests, atrocity will be remembered and thought even when there are no external witnesses and no recourse to the archive. Yet these memories disappear when scholars and activists fail to recognize the traces left by embodied knowledge.

Adios Ayacucho, based on a text by Julio Ortega, takes the question of witnessing further: the dismembered victim is forced to act as sole witness to his own victimization. As the play begins, the members of the audience see

59. Scene from *Adios Ayacucho,* 1990. Photo courtesy of Grupo Cultural Yuyachkani.

a ramp displaying a suit of clothing and candles laid out in a funerary ritual (Figure 59). As their eyes become accustomed to the dim light can they discern movement in a large black plastic bag behind the display. A nameless, almost voiceless figure reconstitutes himself and breaks out of the bag. As he tells his story, his voice becomes strong. He was tortured. His tormented body was cut into bits and discarded, in a garbage bag, by the side of the road. In this crime without an external witness and with no survivors, no one but he himself can demand that justice be served. No documents, photos, or gravestones attest to his annihilation. Only his bones, shoved in plastic, serve as archival proof of an event that left no other material evidence. Only through performance can disappearance be rendered visible. Disappearance, as Latin American activists and artists know full well, becomes itself through performance.

Yet, though no external witnesses exist in *Adios Ayacucho,* the play affirms the vital role of what Dori Laub calls the "the witness from inside" or "the witness to oneself."[16] This witness from inside, though impossible, according to Laub, in the context of the Holocaust that "made unthinkable the very notion that a witness could exist" because it allowed for no "outside," no "other," is nonetheless posited as the only hope for justice in the Andean context (66). The victim reconstitutes himself by finding most of his scattered body parts. Little by little, he reclaims his human form. Finally he finds his face, finally he finds his voice that will proclaim the violence done to him and his community. He not only voices his denunciation, over and over again, but he determines to take a letter to the president of the Republic, outlining the violence he has suffered. This letter, finally, will make it into the archive, a testimony that even the president might acknowledge of the erasure of mestizo and indigenous populations. And, in a final act of personal reconstitution, the victim raids the tomb of the conqueror Pizarro housed in the main cathedral of Lima and helps himself to the bones he still misses. Better that the glorified national body be found wanting than that it be preserved and fetishized in the face of violence against the population. This haunting image from *Adios Ayacucho* suggests the ways Yuyachkani layers its approach to representing violence. The clothes laid out in memory of the dead re-present the missing body of the victim of disappearance, even as they echo an ancient burial practice. These practices are alive; other bodies will perform them just as the man fits himself back into the waiting clothes. Andean performance practices, this shows, are not dead things, fading from view. Nor do they function in a parallel universe.

One of Yuyachkani's most recent productions is the extraordinary one-woman *Antígona* (2000), acted by Teresa Ralli and directed by Miguel Rubio. The spectators readily follow the well-known story as Ralli acts out the various figures—Antigone, Ismene, Creon, Heamon, Tiresias, the messenger—using only a chair as a prop on the otherwise empty stage. Her precise and eloquent movements transform her outfit, a simple tunic over pants and a bodice, into numerous costumes. With a clap of her hands she conjures up the various characters, pulling them out of the archive to incarnate Peru's current woes. Unlike others, such as Anouilh or Griselda Gambaro, however, Yuyachkani does not invoke Antigone primarily to tell of a state divided against itself. As both Rubio and Ralli tell it, no doubt this too would have been their rendition of the play if they had developed it in the 1980s. In the late 1990s, the issues have changed. Now in Peru, as in other countries dealing with the long-term effects of trauma, people struggle to come to terms with their own strategies for surviving in a dehumanizing environment. Ismene, the sister who failed to act in defense of Antigone and her brother, becomes the narrator. "I am the sister whose hands were tied by

 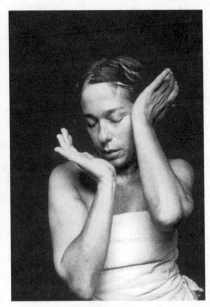

60, 61. Teresa Ralli in *Antígona*, 2000. Photos by Elsa Estremadoyro. Courtesy of Grupo Cultural Yuyachkani.

fear," she says at the end of the play, as she identifies herself.[17] She reenacts the story, not as an outsider looking back, but as a witness who had blinded herself through fear. "This is my own story," she says, as she belatedly assumes her role in the drama, apologizing to her sister and symbolically burying her brother (Figure 60). Through performance, Ismene will complete the actions she could not undertake the first time around. *Antígona* offers hope to those witnesses and participants who were unable to respond heroically in the face of atrocity. Ismene promises to remember every day, as she reenacts her story, again and again.

Yuyachkani based this production on interviews that Ralli conducted with the wives, mothers, and sisters of the disappeared. These survivors tell of inadequate responses and failed attempts in the face of military might. Yet they continue to tell their story. In "Fragments of Memory," a short piece that Ralli wrote about the process, she describes that as she listened to the women's accounts, she felt the best homage she could offer was "to feel all the memories inscribed on their bodies and thus confer them unto Antígona."[18] In the performance, she included the gestures she associated with

the women as a way of signaling the continuity of cultural gestures and behaviors (Figure 61). The women might not identify with Sophocles' Antigone,
yet they would recognize this as their story.

Since the play opened in 2000, Ralli has started to work with Peru's newly
formed Truth Commission to work with women in rural areas. The fact that
there is "no over" in situations of social violence attests to the continuing
effects of trauma, but it also offers survivors the opportunity to reassert their
capacity for intervention, no matter how overdue. In 1999, Grupo Cultural
Yuyachkani won Peru's highest honor for work in human rights.

These performance practices, whether drawn from age-old repertoires or
marginalized traditions, allow for immediate responses to current political
problems. Every response to political violence carries with it a history of responses, conjured up from a vast range of embodied and archival memories.
For Yuyachkani, performance is not about going back, but about keeping
alive. Its mode of transmission is the repeat, the reiteration, the yet again
of "performance." The violence of the past has not disappeared. It has re-
appeared in the violent response against the miners' strike (1971), the massacre of Soccos (1986), the displacement of local populations caught between
Sendero and government forces, on the empty streets of Lima in the 1980s
and early 1990s, torn and made strange by the violence. The remembering
was always past, present, and seemingly future. As Rebeca Ralli puts it, their
work represents the struggle for survival of the Peruvian people even as it
represents their own struggle to survive both as individuals and as a group:
"We put up with so much just to be able to live, just to be able to create."[19]

Yuyachkani's performances make visible a history of cumulative trauma,
an unmarked and unacknowledged history of violent conflict. As in *Adios
Ayacucho*, the attempts at communicating an event that no one cares to acknowledge need to be repeated again and again. For members of traumatized
communities, such as the Andean ones Yuyachkani engages, past violence
blends into the current crisis. As in *Adios Ayacucho*, trauma becomes transmittable, understandable through performance—through the reexperienced
shudder, the retelling, the repeat.

The retelling and reenactment, however, pose problems of legitimacy. Although the performances capture the ongoing nature of the violence against
indigenous peoples, it complicates a historical accounting. What is time

without progression? What is space without demarcation? What happens to a people's concept of history when markers are few? There is no archive or, as in the case of Argentina, no photographs to back these claims of criminal violence. Here, violence is known only through a performatic repeat.

The undifferentiated, reiterative nature of Peru's traumatic history folds seamlessly into the Andean paradigm of memory (summed up in the mythic Inkarrí cycle that replays destruction and recomposition), which defies the fixity of a before and after. "Inkarrí's dismembered body (whose severed head has been taken, variously, to Cusco, Lima or Spain) is coming together again, underground. . . . The lower world, region of chaos and fertility, becomes the source of the future, an extension of the belief that the dead return to present time and space during the growth season."[20] Faced with the consciously deployed strategy of colonial dismemberment, the myths offer the promise of re-membering. "Perú es un país desmemorizado." Who can say, after five hundred years of ongoing conquest and colonization, where the memory of trauma is situated, whether trauma affects the subject or the entire collectively, if it is experienced belatedly or continually embodied, whether it resides in the archive or only in the repertoire, and how it passes from generation to generation? We know from myths and stories only that Peru's indigenous populations see themselves as the product of conquest and violence. Violence is not an event but a worldview and way of life.

Yuyachkani, it seems to me, intervenes in this problematic in two fundamental ways, one having to do with the transmission, the other with the role and function of witnessing. In regard to the first, Yuyachkani understands the importance of performance as a means of re-membering and transmitting social memory. Its use of ethnically diverse performance traditions is neither decorative nor citational; that is, Yuyachkani does not incorporate them as add-ons to complement or "authenticate" its own project. The group's commitment to enter into conversation with rural populations has led them to learn the languages, the music, and the performance modes of these communities. Rather than attempt to restore specific behaviors (i.e., recreating museum pieces that somehow dislocate and replicate an "original"), they follow the traditional usage of reactivating ancient practices to address current problems or challenges. Moreover, Yuyachkani does not participate in the reproduction and commodification of "popular" culture. Their texts do not circulate; other actors and companies do not perform them. The only way to access their work is by participating in it—on the streets as bystander caught up in the action, in Casa Yuyachkani as spectator and discussant, or in the many workshops open to students from around the world. New, younger members are joining the group and they, too, are Yuyachkani. They will not act *like* Yuyachkani, but *be* Yuyachkani, adopting and adapting the character of the group itself. Their performances, just like the performances they draw from, are inseparable from them as people. The "I" who thinks and remembers is the product of these collective pre- and postcolonial performances.

Furthermore, unlike groups that appropriate the performance practices of others, Yuyachkani's work does not separate the performances from their original audiences but, rather, tries to expand the audiences. The productions are not about them, the indigenous and mestizo Others, but about all the different communities that share a territorial space defined by pre-Conquest groups, colonialism, and nationalism. Yuyachkani attempts to make their urban audiences culturally competent to recognize the multiple ways of being "Peruvian." In addressing Lima audiences, however, Yuyachkani feels it has to start "from zero."[21] The country's theatrical memory, much like its historical, cultural, and political memory, has been deracinated. These performances remind urban audiences of the populations they have forgotten. Storing and transmitting these traditions proves essential, because when they disappear, certain kinds of knowledges, issues, and populations disappear with them. These traditions—the street procession, fiestas, songs, masked characters—bring together criollo, mestizo, Afro-Peruvian, and indigenous expressive elements, each vital to the deeply complicated historical, ethnic, and racial configuration of the actual political situation. Performance provides the "memory paths," the space of reiteration that allows people to replay the ancient struggles for recognition and power that continue to make themselves felt in contemporary Peru.

This brings us to a second point. Looking at performance as a retainer of social memory engages history without necessarily being a "symptom of history"; that is, the performances enter into dialogue with a history of trauma without themselves being traumatic. These are carefully crafted works that create a critical distance for "claiming" experience and enabling, as opposed to "collapsing," witnessing.[22] This performance event has an "outside," which, according to Laub, is what allows for witnessing. Yuyachkani, as its name indicates, hinges on the notion of interconnectedness: the "I" who thinks/remembers is inextricable from the "you" whose thought "I" am. The I/you of Yuyachkani promises to be a witness, a guarantor of the link between the I and the you, the inside and the outside. Yuyachkani becomes the belated witness to the ongoing, unacknowledged drama of atrocity, and asks the audience to do the same. The group's practice points to a radically different conclusion from the one Adorno arrived at in "Commitment." Representation, for Yuyachkani, does not further contribute to the desecration of the victims, turning their pain into our viewing pleasure. Rather, without representation, viewers would not recognize their role in the ongoing history of oppression which, directly or indirectly, implicates them. Who, *Adios Ayachuco* asks, will take on the responsibility of witnessing? The hope offered by *Antígona* is that the spectator, like Ismene, will say "I." The witness, like Boal's "spect-actor," accepts the dangers and responsibilities of seeing and of acting on what one has seen. And witnessing is transferable: the theatre, like the testimony, like the photograph, film, or report, can make witnesses of others. The (eye)witness sustains both the archive and the repertoire. So, rather than think of performance primarily as the ephemeral, as that which disappears, Yuyachkani insists on creating a community of witnesses by and through performance. The group counters the performance-as-disappearance model of colonialism that pushes autochthonous practices into the oblivion of the ephemeral, the unscripted, the understudied, the uncontrollable. For many of these communities, on the contrary, when performance ends, so does the shared understanding of social life and collective memory. Performances such as these fiestas, testimony, and theatrical productions warn us not to dismiss the I who remembers, who thinks, who is a product of collective thought. They teach communities not to look away. As the name Yuyachkani suggests, attention to the interconnectedness between thinking subjects and subjects of thought allows for a broader understanding of historical trauma, communal memory, and collective subjectivity.

8

DENISE STOKLOS

The Politics of Decipherability

The stage at La MaMa's annex theatre space is flat, white, and almost bare. Upstage center, a forest of thick ropes hangs from the ceiling. Upstage right, we can barely see the clotheshorse under a heavy fur coat. And off on the opposite side of the stage a small simple clothes rack and chair complete the minimalist effect of this stark setting. Eight TV sets hang suspended above the entire front of the stage, initially hidden by a black partition. The futuristic, gnawing strings of the Kronos Quartet ring out just as the flood of flat white light washes the stage. Off in the corner, poking out from the simple white curtain, we see a black-booted foot. In slow motion, s/he walks on stage in exaggerated, giant steps. Wearing a tuxedo, complete with vest and top hat, her look is enigmatic, androgynous. The suit is male-ish for a woman, though the curved lines and frilled shirt of the tuxedo make it feminine-ish for a man. Red lips prepare us for the mass of blond electric hair with the signature black roots that she sets free as she bows to the audience, removing her top hat. Half Thoreau, half ringmaster, she ushers in her own performance, minimalist in staging, maximalist in the intensity of the corporeal images that fill the space. Using mime, she writes illegible letters in the air (Figure 62). So begins this inquiry into transnational decipherability by Brazil's most renowned solo performer, Denise Stoklos.

Civil Disobedience: Morning Is When I Am Awake and There Is an Aurora in Me, based on texts by Henry David Thoreau and written, directed, and performed by Stoklos, explores the possibilities of freedom—political, individual, sexual, artistic—in a society that keeps people needy and confined. Then—Thoreau's nineteenth-century New England—and now, in the throes of rampant capitalism at the end of the twentieth century, this performance shows people weighed down, cramped, tormented, even driven to the point of madness by society's imperative for compliance. "The twelve labors of Hercules," Stoklos quotes Thoreau, "were trifling in comparison with those which my neighbors have undertaken; for they were only twelve, and had an end."[1] The narrative, like the clotheshorse, serves as a minimalist structure on which to hang her performance. Thoreau's/Stoklos's move to the woods (the forest of ropes bathed in green lighting) was meant as a temporary withdrawal from civilization in order to test those elements of life that were in fact "essential" (Figures 63 and 64). S/he withstands the pangs of loneliness for civilization only to be carted off to jail (again, the ropes, now transformed by red lighting) for not paying taxes. Upon release against her/his will the following day s/he understands that s/he is as "free" in society as out in the woods. The ropes, as both nature and jail, occupy the same mental space. Images of freedom, in Latin America as elsewhere, exist only in proximity to the reality of oppression. In a variety of registers, ranging from humor to poetic introspection to longing, Stoklos's words and body language ask two recurring questions: What is essential to human happiness? How can we communicate with each other? The questions are urgent: Denise Stoklos performs against the clock. She has come, she tells us, to welcome the new millennium. The countdown, made visible on all eight TV sets, makes her hurry to get her message out, "while there is still life" (Figure 65). Theatre, for Stoklos, is neither recreation nor entertainment: "It's to gain time."[2]

What makes this performance so compelling, aside from the urgency of the questions, is Stoklos's conceptual magic act; she juggles signs, images, words, gestures, keeping them all in the air at the same time. Pulling all sorts of modes out of her hat—circus, mime, vaudeville, Brechtian gestus and distanciation, striptease, philosophical declamation, clowning—she creates her own corporeal and verbal system of signs that spin in humorous counterpoint to each other (Figure 66). The text is a composite of Thoreau, Gertrude Stein, Paulo Freire, and scatological passages parodically attributed to the "Guide to Bodily Fluids." As Thoreau, she pays tribute to his civil disobedi-

62. Denise Stoklos walks onstage in slow motion with exaggerated, giant steps in *Civil Disobedience*, 1999. Photo by Denis Leão.

ence, even as she mimes the walls getting smaller. She calls her hilarious reading of Gertrude Stein's story "Miss Furr and . . ." an example of acrobatics for the tongue: "They were gay there—not VERY gay, just gay there . . . She was gay and that was it!" Gaily, she unmoors signifieds from their frenetic signifiers. She saves her rhapsodic voice for the reading of the pseudo-questionnaire asking us in which social situations we allow ourselves to fart. Now she is Elis Regina, the late Brazilian singer, urging us to leave a message inside a bottle in this shipwreck of a civilization. Now she is a socialite, turning herself inside out in front of the mirror to a ferocious tango. Her face transforms into a series of masks, each more grotesque in her efforts to beautify herself (Figures 67–69). An eyebrow pokes up, an eye seems to pop out, the top teeth protrude, the chin disappears in this face that contorts as easily as the body. She mimes adding makeup, then more makeup. She squeezes, prods, and pushes herself into her dress; her body crumbles under the weight of necklaces and rings. Her tormented face in the mirror growls: "Be careful. Be careful." The "meaning" of the words has so little to do with their performative utterance. The whole performance, in the spirit of Pina Bauch, breaks down gesture, word, image, sound to its most essential unit—repeats, refor-

63, 64. Thoreau's/Stoklos's woods—a forest of ropes—is transformed into a jail cell in *Civil Disobedience*. Photos by Denis Leão. Reproduced by permission.

65. Eight TV sets count down to the millennium as Denise Stoklos hurries to get her message out "while there is still life," in *Civil Disobedience*. Photo by Denis Leão. Reproduced by permission.

66. Denise Stoklos turns herself inside out in front of the mirror to a ferocious tango in *Civil Disobedience*. Photo by Denis Leão. Reproduced by permission.

mulates, and rehearses it in another key, another movement—always with the single purpose of establishing communication.

But it's not just these rhythms—corporeal, vocal, and textual—that intersect, converge, and move apart. The Portuguese inflection of the English texts sends the words spinning off in yet another direction. Stoklos widens the distance between the "natural" and the "acquired" language to further disrupt notions of normativity. She prefers to perform in the language of the audience—in Portuguese, English, Spanish, French, German, Russian, or Ukrainian—to facilitate communication. There is always another language coexisting within the language one hears. She has no English script for the performance; she translates as she goes along. In part, this is circumstantial: up until two days before opening Stoklos believed she would perform in Portuguese because the Annex is controlled by Equity, the actors union that prohibits foreign actors from performing in English. But circumstances aside, she has long cultivated both the alienation and freedom produced by speaking in a foreign language.[3] In voluntary exile in England in the late 1970s when she composed her first solo piece, she found English offered her "lightness," one more means for transporting herself from the "vision and vicinity of torture and dictatorship" of the Brazilian military regime (32). When she performs this text in Portuguese, we hear her translate Thoreau's English into her speech. Her ability to perform in these various languages in itself signals the history of migration, exile, and relocation commonly shared by many Latin American artists.

Doubleness, then, is as much strategy as circumstance. Nothing is transparent. We know each other, if at all, only in translation. In multiple registers, her work performs the obstacles to communication that she constantly alludes to. In one scene, she stages an encounter between two people by using only body language and two metal chairs. In a dance, holding the chairs at arm's length, she moves through a sequence of motions and spaces. She then repeats the sequence with language. The language adds some clarity, but it too leaves much to our imagination. "Sometimes," she concludes, addressing us directly, "we achieve communication. Sometimes not." This reflection is followed by a long pause that speaks volumes (Figures 70 and 71). Language thus serves simultaneously as a means of communication, an obstacle to communication, and one more signifying system. As the word *honra* (honor) pops up on all eight TV screens it both reiterates what Stok-

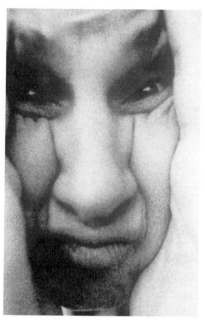

los is saying—"Honor your words, your voice, your communication"—and becomes a visual object in a different communication system. Communication depends on making connections, however ephemeral and haphazard, through this semiotic maze, through this society of the spectacle that produces not clarity but confusion. Sometimes the message arrives, in the face of overwhelming odds, intact in the bottle. Sometimes not. Like the repeated gesture, the words too caution us against believing in completion. One sequence tells of the Chinese Emperor's bathtub, adorned with the mandate *Renew yourself.* With the humor that characterizes the entire piece, Stoklos's spasmodic dives into the tub remind us that the mandate needs to be performed again and again and again.

And through all of this, she looks at us squarely, addresses us directly, questioning our role in the meaning-making process.

So what does this magical juggling act communicate to spectators? And, of course, *which* spectators? Aside from the energy, the humor, and the corporeal and vocal dexterity of the performer, what else is in play? Being (for now) a creature of the new millennium in the United States, I did what

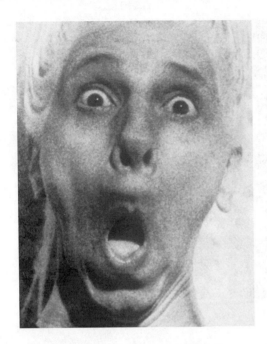

67, 68, 69. Denise Stoklos transforms her face into a series of masks, each more grotesque in her efforts to beautify herself. Photos by Thais Stoklos Kignel. Reproduced by permission.

everyone else does: I polled my friends and acquaintances in New York City who had gone to see it. What did they think of the performance? One performer I know was very taken by the way Stoklos used the grotesque to challenge the social structuring of "white femininity." Her face can twist into every imaginable shape. Some people loved her "cool" hair. Others loved her, passionately, period. One student said her work lacked originality, but he admired the effort she put into it. Is she gay, another wanted to know? Others found her work too "European" in the way it drew from traditions (mime, vaudeville, etc.) or avoided any specific "Latin American" references or issues. Others admired the extraordinary artistic rigor and richness of her performance. Some, including the reviewer from the *New York Times*, found her hilariously funny. A European colleague loved the interaction between Thoreau and Freire and found it wonderful to hear a performer talk about education, poverty, taxes, and other social issues. A friend found the performance "very Latin American" and the English hard to follow. One of my colleagues asked me if Denise Stoklos sought/addressed a "local" or a "global" audience.

The results of my home ethnography test puzzled me. What struck me,

70, 71. Denise Stoklos struggles to achieve communication. Photos by Denis Leão. Reproduced by permission.

of course, were those comments that automatically turned the event into an indicator of a subaltern difference, formulated in terms of too much/too little, and then judged it for failing or succeeding on that level. The subaltern artist, asked to bear the full burden of ensuring communication, was nonetheless denied originality. If commentators recognized the traditions that enabled communication, then the work lacked originality. But if there was something that commentators suspected they didn't grasp, it was deemed excessive and untranslatable. What I had found remarkable about Stoklos's performance was its multicodedness. Ethnically, sexually, politically, aesthetically, and linguistically she refused any simple marking. Her studied plurality was, in itself, an interesting artistic choice, in part because several of the best performance artists of her generation in Latin America—Jesusa Rodríguez and Astrid Hadad, to name two Mexican performers—have chosen to play with and reexamine some of the most "Latin American" of icons. They work to subvert the stereotypical images that have regulated the formulation of gender identity for Mexican women, from sainted mother (the Virgin of Guadalupe or Coatilcue, the Mexica "mother" of all Mexicans) to the macho woman with high heels and spurs (Figure 72). Hadad's recent piece *Heavy Nopal* suggests that the narrow grid provided by the stereotype that reduces and fixes a one-dimensional image serves only as a critique for those who are able to see the violence of the framing. In a tableau vivant of a Diego Rivera painting, she humorously bears the weight of stereotypical accumulation and "anxious" repetition. She is all in one: the Diego Rivera girl holding calla lilies; the *soldadera* (revolutionary fighter); the bejeweled Latina, loaded down with rings, bracelets, and dangling earrings; the India with the hand-embroidered shirt, long black braids, and a bewildered look about her (Figure 73). The overmarked image of telegenic ethnicity signals the rigid structuring of cultural visibility. The parodic self-marking reads as one more repetition of the fact, one more proof of its fixity. Latin America is visible only through cliché, known solely "in translation." Hadad plays with the anxiety behind these images of excess, pushing the most hegemonic of spectators to reconsider how these stereotypes of cultural/racial/ethnic difference are produced, reiterated, and consumed.

And yet Stoklos, who works with Western texts and performance techniques and who explicitly aspires to some "universal" message about communication, is held to how much or how little she displays these same ethnic markings. When my friend said she found Stoklos "very Latin American" I knew that meant "excessive," "emotional," even "hysterical." The comment "too European" (i.e., not Latin American *enough*) meant that the expectations created for the "exotic" or the "emotional" had not been met. My student's comment about the lack of originality (for using some of those Western techniques) carried with it the assumption that Latin Americans do not belong to the West. It also overlooks the troubled issue of originality as applied to Third World contexts. Colonialism strips the original, as denoting cultural belonging and autochthonous expression, from the colonized and transfers it to the colonizer as a marker of cultural taste, privilege, and symbolic capital. Framing the argument in terms of originality not only repeats the charge of colonial mimeticism, but mistakes the cultural gesture of appropriation and transculturation that has characterized Latin American artistic and intellectual formation for an indiscriminate borrowing. Originality in Latin American performance would have to be understood both in terms of autochthonous forms *and* the highly innovative ways artists appropriate forms that come from other cultural repertoires. The "very Latin American," like the "too European," betrays a reductive notion of a natu-

72. Jesusa Rodríguez's version of Coatlicue, the Aztec "mother" of all Mexicans. Photo courtesy of Jesusa Rodríguez.

73. Astrid Hadad, in *Heavy Nopal,* 1998. Photo by Pancho Gilardi.

ralized cultural and group identity in/for Latin America—as if there were *a* Latin American way of being or performing. The degree to which performers resist or take on expectations renders the performance transparent (too European) or untranslatable (too Latin American). Thus, the "Latin American," as I heard it, suggested a way of closing down, rather than expanding, the field of cultural recognition.

The power and originality of Stoklos's work, to my mind, lies in the humor and intensity with which she transforms the most disparate artistic and political traditions into a forceful and highly personal performance project. In her thirty years as an artist, she has explored the quirky mix of Brazilian militarism and postmodern alienation (*Casa*, 1990), responded to the ongoing effects of colonialism (*500 Years—A Fax from Denise Stoklos to Christopher Columbus*, 1992), reflected on the torturous political and personal pulls on women—as political leaders (*Denise Stoklos in Mary Stuart*) and as mothers (*Des-Medéia*, 1995)—and examined the political options facing citizens at the end of the twentieth century (*Civil Disobedience*, 1998; Figures 74–77). Each of these performances draws from the repertoire of artistic traditions that I allude to in relation to *Civil Disobedience*—mime, vaudeville, Brechtian epic theatre, juggling, and other recognizable forms—to convey a message that is uncompromisingly her own. Stoklos makes it a point to cite the traditions that formed her as an artist; thus, she always includes a short mime sequence. However, she rejects the political neutrality of mime and uses it only to further her own project, which is firmly positioned and committed. Her address to Columbus, as the title indicates, is absolutely personal, direct, and contemporary. She explores the role of the artist, the intellectual, the theatre, and the audience in the tragic history of her country. "Read it," she says. "It's all in the books." Later, once the audience fully comprehends the magnitude of her critique, she has the house lights turned up: "The doors of the theatre are open for those who want to abandon this ship in flames."[4] Through her own body, Stoklos explores the ways in which gender, sexuality, power, and familial bonds pull and push in a woman's flesh. Can we undo the historical trajectory of killings and opt for life-affirming strategies, be they ideological, political, or personal/familial? Stoklos's work is polyvalent, allowing for unusually divergent readings.

In Brazil, her audiences recognize her fierce engagement with national

74. Denise Stoklos explores
the quirky mix of Brazilian
militarism and postmodern
alienation in *Casa,* 1990. Photo
by Jay Isla. Reproduced by
permission.

75. In *500 Years—A Fax from
Denise Stoklos to Christopher
Columbus,* 1992, Stoklos
responds to the ongoing effects
of colonialism. Photo by Bel
Pedrosa. Reproduced by
permission.

76. Denise Stoklos in *Mary Stuart*, 1987, a piece reflecting on the torturous pulls of political power. Photo by Jay Islas. Reproduced by permission.

77. *Des-Medéia*, Stoklos's 1995 performance in which Medea chooses not to kill her children. Photo by Sergio Divitis. Reproduced by permission.

78. In 1999, Stoklos's work was featured, as it so often is, in a Brazilian theatre festival. Inside, wall-size photographs of Stoklos's facial expressions taken by her daughter, Thais Stoklos Kignel, surrounded the audience members in the lobby. Photo by Diana Taylor.

politics. A production of hers is an event that receives national attention.[5] At a recent festival of her work in São Paulo that I attended, the audiences of mainly university-age Brazilians were deeply moved by each of her performances. Every show was sold out, and every night brought a thunderous standing ovation. The theatre was plastered inside and out with wall-size photographs of Stoklos's facial expressions, taken by her daughter, Thais Stoklos Kignel. Even the floors and elevators reflected her presence (Figure 78).

Denise Stoklos's status as a national icon stems, in part, from her innovative artistic work. She is the first solo performance artist from Latin America, in the way commentators tend to think of solo performance in the United States, at least. Her precursors there might be the vaudeville artists and cabaret stars of the 1950s and 1960s: Elis Regina, Chavela Vargas, La Lupe, Chabuca Granda. Her book *The Essential Theatre* outlines her project of using minimum resources, "gestures, movement, words, wardrobe, scencry, accessories and effects," to maximum artistic and political effect.[6]

In opting for solo performance, Stoklos went against the prevailing political and artistic style of the late 1960s and the 1970s. The Cuban Revolution had promoted the ethos of collectivity, a concept that organized everything from neighborhoods to theatre groups. Many of Brazil's (and Latin America's) most important artists of the period forged collectives to continue their artistic and political work in the face of criminal politics. Boal worked with other important artists in the Arena Theatre, Buenaventura started TEC in Colombia, Yuyachkani began working in Peru, and so on. It went against the thinking of the times to stage solo work. Even amateur performers formed groups to engage in street theatre, staging pieces that spoke to the current political situation in the *favelas* and other popular neighborhoods. The political instrumentality of performance of this period made it difficult for theatre practitioners and artists who went into exile to continue their work. Deprived of their groups, their audiences, and their contexts, most exiled artists either stopped creating for a time, wrote novels, or taught in theatre schools. Stoklos, however, used the period of exile to train herself as a solo performer. Even so, "solo" doesn't mean "alone." She is always in conversation, artistically and ideologically, with others who have fought for freedom. Her last words to Elis Regina, in her one-woman homage, maps out the trajectory of solidarity. Stoklos quotes Regina, who in turn sings one of Atahualpa Yupanqui's most famous lines, "Yo tengo tantos hermanos que no los puedo contar" (I have so many brothers/sisters that I can't count them all).

In the United States, the issues, the stakes, and the viable spaces of contestation are profoundly different. Although discussions about colonialism, militarism, political freedom, and regulatory systems of gender and sexuality are also intensely politicized in the United States, international dialogue about these issues, even among progressives, usually remains in the realm of wishful thinking. The strategies, the gestures, the corporeal and symbolic languages used to express them reflect the cultural specificity of their articulation and threaten to render them "untranslatable" in another context. In a manner as humorous, but perhaps more difficult to recognize than in *Heavy Nopal*, Stoklos too plays with the epistemological grid of understanding by staging the now-you-see-it-now-you-don't of the seemingly transparent. What makes it through the hegemonic filters, artistically or politically?

This playful hide-and-seek, unnoticed by respondents to my poll, is one of the characteristics I find "very Latin American." Although Stoklos performs it, moving in and out of the ropes, stripping, dressing, moving, camouflaging, transforming before our eyes, it goes unnoticed as a strategy because it's antithetical, according to the grid, to a Latin America that is fixed, known, repeated, and absolutely accessible to us. So, what would it mean to refer to hide-and-seek as a Latin American strategy? It might refer to a broad range of cultural practices that, since the Conquest of the Americas, have seemed suspiciously inaccessible to its colonizers. Even though state and Church authorities imposed strict regulations on how native peoples could dress, live, worship, celebrate, and so forth, the extant writings transmit the uneasy conviction that for all their watchfulness, the Europeans were nonetheless missing the point. The colonizer/colonized spectacle is always double-coded. Something else is always happening beneath the seemingly transparent routines imposed by the new masters. The multicoded cultural practices have, if anything, become even more dynamic with the passing of centuries. The native and African populations of the Americas have always found ways of transmitting their performative practices under the very nose of the ruling groups, as did the conversos, Jews, and other minoritarian groups. This skill, long a survival strategy, has also at times been converted into an art form. For Denise Stoklos, a Brazilian artist who learned her trade during a period of military dictatorship, censorship, and state violence (1964–1985), multivalent virtuosity takes into account both the demand for clarity and the oppositional tactic of selective or partial visibility.

Let's look, for a moment, at the relationship between sexuality and freedom. Brazil, unlike other Latin American countries under dictatorship during the same period, seemed to allow for greater physical and sexual freedom, though people were denied freedom of speech and other civil rights. The image of a sexy, multiracial body was Brazil's greatest export. Carnival and samba, Brazil's two best-known cultural products, both glorify sensuous, undulating, seemingly unrepressed flesh. The body as both an economic and a political commodity functioned as a signifier of a freedom only skin deep, part of a double spectacle or, rather, a spectacle within a spectacle—somewhat along the lines of what Debord calls the military (or "concentrated") spectacle functioning within the more "diffuse" spectacle of global capitalism.[7] The body, for the military, does one thing. The words go someplace else.

Indecipherability, then, has long been a strategy for combating the exigencies that everything be transparent, available for immediate decoding. Ambiguity subverts the demand for decipherability and strict compliance. In a social situation demanding strict gender and sexual formation as integral to the political performance of national "being," not being available for easy reading was both a danger and a form of civil disobedience. Humor, for Stoklos and other Latin American performers, provides the vehicle for the multicoded communication. Predicated on unexpected juxtapositions, subversions, and reconfigurations, her humor hints at other possible meanings, doubleness, multivalence.

Stoklos, who worked in theatre in Brazil as a playwright, actor, and director from 1968 until she left for England in 1979, learned a couple of new languages—one linguistic, one aesthetic. English, as I mentioned previously, offered "lightness." Working on solo performance offered a zone of expressive and political possibility during a period in which group disobedience was dangerous in the extreme. Better to stage one's own, solo act of resistance. Perhaps one point of convergence that drew Stoklos to Thoreau was the similarity of this solo political performance. "The only obligation which I have the right to assume," Stoklos says, quoting from Thoreau's *Civil Disobedience*, "is to do at any time what I think is right."[8] Both withdrew from their world, temporarily, not to escape but to reinterpret it, to disidentify, to retool. Civil disobedience, for Thoreau and for Stoklos, is a solo practice, the politics of nonparticipation, the anti-identity, anticathartic politics of individual resistance, the politics of the *one*. For Stoklos, corporeal language could say what words could not. The "scenic body" assumes the responsibility of communicating, of reopening the venues closed down by the terror systems, silencing, and exile (26).

This political context leads to a somewhat "different" kind of political performance from much of what my friends and acquaintances see in New York. The aims, and thus the strategies, differ. Several of the best U.S. solo performers—Peggy Shaw, Kate Bornstein, Holly Hughes, Karen Finley, John Leguiziamo, Marga Gómez, Carmelita Tropicana, Deb Margolin, Spalding Gray, to name a few—draw from autobiographical material. They write their own material, recalling their personal experiences with menopause, sex changes, coming out, dis/owning one's body, growing up in a dysfunctional family, Alzheimers, exile, and religious formation. Often in the first person, the performances tend to privilege language over corporeality and rely on identification with an audience they recognize as their own. The humor, the intensity, the beauty of these performances often stems from taking the small, the personal, the confessional and making it speak to a community organized around (but not limited to) an "identity." Latino/as, gays/lesbians, and feminists find in these artists a space for identification, for mutual recognition, for being other than that regulated by dominant culture. These performances legitimate alternativity through irony, humor, joy. They are often associated with specific venues (*off off*) and audiences are self-selected around specific "issues."

Stoklos, perhaps more in the vein of Anna Deavere Smith, takes another route in solo performance, allowing her body to channel (rather than own) a whole range of positions. Their work is intensely personal as far as its political and aesthetic project is concerned, but not autobiographical. Nor do they address like-minded audiences. Rather than the inside-out approach described above, these two artists go from the outside in. Smith has stated that an actor can get inside a character through language; if we learn to say the words of another, we will be able to somehow feel what the other feels and understand why others do as they do. Neither of them use their own words, although they very much conceive of and create their own texts. Rather, it is precisely the incorporating of these other words, other languages, other ways of thinking that allows for the interpersonal and intergroup (be it racial or national) communication they both see as key to their political project. Stoklos, somewhat along the lines of many of her Latin American contemporaries, thinks of herself as a revolutionary: she seeks a profound and radical transformation in the individual's way of thinking and acting. But, again ironically, she is more of a revolutionary along the lines of the anarchistic, individualistic Thoreau than of Fidel or Ché or Sandino. Too many failed revolutions later, Stoklos cannot subscribe to the cathartic, identificatory, restrictive programs these have set in motion.

This is not to say that Stoklos doesn't worry about the other issues, such as gender and sexuality, that concern some of these other artists. Even though her reflections are not attached to a personal narrative, they continually spin before our eyes. As a performer, she seems to have equal access to the broad spectrum of genders normally reduced and dichotomized as male/female. But she does not engage in drag, if by that we mean a conscious, parodic masquerading or unmasquerading of "opposite" gender roles. There is nothing parodic in the way she assumes the power, authority, control, and physical strength usually bestowed on the masculine, nor in the way she exalts in the pleasure, vulnerability, and expressivity of the body associated with the feminine. Rather, she challenges the normative system that assigns masculinity exclusively to males and femininity to females. The critique, as the makeup sequence makes clear, lies in the way we are forced to fit into the reductive strictures of stereotypical gender roles.

Androgyny, however, is not a popular category for some queer theorists in the United States. The move that is seen here as most politically radical involves a more explicit, categorical presentation. The disparagement stems from the way androgyny has been mobilized to foreclose, rather than pry open, the complicated relationships between gender and sexual "acts." And there is a way in which Stoklos's performance, while challenging restrictive gender paradigms, stops short of linking gender performances to sexual practice. Besides the Steinian moment of being gay there, not *very* gay, just gay, her sexuality is indecipherable because of the anti-autobiographical nature of her performance. One could argue that, once again, the performance stages the rupture between the corporeal and the speakable. Stoklos's body performs one thing and speaks another. She dismantles normative femininity and masculinity as a dressing up and stripping down; she performs gayness through Stein; she exerts her physical strength in the swinging of the chairs; and she allows for sensuousness and vulnerability. She laments our inability to make use of our full range of body, thought, and being. Her body and her words call for more options, an expansion of our current expressivity. But what works physically as a challenge to limitations can also (as the disparagement about androgyny suggests) be seen as working discursively as its opposite—subsuming issues of sexuality under a blanket of "oppression" —a clumping together, rhetorically, that works against the performance of prying open. However, this discussion too benefits from a broader intercultural dialogue. Rather than dismiss this kind of performance of ambiguity as nonpolitical or unqueer, Sylvia Molloy encourages us to look at "posing" and other forms of "unpatriotic" gender practices as "a significant political performance and a founding queer cultural practice."[9] The discussion that opens up around the seemingly transparent issues of politics, gender, and sexuality, I would argue, highlights the indecipherability produced when two political imperatives run into each other. The politics of ambiguity stemming from Latin America is at odds with the U.S. identity politics that demands definition.

Why is it so urgent that performance theorists focus on intercultural spectatorship, on the ways that we understand or misunderstand each other across cultural and national borders? As systems of circulation—economic, cultural, migratory—undergo change as part of globalization, we are confronted with new systems of control and centralization in which we play a part. Though performances have long traveled (usually one way) from the centers to the colonial peripheries, we now live in an environment of far greater, and seemingly multidirectional, cultural circulation. This circulation takes several shapes. First, we have the prefabricated productions, such as *Cats* and *Miss Saigon*, that play simultaneously in New York, London, and Mexico City. These are cultural commodities, objects that change little if at all in transit. Second, folkloric shows continue to put Third World products onto First World stages: performances of the Ballet Folklórico, tango, and flamenco fall into neat categories that confirm what we already know about these "excessive" cultures. We have some artistically innovative international performances traveling to alternative spaces, such as *Civil Disobedience* playing at La MaMa. Then we have what a colleague calls the "global" circuit, the "world-class" performances by the Robert Wilsons, Pina Bausches, and Tadushi Sasukis showcased in huge productions for the cultural elite in the world's great cities. In short, cultural production plays an important though too often unexamined role in what usually gets talked about as financial "flows." The global city, as Saskia Sassen argues in her book by that title, earns that stature in part through the concentration and diversity of the cultural commodities it can furnish for its affluent, urban, new professionals.[10] Moreover, global cities are linked to each other, sharing more products (including cultural) with each other than they might with the countries in which they happen to be situated. The reterritorialization, however, leads to a different structure of relatively closed systems along new class formations. For, on the other end of the same process, we see the rapidly increasing immigrants and minority groups that take the low-paying jobs servicing these new professionals. These service groups also demand and create cultural products. In New York, for example, mural art, *casitas*, and community sculptures function as ways in which minority communities "up-grade" and "make home" their new environment.

Globalization, then, has furnished us with a variation on the old center-periphery model of colonialism. Now the center and the periphery often occupy the same space, in concentric circles rather than a linear here–there. It has also ushered in new problems in thinking about location and situat-edness, ones that take into account that populations reside in certain places more because of financial and political imperatives than ethnic or national ones. "Latin America" no longer signifies a readily recognizable space or population *over there*. The elite in Latin America have apartments in New York and more ties to other economic leaders worldwide than to the majority of people in their country of origin. The migrant Latin American worker has become the pan-ethnic busboy clearing tables at chic restaurants in SoHo. In Latin American countries too the past five hundred years have been marked by all sorts of invasions, migrations, and other forms of relocation. Brazil has the second largest Japanese population in the world, and Buenos Aires's Jew-ish population is second only to New York in the Americas. There is no one language, artistic or linguistic, associated with either the northern or south-ern hemisphere. What do judgments such as "very Latin American" or "too European" mean in the face of these realities? The urgency for developing a more informed and nuanced *trans-*, *cross-*, or *inter*cultural spectatorship increases as we try to understand our role as intellectuals, theorists, and art-ists in a rapidly changing system that affects our understanding of the local and the international arenas as deeply interconnected. Cultural competence now involves not just an understanding of *transculturation* that explains how cultural systems undergo change through contact with foreign influ-ences—though that would be a start.[11] It requires an understanding of how performances—as commodities, as art objects, as upgrading processes, as ve-hicles for expression and communication—move within and as part of larger economic and ideological networks, linking São Paulo to New York, for ex-ample, or Broadway to the Lower East Side. Broadway shows and Lower East Side murals are flip sides of the same spectacle in Debord's understanding of the term: "The spectacle is not a collection of images, but a social relation among people, mediated by images."[12] The transnational circuits that create one create the other. Cultural production needs to be seen as part of a more mobile, less geographically bound system of interaction and connection.

Performances not only participate in these systemic international flows, they have also long served as a site for intercultural inquiry. Louis Althusser, in *For Marx*, noted that "performance is fundamentally the occasion for a cultural and ideological recognition."[13] This sounds like Victor Turner's utopian claim: "We will know one another better by entering one another's performances and learning their grammars and vocabularies."[14] However, this works only if we do more than extend our existing paradigms to include "other" cultural experiences. Performance, which can literally stage the intragroup encounter, offers a privileged site for this exploration. Performance not only functions as an indicator of global processes, it also opens a space for thinking about them, and about our habits of response. Bad (cultural) habits are thinking about performance as object or commodity, rather than as a collective exercise, and labeling as critical thinking what is, in fact, the reaffirmation of exhausted categories. Performances can challenge our assumptions about our role as spectators and our own cultural positioning.

Intercultural performance, theorists have reiterated throughout most of the past century, requires a new kind of spectatorship, a dialectic spectatorship (for Althusser) that demands a break both with the "identification" model *and* its opposite, the one that places the spectator outside the production: "Mother Courage is presented to you. It is for her to act. It is for you to judge. On the stage the image of blindness—in the stalls the image of lucidity."[15] The identification model, which Althusser critiques as reducing "social, cultural and ideological consciousness" to "a purely psychological consciousness" (149), has also been charged by theorists such as Augusto Boal with disempowering spectators, turning them into passive onlookers of the actions and emotions of the high and mighty. The second model, the nonreflective distancing, seems to me at the heart of the hegemonic spectatorship I alluded to earlier. Here the spectator, not the protagonist, is empowered and claims "absolute consciousness of self" (148). But this is very different from the spectactor Boal advocates for, the disempowered social actor who rightly fights for an active role in the social struggles that involve him or her. Hegemonic spectators profit from nonidentification. As Althusser's image of the judge indicates, these spectators enjoy the superiority and power that accompany the lofty position of sentencing without ever feeling themselves implicated in the proceedings. The problems of hegemonic spectatorship are even more accentuated in the realm of intercultural

performance, where people feel even less implicated in the ideological construction of the performance and even more empowered to demand access.
The onus is on the performance, not the spectator, to create meaning. The
subject matter, style, or language should not be too foreign (but just foreign
enough). This is a different kind of "critical" distancing—power masquerading as aesthetics, taste as value. Spectators, secure in their position of the imperial eye/I outside the frame, pass judgment. Instead of breaking down our
responses as spectators, we might simply repeat them. Cultural habits dress
up as critique. Yet the critique that shakes everyone's assumptions about our
place in the spectacle as "a social relation among people" might be able to
come only from the margins. The aim of our efforts, as one of my students put
it, is "to reeducate the epistemological privilege of the ordinary spectator."[16]

Stoklos's *Civil Disobedience* offers a model for intercultural communication in the face of overwhelming odds. On one hand, this is very much an
international performance, one that travels from São Paulo to New York and
soon to the other great cities. It is also international in its form, drawing from
philosophical texts, circus traditions, mime, and other Western aesthetic and
political repertoires. It stages an international dialogue on topics of universal significance, and its protagonists (Thoreau, Freire, Stein) are well-known.
The words have all been written. They are pronounced in the spectator's own
language. Yet, although on one level the performance functions in the global
circuits of cultural flows, in no way does it sustain the ideology of control
and management that only occasionally tries to pass itself off as communication.

On the contrary: Stoklos whispers, growls, and sings "Be careful." It is not
so easy to achieve communication. Intercultural or international dialogue is
even more difficult, and often treacherous. It turns, too often, into power's
megalomaniacal monologue with itself. Intercultural communication is not
a "thing known"; our grid can't frame or capture "it." A praxis rather than an
episteme, it can never be assumed; access is never given but always learned.
Multiculturalism, erroneously to my mind, held out the promise of cultural
understanding. I propose that we begin with the assumption that we don't
understand, that we always engage in acts of translation. The task of working
toward intercultural communication (as opposed to consuming otherness),
Stoklos proposes, is urgent. She takes the first giant, though careful, step
forward, ushering in the event that brings the past into dialogue with our

future, the over there into the here and now. That here and now is not a stable place but a configuration of elements in constant flux. Some spectators will recognize some of those elements—maybe the Gertrude Stein, or the Paulo Freire, or the mime gestures—and not others. We are all equidistant from the multicultural repertoire of images. How do all the different conversations, signs, movements make sense together? Stoklos, looking at us, communicating with us through languages, images, gestures, movement, challenges us to recognize the urgency with which we too must struggle for communication. Sometimes the words are incomprehensible, the gesture tentative, the meaning fragmented or incomplete. Sometimes we understand each other. Sometimes not. Will we be able to make out the message in the bottle? What if we could? Stoklos's performance demands an act of imagination from us. This is not the Aristotelian urging that we learn to accept the impossible plausibility (as opposed to the possible implausibility) when watching a performance.[17] She demands that we imagine our interrelatedness otherwise; the occasions for interaction and conversation are far more numerous and flexible than we now envision.

Stranger things have happened: Thoreau engages in a contemporary conversation with Freire, a hundred years his junior. The encounter between thinkers, pacifists, educators, and poets from different parts of the world has already produced a transgenerational, transnational discourse about freedom and social justice and has led to social visions and political projects as different as Thoreau's, Gandhi's, Kierkegaard's, and Marx's. Intercultural communication is not just wishful thinking; it's a collective exercise that works toward the creation of what Arjun Appadurai calls a "diasporic public sphere."[18] Through her work, Stoklos affirms not just its potentiality, but its existence. It is with humor, conviction, and courage that she urges us to join her, to add our voices and body language and knowledges to the already vast repertoire of cultural gestures. Together, we will make meaning, or we'll keep trying—again and again and again.

9

LOST IN THE FIELD OF VISION

Witnessing September 11

When I saw the north tower of the World Trade Center in flames, about five minutes after the first plane hit, I thought, "God, it's going to take a lot of time and money to fix that." A small community of watchers gathered in the street. Two women recounted that they had heard the low-flying plane zoom by, then saw it slice into the building. Others joined us. It was a freakishly beautiful day. We stretched closer to hear what others were saying. The women told their story again. Again, we listened. "Are people trapped inside?" it finally occurred to us to ask. Groups formed, dissolved, reformed. I headed home, using my cell phone to contact my family. No signal. Traffic stopped. Then the second plane. Another explosion. Outside of my building, more people. The building manager's wife worked in one of the towers; she was there now, he told us, as we stared dumbfounded down the street at the flames. Even then we didn't start talking about deliberate terrorist attacks. That happened only after word of the Pentagon and Pennsylvania filtered onto the street. We stood transfixed, watching, witnesses without a narrative, part of a tragic chorus that stumbled onto the wrong set. The city stopped. The phones were dead, cars vanished, stores closed.

Like many others, I went inside to turn on the television, trying to find sense in what I was seeing. I could not assimilate it, either live or on TV. As in a sports stadium, I watched both at the same time. The large windows framed

79, 80. World Trade
Center Towers 1 and 2
on fire after attack on
September 11, 2001. Photos
by Diana Taylor.

a surreal and mostly silent scene. The wind was blowing toward Brooklyn, so the smell and smoke had not yet started to leak inside. From the twenty-ninth floor of my NYU housing, a mile or so north of the WTC, I couldn't see people. I'd turn to the television and see the running, the screaming, the collage of frantic yet nonetheless contained images of disaster on the screen. Giuliani was talking, news anchors were talking, foreign correspondents were talking. Then I'd run back to the window. I took a photograph, not knowing why exactly, and started taping the CNN broadcast: TV, window, photo, TV, window, photo, back and forth, my options limited to a back-and-forth, trying to contain and grasp what was happening. Should I go get my daughter? Was she better off at school, a mile uptown, or here? Back and forth, back and forth. I went to get my daughter.

The mood on the street had changed. We were in full crisis mode—the city, still and suddenly stark, in shock. Stunned, people wandered around the streets looking for loved ones. Yet everything was quiet except for the persistent wails of ambulances, fire trucks, police cars.

As we walked back, Marina and I wanted to do something, do anything. We tried to give blood at St. Vincent's, but the line was hours long.

We went home and looked out the window. It was eerie not seeing people. The catastrophe, one could believe for a second perhaps, was about planes and towers, about loss of property rather than loss of life. This looked like one of those surgical strikes that the U.S. military claims to have perfected. Our aviation technology and terror tactics turned against us. Our Hollywood scenarios live—complete with towering infernos and raging sirens—just down the street. Collateral damage, reconfigured. I wondered if my inability to make sense of what I was seeing had been conditioned by the dominance of this virtual repertoire of images, characters, plotlines. I had seen it all before on computer and television monitors. Did this blinding signal the failure of the live as a means of knowing? Or the triumph of what George Yúdice calls the "Military Industrial Media Complex," more commonly known as "entertainment," that has rendered the live one more reiteration? I turned on the TV.

On TV, a narrative sequence was beginning to emerge; people spoke of the attack, the response, "the world reacts," victimization, evil, revenge. But the linear plotline too had little to do with what we were seeing. The images, repeated again and again, froze the moment of impact. Television's multi-

81. The streets emptied out after the attacks. Broadway on September 11. Photo by Diana Taylor.

frames simultaneously conveyed and controlled the crisis: in one tight box, a speaker delivered an opinion; in another, frantic videos taken with handheld cameras caught the panic that I couldn't see from my window. On the bottom of the screen, the information loop also kept repeating, freezing time. The time of the first attack, 8:46 A.M., the time of the second, 9:02 A.M. . . . The loop caught the movement and the stasis of the phenomenon, the obsessive coming back to that one fixed moment. Then the frames shifted again: now a steady Giuliani dominated the foreground, pushing havoc into the tight background box. I ran back to the window.

The Towers smoldered silently in the distance, waves of smoke stuck in the too blue sky. Time itself seemed to have stopped, conjured into fixity perhaps by the TV's invocation of the first strike, then the second. It looked as if the Towers would just keep standing there, smoldering. More photos. Seeing through the lens extended the reach and holding power of my vision.

Aware that a historical event was overtaking my capacity to understand it, I too wanted to contain the moment and freeze it for later: TV, window, photo, TV, window, photo, back and forth. Each click of my camera was my own pause/hold, as I entered into the suspended rhythm of the present. The archival impulse prompted me to save the images to understand them at some future time. One day I would write about it, I told myself, even as I considered taking out my journal and writing about it *now*. But I couldn't. I put the *now* away for later. I envisioned the moment from the post*now*, what I would do with it from a safe distance, sorting through the neat, glossy 4 × 6 images of disaster. Like the TV's *now*, mine was already a repeat, a retrospective as I projected myself into the future, looking back. Photography, at this moment, was paradoxically both action and anti-action, performance and antiperformance, a doing, a click, in the face of the impossibility of doing, about the need to stop everything until I could get a hold of it. I took another photo and thought I really should be writing down the time of each click. But I couldn't do that either. The failures of the archive linked again to the failures of the live. I went back to the TV, my options limited to a back-and-forth. On TV, I heard that the south tower had fallen. I rushed back to the window. I couldn't believe I hadn't seen it live.

The Towers gone, seeing took on a different charge. The TV obsessively repeated images, itself trapped in the traumatic loop. A few newly heroic protagonists, like Giuliani, emerged from the rubble to cordon off the catastrophe, trying to limit it to "ground zero." Almost immediately, he ordered a media blackout at the site.[1] Only designated images would circulate, only professionals allowed to photograph. The signifying objects gone, we had access only to photos of the objects. Instantly, it seemed, newly minted organizations produced glossy journals, passing as weeklies, to circulate the permitted images, the permissible stories. Bylines, photo credits, and authenticating sources disappeared. Unsigned testimonials invoked, yet hid, the seeing "I." Specifics gave way to the ubiquitous footer "God Bless America." Media as vehicle of consumerism partly surrendered to its other, only somewhat less apparent mode: media as delivery system for state ideology.

In spite of all attempts at containability, the catastrophe spread. The attack we had witnessed was now being called a war, albeit a "different kind of war." CNN came up with a logo and a title: the flag toward the bottom left-hand corner, and just under that, "America's New War." The world was sud-

82, 83. One tower folded, then two . . . Photos by Diana Taylor.

denly reshuffled into those who stood by "us" and those who turned against "us." Giuliani, live on TV, spoke of the "tragedy that we're all undergoing right now" and said that his "heart goes out to all the innocent victims." Yet even that first day, when people were walking around in shock, anxious that further devastation might follow, he assured a nervous country that "people in New York City can demonstrate our resolve and our support for all the people viciously attacked today by going about their lives." The "our" immediately shifted into the "their." The roles already assigned: the heroes (Giuliani, the firefighters, etc.), the victims (those who had been "viciously attacked"), and those of us who were neither but who struggled to get on with our lives. As bad as the fear, perhaps, was the physical sensation of being close to the site. We inhaled the Towers, smelled them, tasted them in our mouths, rubbed them from our teary eyes, crunched them with our feet as we walked through the streets. Many people were displaced following the evacuation of lower Manhattan and looking for places to sleep. Was that what Giuliani meant by "going on with our lives"? Giuliani and Bush Jr. soon spelled it out: stay out of the way, buy theatre tickets, eat at restaurants, fly on planes. In a parody of the language of sacrifice that accompanies war, Bush Jr. recognized the sacrifice demanded of us: we were to wait patiently in lines at airports and ballparks, knowing it was for a greater good.[2] If this was a tragedy, we were not recognized as participants. The role of witness, as responsible, ethical, participant rather than spectator to crisis, collapsed in the rubble of talk of victims, heroes, and the rest of us. Even though officials invoked the inclusive "we" to refer to the attack and "our" determination to fight back, there was no place for us, no participation that could conceivably be meaningful.

To *do* something, I kept taking photos, though now mostly photos of photos. I also met regularly with three close friends who were also thinking about photography in relation to September 11: photographer Lorie Novak, cultural theorist Marianne Hirsch, folklorist and performance studies scholar Barbara Kirshenblatt-Gimblett. Speaking about the need to photograph with them made up for what the photos could not communicate in themselves, a recognition, perhaps, that taking a photograph was in itself an act of interlocution, a need to make sense and communicate. It was a way of assessing whether we had all seen the same things, or if our takes on the events—apparently so similar in the photos that we had a hard time remembering who took which—were in fact quite different. Our views had perhaps little connection with the viewfinder—the seeing, again, dislocated from the knowing. Marianne felt uncomfortable about photographing, as if we were further violating the victimized. I felt that the only way I could cope was by photographing, piecing together my own narrative.

The media's inundation of the must-see covered the tensions around the political mustn't-see. The immediate talk about who had *seen* what when (the Towers, the planes), suddenly complicated by the who *knew* what when (FBI, sources close to the White House). If anything, the more we saw the images circulating in the media, the less we had access to. For one thing, too much was going on backstage, out of public view. For another, the intensely mediatized seeing became a form of social blinding: percepticide, a form of killing or numbing through the senses. Our very eyes used against us.

Lost in the field of vision. I think it wasn't until a few days later that some of us started developing hero envy, some trauma envy.

For days, all we saw were images of heroic men in uniform rushing to ground zero. In this time of national bodybuilding, a *New York Times* article on September 12 stated that "the coming days will require [Bush] to master the image of sturdy authority and presidential strength."[3] The photos that followed showed all the determination and polish of the revitalized mise-en-scène. The front-page photo on the *New York Times* on September 13 shows an army of men amid a sea of debris. On September 15, it's Giuliani, Bush, and Fire Commissioner Von Essen looking at the wounded site with grim courage. "Bush tells the military to 'get ready,'" says the *New York Times* headline of September 16. The front cover of *Time* magazine's special issue of September 24 depicts Bush standing on the ruins, holding the U.S. flag resolutely over his head with his right hand. *U.S. News and World Report* that same week shows a firefighter hanging an enormous flag high over the eerie remains of the crumbled towers.

Women were noticeably absent that first week, except for the front cover of the *New Republic*, which featured a woman, well, a symbolic woman. The Statue of Liberty holds her burning beacon high with her right hand, the tall towers lit up behind her. On her body, the words "It happened here." Should the instant feminization of loss surprise us? Or the masculinist rush to save the day? Soon images of weeping widows and women in burkhas appeared in the media, strengthening "our" national resolve. It is interesting how quickly the official scenario of active men rescuing vulnerable women got reactivated. For an event labeled "unprecedented," "singular," a watershed that changed everything forever, it is clear how little the logic of justification had changed and how much it relied on gendering self and other. The attacks immediately triggered the same old scenario drawn from a repertoire of frontier lore: evil barbarians, threatened damsels protected by heroic males. Wanted: Dead or Alive.

Arts and sports fully engaged in the patriotic and militaristic spectacle. The Concert for the City of New York that October, highlighting artists such as Paul McCartney, the Rolling Stones, and the Who (to name a few), paraded police officers, firefighters, emergency and rescue workers, along with dozens of uniformed athletes to perform the heroics of the hitherto ordinary. Male bonding was not only okay again but sanctified. A handful of women appeared among the sea of uniforms. From our seats, we could feel the craving for protagonism on the part of the audience. Many of us had dutifully accepted our nonheroic roles by taking out our credit cards and paying to participate. The 800-number for contributions flashed on the screens around the stage, addressing the intended audience sitting at home watching TV rather than those of us physically there. We, the live, served as an enthusiastic background for the real show taking place in the public arena, a show of national unity and directionality that by-passed the public itself. As in the political arena, where daily polls tracked the growing support for war, our role was to sit back and clap. Sports clamored to get in the act. The Mets' first game after September 11 included a ceremony featuring uniformed men and flags in honor of those who had contributed to the rescue efforts. So, of course, did the Yankees'. Moments of silence and other commemorative acts froze us again in that forever time, September 11.

So what about us, the nonheroes who were not allowed to play, who were trying to do what the Mayor asked of us, that is, get on with our lives? At Tisch School of the Arts, some students lamented that they had chosen to pursue arts rather than medicine. At Bellevue Hospital, I heard a doctor say he was sorry he'd gone into medicine rather than rescue work.

But there was a competing spectacle on the streets. The entire surface of lower Manhattan was wrapped in images of the missing—the missing towers, the missing people.

84, 85. The first Mets game after September 11. Photos by Diana Taylor.

86. Someone drew the towers and inserted them where the Towers once stood, Brooklyn, September 2001. Photo by Lorie Novak. Reproduced by permission.

The loss of the Towers triggered a phantom limb phenomenon: the more people recognized the lack, the more they felt the presence of the absence.

Never had the Towers been so visible. Photos, postcards, T-shirts, banners, and street art immediately hit the streets, performing the existence of what no longer was physically there. Their ghostly presence, by definition a repetition, like Derrida's revenant, filled the vacuum. Instead of their ontology, we can think about their hauntology. At this moment, in New York, we were haunted.

The smiling faces of the missing also haunted. They were everywhere, but they were nowhere to be found: 8 × 10 Xerox and laser fliers taped on streetlamps, at bus stops, on mailboxes and hospital walls; theirs were the only happy faces in the city. The photos multiplied endlessly, making the absence of those in them more palpable. From the fliers, it looked as if the people in them came from every imaginable background and part of the world. Most were young. All were "legal" immigrants or citizens. Families of undocumented workers who worked in the Towers did not dare display their photos—yet one more disappearance. Mexicans would sometimes simply post an anonymous Virgen de Guadalupe to show that their loved one belonged among the missing.

87, 88. From the fliers, it looked as if the people in them came from every imaginable background and part of the world. Most were young. The undocumented victims disappeared from the walls much as they had disappeared from the Towers. Photo by Diana Taylor.

The photographs of the missing were recent: a man holding his newborn, a joyous family gathering with an arrow pointing to the lost person, a woman proudly holding up the fish she'd caught. The photos now had an entirely different function; we, the passersby, are begged to recognize and help locate the missing. In a sudden reversal, the relatively inanimate and flimsy photograph had outlasted its more "permanent" subject: the living person, the towering buildings.

On or around the photographs, someone had added text to convey something not in the photos themselves. The captions all note exact positions: "Last seen 85th floor, WTC 2." As with the September 11 crisis in general, the emphasis was on *where* people were. All but the essential particularities vanished, leaving the where, the when. The photos, as Barbara Kirshenblatt-Gimblett noted, conveyed hope; the captions anticipated the worst. They painfully mixed the intimate and forensic. They included physical descriptions as well as identifying body marks, envisioning that the loved ones, though, it was hoped, alive, would not be able to identify or speak for themselves. Sometimes the possible scenarios were explicitly spelled out. If you have any Jane Does please call. . . . Maybe the loved one was wandering around in shock? Sometimes, the captions imagined a body lying unconscious, exposed to the medical gaze: mole on back of thigh, heart-shaped tattoo on pelvic area, appendectomy scar. Family members made the rounds with stacks of fliers—St Vincent's, Bellevue, the VA—taping the fliers on all available surfaces as they went.

As opposed to the language of heroism, the fliers avoided the gendered pitfalls. Lorie Novak notes that men were identified as fathers, husbands, and brothers as often as women were described as executives, managers, and office assistants. Family photos included the missing in a wide variety of poses—fishing, holding children, cutting the birthday cake—few of them conventionally gendered. Both male and female photos and captions showed the loving perspective of a family member, intimately connected to that lost body.

The walls near Bellevue and St. Vincent's were called the Wall of Prayers and the Wall of Hope and Remembrance. On Wednesday, September 12, and Thursday the 13th, the areas were filled with family members searching for loved ones, pasting up fliers.

City officials couldn't use the photos; they asked family members to bring

89. Bellevue Hospital's Wall of Prayers. Photo by Diana Taylor.

in toothbrushes, cigarette butts, and hair clippings. Recognition in this day and age has more to do with DNA than with body marks and photography.

But the photographs fulfilled an enormous public function: they involved us, the nonheroes, nonvictims, in the search, in the hope, in the mourning. They enabled acts of transfer: the missing were now "ours," and New York City suddenly part of "America."

After the rain on Thursday and Friday, the fliers were covered with plastic sheets, shrouds for the victims, protection against further damage. The photos occupied the space of the missing bodies.

The "missing" signs turned into memorials: "In Loving Memory of . . ." Tiny shrines emerged, with messages, poems, photos, religious passages, flowers, stuffed bears, and children's drawings. People arrived with cameras, ready to memorialize in their own ways. Television cameras clogged the passageways.

The *New York Times* had started running portraits of the missing on September 15 as "Snapshots of Their Lives," a section that became "Portraits of Grief" after hope of the "lives" was gone.

Soon, the missing were officially declared dead. In October, the government handed small mahogany urns to the families of the victims, each one

90. New York City suddenly became part of "America." Photo by Diana Taylor.

91. The plastic shrouds for the victims' photographs protected them against further damage. Photo by Diana Taylor.

containing debris from the site. Although there were some strong parallels with countries such as Argentina, where victims were also pawns of terrorist violence and their bodies never found, the U.S. government wanted no "disappeared." Photographs of the victims' faces, unlike in the case of Argentina, have not been used in pro- or antimilitary demonstrations or to bring a performance claim against any individual, party, or political platform. This is not to say that financial claims have not been made on behalf of the victims. References to them continue to permeate our daily lives, but these have not involved the photographs. Somehow, the images remained particularized, cordoned off, a testimony to lives, now lost.

Loved ones used photographs to create portals for their dead. Tiny shrines, adorned with teddy bears and flowers, became the point of contact where the living went to communicate recent events with those no longer here to witness them. Somebody left a sonogram of their unborn child; someone else took a recent photo of the newborn baby to show the missing father. A son wrote a message to his dead mother. These sites became privileged conduits between here and there.

But where did the rest of us fit? And what was our role in this event, so often referred to as a tragedy? Because of the time lag between the first hit and the fall of the second tower, September 11 was an event that produced a huge number of eyewitnesses. The attack had also inscribed our positions. Everyone started their description by stating where they were, what they had seen. Yet it was clear from early on that "we" had no neat place in all of this. A photograph published in the *New York Times* the day after the attack had already converted witnesses into spectators. The caption read: "Spectators walking through debris from the World Trade Center." Those of us who lived here were deterritorialized, not just by the events but by official pronouncements that turned us into tourists, walking through.

People responded as citizens, however, wanting to help by giving blood or volunteering. But the city could not cope with the outpour of public participation. There were very few survivors in the hospitals, which already had more than enough blood. When the fliers of the missing started appearing, we were interpolated as potential heroes: PLEASE HELP!!! some fliers begged. The new spatial inscriptions asked us to interact with the city in a different way, as actors in the public space and not merely passive recipients or consumers. Many people responded by turning themselves into the embodi-

92, 93. Memorial shrines and portals for the dead. Photos by Lorie Novak.

94. (*left*) A photograph published in the *New York Times* the day after the attack had already converted witnesses into spectators. The caption reads: "Spectators walking through debris from the World Trade Center." Photo by Justin Lane for the *New York Times*.

95. (*below*) New Yorkers started interacting with the city in a different way, as active participants in a crisis. Photo by Diana Taylor.

96. A man reading the inscription on a mural by Chico, Lower East Side, New York City. Photo by Diana Taylor.

ment of unity and national fervor, wearing flags on jackets, as headscarves, as T-shirts; FDNY and NYPD baseball caps magically appeared on every street corner. Immigrants and people of color knew they would be targeted as terrorists and preemptively protected themselves behind the American flag. Artists, like mural artist Chico, offered their homage by painting walls and erecting shrines throughout the city. Public interventions in the parks gave people a place to participate actively and put forward their views about the escalating war talk and ethnic tensions. Thousands of people gathered daily in Union Square (among other places), turning every inch into a shrine, a protest, a performance event. This live interaction showed a far greater range of opinion than the TV coverage did, and soon the media stopped referring to this show of popular opinion.

Politicians hurried to interpret this show of civil activity in specific ways. Senator Lewis, who sits on the Senate Appropriations Committee, claimed he got the bellicose message of "the American people" behind these demonstrations: they're being patient, but they're not going to wait forever. Nonetheless, the show of activity made many officials nervous. Giuliani ordered the Park Service to take away the flowers, posters, candles, and other offerings, claiming that, after the rain, they made the city look dirty. Why would tourists visit a dirty city?

Many people participated by taking photographs. Inundated in images, we created our own. Thousands upon thousands of photographs flooded the public sphere, some highly professional and aesthetically compelling, but many more of them like mine, undistinguished and indistinguishable snapshots of the Towers, the fliers, the memorials. Photography was evidence, proof not so much of the existence of the object of the photograph but of our own existence. We, the backgrounded participants in this drama, were nonetheless *there*. In photography, some of us found an act of unity of sorts: we were all focused on the same thing, we were all framing what we saw from our position. Photography was also democratic: we could all point and shoot. Taking photos, for some, surely represented an effort to gain access, to gain understanding, both officially denied. It allowed people like me to formulate our own take in response to those circulated through the media. Maybe, too, it allowed us to confine disaster to pocket-size dimensions, 4 × 6s and 8 × 10s. It was a way of doing *something* when it seemed that nothing could be done. At the same time, photo taking has become a cultural habit,

97. Drawing by Marina Manheimer-Taylor. The writing on the flag reads: "bigotry/hate crimes/discrimination."

98. Local mural artists, like Chico from the Lower East Side, offered their homage. Photo by Diana Taylor.

99, 100, 101. The "live" performances, installations, and protests showed a far greater range of opinion than the TV coverage did. Photos by Diana Taylor.

102, 103. Towers for peace, towers for war . . . Photos by Diana Taylor.

a way of documenting without necessarily seeing, a way of entering into the structured frame of visibility: pointing, shooting, and posing. Two students recounted, with utter disbelief and self-disgust, that they had posed, smiling at the camera, with the burning towers behind them.

A gallery in SoHo offered space to *This Is New York,* an exhibit that understood the democratizing and testimonial role of photography in a time of social crisis by anonymously displaying all the photos submitted in relation to September 11. Those by famous professionals hung clipped to clotheslines next to those by everyone else.

Signs went up prohibiting photography near ground zero, which had been turned simultaneously into a battle zone, a crime scene, "a tragedy site," and a sacred site. The Mayor accused us of "gawking."

What I most remember of the months following September 11 is all about seeing, about the failure to understand what I was seeing with my own eyes, to make sense of the images in the media, and the downright prohibition of seeing and knowing imposed by the government. It wasn't just ground zero and popular protest that was blocked out. Coverage of the U.S. attacks on

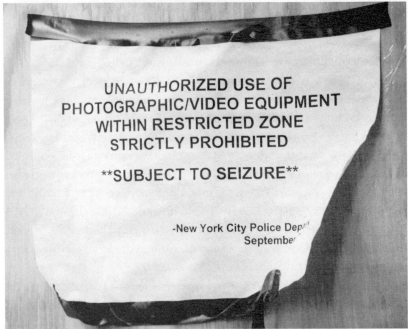

UNAUTHORIZED USE OF
PHOTOGRAPHIC/VIDEO EQUIPMENT
WITHIN RESTRICTED ZONE
STRICTLY PROHIBITED

SUBJECT TO SEIZURE

-New York City Police Dep···
Septembe···

104, 105. Signs went up prohibiting photography near ground zero. Photos by Diana Taylor.

Afghanistan was highly censored; surveillance was turned back on the public at home. The group Americans for Victory over Terrorism (AVOT) urged people to "support democratic patriotism when it is questioned; and take to task those groups and individuals who fundamentally misunderstand the nature of the war we are facing." University professors and public intellectuals critical of the war efforts were silenced and, at times, lost their jobs. Ashcroft announced that our democratic system made us vulnerable to the enemy. Like our airplanes and popular entertainment, our democracy had turned against us.

In the midst of this crackdown on dissent, we hear that "we" are indeed also actors in this tragedy, also victims of trauma. Victimization has been expanded to include not only "those who were viciously attacked" but an increasing number of others affected by the attacks. The *New York Times* included a small brochure inside the paper several times, *New York Needs Us Strong: Coping after Sept. 11,* that outlined the stress and trauma affecting "those who saw it happen from the street, or from their window, or over and over again on television." Funded by Project Liberty: Feel Free to Feel Better, the brochure adds that the disaster seems uncontainable: "Unlike other disasters that seem to have an end, the attacks on New York and Washington have been followed by other disturbing events, including the threat of bioterrorism." The anxiety, detachment, forgetfulness, and lack of concentration that the brochure links to the crisis are, of course, common symptoms of trauma. But what, I wonder, are the political ramifications of such a public discourse of victimhood in the face of the United States' expanding, and undefined, war against terrorism? Many of us have experienced trauma and struggled to regain some sense of balance in the face of accelerated global violence after September 11, but we might find more enabling models than the one put forth by Project Liberty. The Mothers of the Plaza de Mayo, to go back to Argentina for a moment, coped with their grief through the weekly, ritualized protest against the government. Women in Black meet weekly to protest and mourn the loss of life in the Middle East. Yet, amid talk of anxiety and detachment, we have been slow to mobilize against the escalating politics of violence, largely perpetuated by the U.S. government. Where is our ethical engagement?

If this is a tragedy, whose tragedy? As an aesthetic category, tragedy turns around the challenge of containment. Can Oedipus curb the tide of devasta-

106. People on the World Trade Center viewing platform. Photo by Diana Taylor.

tion that has wrecked Thebes? Hamlet's inability to act decisively leads to generalized death and the loss of the kingdom. Yet, tragedy is not just *about* containment, it functions as a structure of containment. Tragedy cuts catastrophe down to size. It orders events into comprehensible scenarios. Aristotle specifies that tragic events are of a certain magnitude, carry serious implications, and have an air of inevitability about them; protagonists have a "defined moral character," and the plot leads to recognition in the tragic hero as well as the spectator.[4] Most theories of tragedy identify the hero as committing a huge mistake, related to a tragic flaw or hubris. The massive potential for destruction depicted in tragedy is contained by the form itself, for tragedy delivers the devastation in a miniaturized and "complete" package, neatly organized with a beginning, middle, and end. Ultimately, tragedy assures us, the crisis will be resolved and balance restored. The fear and pity we, as spectators, feel will be purified by the action.

The events of September 11, however, make me think that we're looking at not only a different kind of war but a different kind of tragedy. When people refer to "the tragedy," they usually are referring to the unexpected fall of the mighty, to that awesome spectacle of pity and fear so brilliantly executed by the suicide pilots and so efficiently delivered nationally and globally by the U.S. media. They refer to the hijacked planes and the thousands of victims, to Bush Jr., hastily recast as a leader with a definable moral character, gearing up to set time right. Tragedy also allows us to stress the exceptional and isolated nature of the catastrophe and dovetails neatly with the language of the "unprecedented" and "watershed" occurrence. The catastrophe was certainly tragic in the vernacular sense, and the term offers us a vocabulary for fear and sorrow. Yet, I think that using *tragedy* in its aesthetic connotation not only structures the events but also blinds us to other ways of thinking about them.

Take tragedy's organizational timetable: beginning, middle, and end. Did the tragic action really start on September 11? Some might argue that we were hijacked long before, maybe starting in fall 2000, when the elections were pulled off course. Important items on the national agenda, such as improving education and health care, went up in smoke. The victims from that catastrophe remain uncounted, although they are certainly identified. New victims are created daily: antiterrorist legislation, anti-immigrant sentiment, racial profiling, and unaccountable military tribunals seep into our social system even as corporate welfare packages wind their way through the Congress. Others might point out that we have been on a seemingly inevitable collision course with Islamic oil-producing nations for decades. Should the civilian losses they have sustained figure among the victims? What about their trauma? As for the ending, nothing seems certain except that it won't be speedy, make sense, or bring purification and release.

And if this is a tragedy, who is the tragic hero? Bush Jr., as the representative of the United States, cannot take on the role because that would entail assuming a position of recognition and self-indictment. "Fearful and pitiable happenings," as Aristotle notes, involve a change "from good fortune to bad, and not thanks to wickedness but because of some mistake of great weight and consequence, by a man such as we have described" (38–39). Rather than owning that many of the events leading to September 11 resulted from a mistaken politics of great weight and consequences, however, the administration has stressed that this is about "good" fighting "evil." The struggle, moreover, lacks the linear directionality of tragedy. The war, too, is a revenant, a haunting: in simple terms, it's a replay of an earlier Bush war. More subtly, it's a recycling of Manifest Destiny ideology that justifies ("our") annihilating "evil" under the banner of righteousness. The victims lost in the World Trade Center, on the other hand, can't be the heroes unless we can pinpoint their tragic stature, their mistake, their recognition.

The events of September 11 become tragedy through claims to universality. The U.S. government and the media present it as a limit case, as "incommensurable," the greatest, worst, most unimaginable and unspeakable crisis ever. Commentators tend to place limit cases at the outer edges of intelligibility, at the very boundaries of representation. We can talk about them only in the language of exceptionalism. Limit cases are paradigmatic. They signal models to which many disparate issues can be related, but only by illustration. However, it is clear to most commentators outside the United States that the attacks, though criminal, were in no way exceptional. For many Latin Americans, for example, September 11 was all too familiar.[5] State terrorism and antistate terrorism vie for public control through escalating attacks on the civilian population, whether it's the bombing of buildings or the silencing of dissent. Talk of ground zero, moreover, illuminates what it most seeks to hide: that "ground zero" originally referred to Hiroshima and Nagasaki, the two sites bombed by U.S. nuclear forces that killed between one hundred thousand and three hundred thousand innocent people. The government's performance of innocence and Giuliani's cordoning off of the site urge the public to forget historical precedence. So, instead of the language of exceptionalism, there is a political argument to be made against the discourse of incommensurability. The language of tragedy and limit cases works against broader emancipatory politics because it detaches events, refusing to see connections and larger frameworks. Insulated claims to protagonism and universality work at odds with coalition building that enables cross-event understanding.

Finally, none of the tragic events seems destined to occasion recognition or insight in the spectators. On the contrary: September 11 created a revealing paradox. This is an event that banished and blinded the witnesses, even as it created them. Will purification and release come from participating in polls asking whether we support war efforts? What insights can we salvage from the rubble?

During the final phases of the cleanup, ground zero was open for viewing. The massive rubble that was the World Trade Center took on a life of its own. The twisted steel and pulverized concrete reminded us that the event was "real." Now that all that has been cleared away, the fenced-in display of sacralized remains provides the authenticating materiality that animates the resuscitations and sustains the performance of retribution. The Towers live. This moment of postdisappearance functions politically; the endless re-visualizations of the Towers will continue to motivate foreign and domestic policy. City officials and business advocates balance the demands of tourism with those of commercial real estate. Sixteen acres in lower Manhattan are too valuable to remain sacred for long. But the 7,700 viewers who visit the site daily need to have something to commemorate.[6] The negotiations demand yet more shifts in language and the creative concentration of the aura in one discrete place.

A few weeks before the final cleanup, I walked down to the site, stood in line for a ticket, waited hours for my assigned time, snaked through the viewing platform with dozens of other people. I took a photograph. There was nothing to see.

107. Debris from the World Trade Center, on display on the viewing platform. Photo by Diana Taylor.

108. Ground zero. There was nothing to see. Photo by Diana Taylor.

10

HEMISPHERIC PERFORMANCES

Sunday afternoon, September 20, 1998. Central Park. On this late summer afternoon, the sun was shining, the trees enclosed the idyllic lake before us, the Rollerbladers rushed behind us, the majestic apartments that frame the park boasted that we were in one of the world's great cities that can afford to stage the rural in the very heart of the urban. The music playing off to the side—the drums, the sticks, the complicated rhythm, the call-and-response singing—reminded us that other worlds coexist right in the middle of this one. The Marielitos, the Cuban boat people whom Castro had expelled as social deviants in 1980, were now playing rumba on Sundays alongside Puerto Ricans, Nuyoricans, and other Caribbean musicians who had been making music in the park for thirty years. It was them we had come to see, my students from the "Borders and Barrios" course I teach in performance studies. How, we wondered, did the music of resistance that originated among Afro-Cubans during slavery undergo transformation into an "event," a "fiesta," a celebration that involves improvisation, movement, singing, eating, drinking, and dancing, that included not just other Latinos but a whole community of spectators?

Berta Jottar, then a doctoral student in the department who is writing a book on rumba, described how René López, a musical historian, started bringing tapes of rumba to Puerto Rican musicians playing Latino jazz (blues, jazz, and funk) in the park. Previously, these musicians had picked up ideas about rumba through the mass media, shows such as *I Love Lucy* and other forms of popular culture. In other words, they had learned their music through what I have been calling the archive. In 1994, the Marielitos finally started playing with the Nuyoricans in Central Park. Their music, drawn from the repertoire of embodied performance, transmitted its handed-down rhythms and its own particular history. Initially, the Marielitos resisted invitations to play in the park. "My speculation," said Jottar, "is that they didn't want to be criminalized again, associated with a form that had been absolutely marginalized in the place they had come from. For them, rumba meant going back to a space of criminality that they were trying to erase."

The rumba had undergone another process of transformation in its found home in Central Park. The archive and the repertoire combined to produce new, transcultured rhythms to respond to this new, transcultured reality. And it retained its fiesta atmosphere. Cuban women sold Cuban *pasteles* on one side; Puerto Rican women sold their *arroz con gandules* on the other. We all stood around, swaying, some clapping, looking at the musicians, the lake, looking at each other looking, and enjoying the unlikely background for this outdoor performance. It was all so incongruous: Afro-Caribbeans playing music against the pines, rowboats, and luxury buildings. The Museum of Natural History across the street was hosting a major exhibit on Haiti that included musicians and voodun practitioners. When I looked out at the lake, I could almost imagine the music being a new version of the Buenavista Social Club variety, coming from some upscale sound system. Rumba, Jottar concluded, functioned as a space of identification and cross-identification. The music, a product of hybridization, was not concerned with maintaining "authenticity" or tradition. It was, by definition, about change and cultural contact. Because this was a performance event, I had brought my video camera. I taped the musicians' hands running authoritatively and expressively over the drums, their smiles and laughs as they communicated with each other. I talked to my daughter, Marina, to friends and students, and wondered why we didn't come to the park more often.[1]

The arrival of the NYPD ushered in a different kind of noise, a different kind of performance. The musicians dispersed, and the men in blue took center stage. Three police vehicles drove up. Instead of music, we had officers talking about permits, drugs, alcohol, and urination. Confusion. Cacophony.

109. Diana Taylor filming police in Central Park, New York City, 1998. Photo by Rosa G. Lizarde.

Everyone talking at once. What happened, we all asked? Queries, expressions of disbelief, demands for answers about *right to public space, right to assembly* were met with talk of Rules. Regulations. Rank. Superiors. Out comes the codebook—Sec 105 A subdivision 1, Assemblies, Meetings, Exhibitions, etc. "No Person shall hold or sponsor exhibit or contest, dramatic reading, poetry reading etc. unless fewer than twenty people can reasonably be expected to be in attendance." "We've been coming here for seventeen years," one musician pointed out. "And all of a sudden you come here and tell us we can't play? Come on. You know we're going to ask why." The more answers the officers gave us, the more confusing it became. Sometimes it was about the permit, other times about the number of people in attendance, sometimes about the beer, and still other times it had to do with people selling food. It was a bad joke: How many police officers and police cars does it take to inquire after a permit?

The police were also performing. "We're all professionals here," one officer said, acting for my camera. Would he have been so polite if I weren't white? Or in the pre–Rodney King era? Certain performances become especially problematic when they make it into the archive.

Another officer stressed the importance of etiquette, pointing out that he was addressing us with respect (another look at the camera). He prefaced each remark with a Miss or a Ma'am. An officer read from his little book, performing the proof of his legitimacy. (I was wondering if this dramatic reading too was unlawful, as there were certainly more than twenty of us in attendance.) "See?" he insisted; he was right and we were wrong. "What can we do or say to secure your lawful cooperation?" But what laws have been broken? It's not against the law to play music. "We're breaking the law because we're watching. If there weren't more than twenty people watching, no laws would be broken, right? So we're the criminals. You should harass us," I offered.

All of us there knew this was about race, language, and class—not about music, listeners, or even beer. One woman asked, "Do you arrest people who drink beer or wine as they watch Shakespeare in the Park?" The police talked about *discretion:* "There's a lot of rules and regulations being broken. We don't bother with them all." One musician laughed, saying he wished he'd worn a blonde wig. An officer approached an African American man, demanding to know if he worked. "I'm an electrical engineer," said the stunned bystander. The idyllic park, that appeared so incongruously open to all, was in fact what it seemed: a haven for the affluent city dwellers, anxious to enjoy the trees, grass, and water without the likes of "them/us." While everyone, it seems, loves Latin music, propelling world music CDs to the top of the charts, they don't want to deal with the brown bodies producing that music. Cultural taste prefers disembodied music and staged ethnicity in the Museum of Natural History.

This little corner, consisting of some 25 square feet facing the lake, had become only the latest site for Mayor Giuliani's free-floating practice of criminalization. One week the vehemence was directed at cab drivers, the next at methadone users, the next at the *rumberos.* What do they all have in common? Their groups are largely made up of men of color, the disenfranchised, the poor, the immigrants. Few people—people who matter to the politicians, that is—care about them.

Everyone was talking. The officers didn't like the discussion. They "don't want to split hairs," an increasingly impatient Officer Federico says. They just want us to go away. Aside from the three or four officers in uniform and the two out of uniform (who showed their badges on request), another two or three officers in uniform stood by, attentive. Two of them, an African

American and a Caucasian, had their hands on their pistols. They whispered into their walkie-talkies without taking their eyes off of us. Of course, we were all talking to each other too, resolving to do something. Write. Call the American Civil Liberties Union. The *New York Times.* A new community formed, new lines drawn in the sand between the suddenly all of "us" and the blue "them."

The history of criminalization of minority groups, we knew through our academic discussion on rumba, was inseparable from the history of rumba as resistance. Maybe the musicians had read the book? In a spontaneous movement that seemed to spark simultaneously in all the musicians, they returned to their drums, their sticks, their song, and suddenly we were all clapping, singing, celebrating the triumph of art over oppression. The police dispersed the group, "arrested" some instruments, and started hauling them away. When one of the musicians asked for his drum back, they arrested and handcuffed him without reading him his rights. "Why?" we demanded again, as they pushed him into one of three police vehicles and started driving away. The officers said something about there being a warrant out for his arrest. As some musicians quickly removed the remaining drums, others with sticks kept playing, using the back of the bench as their instrument. They sang, swayed, and we joined them in the last, sorrowful act of resistance. "You can take away our drums, but you can't take away our music," they said. "You can arrest one of us, but you'll have to come back forty thousand times to get us all." So this history of rumba continues, rumba persecuted during the period of slavery, rumba persecuted under Castro's Cuba of 1980, rumba persecuted now in this, our cleaner, whiter, safer New York. Safe for whom, I wonder? My daughter cried angrily as we took the subway home. "Mommy, you shouldn't have talked to the policeman like that. I was afraid he was going to kill you." "You didn't plan that, did you?" my students asked once we were back at NYU.

As it turned out, that was in fact the last performance of rumba in the park. We called the *New York Times,* and a reporter interviewed us and asked for our videotapes, now archival evidence. A short piece appeared a few days later. "Parks Commissioner Henry J. Stern said it was important to maintain quiet areas in the park. 'You can't play on the lake. . . . I know that Olmstead did not design Central Park as a rumba stage.'"[2] The charges against playing rumba in the park stuck. This is a park, not a stage, designed for certain kinds of performances and not others. Case closed.

This event in Central Park illuminates many of the issues that I've focused on throughout this study. The Americas, I had been taught to believe, are one—and I still believe it. Produced and organized through mutually constitutive scenarios, acts, transactions, migrations, and social systems, our hemisphere proves a contested and entangled space. The First World is in the Third World just as the Third World lives in the First. The apparent discreetness of nation-states, national languages, and official religions barely hides the deep intermingling of peoples, languages, and cultural practices. That day, Central Park provided one of the infinite sites of encounter and disencounter in which the dramas of unequal power relations, access, and legitimacy take place daily. Which scenarios become conceivable? How does performance make and legitimate its claim? What kinds of exchanges become admissible in designated spaces?

Histories and trajectories become visible through performance, although recognizing the challenges and limits of decipherability remains a problem. For example, we could trace resistant practices such as rumba to the middle passage, slavery, and the continued exploitation and criminalization of black peoples in various parts of the Americas. Repertoires of resistance would include additional forms—capoeira, samba, carnival, and hip-hop, to name a few.[3] Simultaneously, of course, other histories come into play. We would have to focus on the legacies of the cold war, especially the preferential treatment awarded to exiled Cubans in the United States, to explain the presence of the Marielitos in the park. Castro turned the tables on U.S. immigration policy that automatically welcomed the well-educated, politically conservative, white Cubans who fled communism by allowing impoverished people, many of them black and some of them released from prisons or mental institutions, to leave the island on flimsy rafts. The history of cold war tensions intersects at the same time with that of U.S. colonialism: Puerto Rico continues to be a colony and its population U.S. citizens. The Nuyoricans playing rumba in the park are living proof that postcolonial studies needs to address concomitant colonial and neocolonial realities to be relevant in the Americas. The ethnicity of the police officers bespeaks other waves of migration—Italian, Mexican, Irish—that in turn reflect crises in their lands of origin. Those of us standing around listening to the music signal other flows and circulations: international students hoping for a better education; people like me drawn to the United States by increased professional opportunities; tourists; those born in New York or attracted to its cosmopolitanism.

These many histories inform all the performances taking place simultaneously. Although each performance has its own tradition, they come together in the here and now in very specific ways. As I have argued throughout this study, embodied performance may draw from a rich repertoire, and illuminate a complex history, but it is always in situ, every particular instantiation marked by the confluence of traditions in a particular scenario. The architect Olmstead envisioned a certain type of performance when he designed Central Park. The Museum of Natural History continues its historical practice of including socially marginalized groups as exhibits. The police officers legitimate their performance by pointing to their *rules and regulations* book. My graduate class followed the academic ritual of the semiethnographic fieldtrip. Tourists enjoyed the rowboats, the food, and the music on this beautiful afternoon in September. The musicians were improvising on materials drawn from their cultural backgrounds, and the women who cooked under the pine trees drew from their repertoire of typical Caribbean foods. Rumba was just one of the traditions circulating that day, changing and adapting to its local circumstance.

Because performances always participate in social systems, they elucidate power relations. Rumba in the park clarified the positions occupied by the many social actors: the musicians displaced by the NYPD, who dominated the rest of the scene; the intervention of us spectators, who clearly saw ourselves implicated in the scenario. In fact, the rules and regulations book made it clear how central we all were. The fact that there were more than twenty of us had turned the episode into a criminal offense. The video and the photos recorded the happenings for posterior viewing by an unintended audience: the readers of the *New York Times*. Yet, although the event revealed the workings of power, it didn't do so in any straightforward way. The police could and could not stamp out the embodied performance of resistance offered by the musicians. While the musicians kept playing, affirming the near impossibility of fully policing the live ("You'll have to come back forty thousand times to get us all"), the police succeeded in prohibiting future access to Central Park.

But rumba plays on, in different street corners and bars throughout New York and throughout parts of the Americas, attracting new audiences. Racism, too, plays on, as does racial profiling, police misconduct, and official policies of exclusion. The trajectories continue their discontinuous, disjointed routes of encounters and disencounters. These tangled interactions make visible the many points of conflict and contact that have become constitutive of the Americas.

I close my study with this event in Central Park because, for most people, this was a nonevent. The little article tucked away in the City section of the Sunday *New York Times* did not provoke discussion or even a letter to the editor. As I wrote in chapter 3, "Public attention focuses on the 'event,' as a limit case that epitomizes the sensational and the extreme, but overlooks the crime of poverty, marginalization, and social inequality." Our explanatory models privilege the *paradigmatic* as a standout, exemplary instance to think about our hemisphere. We can think of the "discovery" of the Americas, the Conquest, the Dirty War in Argentina, the death of Diana, Princess of Wales, and the attacks on the World Trade Center as isolated limit cases. In dealing with limit cases, commentators resort to the language of exceptionalism and incommensurability. Todorov, for example, writes of the "discovery [as] the most astonishing encounter of our history" and the Conquest as "the greatest genocide in human history."[4] Descriptions of the attack on the World Trade Center overflow with superlatives: the worst, deadliest, unimaginable, unspeakable, unthinkable act of terror. *Nunca Más: The Report of the Argentine National Commission on the Disappeared* announced the closure of a singular and unprecedented period of state terrorism, never to be repeated. The death of Princess Diana, in its own way, pressed the limits. No royal figure, it seemed, had been so misunderstood, so loved, so mourned.

Thinking about events as limit cases insulates them. How can one place the incommensurable in a wider context? Limit cases signal models to which many disparate issues can be related, but only as illustration. We might say that someone is as egomaniacal as Caligula without suggesting a link. These cases, then, provide an example rather than elucidate causality. Clearly, in some instances, it seems politically urgent to emphasize the singularity and particularism of an event. The political organization of the children of the disappeared (H.I.J.O.S.), along with Grupo Arte Callejero (the activist artists who work with them), made a map of Buenos Aires using red dots to mark the exact location of torturers' homes and workplaces, as well as the many sites used as detention centers during the dictatorship. During the two-week encuentro of the Hemispheric Institute in Mexico, I proposed we extend the map to include all the Americas. The Argentine activists agreed in principle, though they made it clear that the larger mapping was not their project. Though recognizing the importance of positioning the Dirty War in Argentina as a limit case, I am convinced that a map of the Americas signaling the location of all those who participated in Plan Condor—from Washington, D.C., to Patagonia—would elucidate an important network of criminal collusion, including but not confined to economic and military trafficking. So there is also a political argument to be made against the discourse of incommensurability. As I have suggested throughout, the language of tragedy and uniqueness works against broader emancipatory politics because it detaches events from the context that might help explain them.

In this study, I have tried to put limit events into conversation with the daily, noneventful enactments of embodied practice. Instead of isolationist perspectives and politics, I've tried to focus on the messy entanglements that constitute hemispheric relations. If limit cases play well as tragedy, the perspective I'm advancing might best be represented in the simultaneous, jumbled, episodic practice of accumulation and saturation: *Now playing everywhere.* Instead of having all the elements of the plot tightly interwoven to culminate in crisis and dénouement, the episodic places events in a multilayered, concurrent, loosely structured arrangement. What happens in Scene A might not be causally related to Scenes B and C, but their placement either in space or time asks us to think them together. How can cultures of criminality originate in slavery, get reactivated in capitalist and "revolutionary" discourses, and migrate from Cuba to Central Park; that is, what scenarios perpetuate the notion and conditions of the disenfranchised as criminal? How, in turn, does that scenario contribute to the official criminalization of poverty that we saw played out in Castro's release of the Marielitos and in Giuliani's war on panhandlers?

Or let's rehearse a hemispheric analysis of two other events that I look at separately in this study: the attacks on the World Trade Center and the aftermath of the Dirty War. Unlike rumba in the park, they do not constitute one definable experience. The attack on the towers does not directly relate to the state terrorism in Argentina that the Abuelas, Madres, and H.I.J.O.S.

continue to protest. However, placing them together in a loose, episodic relationship makes evident their hemispheric linkage and encourages us to use them to understand each other. What do we mean by "terrorist"? Usually, governments use the term to refer to antistate "barbarians" and unassimilatable Others who use "illegitimate" forms of violence against them. The language against terrorism, however, immediately tends to slip over into the justification of state terrorism. This discourse, as we learn from both the Argentine and U.S. governmental response to terrorism, includes the decimation of civil liberties, the surveillance of national populations, the escalation in racial profiling, the use of increasingly suspect judicial and police procedures, and governmental association with known torturers and murderers.[5] What would distinguish legitimate from illegitimate forms of violence, appropriate from inappropriate targets, state precaution from state persecution? There is also a recognizable discourse of and about terrorism that relies on the language of good and evil, us versus them, the greater good, sacrifice, stifling dissent, and so forth. The links might prove helpful to populations dealing with issues of witnessing and collective trauma. The families of the missing in Argentina and the United States, to single out a specific subgroup, faced similar experiences: they used photographs to identify their missing and mourned their dead without being able to bury their bodies. Those who are not victims or perpetrators but witnesses to atrocities—another subgroup—are often blinded by governmental efforts to contain the situation. The "war on terror" produces public percepticide. Artists, activists, and scholars who live, work, or study situations of terror also need to explore how their work intervenes in this scenario. The points of contact abound, even though explorations beyond the designated limits remain few.

Downplaying the linear thrust of tragedy and presenting events episodically also permits us to see them as extending and overlapping horizontally, in temporal circles that continue to ripple outward. From this optic, we might well recognize a clear economic link between the World Trade Center catastrophe and the economic impact and aftermath of the Dirty War in Argentina. José Martínez de Hoz, the mastermind of the economic project behind the brutal military junta in the 1970s, forced the country to enter into a neoliberal, "global" economic system. That insertion produced its own form of social violence, as the country's population grew increasingly polarized into the haves and have-nots. The conditions that have been imposed through the International Monetary Fund have led to other disappearances, among them certain social services such as retirement benefits, health care, child care, and other forms of social security. The escalating social crisis prompted some newly impoverished retirees to commit suicide on Wednesday afternoon in front of the Casa Rosada in the Plaza de Mayo, the same place where the Madres de la Plaza de Mayo meet on Thursdays to protest the amnesty granted to the torturers and war criminals from the Dirty War. The terrorism unleashed by the state has given way to a more invisible form of violence unleashed through these fiscal policies. The Argentine economy collapsed. So, shortly thereafter, did the towers, symbols of global capitalism. Both crashes reflect an indictment of the hubris of promoting "world" economic systems that are thoroughly identified with the United States and its interests. Although IMF policies have left Argentina in shambles, Condoleezza Rice, Bush Jr.'s national security advisor, recently remarked, "We truly believe that if they [the Argentines] can just do the things that the IMF is requesting that they do [they can] find a way back to sustainable growth."[6]

The episodic modality expresses itself as a cacophony of voices, not as a monologue. The simultaneity of reactions and perspectives complicates any preferred interpretation. Unlike tragedy, the episodic structure works against the bracketing of a clear beginning and end, cause and effect, before and after. The beginning can be as arbitrary as the end is tentative. The ongoingness and continual juxtaposition of elements keep the framework open and flexible. As with rumba, improvisations build on earlier frameworks and traditions, and for a second, they come alive in the now of performance, only to keep moving, finding new audiences, making new claims. As opposed to tragedy, which imposes its brackets to accentuate the singularity of the limit case, the malleable episodic links reflect how the fallout of the attacks widen daily, affecting hemispheric relations as well as the rest of the world. The "war on terrorism" has expanded to Latin America, particularly Colombia, where it has replaced the militarized "war on drugs." Undocumented immigrants in the United States have either returned to their home country or risk being arrested for working without permits.[7] The Patriot Act authorizes the government to imprison "aliens" "potentially indefinitely, on mere suspicion, without any hearing."[8] The commitment to promoting democracy in the Americas, announced by Ronald Reagan in 1982, has noticeably waned. The attempted ouster of President Hugo Chavez of Venezuela in April 2002, first applauded as a "resignation" by U.S. government officials, was later declared a coup supported and financed by the U.S. government.[9] The loss of enthusiasm for supporting democratic principles in Latin America, under the guise of the new urgency for national self-interest, echoes U.S. Attorney General John Ashcroft's ambivalent relationship to democracy and constitutional protections at home. The examples go on and on.

A hemispheric perspective stretches the spatial and temporal framework to recognize the interconnectedness of seemingly separate geographical and political areas and the degree to which our past continues to haunt our present. The reassuring slash between past/present cannot, in fact, keep these distinct. Talk of tragedy, like references to limit cases, gives these events an aesthetic wholeness and a political insularity that obfuscates our understanding of them.

Now is a time for remapping the Americas. This means reconfiguring cold war area studies into hemispheric studies, even while we recognize that cold war ideologies continue under more modern guise. Without ever assuming that "new" methodologies and configurations free themselves from the ideological shackles of their originating condition, the shift at least allows us to illuminate some blind spots. Decentering a U.S. *America* for a hemispheric *Americas* seems urgent and overdue. This remapping would also show histories and trajectories omitted from earlier maps; we could include the routes made through specific migrations by exploring embodied performances such as the pastorela, moros y cristianos, carpa, and other performances I've mentioned in passing here. We might look at how ancient rural performances, such as the Fiesta de la Virgen del Carmen in Paucartambo, Peru, migrate from the Andes to the capital as escalating economic demands disperse local populations. These migrants take their performances with them, establishing an urban version of their traditional fiesta. When these migrants disperse further, to the New York area, for example, their fiesta travels too, changing once again in transmission. All these changes are multidirectional; that is, they in turn affect the way the performances function back home, whether home is now Lima or Paucartambo. The ways the organizing principles of the fiesta change or adapt—in terms of leadership, funding, decision making, the formation of the comparsas, the changes in tradition that need to be justified by competing, often invented, traditions—illuminate much about the multiple pressures and pulls of the local by the global. These repertoires show migrations left out of histories that base themselves solely on archival materials and offer us additional sites and critical tools for understanding.

Recognizing performance as a valid focus of analysis contributes to our understanding of embodied practice as an episteme and a praxis, a way of knowing as well as a way of storing and transmitting cultural knowledge and identity. Performance as a lens enables commentators to explore not only isolated events and limit cases, but also the scenarios that make up individual and collective imaginaries. Performances such as rumba in the park make visible those social actors, scenarios, and power relations that have been overlooked and disappeared over and over again. Performance studies can allow us to engage in a sustained historical analysis of the performance practices that both bind and fragment the Americas. As such, it plays a vital role in the remapping. That's what I'm asking it to do.

NOTES

CHAPTER ONE. ACTS OF TRANSFER

1   The Hemispheric Institute of Performance and Politics is a consortium of institutions, scholars, artists, and activists in the Americas who explore the intersections of "performance" and politics (both broadly construed) in the Americas since the sixteenth century. For more information, see http://hemi.nyu.edu.

2   Tim Weiner, in "Pummeling the Powerful, with Comedy as Cudgel," *New York Times*, June 15, 2001, A4, writes that "when Jesusa Rodríguez is on—onstage, on camera, in the streets protesting the latest outrage—she may be the most powerful woman in Mexico."

3   Richard Schechner, *Between Theater and Anthropology* (Philadelphia: U of Pennsylvania P, 1985), 36. I am indebted to Paul Connerton for the term "acts of transfer," which he uses in his excellent book, *How Societies Remember* (Cambridge: Cambridge UP, 1989), 39.

4   The as/is distinction is Richard Schechner's; see his *Performance Studies: An Introduction* (London: Routledge, 2002), 30–32. However, we disagree on whether the *is* reflects an ontology. For Schechner, "performance is anything but ontological. . . . It is socially constructed through and through" (personal correspondence). I find the tension between the ontological and constructed more ambiguous and constructive, underlining the field's understanding of performance as both "real" and "constructed."

5   "Here the etymology of 'performance' may give us a helpful clue, for it has nothing to do with 'form,' but derives from Old French parfournir, 'to complete' or 'carry out thoroughly.'" Victor Turner, *From Ritual to Theatre* (New York: Performing Arts Journal Publications, 1982), 13.

6   *The Barnhart Dictionary of Etymology* states that Steele, writing in *Tatler* in 1709, used the term in "the sense of a public exhibition or entertainment" and in 1711 to refer to "the one who performs" (777).

7   "We will know one another better by entering one another's performances and learning their grammars and vocabularies." Victor Turner, "From a Planning Meeting for the World Conference on Ritual and Performance," quoted in introduction to *By Means of Performance: Intercultural Studies of Theatre and Ritual*, ed. Richard Schechner and Willa Appel (New York: Cambridge UP, 1990), 1.

8   Susan Blackmore, "The Power of Memes," *Scientific American* (October 2000): 65.

9   Peggy Phelan, *Unmarked: The Politics of Performance* (London: Routledge, 1993), 146.

10   Joseph Roach, *Cities of the Dead: Circum-Atlantic Performance* (New York: Columbia UP, 1996), 26.

11   J. L. Austin, *How to Do Things with Words*, 2d ed. (Cambridge, MA: Harvard UP, 1975), 6.

12   As Jacques Derrida put it in writing about Austin's performative: "Could a performative utterance succeed if its formulation did not repeat a 'coded' or iterable utterance?" "Signature Event Context," in *Margins of Philosophy*, trans. Alan Bass (Chicago: U of Chicago P, 1982).

13   Ibid., 326.

14   See, for example, Emile Durkheim, *The Elementary Forms of the Religious Life* (New York: Free Press, 1915).

15   See John Searle, "What Is a Speech Act," in *Philosophy in America*, ed. Max Black (Ithaca: Cornell UP, 1965); Dell Hymes, "Breakthrough into Performance," in *Folklore, Performance and Communication*, ed. D. Ben-Amos and K. S. Goldstein (Hague: Mouton, 1975); Dell Hymes, "The Ethnography of Speaking," in *Anthropology and Human Behavior*, ed. T. Gladwin and W. Sturtevant (Washington: Anthropological Society of Washington, 1982); Richard Bauman, *Verbal Art as Performance* (Rowley, MA: Newbury House, 1977); Charles Briggs, *Competence in Performance* (Philadelphia: U of Pennsylvania P, 1988); Michele Rosaldo, "The Things We Do with Words," *Language in Society* 11 (1982): 203–35. I am indebted to Faye Ginsburg and Fred Myers for helping me sort out the various streams in anthropology dealing with performance and performativity. I am also indebted to Aaron Glass's unpublished manuscript, "Performance and Performativity: Cultural and Linguistic Models" (June 2002), for clarifying some of the influences in these streams.

16   Turner, *From Ritual to Theatre*, 9.

17   Michael Kirby, "Environmental Theatre," in *Total Theatre*, ed. E. T. Kirby (New York: Dutton, 1969), 265.

18   "They had one very striking thing. At each of four corners or turns that the road made, there was constructed a mountain and from each mountain there rose a high cliff. The lower part was made like a meadow, with clumps of herbs and flowers and everything else that there is in a fresh field; the mountain and the cliff were as natural as if they

had grown there. It was a marvellous thing to see, for there were many trees: wild trees, fruit trees, and flowering trees, and mushrooms and fungus and the lichen that grows on forest trees and rocks. There were even old broken trees; in one place it was like a thick wood and in another it was more open. On the trees were many birds, both big and small: falcons, crows, owls; and in the wood much game; there were stags, hares, rabbits, coyotes, and very many snakes. These last were tied and their fangs drawn, for most of them were of the genus viper, a fathom in length and as big around as a man's arm at the wrist. . . . In order that nothing might be lacking to make the scene appear completely natural, there were hunters with their bows and arrows well concealed on the mountain. . . . One had to look sharply to see these hunters, so hidden were they and so covered with branches and lichen from the trees, for the game would easily come right to the feet of men so concealed. Before shooting, these huntsmen made many gestures which aroused the attention of the unsuspecting public." Fray Toribio Motolinía, *History of the Indians of New Spain*, ed. and trans. Elizabeth Andros Foster (New York: Cortés Society, 1950), 102–3.

19 Fernando Ortiz, *Contrapunteo cubano del tabaco y el azucar* (Caracas: Biblioteca Ayacucho, 1978).

20 Patrice Pavis, ed., *The Intercultural Performance Reader* (London: Routledge, 1996), 25.

21 Clifford Geertz, *The Interpretation of Cultures* (New York: Basic Books, 1973), 10.

22 *El* performance usually refers to events coming out of business or politics, whereas the feminine *la* usually denotes those that come from the arts. I am indebted to Marcela Fuentes for this observation.

23 Michel de Certeau, *The Writing of History*, trans. Tom Conley (New York: Columbia UP, 1988), xxv.

24 In *Colonial Encounters: Europe and the Native Caribbean, 1492–1797* (London: Routledge, 1986), for example, Peter Hulme discusses the narrative of the encounter within the general rubric of "colonial discourse," thereby accentuating the tropes and "linguistically-based practices" that stemmed from it (2).

25 Guy Debord, *Society of the Spectacle* (Detroit: Black and Red, 1983), 4; Diana Taylor, *Disappearing Acts: Spectacles of Gender and Nationality in Argentina's Dirty War* (Durham: Duke UP, 1997), 119.

26 Angel Rama, *The Lettered City*, trans. John Charles Chasteen (Durham: Duke UP, 1996), 29–30.

27 Enrique Florescano, *Memory, Myth, and Time in Mexico: From the Aztecs to Independence*, trans. Albert G. Bork (Austin: U of Texas P, 1994), 39.

28 De Certeau, *Writing of History*, 216.

29 Walter W. Skeat, *A Concise Etymological Dictionary of the English Language* (New York: Perigee, 1980), 24.

30 Ibid., 443. I use *repertoire* rather than *repertory* for somewhat obscure reasons. *Repertoire*, according to the *OED*, refers to "a stock of dramatic or musical pieces which a company or player is accustomed or prepared to perform" (2: 466). *Repertory*, on the other hand, refers to more "archival" kinds of knowledge: "An index, list, cata-

logue or calendar" and a "storehouse, magazine or repository, where something may be found" (467).

31 Richard Flores, *Los Pastores: History and Performance in the Mexican Shepherd's Play of South Texas* (Washington: Smithsonian Institution Press, 1995).

32 Max Harris, *Aztecs, Moors, and Christians: Festivals of Reconquest in Mexico and Spain* (Austin: U of Texas P, 2000).

33 Rebecca Schneider, in "Archives Performance Remains," asks whether "in privileging an understanding of performance as a refusal to remain, do we ignore other ways of knowing, other modes of remembering, that might be situated precisely in the ways in which peformance remains, but remains differently?" *Performance Research* 6, no. 2 (2001): 101.

34 Jesús Martín-Barbero, "Memory and Form in the Latin American Soap Opera," trans. Marina Elias, in *To Be Continued . . . Soap Operas around the World,* ed. Robert C. Allen (London: Routledge, 1995), 276–84.

35 Quoted in Thomas A. Abercrombie, *Pathways of Memory and Power: Ethnography and History among an Andean People* (Madison: U of Wisconsin P, 1998), 12.

36 Pierre Nora, "Between Memory and History: Les Lieux de Mémoire," in *History and Memory in African-American Culture*, ed. Geneviève Fabre and Robert O'Meally (New York: Oxford UP, 1994), 284, 289.

37 Though it seems intuitive that the live event associated with the repertoire would pre-cede the documentation of the archive, this is not necessarily the case. An original live theater performance might well interpret an ancient text. Or, to give a very different kind of example, obituaries of famous people are usually written before they die, so that the media immediately have the materials when the time comes.

38 "Masterpieces of the Oral and Intangible Heritage of Humanity," http://www.unesco.org/culture/heritage/intangible/index.shtml, accessed in 2002. The UNESCO docu-ment continues: "UNESCO seeks to draw attention to cultural spaces or traditional and popular forms of cultural expression. We have to be quite clear about the difference be-tween a cultural space and a site. From the standpoint of the cultural heritage, a site is a place at which physical remains created by human genius (monuments or ruins) are to be found. A 'cultural space' is an anthropological concept that refers to a place or a series of places at which a form of traditional or popular cultural expression occurs on a regular basis. But the value of such cultural expression is not necessarily dependent on a particular space. For example, when storytellers traditionally ply their art either at the same place or at fixed times, we have a cultural space. But other storytellers may by tradition be iterant performers and their performance a cultural expression. Both cultural spaces and cultural expressions qualify to be regarded as masterpieces of the oral and intangible heritage of humanity."

39 Mary Carruthers, *The Book of Memory: A Study of Memory in Medieval Culture* (New York: Cambridge UP, 1990), 16.

40 De Certeau, *Writing of History*, 216.

41 Sigmund Freud, "A Note upon the 'Mystic Writing-Pad,'" in *The Standard Edition of*

the Complete Psychological Works of Sigmund Freud, ed. James Strachey (London: Hogarth Press, 1953–74), 19: 229.

42   Jacques Derrida, "Freud and the Scene of Writing," in *Writing and Difference,* trans. Alan Bass (Chicago: U of Chicago P, 1978), 197.

43   Roland Barthes, *Image-Music-Text,* trans. Stephen Heath (New York: Hill and Wang, 2001), 32.

44   Roland Barthes, *Mythologies,* trans. Annette Lavers (New York: Noonday Press, 1988), 110. He adds: "We shall therefore take language, discourse, speech etc., to mean any significant unit or synthesis, whether verbal or visual . . . even objects will become speech, if they mean something" (111). In his posthumous work, *Empire of Signs,* trans. Richard Howard (New York: Hill and Wang, 2000), Barthes refers to "three writings" in Bunraku performance to signal "three sites of spectacle: the puppet, the manipulator, the vociferant: effected gesture, effective gesture, and the vocal gesture" (48–49).

45   Barbara Kirshenblatt-Gimblett, "Folklore's Crisis," *Journal of American Folklore* 111, no. 441 (1998): 309–11.

46   This is not the same project as many so-called interdisciplinary programs in the United States, where teams of scholars, training in one traditional field, coteach students in a particular course. Rather, performance studies helps students acquire the training they need to rigorously examine materials in the archive and the repertoire even as they challenge the boundedness of the "field."

47   See Dwight Conquergood, "Interdisciplinary Interventions and Radical Research," paper presented at the Cultural Intersections Conference, Northwestern University, October 9, 1999.

48   *Oxford English Dictionary,* 1976 ed.

49   See D. Taylor, *Disappearing Acts,* ch. 5. I return to the concept of percepticide in the last chapter of this study.

50   V. Propp. *Morphology of the Folktale,* trans. Laurence Scott (Austin: U of Texas P, 1988).

51   My thanks to Doris Sommer for this observation.

52   Michel de Certeau, *The Practice of Everyday Life* (Berkeley: U of California P, 1984), 117.

53   See Richard Trexler, "We Think, They Act: Clerical Readings of Missionary Theatre in Sixteenth-Century New Spain," in *Understanding Popular Culture: Europe from the Middle Ages to the Nineteenth Century,* ed. Steven L. Kaplan (Berlin: Mouton, 1984). See also Max Harris's critique of Trexler's argument in his essay, "Disguised Reconciliations: Indigenous Voices in Early Franciscan Missionary Drama in Mexico," *Radical History* 53 (spring 1992): 13–22.

54   See Max Harris, *Aztecs, Moor, and Christians,* 23.

55   See Motolinía, *History,* ch. 15; Max Harris, *The Dialogical Theatre* (New York: St. Martin's Press, 1993), ch. 6; and James C. Scott, *Domination and the Arts of Resistance* (New Haven: Yale UP, 1990).

56   See Jill Lane's essay, "On Colonial Forgetting: The Conquest of New Mexico and Its Historia," in *The Ends of Performance,* ed. Peggy Phelan and Jill Lane (New York: New York UP, 1998).

57 Ibid., 58.

58 Bourdieu defines habitus: "The structures constitutive of a particular type of environ-ment (e.g. the material conditions of existence characteristic of a class condition) pro-duce *habitus*, systems of durable, transposable *dispositions*, structured structures pre-disposed to function as structuring structures, that is, as principles of the generation and structuring of practices and representations which can be objectively 'regulated' and 'regular' without in any way being the product of obedience to rules, objectively adapted to their goals without presupposing a conscious aiming at ends or an express mastery of the operations necessary to attain them and, being all this, collectively orchestrated without being the product of the orchestrating action of a conductor." Pierre Bourdieu, *Outline of a Theory of Practice*, trans. Richard Nice (Cambridge, En-gland: Cambridge UP, 1989), 72.

59 For a reflection on this issue, see James Clifford, "Introduction: Partial Truths," in *Writing Culture: The Poetics and Politics of Ethnography*, ed. James Clifford and George E. Marcus (Berkeley: U of California P, 1986), 1–26.

60 Saidiya V. Hartman, *Scenes of Subjection: Terror, Slavery, and Self-Making in Nine-teenth-Century America* (New York: Oxford UP, 1997), 4.

61 Friar Francisco de Avila, *The Huarochiri Manuscript: A Testament of Ancient and Colonial Andean Religion*, ed. Frank Salomon (Austin: U of Texas P, 1991), 41.

62 Fray Diego Durán, *History of the Indies of New Spain*, trans. Doris Heyden (Norman: U of Oklahoma P, 1994), 3.

63 José de Acosta, *Historia natural y moral de las Indias* (Mexico City: Fondo de Cultura Económica, 1962).

64 Patrick Johansson, ed., *Teatro mexicano: Historia y dramaturgia*, vol. 1: *Festejos, ritos propiciatorios y rituals prehispáncios* (Mexico City: Consejo para la Cultura y las Artes, 1992), 30, quoting Fray Juan de Torquemada.

65 Fernando Alvarado Tezozómoc, "Thus They Have Come to Tell It," in *Crónica mexi-cana* (4–6), quoted in Miguel León-Portilla, *Pre-Columbian Literatures of Mexico*, trans. Grace Lobanov and Miguel León-Portilla (Norman: U of Oklahoma P, 1969), 117.

66 Abercrombie, *Pathways*, 6.

67 Barbara Kirshenblatt-Gimblett, *Destination Culture: Tourism, Museums, and Heritage* (Berkeley: U of California P, 1998).

68 Bruno Latour, "A Few Steps toward an Anthropology of the Iconoclastic Gesture," *Sci-ence in Context* 10, no. 1 (1997): 63.

69 Bernardino de Sahagún, *Florentine Codex*, ed. and trans. Arthur J. O. Anderson and Charles E. Dibble (Santa Fe, NM: School of American Research and University of Utah, 1982), *Introductions and Indices*, prologue to book 1, 56, 57.

70 Ibid.

71 "Ĭmĭtāri . . . de la misma familia que *imago* 'imagen.'" Joan Corominas, *Breve diccio-nario etimológico de la lengua castellana* (Madrid: Gredos, 1961), 332.

72 James Lockhart, *The Nahuas after the Conquest* (Stanford: Stanford UP, 1992), 238.

73 "Ixiptlas were everywhere, the sacred powers represented in what we would call mul-

tiple media in any particular festival—a stone image, richly dressed and accoutred for the occasion; in elaborately constructed seed-dough figures; in the living body of the high priest in his divine regalia, and in the living god-image he would kill: human, vegetable and mineral ixiptlas." There were three criteria: (1) it was "a made, constructed thing"; (2) "it was formally 'named' for the particular sacred power, and adorned with some of its characteristic regalia"; and (3) "it was temporary, concocted for the occasion, made and unmade during the course of the action. (The great images within the shrines . . . were not described as ixiptlas, nor were they processed or publicly displayed.)" Inga Clendinnen, *The Aztecs: An Interpretation* (Cambridge: Cambridge UP, 1991), 252.

74 Ibid.

75 Rémi Siméon, *Diccionario de la lengua náhuatl o mexicana* (Mexico City: Siglo Veintiuno, 1977); Clendinnen, *The Aztecs*, 253.

76 Sahagún, *Florentine Codex*, prologue to book 2, *The Ceremonies*, 53.

77 Performance was certainly crucial to maintaining sociopolitical order. Political power was sustained by hegemony rather than force. See Ross Hassig, *Aztec Warfare* (Norman: U of Oklahoma P, 1988), 19. Given the need to maintain hegemonic order, performance served to maintain and communicate dominance (military, political, social). Power was made visible through the show of force and order (Flower Wars, conquest wars, dress codes).

78 Sahagún, *Florentine Codex*, prologue to book 1, 45.

79 See Steven Mullanay, *The Place of the Stage* (Ann Arbor: U of Michigan P, 1988), for an analysis of "the spectacle of strangeness" and the politics of repudiation (particularly ch. 3, "The Rehearsal of Cultures").

80 Maya Ramos Smith, Tito Vasconcelos, Luis Armando Lamadrid, and Xabier Lizarraga Cruchaga, eds., *Censura y teatro novohispano (1539–1822): Ensayos y antología de documentos* (Mexico City: Conaculta, INBA, Citru, 1998), 239–40. Quotations that follow are from this source; all translations are mine.

81 "The Ordinances of Tomás López, of the Royal Audience of Confines, promulgated in 1552," in Friar Diego de Landa, *Yucatán: Before and after the Conquest*, trans. William Gates (Mexico City: San Fernando, 1993).

82 Halbwach, *On Collective Memory*, ed. and trans Lewis A. Coser (U of Chicago P, 1992), 38.

83 Roach, *Cities*, 26.

84 See Maria Concepcion García Saiz, *Las castas mexicanas/The Mexican Castes* (Milan: Olivetti, 1989).

85 Durán, for example, claimed that religious conversion was happily accepted, that Indians "began to abandon their idols. They broke them, mocked them, stepped on them, and demolished the cues where these images had been. . . . it was an amazing thing to see the millions who came for this baptism and who gave up the blindness in which they had lived" (*History*, 562).

86 Sahagún, *Florentine Codex*.

87 Fray Diego Durán, *Book of the Gods and Rites and the Ancient Calendar*, ed. and trans. Fernando Horcasitas and Doris Heyden (Norman: U of Oklahoma P, 1971), 51.

88 The quotation is "andan mirando como monos para contrahacer todo cuanto ven." Fray Toribio Motolinía, *Historia de los Indios de la Nueva España* (Mexico City: Editorial Porrúa, 1969); Motolinía, *History*, book 1, 104.

89 See W. J. T. Mitchell, *Iconology: Image, Text, Ideology* (Chicago: U of Chicago P, 1986), "The Rhetoric of Iconoclasm" (final chapter).

90 Lockhart, *The Nahuas* (237–38), describes the transmission of social, administrative, and individual memory through the indigenous practice of keeping images of saints in small sacred spaces. These practices, which looked Christian, continued to organize the community after the Conquest. The *santopan* ("where the saint is," a term for a sub-entity of the *altepetl*, an administrative area or "sociopolitical entity"), the *teocalli* or god's house, and little individual saint houses ("my little building where an image is") all helped transmit communal and "household identity" from one generation to the next. The saints, Lockhart argues, also supported claims to land rights, as they were seen as "parents of their people and as true owners of the unit's land" (237).

91 Roach, *Cities*, 2.

92 See Stafford Poole, *Our Lady of Guadalupe: The Origins and Sources of a Mexican National Symbol, 1531–1797* (Tucson: U of Arizona P, 1996), 12.

93 There are particular Virgins for many parts of the world colonized by the Catholics: Virgen de la Candelaria, Virgen del Carmen, Virgen del Camino, Virgen de la Soledad, and Virgen de Zapopan (Guadalajara) that Mary Louise Pratt studies. Pratt traces the ways the Virgen de Zapopan has "multiplied" since 1734 to reach her new worshippers. She most recently appeared in Los Angeles in 1998 as "La Viajera" (the traveler) to be near the Mexican population that could not safely come to her.

94 Diego de Landa, quoted in Inga Clendinnen, *Ambivalent Conquests* (Cambridge, England: Cambridge UP, 1987), 194.

95 Clendinnen, *Ambivalent Conquests*, 83.

96 Ramos Smith et al., *Censura y teatro*, 260.

CHAPTER TWO. SCENARIOS OF DISCOVERY: REFLECTIONS ON PERFORMANCE AND ETHNOGRAPHY

1 Gary Richman, "Expedition Claims to Have Found New Tribe in Amazon Rain Forest," *Valley News* (Lebanon, NH), September 11, 1995, A8.

2 Connerton, *How Societies Remember*, 64.

3 Propp, *Morphology*, 20ff.

4 References to this letter are from B. W. Ife, ed. and trans., *Letters from America: Columbus's First Accounts of the 1492 Voyage* (London: King's College London, School of Humanities, 1992), 25; and R. H. Major, ed., *Christopher Columbus: Four Voyages to the New World, Letters and Selected Documents* (Gloucester, MA: Peter Smith, 1978). Columbus's original letter to the King and Queen, written in 1493, was his first account

of his voyage. In the introduction to the Major edition, John E. Fagg notes the instability of the text: "This letter was apparently enclosed with another that has been lost, one dispatched by Columbus to Ferdinand and Isabella. The original of our letter has also disappeared, though eight copies of it remain extant. In 1847, when R. H. Major edited this selection of documents for the Hakluyt Society, he relied on Martin Fernández de Navarrete's invaluable collection. Much later, the Hakluyt Society issued a similar publication but, in the case of the Letter on the First Voyage, was able to use a more accurate text based on a folio unknown to Major" (vii).

5   Christopher Columbus, *The Journal of Christopher Columbus*, trans. Cecil Jane (New York: Clarkson N. Potter, 1960), 23.

6   Christopher Columbus, *The Four Voyages of Christopher Columbus*, ed. and trans. J. M. Cohen (Middlesex, England: Penguin Books, 1969), 53.

7   Major, *Columbus*, first letter, 16–17.

8   B. W. Ife, translator and editor of the King's College edition of Columbus's "Letter to the Monarchs," writes that the act of possession included three essential steps: "It took a physical, symbolic form (cutting the branch of a tree, drinking water or eating fruit), and, to be valid in law, had to be witnessed, preferably by Crown representatives. In addition, those who were being dispossessed had themselves to give permission; hence the significance of Columbus' insistence that there had been no opposition" (*Letters*, 25, n.2).

9   Stephen Greenblatt, ed., *New World Encounters* (Berkeley: U of California P, 1991), 55; Tzvetan Todorov, *The Conquest of America*, trans. Richard Howard (New York: Harper Colophon, 1984).

10   Patricia Seed, *Ceremonies of Possession in Europe's Conquest of the New World, 1442–1640* (New York: Cambridge UP, 1995), makes the important point that though these scenarios were "readily understood" by the colonizers' countrymen, the scenarios differed significantly among the various colonizing groups in the Americas—Spanish, British, Portuguese, French and Dutch. "Their rituals, ceremonies, and symbolic acts of possession overseas were based upon familiar actions, gestures, movements or speeches, and as such were readily understood by themselves and their fellow countrymen without elaboration, and often without debate as well" (3). But it would be a mistake, she warns, to extend that familiarity to "homogenize the five major powers colonizing the Americas into a single identity: 'Europe'" (3). The scenarios of discovery share notable features but also manifest important variations of a theme.

11   Major, *Columbus*, first letter, 29.

12   Columbus, *Journal*, 23–24.

13   Ife, *Letters*, 27.

14   Columbus, *Four Voyages*, 57. Quotations that follow are from this source.

15   Greenblatt, *New World*, 61.

16   For example, Durán's assertion that they were Jews (chapter 1).

17   Anthony Pagden, "Translator's Preface" to *Hernán Cortés: Letters from Mexico*, by Hernán Cortés (New Haven: Yale UP, 1986), states, "Like Columbus and Vespucci be-

fore him, Cortés realized the full political importance of the printing press. The open public legitimation of his behavior would be harder for the crown to ignore than a public request, which is probably one of the reasons why the letters were banned in 1527. But Cortés was also aware of the importance of arguing his case before posterity. If his *fama et gloria* which, as he knew, were the nobleman's most precious, and most precarious, possessions were to survive they had to be preserved for a later generation on his own terms, and in print" (xliv).

18   Susanne Zantop, *Colonial Fantasies* (Durham: Duke UP, 1997), 2.

19   See Patricia Seed, "The Requirement: A Protocol for Conquest," in *Ceremonies of Possession.*

20   Bartolomé de las Casas, *Obra indigenista* (Madrid: Alianza Editorial, 1985), 165; Juan Ginés de Sepúlveda, *Demócrates segundo, o de las justas causas de la guerra contra los indios* (Madrid: Consejo Superior de Investigaciones Científicas, 1951).

21   David E. Stannard, *American Holocaust: The Conquest of the New World* (New York: Oxford UP, 1992), x.

22   Coco Fusco, *English Is Broken Here: Notes on Cultural Fusion in the Americas* (New York: New Press, 1995), 39.

23   See chapter 1 for a discussion of performance as an object of study in performance studies and as a theoretical lens.

24   See James Clifford, *The Predicament of Culture: Twentieth-Century Ethnography, Literature, and Art* (Cambridge, MA: Harvard UP,1988).

25   For a discussion of the ethnographic fairs, see Fatimah Tobing Rony, *The Third Eye: Race, Cinema, and Ethnographic Spectacle* (Durham: Duke UP, 1996).

26   Jorge Portilla, *La fenomenología del relajo* (Mexico City: Fondo de Cultura Economica, 1986), describes relajo as a three-part process: (1) a displacement of attention from what is being offered as the value/topic to be accepted; (2) the subject assumes a position of dis-solidarity with the value/topic, as (3), by means of gestures or words, he or she invites others to join in the act of dis-solidarity (19).

27   Fusco, *English,* 57.

28   The comment was made during a discussion following my lecture, "A Savage Performance," in the "Performing Identities" lecture series, Center for Ideas and Society, University of California, Riverside, February 28, 1997.

29   Fusco, *English,* 51; Guillermo Gómez-Peña, *Warrior for Gringostroika* (St. Paul, MN: Graywolf Press, 1993), 112.

30   For all the parodic staging and acting, many in the audience believed the performance. Although Fusco and Gómez-Peña had intended to play "the identity of an other for a white audience" (Fusco, *English,* 37), it never occurred to them that they would be taken literally. In her essay written after the experience, Fusco notes that more than half of their 150,000 spectators believed the Guatinauis were "real." This was in spite of the fact that the information on the walls around the cage specifically set the piece in a tradition of a representational practice, that nonwhites and "freaks" have been exposed for centuries.

31 See the video by Coco Fusco and Paula Heredia, *The Couple in the Cage: A Guatinaui Odyssey*, 1993.

32 Homi Bhabha, *The Location of Culture* (New York: Routledge, 1994), 9.

33 Gomez-Peña, public lecture, Dartmouth College, 1995.

34 Fusco, *English*, 50.

35 Ibid., 40.

36 Portilla, *La fenomenolgía del relajo*, 19.

37 See Schechner, *Between Theater and Anthropology*, 109.

38 Victor Turner, *The Anthropology of Performance* (New York: PAJ Publications, 1986), 37.

39 Applying terms such as "real" and "authentic" to cultural behavior has been continually problematized by people such as Clifford, *Predicament*; Schechner, *Between Theater and Anthropology*; Ella Shohat and Robert Stam, *Unthinking Eurocentrism: Multiculturalism and the Media* (New York: Routledge, 1994); Rony, *Third Eye*, and many others. They therefore require no further elaboration here.

40 Fusco, *English*, 37, 40, 50.

CHAPTER THREE. MEMORY AS CULTURAL PRACTICE: MESTIZAJE, HYBRIDITY, TRANSCULTURATION

1 All translations from the Spanish are my own. My translation of passages from *I, Too, Speak of the Rose* draws on William I. Oliver's translation in George Woodyard, ed., *The Modern Stage in Latin America: Six Plays* (New York: Dutton, 1971). This is the second time I write about this play. Another interpretation appeared in my *Theatre of Crisis* (1991).

2 Bernal Díaz del Castillo, in *The Conquest of New Spain*, trans. J. M Cohen (London: Penguin, 1963), describes many of the wonders of Tenochtitlán, citing among them the remarkable "large canoes that could come into the garden from the lake, through a channel they had cut" (215).

3 Connerton, *How Societies Remember*, 37.

4 Lockhart, in *The Nahuas after the Conquest*, relates the following: "In the legend of Sula (Tlalmanalco area, on the northwestern edge of Chalco), as it was written down sometime in the late seventeenth century, the choice of Santiago as a patron took place in the following manner. When the Spaniards not long after the conquest said that it was time for Sula to decide on a saint, the people delegated the task to the two oldest and wisest among them. Sleeping on the matter, each had a dream in which Santiago appeared in great splendor, declaring himself to be from Persia (i.e., far away), and announced that he would be Sula's saint. Still in doubt the next morning, the two elders questioned each other, and on discovering that their dreams had been identical, proclaimed the choice of Santiago to the populace. These two eldest citizens are (though named differently) an embodiment of the autochthonous pair, representing Sula's dual organization . . . ; one of them as 'Quail-lord' and 'Quail-serpent' also represents the

preconquest totemic deity. Thus the indigenous bearers of ethnic identity are made to endorse and become associated with the saint, who can be viewed as having been thereby consecrated in the role of the sacred symbol of the community" (236).

5   Marianne Hirsch and Valerie Smith edited a special issue of *Signs*, "Gender and Cultural Memory" (vol. 28, no. 1 [autumn 2002]), dedicated to the question of the gendering of cultural memory. They note in the introduction that to their knowledge, their volume provides the first occasion since 1987 [*Michigan Quarterly Review's* special issue "Women and Memory"] for an interdisciplinary and international dialogue between feminist theories and theories of cultural memory (4).

6   Most of the population of Mexico is mestizo. As Alan Knight notes, "The 'pure' Indian was as rare culturally as biologically" (76). The same could be said of the European. For a discussion of the history of racial formation in Mexico see Alan Knight, "Racism, Revolution, and Indigenismo: Mexico, 1910–1940," in *The Idea of Race in Latin America, 1870–1940*, ed. Richard Graham (Austin: U of Texas P, 1990); R. Douglas Cope, *The Limits of Racial Domination: Plebeian Society in Colonial Mexico City, 1660–1720* (Madison: U of Wisconsin P, 1994); and Robert H. Jackson, *Race, Caste, and Status* (Albuquerque: U of New Mexico P, 1999).

7   See García Saiz, *Las castas mexicanas*.

8   Race was theoretically about blood and skin color, but practically it was about lifestyle, class, and environment. As Robert H. Jackson writes, the castas were "based on documented bloodlines as well as skin color that established legal distinctions between people of predominantly European ancestry and of indigenous or African ancestry. . . . However, other criteria also figured in the creation of racial identity such as stereotypical assumptions about culture, behavior, and . . . place of residence" (*Race*, 4). "Indian," as Knight notes, was an ethnic rather than racial designation, grounded in "language, dress, religion, social organization, culture, and consciousness" ("Racism," 73).

9   Cope, *The Limits of Racial Domination*, 18.

10 For a detailed analysis of the caste system, see ibid., ch. 1; Jackson, *Race*, ch. 2.

11 Justo Sierra, for example, one of Mexico's great educators of the late eighteenth and early nineteenth centuries, promoted European immigration "so as to obtain a cross with the indigenous race, for only European blood can keep the level of civilization . . . from sinking, which would mean regression, not evolution." *Political Evolution of the Mexican People*, quoted in Knight, "Racism," 78.

12 Miguel León-Portilla, ed., *Huehuehtlahtolli, testimonios de la antigua palabra* (Mexico City: SEP y Fondo de Cultura Económica, 1991), 91.

13 Alfredo López Austin, *Cuerpo humano e ideología* (Mexico City: Universidad Nacional Autónoma de México, 1989), 1:71.

14 Connerton, *How Societies Remember*, ch. 3.

15 I understand the difference between Mexican-American women and Chicanas as one of political positioning. Woman is to feminist what Mexican American is to Chicana; the latter reflects a commitment to issues of social justice and equality.

16 Alfredo López Austin, "La parte feminina del cosmos," *Arqueología Mexicana* 5, no. 29 (1998), notes, "As in other conceptions of the world, Mesoamerican thought did not accept the possibility of pure beings. Everything that existed, even the gods, were a mix of the essence of the masculine and the feminine. It was the predominance of one of these that determined classification" (6).

17 Ibid.

18 Sahagún, *Florentine Codex*, book 1, 17, 21, 11, 19.

19 See Rosemary A. Joyce, *Gender and Power in Prehispanic Mesoamerica* (Austin: U of Texas P, 2000), especially ch.5, "Becoming Human," where she notes how "the cosmological patterns of gender complementarity inscribed in Aztec myth, ritual practice, and monumental representation were also embodied in the monumental temporal scale of narratives of royal origins of the Mexica. Susan Gillespie shows that official Aztec genealogies relied on the transmission of the right to rule through women, who are specifically treated as links to traditions of creation" (172).

20 See Cecelia F. Klein, "Fighting with Femininity: Gender and War in Aztec Mexico," in *Gender Rhetorics*, ed. Richard Trexler (Binghamton, NY: MRTS, 1994), 107–46; Richard C. Trexler, *Sex and Conquest* (New York: Cornell UP, 1995).

21 Joyce, *Gender and Power*, 172.

22 See Codex Mendoza, in Sahagún's *Florentine Codex*, books 2 and 6; Alfredo López Austin, *La educación de los antiguos Nahuas*, 2 vols.(Mexico City: Ediciones El Caballito, 1985); Joyce, *Gender and Power*, ch. 5.

23 Díaz del Castillo, "Doña Marina's Story," in *The Conquest of New Spain*, 85.

24 Contemporary references to her can be found in Sahagún, *Florentine Codex*; Díaz del Castillo, *The Conquest of New Spain*; Francisco López de Gómara, *Cortés: The Life of the Conqueror by His Secretary*, trans. Lesley Byrd Simpson (Berkeley: U of California P, 1964); and in a letter from Cortés to the King of Spain. Innumerable books, articles, plays, poems, essays, and newspaper articles also have been written about her. The Mexican and Mexican American repertoire is also full of masked dances and other kinds of performances in which La Malinche plays a prominent (though often wildly divergent) role.

25 Octavio Paz, *The Labyrinth of Solitude: Life and Thought in Mexico*, trans. Lysander Kemp (New York: Grove Press, 1961), 80.

26 Ibid.

27 D. A. Brading, *Mexican Phoenix: Our Lady of Guadalupe* (Cambridge, England: Cambridge UP, 2001), 9.

28 Roger Bartra, *La jaula de la melancolía* (Mexico City: Grijalbo, 1987), 173.

29 María Moliner, *Diccionario de uso del español* (Madrid: Editorial Gredos, 1967), defines mestizo/a as follows: "(Del lat. tardío <mixticius> deriv. de <mixtus>, partic. de <miscere>; v. <mixto>.) Hijo de padres de disticta raza. Particularmente, hijo de indio y blanco. También se aplica a los animales y a las plantas procedentes del cruce de individuos de distinta raza" (402). The verb *mestizar* is more judgmental, defined as

"Adulterar la pureza de una raza por el cruce con otras" (402). *Mestizaje*, the dictionary notes, has only recently been admitted into the official language as controlled by the *Diccionario de la Real Academia Española*.

30 Gilberto Freyre, in the 1930s, for example, declares the following: "Hybrid from the beginning, Brazilian society is, of all those in the Americas, the one most harmoniously constituted so far as racial relations are concerned, within the environment of a practical cultural reciprocity that results in the advanced people deriving the maximum of profit from the values and experiences of the backward ones, and in a maximum of conformity between the foreign and the native cultures, that of the conqueror and the conquered." *The Master of Slaves: A Study in the Development of Brazilian Civilization* (Berkeley: U of California P, 1986), 83.

31 Corominas, *Breve diccionario etimológico*.

32 Eric Wolf, *Sons of the Shaking Earth* (Chicago: U of Chicago P, 1959), 238.

33 See Rachel Phillips, "Marina/Malinche: Masks and Shadows," in *Women in Hispanic Literature: Icons and Fallen Idols*, ed. Beth Miller (Berkeley: U of California P, 1983).

34 Robert J. C. Young, *Colonial Desire: Hybridity in Theory, Culture and Race* (London: Routledge, 1995), 19.

35 Ignacio Ramírez, *Discursos y artículos* (Mexico City: Imprenta Victoria, 1915), 5, quoted in Phillips, "Marina/Malinche," 111.

36 A new journal of Latin/o American studies, *Nepantla*, is being published by Duke University Press. Mexican and Chicano/a artists such as Guillermo Gómez-Peña and Gloria Anzaldúa also write of their experience of nepantla.

37 Robert Stam, "Specificities: From Hybridity to the Aesthetics of Garbage," *Social Identities* 3, no. 2 (1997): 277.

38 José Vasconcelos, *The Cosmic Race/La raza cósmica*, trans. Didier T. Jaén (Baltimore: Johns Hopkins UP, 1997), 102.

39 Todorov, *The Conquest of America*, 101.

40 Quoted in Brading, *Mexican Phoenix*, 297.

41 I argue this point more fully in Diana Taylor, *Theatre of Crisis: Drama and Politics in Latin America* (Lexington, U of Kentucky P, 1990), ch. 4.

42 Gloria Anzaldúa, *Borderlands/La Frontera: The New Mestiza* (San Francisco: Spinsters/Aunt Lute, 1987), 78.

43 Cherríe Moraga, *Loving in the War Years* (Boston: South End Press, 1983), 100.

44 Sandra Cisneros, "Little Miracles, Kept Promises," in *Woman Hollering Creek* (New York: Random House, 1991), 124.

45 Néstor García Canclini, *Hybrid Cultures: Strategies for Entering and Leaving Modernity*, trans. Christopher L. Chiappari and Silvia L. López (Minneapolis: U of Minnesota P, 1995), 11, n. 1.

46 Skeat, *Concise Etymological Dictionary*.

47 The debates about the inferiority, even nonhumanness of a hybrid species (rather than race) is described in Young, *Colonial Desire*, ch. 1.

48 William Rowe and Vivian Schelling, *Memory and Modernity: Popular Culture in Latin America* (London: Verso, 1991), 231.

49 Stannard, in *American Holocaust*, estimates that 95 percent of the native populations of the Americas died in the fifty years following the conquest (x).

50 Bhabha, *The Location of Culture*, 112.

51 Anthropologists in the United States have not taken up the term transculturation, and theater scholar Carl Weber erroneously argued in 1989 that the word "is as new as the phenomenon" of intercultural festivals that date from the 1950s onwards. "AC/TC: Current of Theatrical Exchange," Performing Arts Journal, nos. 33–34 (1989):11. For my critique of his essay, see Diana Taylor, "Transculturating Transculturation," in *Performance Arts Journal* 13, no. 2 (1989): 90–104. For a study of transculturation, see Silvia Spitta, *Between Two Waters: Narratives of Transculturation in Latin America* (Houston: Rice UP, 1995), and Pratt, *Imperial Eyes.*

52 Angel Rama, *Transculturación narrativa en América Latina* (Mexico City: Sigo XXI, 1982), 33.

53 For a much earlier discussion of this play and the scholarship, see D. Taylor, *Theatre of Crisis*, ch. 4.

54 Walter Ong, *Orality and Literacy* (London: Methuen, 1982), 73.

55 Bertolt Brecht, *Brecht on Theatre*, trans. John Willett (New York: Hill and Wang, 1964), 201.

56 Sahagún, "Exclamation of the Author," introduction to book 2, *Florentine Codex.*

57 Antonin Artaud, *The Theater and Its Double* (New York: Grove Press, 1958), 10–11.

58 See Guillermo Bonfil Batalla, *México Profundo: Reclaiming a Civilization* (Austin: U of Texas P, 1996), part 1.

CHAPTER FOUR. LA RAZA COSMÉTICA: WALTER MERCADO PERFORMS LATINO PSYCHIC SPACE

I want to thank Doris Sommer for the Wardy epigraph at the beginning of this chapter.

1 Sahagún, *Florentine Codex*, book 1, ch. 12, p. 24.

2 See, for example, Noemí Quezada, "The Inquisition's Repression of Curanderos," and María Helena Sánchez Ortega, "Sorcery and Eroticism in Love Magic," both in *Cultural Encounters: The Impact of the Inquisition in Spain and the New World*, ed. Mary Elizabeth Perry and Anne J. Cruz (Berkeley: U of California P, 1991).

3 Moctezuma, the Nahua ruler at the time of the arrival of the Spaniards in 1519, called before him his soothsayers, "you [who] study the night sky . . . and observe the movement of the celestial bodies, the course of the stars," begging them "not to hide anything from me, but to tell me all" (Durán, *History of the Indies of New Spain*, 493). Furious at their evasive answer, Moctezuma threw them in jail. When the soothsayers disappeared from jail, apparently through the strength of their own magic, Moctezuma had their wives and children killed and their possessions destroyed.

4   Florescano, *Memory, Myth, and Time in Mexico,* focuses on these visionary move-
    ments to explain the ways orality and myth shape social identity in Mexico. He writes:
    "One characteristic distinguishes these movements: they are born and gain strength
    under the impulse of a sacred event that has occurred or is about to occur—the an-
    nouncement of a miracle, the appearance of a Virgin, the prophecy of an apocalyptic
    ending, the arrival of a savior who will wipe out injustice and establish an Indian mil-
    lennium. In all these cases, the sacred event appears as an exceptional occurrence, as
    an extraordinary privilege reserved to the group that lives the event" (167).

5   *Aprenda Sanaciones Espirituales,* video, Amazonas Corp., New York, 1997.

6   José Vasconcelos, *The Cosmic Race,* 6.

7   Grant Tume, "The Caped Crusader," *Detour,* May 1996, 34.

8   In contrast to the story of the miraculous childhood circulated by Walter himself,
    people remember him as a young television personality who starred in soap operas in
    Puerto Rico. However, the refashioning has been so successful that few people remem-
    ber the preprophetic Walter, and it's difficult to locate materials pertaining to that past.

9   Sigmund Freud, *Civilization and Its Discontents,* ed. and trans. James Strachey (New
    York: Norton, 1962), 39.

10 See Judith Butler, *The Psychic Life of Power: Theories of Subjection* (Stanford: Stanford
    UP, 1997), 13.

11 On casta paintings, see García Saiz, *Las castas mexicanas,* and Deborah Poole, *Vision,
    Race and Modernity: A Visual Economy of the Andean Image World* (Princeton: Prince-
    ton UP, 1997).

12 Andrew Friedman, "Behind the Big Numbers, a Million Little Stories," *New York
    Times,* March 18, 2001, CY6.

13 The Census 2000 officials "acknowledged that 97% of the 15.4 million people who
    checked the 'some other race' box were Hispanics who ignored requests by federal offi-
    cials to indicate their Hispanic origin in the ethnic category, not racial category. 'His-
    panic' is a catch-all term designated to cover an array of Spanish-speaking people." Eric
    Schmitt, "For 7 Million People in Census, One Race Category Isn't Enough," *New York
    Times,* May 13, 2001, A1.

14 Vasconcelos, *The Cosmic Race,* 40.

15 See Lynette Clemeston, "Hispanics Now Largest Minority," *New York Times,* Janu-
    ary 22, 2003, A1.

16 Luis Valdéz, *The Shrunken Head of Pancho Villa,* in *Necessary Theater,* ed. Jorge
    Huerta (Houston: Arte Público Press, 1989); Cherríe Moraga, *Heroes and Saints* (Albu-
    querque, NM: West End Press, 1994).

17 Cherríe Moraga, *Loving in the War Years* (Boston: South End Press, 1983), 120.

18 As Latin America has historically been a site of intense migrations, the populations
    are very mixed. There are large European communities in countries such as Argentina,
    Chile, and Mexico who might also be considered Latino/as in the United States.

19 In one noteworthy case in Texas, two Latina women, Ester Hernandez and Rosa Gon-

zalez, were fired from their jobs for refusing to sign a pledge to speak only English in their workplace, even though they had been hired because they spoke Spanish. Gonzales refused on the basis that she speaks both English and Spanish in her daily life: "I told him no. This is what I am; this is what I do. This is normal to me. I'm not doing it to offend anybody. It just feels comfortable." Sam Howe Verhovek, "Clash of Cultures Tears Texas City," *New York Times*, September 30, 1997, A14.

20 Austin, *How to Do Things with Words*, 7.

21 *Rascuache* or *rasquache* is a word (of unknown etymology) used in Mexico and Guatemala to describe that which is vulgar, ridiculous, trite, poor. See Tomás Ybarra-Frausto, "Rasquachismo: A Chicano Sensibility," in *Chicano Art: Resistance and Affirmation, 1965-1985*, ed. Teresa McKenna, Yvonne Yarbro-Bejarano, and Richard Griswold del Castillo (Los Angeles: UCLA Wight Art Gallery, 1991), 155–62.

22 Susan Sontag, "Notes on Camp," *Against Interpretation* (New York: Dell, 1966). See Marcie Frank, "The Critic as Performance Artist: Susan Sontag's Writing and Gay Cultures," in *Camp Grounds: Style and Homosexuality*, ed. David Bergman (Amherst: U of Massachusetts P, 1994). See also Moe Meyer's rejection of camp as "apolitical, aestheticized, and frivolous" (1), "Introduction: Reclaiming the Discourse of Camp," in *The Politics and Poetics of Camp*, ed. Moe Meyer (London: Routledge, 1994).

23 Meyer, "Introduction: Reclaiming the Discourse of Camp," 6.

24 Ybarra-Frausto, "Rasquachismo."

25 Ibid., 155.

26 Sigmund Freud, *The Future of an Illusion*, trans. James Strachey (New York: Norton, 1961), 30.

27 Walter Mercado, *Beyond the Horizon* (New York: Warner, 1997), 229.

28 Jorge Portilla, *La fenomenología del relajo*, 2d ed. (Mexico City: Fondo de Cultura Económica, 1986), 24.

29 Treaty of Guadalupe Hidalgo and the original texts of Articles VIII and IX in Richard Griswold del Castillo, *The Treaty of Guadalupe Hidalgo: A Legacy of Conflict* (Norman: U of Oklahoma P, 1990), 179–99. The treaty, in fact, reneged on an earlier promise to grant Mexicans who stayed on their lands—which were now U.S. territory—citizenship within a year. "Those [Mexicans] who shall prefer to remain in the said territories [previously belonging to Mexico, and which remain for the future within the limits of the United States] may either retain the title and rights of Mexican citizens, or acquire those of citizens of the United States" (Article VIII). These Mexicans had one year to decide whether to stay on their land as U.S. citizens or migrate south, to the newly defined Mexico. Those who remained did not in fact enjoy "all the rights of citizens of the United States," as guaranteed by Article IX, which was stricken from the treaty by the U.S. government.

30 Alberto Ledesma, "Undocumented Crossings: Narratives of Mexican Immigration to the United States," in *Culture across Borders: Mexican Immigration and Popular Culture*, ed. David R. Maciel and Maria Herrera-Sobek (Tucson: U of Arizona P, 1998), 75.

31   Jean Baudrillard, *Seduction*, trans. Brian Singer (New York: St. Martin's Press, 1979),
      132.

CHAPTER FIVE. FALSE IDENTIFICATIONS:
MINORITY POPULATIONS MOURN DIANA

1   Guy Debord, *Society of the Spectacle*, 3.
2   Victor Turner, *Dramas, Fields, and Metaphors: Symbolic Action in Human Society*
     (Ithaca: Cornell UP, 1974), 37–42.
3   Winston S. Churchill, "Modernizing Britain, the Tony Blair Way," *New York Times*,
     January 2, 1998, A17.
4   Roach, *Cities of the Dead*, 2.
5   Jacques Derrida, *Specters of Marx* (London: Routledge, 1994), 4.
6   Phelan, *Unmarked*, 146.
7   Warren Hoge, "Diana's Hereafter, an Eternity of Newsstand Life," *New York Times*,
     February 9, 1998, A4.
8   Phelan, *Unmarked*, 146.
9   Michael Taussig, *Mimesis and Alterity* (New York: Routledge, 1993), 10.
10   See Elisabeth Bronfen, *Over Her Dead Body: Death, Femininity and the Aesthetic* (New
     York: Routledge, 1992), 181.
11   Debord, *Society of the Spectacle*, 4.
12   Bronfen, *Over Her Dead Body*, 181.
13   Quoted in Maria Celeste Arraras, *Selena's Secret* (New York: Simon and Schuster, 1997),
     24.
14   Walter Benjamin, *Illuminations: Essays and Reflections* (New York: Harcourt, Brace
     and World, 1955), 72.
15   Aristotle, *Poetics*, trans. Gerald F. Else (Ann Arbor: U of Michigan P, 1973), 25.
16   Judith Butler, "Performative Acts and Gender Constitution: An Essay in Phenome-
     nology and Feminist Theory," in *Performing Feminisms: Feminist Critical Theory and
     Theatre*, ed. Sue-Ellen Case (Baltimore: Johns Hopkins UP, 1990), 270.
17   Sarah Lyall, "Diana's Hunters: How Quarry Was Stalked," *New York Times*, Septem-
     ber 10, 1997, A1.
18   "She Didn't Have to Die!" *Globe*, September 16, 1997, cover; "The Love She Died For,"
     Globe, September 16, 1997, 22.
19   Barbara Kirshenblatt-Gimblett, "Issues and Methods" class, Performance Studies, New
     York University, September 1997.
20   Kamal Ahmed, "Charles and the Queen at War over Diana," *The Guardian*, Interna-
     tional ed., September 9, 1997, 1.
21   García Canclini, *Hybrid Cultures*, 191.
22   "Princess Diana Fax Poll," *New York Post*, September 4, 1997, 5.
23   Warren Hoge, "Flower Power," *New York Times*, September 9, 1997, A1.

24 Frank Rich, "101 Evitas," *New York Times,* December 11, 1996, A27.

25 Bhabha, *The Location of Culture,* 86.

26 Max Frankel, "No Pix, No Di," *New York Times Magazine,* September 21, 1997, 53.

27 Susan Stewart, "TV Bids Farewell to Its Princess," *TV Guide,* September 20, 1997, 24.

CHAPTER SIX. "YOU ARE HERE":
H.I.J.O.S. AND THE DNA OF PERFORMANCE

1 The acronym H.I.J.O.S. stands for Hijos por la Identidad y la Justicia, contra el Olvido y el Silencio (Children for Identity and Justice, against Forgetting and Silence).

2 See, for example, Shoshana Felman and Dori Laub, *Testimony: Crisis of Witnessing in Literature, Psychoanalysis, and History* (New York: Routledge, 1992); Cathy Caruth, *Unclaimed Experience: Trauma, Narrative, and History* (Baltimore: Johns Hopkins UP,1996).

3 Laub, in Felman and Laub, *Testimony,* 57.

4 As Richard Schechner points out, "Behavior is separate from those who are behaving; the behavior can be stored, transmitted, manipulated, transformed" (*Between Theater and Anthrophology,* 36).

5 Marcelo Suárez-Orozco, "The Heritage of Enduring a 'Dirty War': Psychosocial Aspects of Terror in Argentina, 1976–1983," *Journal of Psychohistory* 18, no. 4 (1991): 491. I have developed this at greater length in D. Taylor, *Disappearing Acts,* ch. 7.

6 For a succinct discussion of DNA, see Brian L. Silver, *The Ascent of Science* (New York: Oxford UP, 1998), especially ch. 24, "The Gene Machine." Silver notes that "your DNA, unless you are an identical twin, is distinct from everyone else's in the whole Creation, the difference being, as we said, in the order of the bases. . . . DNA carries all your genetic information, a collection of genes that contain a set of instructions for building you" (295). See, too, Matt Ridley, *Genome* (New York: Harper Collins, 1999). Ridley defines DNA as a filament of information, "a message written in a code of chemicals, one chemical for each letter" (13), that includes four bases: A, T, C, and G. Sections of the filament, known as genes, form units of 120 "letters" that are "constantly being copied into a short filament of RNA. The copy is known as 5S RNA. It sets up residence with a lump of protein and other RNAs, carefully intertwined, in a ribosome, a machine whose job it is to translate DNA recipes into proteins. And it is the proteins that enable DNA to replicate" (16). For speed and accuracy when referencing them, the genes were clumped into three-letter genetic codes, each letter "spelling out a particular one of twenty amino acids as part of the recipe for a protein" (19). "Life consists of the interplay of two kinds of chemicals: proteins and DNA" (16–17). It is interesting to note that both Ridley's description and the image below (from Andrew Pollack, "Scientists Are Starting to Add Letters to Life's Alphabet," *New York Times,* July 24, 2001, F1) stress the metaphors of language and writing in explaining the composition and workings of DNA. This supports my argument that epistemic systems need each other in order

to make their claims. DNA is not a "language," though that word is repeatedly used to describe it, but the relationship is not simply metaphoric. Both codes—DNA and linguistic—are interrelated modes of thinking about and organizing knowledge.

7   Quoted in David Gonzalez, "New Violence over Rights Raise Fear in Guatemala," *New York Times*, May 3, 2002, A7. Although Snow was referring to the Guatemalan generals, this holds for the junta during Argentina's Dirty War. Snow participated in efforts there too to identify the disappeared.

8   *Nunca Más: The Report of the Argentine National Commission of the Disappeared* (New York: Farrar Straus Giroux, 1986). By this insistence on the live, I don't want to lessen the importance of the video and virtual testimonies that have gained currency in the past decade. The Video Archive for Holocaust Testimonies at Yale and Web sites such as *www.witness.org* and The Vanished Gallery (http://www.yendor.com/vanished.html), which include materials from Argentina, are only three of the many initiatives designed to expand our ability to archive and recapture the act of testifying. They store knowledge and make it available to a far greater number of people than any live scenario permits. But the *re* in recapture is not the reiterative repeat of either trauma or performance; it is, rather, a transfer into the archive—a different economy of storage and representation. The replay will always be the same, a record of an earlier moment, an anterior utterance that is frozen for posterior use. I am not suggesting that the transmission of traumatic memory happens only in the live encounter. But I do want to distinguish between different, though intertwined, systems of knowledge—the archival and the embodied—that participate in the transmission and politicization of traumatic memory.

9   Richard Dawkins, *The Selfish Gene* (New York: Oxford UP, 1976).

10 "When we die there are two things we can leave behind us: genes and memes. We were built as gene machines, created to pass on our genes. But that aspect of us will be forgotten in three generations. . . . But if you contribute to the world's culture, if you have a good idea, compose a tune, invent a sparking plug, write a poem, it may live on, intact, long after your genes have dissolved in the common pool" (ibid., 214).

11 Roach, *Cities of the Dead*, 2.

12 Through photography, as Allan Sekula argues in his analysis of the nineteenth-century convergence of police work and eugenics, the body becomes constructed and contained in the archive. "The Body and the Archive," *October*, no. 39 (1987): 3.

13 Julio Pantoja, "Los Hijos, Tucumán veinte años después," http://www.juliopantoja.com.ar/.

14 D. Taylor, *Disappearing Acts*, 277 n. 13.

15 Barthes, *The Responsibility of Forms: Critical Essays on Music, Art, and Representation*, trans. Richard Howard (New York: Hill and Wang, 1985), 10.

16 The archive in the body is related to what I have elsewhere called the repertoire: the embodied images and behaviors that get transmitted through performance. Here, the embodied performance consciously displays the archival both as it promises to preserve materials and threatens to erase them.

17   Postcard/flier, *Teatro por la identidad*, Abuelas de Plaza de Mayo.

18   See the Web site www.hijos.org.

19   Video interview, Hemispheric Institute of Performance and Politics, Encontro Brazil, 2000, http://hemi.nyu.edu.

20   José Gobello, *Diccionario Lunfardo* (Buenos Aires: Peña Lillo Editor, 1982).

21   Julio Pantoja writes that when Antonio Domingo Bussi, a known torturer during the dictatorship, was democratically voted in as Tucumán's governor, he decided he had to do something using his own instrument: photography. "Durante los cuatro años que duró el formalmente democrático gobierno de Bussi, me dediqué sistemáticamente a retratar a los hijos de víctimas de la represión en Tucumán, que según los organismos de Derechos Humanos deben ser alrededor de mil. Al principio fue tal vez sólo un impulso casi ingenuo de resistencia empujado por la indignación, pero de a poco fue consolidándose y tomando forma de una toma de posición lúcida usando mi herramienta: la fotografía" ("Los Hijos, Tucumán veinte años después").

22   While members of H.I.J.O.S. officially endorse the political activism of their parents, and vow to continue it, they had until recently avoided some of the pitfalls of other movements. Like the Madres, H.I.J.O.S. also split in two, with a new group, called HIJOS (or HIJOS ROJOS, red), taking a more radical political position.

CHAPTER SEVEN. STAGING TRAUMATIC MEMORY: YUYACHKANI

1   Hugo Salazar del Alcazar, "Los músicos ambulantes," *La escena latinoamericana*, no. 2 (August 1989): 23.

2   Dori Laub, quoted in Cathy Caruth, Introduction to *Trauma: Explorations in Memory* (Baltimore: Johns Hopkins UP, 1995), 6.

3   See, for example, the essays in Mark Rogers, ed., "Performance, Identity, and Historical Consciousness in the Andes," special issue of *Journal of Latin American Anthropology* 3, no. 2 (1998), especially the essay by Mark Rogers, "Spectacular Bodies: Folkorization and the Politics of Identity in Ecuadorian Beauty Pageants."

4   Ernest Renan, "What Is a Nation?" in *Nation and Narration*, ed. Homi Bhabha (London: Routledge, 1990), 11.

5   Personal interview, Paucartambo, Peru, July 1999.

6   Deborah Poole and Gerardo Rénique, *Peru: Time of Fear* (London: Latin American Bureau, 1992), 6.

7   The antistar sentiment was, of course, often contradicted in the group's makeup, with the director functioning as leader and even guru. See Yolanda González-Broyles's study of the Teatro Campesino as an example, *El Teatro Campesino: Theater in the Chicano Movement* (Austin: U of Texas P, 1994).

8   D. Taylor, *Theatre of Crisis*, ch. 1.

9   Miguel Rubio, "Encuentro con el hombre andino," in *Grupo Cultural Yuyachkani, Allpa Rayku: Una experencia de teatro popular*, 2d ed. (Lima: Edición del Grupo Cultural Yuyachkani y Escuelas Campesinas de la CCP, 1985), 9.

10 Quoted in Brenda Luz Cotto-Escalera, "Grupo Cultural Yuyachkani: Group Work and Collective Creation in Contemporary Latin American Theatre" (Ph.D. diss., University of Texas, Austin, 1995), 116.

11 Hugo Salazar del Alcazar, interview in *Persistencia de la Memoria*, documentary video on Yuyachkani, dir. Andrés Cotler.

12 *Encuentro de zorros* is based on a text by José María Arguedas entitled "El zorro de arriba y el zorro de abajo" and cowritten by the group and Peter Elmore. *Adios Ayacucho* is based on a text of the same name by Julio Ortega.

13 Quoted in Cotto-Escalera, "Grupo Cultural Yuyachkani," 156.

14 D. Taylor, *Disappearing Acts*.

15 Theodor Adorno, "Commitment," in *Aesthetics and Politics*, ed. Ernst Bloch et al. (London: Verso, 1977), 189.

16 Dori Laub, "Truth and Testimony: The Process and the Struggle," in Caruth, *Trauma: Explorations in Memory*, 66.

17 José Watanabe, *Antígona*, trans. Margaret Carson, in *Holy Terrors: Latin American Women Perform*, ed. Diana Taylor and Roselyn Costantino (Durham: Duke UP, 2003).

18 Teresa Ralli, "Fragments of Memory," trans. Margaret Carson, in D. Taylor and R. Costantino, *Holy Terrors*.

19 Interview, Rebeca Ralli, Casa Yuyachkani, June 1996.

20 Rowe and Schelling, *Memory and Modernity*, 55.

21 Rubio, *Allpa Ravku*, quoted in Cotto-Escalera, "Grupo Cultural Yuyachkani," 115.

22 See Caruth, *Unclaimed Experience*, and Laub's notion of the "collapse of witnessing" in "Truth and Testimony," 65.

CHAPTER EIGHT. DENISE STOKLOS: THE POLITICS OF DECIPHERABILITY

1 Henry David Thoreau, *Walden* and *Civil Disobedience* (New York: Penguin Classics, 1986), 47.

2 Denise Stoklos, *The Essential Theatre* (São Paulo: Denise Stoklos Productions, 1992), 47.

3 "I worked on two performances in England. Those two plays have been, for me, technically important. They incited the beginning of my personal research on graphic projection of the text. By this I mean the alienated verbal representation of a text that occurs, for instance, when a text is delivered in a foreign language. On this occasion, the experience of 'feeling in Portuguese and expressing in English' revealed the denial of that emotional flowing that happens spontaneously when using the music of the first language. I perceived that this new alienation dramatized the encounter with oral signs contained in the musicality inherent to a foreign language. Within my research on the essentialities of the theatre, the perception of 'schizophrenia' caused by the clash between the sound and the meaning of the word shed a light on the verbal path I would pursue in my future work" (ibid., 30).

4   Denise Stoklos, *500 Anos—Um Fax de Denise Stoklos para Cristóvão Colombo* (São Paulo: Denise Stoklos Productions, 1992), 9; my translation.

5   Media coverage on Stoklos's most recent festival. Denise Stoklos has won the Best Actress award nine times in Brazil; she has been the recipient of a Guggenheim award and a Fulbright Scholarship and her work has been translated and staged in thirty-one countries. For texts, see Taylor and Costantino, eds., *Holy Terrors* (Durham: Duke UP, 2003).

6   Stoklos, *Essential Theatre*, 5.

7   Debord, *Society of the Spectacle*, 63. At the time of writing this piece, Debord did not see the two spectacles as connected. Only in his later work, *Comments on the Society of the Spectacle*, trans. Malcolm Imrie (London: Verso, 1998), did he see the two as working together, as the "integrated" spectacle. "The controlling centre," he writes, "has now become occult: never to be occupied by a known leader, or a clear ideology. And on the more diffuse side, the spectacle has never before put its mark to such a degree on almost the full range of socially produced behaviour and objects. . . . When the spectacle was concentrated, the greater part of surrounding society escaped it; when diffuse, a small part; today, no part" (*Comments on the Society of the Spectacle*, 9).

8   Thoreau, *Civil Disobedience*, 387.

9   Sylvia Molloy and Robert McKee Irwin, eds., *Hispanisms and Homosexualities* (Durham: Duke UP, 1998), xiv.

10 Saskia Sassen, *The Global City* (Princeton: Princeton UP, 1991).

11 See my chapter on transculturation (ch. 4) in D. Taylor, *Theatre of Crisis*.

12 Debord, *Society of the Spectacle*, 4.

13 Louis Althusser, *For Marx*, trans. Ben Brewster (Harmondsworth, England: Penguin, 1969), 149.

14 Victor Turner, quoted in Schechner and Appel, *By Means of Performance*, 1.

15 Althusser, *For Marx*, 148.

16 Abdul-Karim Mustapha, "Rumba in the Park," unpublished paper for "Borderlands and Barrios" course, New York University, December 1998.

17 Aristotle, *Poetics*, 66.

18 Arjun Appadurai, *Modernity at Large: The Cultural Dimension of Globalization* (Minneapolis: U of Minnesota P, 1996), 22.

CHAPTER NINE. LOST IN THE FIELD OF VISION:
WITNESSING SEPTEMBER 11

1   C. J. Chivers, "Ground Zero Diary: 12 Days of Fire and Grit," *New York Times*, September 30, 2001, A1.

2   R. W. Apple Jr., "So Far, Bush Has Asked Not What You Can Do," *New York Times*, October 15, 2001, B1.

3   Elizabeth Bumiller, with David E. Sanger, "A Somber Bush Says Terrorism Cannot Prevail," *New York Times*, September 12, 2001, A1.

4   Aristotle, *Poetics*, 30.

5   Ariel Dorfman, the Chilean writer, relates September 11 to another September 11, in 1973, the day President Salvador Allende's democratic government was toppled by military forces backed by the CIA: "I have been through this before. . . . The resemblance I am evoking goes well beyond a facile and superficial comparison, for instance, that both in Chile in 1973 and in the States today, terror descended from the sky to destroy the symbols of national idenity. . . . No, what I recognize is something deeper, a parallel suffering, a similar pain, a commensurate disorientation" (*NACLA Report on the Americas* 35, no. 3 [2001]: 8). Eduardo Galleano also connects the dots: "There is a lot of similarity between homemade terrorism and high-tech terrorism, that of religious fundamentalists and that of fundamentalist believers in the market, that of the desperate and that of the powerful, that of crazies-on-the-loose and that of the military in uniform. They all share the same disdain for human life" (*NACLA Report on the Americas* 35, no. 3 [2001]: 9).

6   The estimate comes from Jayson Blair, "Here, Dignity Rubs Elbows with Demand," *New York Times*, June 26, 2002, B1.

CHAPTER TEN. HEMISPHERIC PERFORMANCES

1   For a video of Berta Jottar's talk and images of rumba in Central Park, visit the Web site of the Hemispheric Institute of Performance and Politics *http://hemi.nyu.edu* in the Web Cuaderno section.

2   David Kirby, "Police Officers Put Abrupt End to Rumba Beat," *New York Times*, October 11, 1998, City sec., 6.

3   For specific examples, see Barbara Browning, *Samba: Resistance in Motion* (Bloomington: Indiana UP, 1995), and *Infectious Rhythms* (New York: Routledge, 1998); Roach, *Cities of the Dead*.

4   Todorov, *The Conquest of America*, 4, 5.

5   See Kate Doyle and Adam Isacson, "A *New* New World Order? U.S. Military Mission Grows in Latin America," *NACLA Report on the Americas* 35, no. 3(2001):14–20.

6   Larry Rohter, "Back in Business, Argentina Calms Down and the Peso Perks Up," *New York Times*, April 30, 2002, A5.

7   Matthew L. Wald, "Officials Arrest 104 Airport Workers in Washington Area," *New York Times*, April 24, 2002, A13.

8   David Cole, "National Security State," *The Nation*, December 17, 2001, 4.

9   Christopher Marquis, "U.S. Bankrolling Is Under Scrutiny for Ties to Chávez Ouster," *New York Times*, April 25, 2002, A6.

BIBLIOGRAPHY

Abercrombie, Thomas A. *Pathways of Memory and Power: Ethnography and History among an Andean People.* Madison: University of Wisconsin Press, 1998.

Acosta, Joseph de. *Historia natural y moral de las Indias.* Mexico City: Fondo de Cultura Económica, 1962.

Adorno, Theodor W. *Aesthetic Theory.* Trans. Robert Hullot-Kentor. Minneapolis: University of Minnesota Press, 1997.

———. "Commitment." In *Aesthetics and Politics.* Ed. Ernst Bloch et al. London: Verso, 1977.

Agamben, Giorgio. *Remnants of Auschwitz: The Witness and the Archive.* Trans. Daniel Heller-Roazen. New York: Zone Books, 1999.

Ainley, Rosa, ed. *New Frontiers of Space, Bodies and Gender.* London: Routledge, 1998.

Allard, Genevieve, and Pierre Lefort. *La Máscara.* Mexico City: Fondo de Cultura Económica, 1984.

Althusser, Louis. *For Marx.* Trans. Ben Brewster. Harmondsworth, England: Penguin Books, 1969.

Althusser, Louis, and Etienne Balibar. *Reading Capital.* London: Verso, 1968.

Alvar, Manuel, and Rodolfo A. Borello. *Epoca colonial: Historia de la literatura hispanoamerica.* Madrid: Ediciones Cátedra, 1982.

Alvarado Tezozomoc, Hernando. *Crónica mexicana: Codice Ramirez.* Mexico City: Porrúa, 1987.

Anzaldúa, Gloria. *Borderlands/La Frontera: The New Mestiza.* San Francisco: Spinsters/Aunt Lute, 1987.

Appadurai, Arjun. *Modernity at Large.* Minneapolis: University of Minnesota Press, 1996.

Arguedas, José María. *Indios, mestizos y señores.* Lima: Editorial Horizonte, 1989.

Aristotle. *Poetics.* Trans. Gerald F. Else. Ann Arbor: University of Michigan Press, 1973.

———. *The Politics.* Trans. T. A. Sinclair. London: Penguin Books, 1962.

Arraras, Maria Celeste. *Selena's Secret.* New York: Simon and Schuster, 1997.

Arriaga, Pablo José de. *La extirpación de la Idolatria en el Perú.* Cuzco: Bartolomé de las Casas, 1999.

Artaud, Antonin. *The Theater and Its Double.* New York: Grove Press, 1958.

Auslander, Philip. *Liveness: Performance in a Mediatized Culture.* London: Routledge, 1999.

———. *Presence and Resistance.* Ann Arbor: University of Michigan Press, 1994.

Austin, J.L. *How to Do Things with Words.* 2d ed. Cambridge, MA.: Harvard University Press, 1975.

Avila, Friar Francisco de. *The Huarochiri Manuscript: A Testament of Ancient and Colonial Andean Religion.* Ed. Frank Salomon. Austin: University of Texas Press, 1991.

Ayllon, Fernando. *El tribunal de la Inquisición.* Lima: Ediciones del Congreso del Perú, 1999.

Azor, Ileana. *Origen y presencia del teatro en nuestra America.* La Habana: Editorial Letras Cubanas, 1988.

Bakhtin, Mikhail. *Rabelais and His World.* Trans. Helene Iswolsky. Bloomington: Indiana University Press, 1984.

Balderston, Daniel, and Donna J. Guy, eds. *Sex and Sexuality in Latin America.* New York: New York University Press, 1997.

Barnhart, Robert K., ed. *The Barnhart Dictionary of Etymology.* New York: H.W. Wilson, 1988.

Barthes, Roland. *Camera Lucida.* Trans. Richard Howard. New York: Hill and Wang, 1985.

———. *Empire of Signs.* Trans. Richard Howard. New York: Hill and Wang, 2000.

———. *The Fashion System.* Trans. Matthew Ward and Richard Howard. Berkeley: University of California Press, 1990.

———. *Image-Music-Text.* Trans. Stephen Heath. New York: Hill and Wang, 2001.

———. *Mythologies.* Trans. Annette Lavers. New York: Noonday Press, 1988.

———. *The Responsibility of Forms: Critical Essays on Music, Art, and Representation.* Trans. Richard Howard. New York: Hill and Wang, 1985.

Bartra, Roger. *La jaula de la melancolía.* Mexico City: Grijalbo, 1987.

Bataille, Georges. *The Accursed Share.* Trans. Robert Hurley. New York: Zone Books, 1991.

———. *Eroticism: Death and Sensuality.* Trans. Mary Dalwood. San Francisco: City Lights Books, 1986.

———. *Visions of Excess: Selective Writings, 1927–1939.* Trans. Allan Stoekl. Minneapolis: University of Minnesota Press, 1985.

Baudrillard, Jean. *Seduction.* Trans. Brian Singer. New York: St. Martin's Press, 1979.

———. *Simulacra and Simulation.* Trans. Sheila Faria Glaser. Ann Arbor: University of Michigan Press, 1994.

Bauman, Richard. *Verbal Art as Performance.* Rowley, MA: Newbury House, 1977.

Bell, Catherine. *Ritual Theory, Ritual Practice.* New York: Oxford University Press, 1992.

Benjamin, Walter. *Illuminations: Essays and Reflections.* New York: Harcourt, Brace and World, 1955.

Berger, John. *Ways of Seeing.* London: Penguin, 1972.

Bernabe, Jean, Patrick Chamoiseau, and Raphael Confiant. *Eloge de la Creolite/In Praise of Creoleness.* Baltimore: Gallimard, 1990.

Bernard, Carmen. *The Incas: Empire of Blood and Gold.* New York: Thames and Hudson/New Horizons, 1988.

Bhabha, Homi. *The Location of Culture.* New York: Routledge, 1994.

———. *Nation and Narration.* London: Routledge, 1990.

Blackmore, Susan. "The Power of Memes." *Scientific American* (October 2000): 64–73.

Blau, Herbert. *The Audience.* Baltimore: Johns Hopkins University Press, 1990.

Boal, Augusto. *Legislative Theatre.* Trans. Adrian Jackson. New York: Routledge, 1998.

———. *Theatre of the Oppressed.* Trans. Charles McBride and Maria-Odilia Leal McBride. New York: Theatre Communications Group, 1965.

Bond, George C., and Angela Gilliam, eds. *Social Construction of the Past.* London: Routledge, 1994.

Bonfil Batalla, Guillermo. *Mexico Profundo: Reclaiming a Civilization.* Austin: University of Texas Press, 1996.

Bonilla, Heraclio. *Los Conquistados.* Bogotá: Tercer Mundo Editores, 1992.

Bourdieu, Pierre. *Distinction: A Social Critique of the Judgement of Taste.* Trans. Richard Nice. Cambridge, MA: Harvard University Press, 1984.

———. *The Field of Cultural Production.* New York: Columbia University Press, 1993.

———. *Outline of a Theory of Practice.* Trans. Richard Nice. Cambridge, England: Cambridge University Press, 1989.

Brading, D.A. *The First America: The Spanish Monarchy, Creole Patriots, and the Liberal State 1492–1867.* Cambridge, England: Cambridge University Press, 1991.

———. *Mexican Phoenix: Our Lady of Guadalupe.* Cambridge, England: Cambridge University Press, 2001.

Brecht, Bertolt. *Brecht on Theatre.* Trans. John Willett. New York: Hill and Wang, 1964.

Brenneis, Donald, and Fred R. Myers, eds. *Dangerous Words: Language and Politics in the Pacific.* Prospect Heights, IL: Waveland Press, 1984.

Breton, Andre. *Manifestoes of Surrealism.* Trans. Richard Seaver and Helen R. Lane. Ann Arbor: University of Michigan Press, 1972.

Briggs, Charles. *Competence in Performance.* Philadelphia: University of Pennsylvania Press, 1988.

Bronfen, Elisabeth. *Over Her Dead Body: Death, Femininity and the Aesthetic.* New York: Routledge, 1992.

Browning, Barbara. *Infectious Rhythms.* New York: Routledge, 1998.

———. *Samba: Resistance in Motion.* Bloomington: Indiana University Press, 1995.

Broyles-González, Yolanda. *El Teatro Campesino: Theater in the Chicano Movement.* Austin: University of Texas Press, 1994.

Burckholder, Mark A., and Lyman L. Johnson. *Colonial Latin America.* New York: Oxford University Press, 1998.

Burkhart, Louise M. *Before Guadalupe: The Virgin Mary in Early Colonial Nahuatl Literature.* Monograph 13. Albany, NY: Institute for Mesoamerican Studies., 2001.

———. *Holy Wednesday: A Nahua Drama from Early Colonial Mexico.* Philadephia: University of Pennsylvania Press, 1996.

Butler, Judith. *Bodies That Matter: On the Discursive Limits of "Sex."* New York: Routledge, 1993.

———. *Excitable Speech: A Politics of the Performative.* New York: Routledge, 1997.

———. "Performative Acts and Gender Constitution." In *Performing Feminisms: Feminist Critical Theory and Theatre,* ed. Sue-Ellen Case. Baltimore: Johns Hopkins University Press, 1990.

———. *The Psychic Life of Power: Theories of Subjection.* Stanford: Stanford University Press, 1997.

Caillois, Roger. *Man, Play and Games.* Trans. Meyer Barash. New York: Schocken Books, 1979.

Campa, Román de la. *Latin Americanism.* Minneapolis: University of Minnesota Press, 1999.

Carlos, Juan, and Garcia Cabrera. *Ofensas a dios: Pleitos e injurias.* Cuzco: Bartolomé de Las Casas, 1994.

Carlson, Marvin. *Performance: A Critical Introduction.* London: Routledge, 1996.

———. *Theories of the Theatre.* Ithaca: Cornell University Press, 1984.

Carruthers, Mary. *The Book of Memory: A Study of Memory in Medieval Culture.* New York: Cambridge University Press, 1990.

Caruth, Cathy. *Unclaimed Experience: Trauma, Narrative, and History.* Baltimore: Johns Hopkins University Press, 1996.

———, ed. *Trauma: Explorations in Memory.* Baltimore: Johns Hopkins University Press, 1995.

Case, Sue-Ellen. *The Domain-Matrix.* Bloomington: Indiana University Press, 1996.

———. *Feminism and Theatre.* New York: Methuen, 1988.

———, ed. *Performing Feminisms: Feminist Critical Theory and Theatre.* Baltimore: Johns Hopkins University Press, 1990.

———, ed. *Split Britches.* London: Routledge, 1996.

Case, Sue-Ellen, and Janelle Reinelt, eds. *The Performance of Power.* Iowa City: University of Iowa Press, 1991.

Caso, Alfonso. *El pueblo del sol.* Mexico City: Fondo de Cultura Economica, 1953.

Cervantes, Fernando. *The Devil in the New World.* New Haven: Yale University Press, 1994.

Chow, Rey. "Where Have All the Natives Gone?" In *Writing Diaspora.* Bloomington: University of Indiana Press, 1993.

Cieza de Leon, Pedro de. *The Discovery and Conquest of Peru.* Trans. Alexandra Parma Cook, and Noble David Cook. Durham: Duke University Press, 1998.

Cisneros, Sandra. *Woman Hollering Creek.* New York: Random House, 1991.

Clendinnen, Inga. *Ambivalent Conquests.* Cambridge, England: Cambridge University Press, 1987.

———. *The Aztecs: An Interpretation.* Cambridge, England: Cambridge University Press, 1991.

Clifford, James. *The Predicament of Culture: Twentieth-Century Ethnography, Literature, and Art.* Cambridge, MA: Harvard University Press, 1988.

Clifford, James, and George E. Marcus, eds. *Writing Culture: The Poetics and Politics of Ethnography.* Berkeley: University of California Press, 1986.

Columbus, Christopher. *The Four Voyages of Christopher Columbus.* Ed. and trans. J. M. Cohen. Middlesex, England: Penguin Books, 1969.

———. *Four Voyages to the New World: Letters and Selected Documents: A Bilingual Edition.* Ed. and trans. R. H. Major. Gloucester, MA: Peter Smith, 1978.

———. *The Journal of Christopher Columbus.* Trans. Cecil Jane. New York: Clarkson N. Potter, 1960.

———. *Letters from America: Columbus' First Accounts of the 1492 Voyage.* Trans. B. W. Ife. London: King's College London, 1992.

Connerton, Paul. *How Societies Remember.* Cambridge, England: Cambridge University Press, 1989.

Conquergood, Dwight. "Interdisciplinary Interventions and Radical Research." Paper presented at the Cultural Intersections Conference, Northwestern University, October 9, 1999.

Cooper Alarcón, Daniel. *The Aztec Palimpsest.* Tuscon: University of Arizona Press, 1997.

Cope, R. Douglas. *The Limits of Racial Domination.* Madison: University of Wisconsin Press, 1994.

Corominas, Joan. *Breve diccionario etimologico de la lengua castellana.* Madrid: Gredos, 1961.

Cortés, Hernán. *Cartas de relación.* Mexico City: Porrúa, 1981.

———. *Letters from Mexico.* Trans. Anthony Pagden. New Haven: Yale University Press, 1986.

Cotto-Escalera, Brenda Luz. "Grupo Cultural Yuyachkani: Group Work and Collective Creation in Contemporary Latin American Theatre." Ph.D. diss., University of Texas, Austin, 1995.

Cypess, Sandra Messinger. *La Malinche in Mexican Literature.* Austin: University of Texas Press, 1991.

Davis, Darien J., ed. *Slavery and Beyond: The African Impact on Latin America and the Caribbean.* Wilmington, DE: SR Books, 1995.

Dawkins, Richard. *The Selfish Gene.* New York: Oxford University Press, 1976.

de Certeau, Michel. *Heterologies: Discourse on the Other.* Trans. Brian Massumi. Minneapolis: University of Minnesota Press, 1986.

———. *The Practice of Everyday Life.* Trans. Steven Rendall. Berkeley: University of California Press, 1984.

———. *The Writing of History.* Trans. Tom Conley. New York: Columbia University Press, 1988.

Debord, Guy. *Comments of the Society of the Spectacle.* Trans. Malcolm Imrie. London: Verso, 1998.

———. *Society of the Spectacle.* Detroit: Black and Red, 1983.

Derian, James Der. *Virtuous War: Mapping the Military-Industrial-Media-Entertainment Network.* Boulder, CO: Westview, 2001.

Derrida, Jacques. *Archive Fever.* Trans. Eric Prenowitz. Chicago: University of Chicago Press, 1995.

———. *Margins of Philosophy.* Trans. Alan Bass. Chicago: University of Chicago Press, 1982.

———. *Of Grammatology.* Trans. Gayatri Chakravorty Spivak. Baltimore: Johns Hopkins University Press, 1974.

———. *Specters of Marx.* Trans. Peggy Kamuf. London: Routledge, 1994.

———. *Writing and Difference.* Trans. Alan Bass. Chicago: University of Chicago Press, 1978.

Díaz del Castillo, Bernal. *The Conquest of New Spain.* Trans. J. M Cohen. London: Penguin, 1963.

Dolan, Jill. *Geographies of Learning: Theory and Practice, Activism, and Performance.* Middletown, CT: Wesleyan University Press, 2001.

Doyle, Kate, and Adam Isacson. "A *New* New World Order? U.S. Military Mission Grows in Latin America." *NACLA Report on the Americas* 35, no. 3 (2001): 14–20.

Durán, Fray Diego. *Book of the Gods and Rites and the Ancient Calendar.* Ed. and trans. Fernando Horcasitas and Doris Heyden. Norman: University of Oklahoma Press, 1971.

———. *Historia de las Indias de Nueva España e islas de la Tierra Firme.* Mexico City: Porrúa, 1984.

———. *History of the Indies of New Spain.* Trans. Doris Heyden. Norman: University of Oklahoma Press, 1994.

Durkheim, Emile. *The Elementary Forms of the Religious Life.* New York: Free Press, 1915.

Eisenhower, John S. D. *So Far from God.* Norman: University of Oklahoma Press, 1989.

Felman, Shoshana, and Dori Laub. *Testimony: Crisis of Witnessing in Literature, Psychoanalysis, and History.* New York: Routledge, 1992.

Fernández, Amaya, and Lourdes Leiva Viacava. *La mujer en la conquista y la evangelización en el Perú.* Lima: Fondo Editorial.

Fernández Retamar, Roberto. *Calibán: Apuntes sobre la cultura en nuestra América.* Mexico City: Editorial Diogenes, 1974.

Flores, Richard. *Los Pastores: History and Performance in the Mexican Shepherd's Play of South Texas.* Washington, DC: Smithsonian Institution Press, 1995.

Florescano, Enrique. *La bandera mexicana: Breve historia de su formación y simbolismo.* Mexico City: Fondo de Cultura Económica, 1999.

———. *Etnia, estado y nación.* Mexico City: Aguilar, 1996.

———. *Memory, Myth, and Time in Mexico: From the Aztecs to Independence.* Trans. Albert G. Bork. Austin: University of Texas Press, 1994.

———. *The Myth of Quetzalcoatl.* Baltimore: Johns Hopkins University Press, 1984.

Franco Sodja, Carlos. *Leyendas mexicanas de antes y después de la conquista.* Mexico City: Edamex, 1993.

Frank, Marcie. "The Critic as Preformance Artist: Susan Sontag's Writing and Gay Cultures." In *Camp Grounds: Style and Homosexuality,* ed. David Bergman. Amherst: University of Massachusetts Press, 1994.

Frankovits, Andre, ed. *Seduced and Abandoned.* New York: Stonemoss, 1984.

Freud, Sigmund. *Civilization and Its Discontents.* Trans. James Strachey. New York: Norton, 1961.

———. *The Future of an Illusion.* Trans. James Strachey. New York: Norton, 1961.

———. "A Note upon the 'Mystic Writing Pad.'" In *The Standard Edition of the Complete Psychological Works of Sigmund Freud.* Ed. and trans. James Strachey. London: Hogarth Press, 1953–1966.

Freyre, Gilberto. *The Master of Slaves: A Study in the Development of Brazilian Civilization.* Berkeley: University of California Press, 1986.

Fusco, Coco. *English Is Broken Here: Notes on Cultural Fusion in the Americas.* New York: New Press, 1995.

García Canclini, Néstor. *Hybrid Cultures: Strategies for Entering and Leaving Modernity.* Trans. Christopher L. Chiappari and Silvia L. López. Minneapolis: University of Minnesota Press, 1995.

García Saiz, María Concepción. *Las castas mexicanas/The Mexican Castes.* Milan: Olivetti, 1989.

Gardina Pestana, Carla, and Sharon V. Salinger, eds. *Inequality in Early America.* Hanover, NH: University Press of New England, 1999.

Garibay K., Angel Maria. *Historia de la literatura náhuatl.* Mexico City: Porrúa, 1987.

———. *Llave del náhuatl.* Mexico City: Porrúa, 1994.

———. *Panorama literario de los pueblos nahuas.* Mexico City: Porrúa, 1987.

Garza Cuaron, Beatriz, and Georges Baudot. *Historia de la literatura mexicana 1.* Mexico City: Siglo Veintiuno Editores, 1996.

Geertz, Clifford. *The Interpretation of Cultures.* New York: Basic Books, 1973.

———. *Local Knowledge: Further Essays in Interpretive Anthropology.* New York: Basic Books, 1983.

Géronimo de Mendieta, Fray. *Historia eclesiastica indiana.* Vol. 1. Mexico City: Cien de México, 1997.

Gillespie, Susan D. *The Aztec Kings.* Tucson: University of Arizona Press, 1989.

Glass, Aaron. "Performance and Performativity: Cultural and Linguistic Models." Unpublished paper, 2002.

Gobello, José. *Diccionario Lunfardo*. Buenos Aires: Pena Lillo Editor, 1982.

Goffman, Erving. *The Presentation of Self in Everyday Life*. New York: Doubleday, 1959.

Gómez-Peña, Guillermo. *Warrior for Gringostroika*. St. Paul, MN: Graywolf Press, 1993.

González Torres, Yolotl. *El sacrificio humano entre los Mexicas*. Mexico City: Fondo de Cultura Económica, 1985.

Graham, Richard, ed. *The Idea of Race in Latin America*. Austin: University of Texas Press, 1990.

Greenblatt, Stephen. *Marvelous Possessions: The Wonder of the New World*. Chicago: University of Chicago Press, 1991.

———, ed. *New World Encounters*. Berkeley: University of California Press, 1993.

Griswold del Castillo, Richard. *The Treaty of Guadalupe Hidalgo: A Legacy of Confict*. Norman: University of Oklahoma Press, 1990.

Gruzinski, Serge. *The Aztecs: Rise and Fall of an Empire*. New York: Harry N. Abrams, 1987.

———. *La colonización de lo imaginario*. Mexico City: Fondo de Cultura Económica, 1991.

———. *The Conquest of Mexico*. Trans. Eileen Corrigan. Cambridge, England: Polity Press, 1993.

Guibovich Perez, Pedro. *En defensa de dios*. Lima: Ediciones del Congreso del Perú, 1998.

Gutiérrez, Ramón A. *When Jesus Came, the Corn Mothers Went Away*. Stanford: Stanford University Press, 1991.

Hampe Martínez, Teodoro. *Santo oficio e historia colonial*. Lima: Ediciones del Congreso del Perú, 1998.

Hanke, Lewis, and Jane M. Rausch, eds. *People and Issues in Latin American History: The Colonial Experience*. New York: Markus Wiener Publishing, 1999.

Harris, Max. *Aztecs, Moors, and Christians: Festivals of Reconquest in Mexico and Spain*. Austin: University of Texas Press, 2000.

———. *The Dialogical Theatre*. New York: St. Martin's Press, 1993.

———. "Disguised Reconciliations: Indigenous Voices in Early Franciscan Missionary Drama in Mexico." *Radical History* 53 (spring 1992): 13–22.

Hartman, Saidiya V. *Scenes of Subjection: Terror, Slavery, and Self-Making in Nineteenth-Century America*. New York: Oxford University Press, 1997.

Haslip-Viera, Gabriel. *Crime and Punishment in Late Colonial Mexico City*. Albuquerque: University of New Mexico Press, 1999.

Hassig, Ross. *Aztec Warfare: Imperial Expansion and Political Control*. Norman: University of Oklahoma Press, 1988.

———. *Time, History, and Belief in Aztec and Colonial Mexico*. Austin: University of Texas Press, 2001.

Hemming, John. *The Conquest of the Incas*. San Diego: Harcourt Brace, 1970.

Herren, Ricardo. *Doña Marina, la Malinche*. Mexico City: Planeta, 1993.

Hirsch, Marianne, and Valerie Smith, eds. "Gender and Cultural Memory." Special issue of *Signs* (fall 2002).

Hoberman, Louisa Schell, and Susan Migden Socolow, eds. *Cities and Society in Colonial Latin America*. Albuquerque: University of New Mexico Press, 1986.

Horcasitas, Fernando. *El teatro náhuatl*. Mexico City: Universidad Nacional Autónoma de México, 1974.

Hulme, Peter. *Colonial Encounters: Europe and the Native Caribbean, 1492-1797*. London: Routledge, 1986.

Hymes, Dell. "Breakthrough into Performance." In *Folklore, Performance and Communication*, ed. D. Ben-Amos and K. S. Goldstein. Hague: Mouton,1975.

Ife, B. W., ed. *Letters from America: Columbus's First Accounts of the 1492 Voyage*. London: King's College London, School of Humanities, 1992.

Inés de la Cruz, Sor Juana. *Autos sacramentales*. Mexico City: Universidad Nacional Autónoma de México, 1995.

———. *The Divine Narcissus*. Trans. Patricia A. Peters and Renee Domeier, OSB. Albuquerque: University of New Mexico Press, 1998.

Itier, Cesar. *El teatro quechua en el Cuzco*. Cuzco: Bartolomé de Las Casas, 1995.

Jackson, Robert H. *Race, Caste, and Status*. Albuquerque: University of New Mexico Press, 1999.

Jameson, Fredric. *Brecht and Method*. London: Verso, 1998.

Johansson, Patrick, ed. *Teatro mexicano: Historia y dramaturgia*. Vol. 1, *Festejos, ritos propiciatorios y rituals prehispáncios*. Mexico City: Consejo para la Cultura y las Artes, 1992.

Joyce, Rosemary A. *Gender and Power in Prehispanic Mesoamerica*. Austin: University of Texas Press, 2000.

Katz, Friedrich. *The Ancient American Civilizations*. Trans. K. M. Lois Simpson. New York: Praeger, 1974.

Kear, Adrian, and Deborah Lynn Steinberg, eds. *Mourning Diana: Nation, Culture, and the Performance of Grief*. London: Routledge, 1999.

Kirby, Michael. "Environmental Theatre." In *Total Theatre*, ed. E. T. Kirby. New York: Dutton, 1969.

Kirshenblatt-Gimblett, Barbara. *Destination Culture: Tourism, Museums, and Heritage*. Berkeley: University of California Press, 1998.

———. "Folklore's Crisis." *Journal of American Folklore* 111, no. 441 (1998): 281–327.

Klein, Cecelia F. "Fighting with Femininity: Gender and War in Aztec Mexico." In *Gender Rhetorics*, ed. Richard Trexler. Binghamton, NY: MRTS, 1994.

Klein, Herbert S. *African Slavery in Latin America and the Caribbean*. New York: Oxford University Press, 1986.

Knight, Alan. "Racism, Revolution, and Indigenismo: Mexico, 1910–1940." In *The Idea of Race in Latin America, 1870–1940*, ed. Richard Graham. Austin: University of Texas Press, 1990.

Kobayashi, José María. *La educación como conquista*. Mexico City: El Colegio de México, 1997.

Krauze, Enrique. *Mexico: Biography of Power.* Trans. Hank Heifetz. New York: HarperPerennial, 1997.

Lafaye, J. *Quetzalcoatl y Guadalupe.* Mexico City: Fondo de Cultura Económica, 1977.

Landa, Fray Diego de. *Relación de las cosas de Yucatán.* Mexico City: Porrúa, 1986.

———. *Yucatán: Before and after the Conquest.* Trans. William Gates. Mexico City: San Fernando, 1993.

Lane, Jill. "On Colonial Forgetting: The Conquest of New Mexico and Its Historia." In *The Ends of Performance,* ed. Peggy Phelan and Jill Lane. New York: New York University Press, 1998.

Las Casas, Bartolomé de. *Obra indigenista.* Madrid: Alianza Editorial, 1985.

———. *A Short Account of the Destruction of the Indies.* Trans. Nigel Griffin. London: Penguin Books, 1992.

Latour, Bruno. "A Few Steps toward an Anthropology of the Iconoclastic Gesture," *Science in Context* 10, no. 1 (1997).

Laub, Dori. "Truth and Testimony: The Process and the Struggle." In *Trauma: Explorations in Memory,* ed. Cathy Caruth, Baltimore: Johns Hopkins University Press, 1995.

Lazo, Raimundo. *Historia de la literatura hispanoamericana.* Mexico City: Porrúa, 1965.

Ledesma, Alberto. "Undocumented Crossings: Narratives of Mexican Immigration to the United States." In *Culture across Borders: Mexican Immigration and Popluar Culture,* ed. David R. Maciel and Maria Herrera-Sobek. Tucson: University of Arizona Press, 1998.

Léon-Portilla, Miguel. *Los antiguos Mexicanos.* Mexico City: Fondo de Cultura Económica, 1961.

———. *The Aztec Image of Self and Society.* Salt Lake City: University of Utah Press, 1992.

———. *Aztec Thought and Culture.* Trans. Jack Emory Davis. Norman: University of Oklahoma Press, 1963.

———. *Bernardino de Sahagun.* Mexico City: Universidad Nacional Autónoma de México, 1999.

———. *Fifteen Poets of the Aztec World.* Norman: University of Oklahoma Press, 1992.

———. *Literaturas indigenas de Mexico.* Mexico City: Fondo de Cultura Económica, 1992.

———. *México Tenochtitlán: Su tiempo y espacio sagrados.* Mexico City: Plaza y Valdes Editores, 1987.

———. *Pre-Columbian Literatures of Mexico.* Trans. Grace Lobanov and Miguel Léon-Portilla. Norman: University of Oklahoma Press, 1969.

———. *El reverso de la conquista.* Mexico City: Joaquin Mortiz, 1964.

———. *Visión de los vencidos.* Mexico City: Universidad Nacional Autónoma de México, 1982.

———, ed. *The Broken Spears: The Aztec Account of the Conquest of Mexico.* Boston: Beacon Press, 1962.

Lévi-Strauss, Claude. *Tristes Tropiques: An Anthropological Study of Primitive Societies in Brazil.* Trans. John Russell. New York: Atheneum, 1967.

Lipsitz, George. *Time Passages: Collective Memory and American Popular Culture.* Ed. Stanley Aronowitz, Sandra M. Gilbert, and George Lipsitz. Minneapolis: University of Minnesota Press, 1990.

Lockhart, James. *The Nahuas after the Conquest.* Stanford: Stanford University Press, 1992.

———. *Of Things of the Indies.* Stanford: Stanford University Press, 1999.

Lohmann Villena, Guillermo. *Inquisidores, virreyes y disidentes.* Lima: Fondo Editorial del Congreso del Perú, 1999.

Lope de Vega, Tirso de Molina, and Calderón de la Barca. *Teatro indiano.* Mexico City: Trillas, 1988.

López Austin, Alfredo. *Cuerpo humano e ideologia.* Vols. 1 and 2. Mexico City: Universidad Nacional Autónoma de México, 1989–90.

———. *La educación de los antiguos Nahuas.* 2 vols. Mexico City: Ediciones El Caballito, 1985.

———. "La parte feminina del cosmos." *Arqueología Mexicana.* 5, no. 29 (1998): 6–13.

———. *The Rabbit on the Moon.* Trans. Bernard R. Ortiz de Montellano and Thelma Ortiz de Montellano. Salt Lake City: University of Utah Press, 1996.

López de Gomara, Francisco. *Cortés: The Life of the Conqueror by His Secretary.* Trans. Lesley Byrd Simpson. Berkeley: University of California Press, 1964.

Luis Martínez, José. *Nezahualcoyotl, vida y obra.* Mexico City: Fondo de Cultura Económica, 1972.

Maciel, David R., and Maria Herrera-Sobek, eds. *Culture across Borders: Mexican Immigration and Popular Culture.* Tucson: University of Arizona Press, 1998.

Major, R. H., ed. and trans. *Christopher Columbus: Four Voyages to the New World, Letters and Selected Documents: A Bilingual Edition.* Gloucester, MA: Peter Smith, 1978.

Manrique, Nelson. *El universo mental de la conquista de América.* Lima: Desco, 1993.

Marti, Samuel. *Music before Columbus.* Mexico City: Ediciones Euroamericanas, 1978.

Martín-Barbero, Jesús. *De los medios a las mediaciones: Comunicación, cultura y hegemonia.* Mexico City: Ediciones G. Gill, 1987.

———. "Memory and Form in the Latin American Soap Opera." Trans. Marina Elias. In *To Be Continued . . . : Soap Operas around the World,* ed. Robert C. Allen. London: Routledge, 1995.

Matos Moctezuma, Eduardo. *Guia Oficial: Templo Mayor.* Mexico City: Inah-Salvat, 1989.

McKendrick, Melveena. *Theatre in Spain.* Cambridge, England: Cambridge University Press, 1989.

McKenzie, Jon. *Perform or Else: From Discipline to Performance.* London: Routledge, 2001.

Meyer, Moe. "Introduction: Reclaiming the Discourse of Camp." In *The Politics and Poetics of Camp,* ed. Moe Meyer. London: Routledge, 1994.

Miller, Beth, ed. *Women in Hispanic Literature: Icons and Fallen Idols.* Berkeley: University of California Press, 1983.

Millones, Luis. *Dioses familiares.* Lima: Ediciones del Congreso del Perú, 1999.

Milliones, Luis, et al. *Retorno de las huacas.* Lima: IEP/SPP, 1990.

Mitchell, W. J. T. *Iconology: Image, Text, Ideology.* Chicago: University of Chicago Press, 1986.

Moliner, María. *Diccionario de uso del español.* Madrid: Editorial Gredos, 1967.

Molloy, Sylvia, and Robert McKee, eds. *Hispanisms and Homosexualities.* Durham: Duke University Press, 1998.

Montemayor, Alma. *Teatro y maroma Chihuahua: Siglos XVIII y XIX.* Chihuahua: Instituto Chihuahuense de la Cultura, 1998.

Moraga, Cherríe. *Heroes and Saints and Other Plays.* Albuquerque, NM: West End Press, 1994.

———. *Loving in the War Years.* Boston: South End Press, 1983.

Motolinía, Fray Toribio. *Historia de los Indios de la Nueva España.* Mexico City: Editorial Porrúa, 1969.

———. *History of the Indians of New Spain.* Ed. and trans. Elizabeth Andros Foster. [Berkeley, CA]: Cortés Society, 1950.

Mullanay, Steven. *The Place of Stage.* Ann Arbor: University of Michigan Press, 1988.

Muñoz, José Esteban. *Disidentifications: Queers of Color and the Performance of Politics.* Minneapolis: University of Minnesota Press, 1999.

Myers, Kathleen A., and Amanda Powell, eds. *A Wild Country Out in the Garden.* Bloomington: Indiana University Press, 1999.

Nájera-Ramírez, Olga. *La fiesta de los Tastoanes.* Albuquerque: University of New Mexico Press, 1997.

Noguez, Xavier. *Documentos guadalupanos: Un estudio sobre las fuentes de información tempranas en torno a las mariofanias en el Tepeyac.* Mexico City: El Colegio Mexiquense y Fondo de Cultura Económica, 1995.

Nora, Pierre. "Between Memory and History: Les Lieux de Mémoire." In *History and Memory in African-American Culture,* ed. Genevieve Fabre and Robert O'Meally. New York: Oxford University Press, 1994.

Novo, Salvador. *The War of the Fatties and Other Stories from Aztec History.* Trans. Michael Anderson. Austin: University of Texas Press, 1994.

Nunca Más: The Report of the Argentine National Commission of the Disappeared. New York: Farrar Straus Giroux, 1986.

O'Gorman, Edmundo. *La invención de América.* Mexico City: Tierra Firma, 1958.

Ortíz, Fernando. *Contrapunteo cubano del tabaco y el azucar.* Caracas: Biblioteca Ayacucho, 1978.

Padial Guerchoux, Anita, and Manuel Vazquez-Bigi. *Quiche Vinak.* Mexico City: Fondo de Cultura Económica, 1991.

Palma, Ricardo. *Anales de la inquisición de Lima.* Lima: Edicones del Congreso de la Republica, 1997.

Pané, Fray Ramón. *An Account of the Antiquities of the Indians.* Ed. José Juan Arrom. Durham: Duke University Press, 1999.

Pantoja, Julio. "Los Hijos, Tucumán veinte años después." Available http://www. juliopantoja.com.ar/, 1999.

Partida, Armando, ed. *Teatro mexicano: Historia y dramaturgia.* Mexico City: Consejo Nacional para las Artes, 1993.

Pavis, Patrice, ed. *The Intercultural Performance Reader.* London: Routledge, 1996.

Paz, Octavio. *El laberinto de la soledad.* Mexico City: Fondo de Cultura Económica, 1950.

———. *The Labyrinth of Solitude: Life and Thought in Mexico.* Trans. Lysander Kemp. New York: Grove Press, 1961.

Perry, Mary Elizabeth, and Anne J. Cruz, eds. *Cultural Encounters: The Impact of the Inquisition in Spain and the New World.* Berkeley: University of California Press, 1991.

Phelan, Peggy. *Unmarked: The Politics of Performance.* London: Routledge, 1993.

Phelan, Peggy, and Jill Lane, eds. *The Ends of Performance.* New York: New York Unversity Press, 1998.

Phillips, Rachel. "Marina/Malinche: Masks and Shadows." In *Women in Hispanic Literature: Icons and Fallen Idols,* ed. Beth Miller. Berkeley: University of California Press, 1983.

Pino Iturrieta, Elias. *Fueros, civilizacion y ciudadania.* Caracas: Universidad Católica Andres Bello, 2000.

Poole, Deborah. *Vision, Race and Modernity: A Visual Economy of the Andean Image World.* Princeton: Princeton University Press, 1997.

Poole, Deborah, and Gerarado Renique. *Peru: Time of Fear.* London: Latin American Bureau, 1992.

Poole, Stafford. *Our Lady of Guadalupe: The Origins and Sources of a Mexican National Symbol, 1531-1797.* Tucson: University of Arizona Press, 1996.

Portilla, Jorge. *La fenomenología del relajo.* 2d ed. Mexico City: Fondo de Cultura Económica, 1986.

Pratt, Mary Louise. *Imperial Eyes: Travel Writing and Transculturation.* London: Routledge, 1992.

Propp, V. *Morphology of the Folktale.* Trans. Laurence Scott. Austin: University of Texas Press, 1988.

Queiros Mattoso, Katia M. de. *To Be a Slave in Brazil: 1550-1888.* Trans. Arthur Goldhammer. New Brunswick, NJ: Rutgers University Press, 1986.

Quezada, Noemí, Martha Eugenia Rodriguez, and Marcela Suarez. *Inquisición novohispana.* Vol. 1. Mexico City: Universidad Nacional Autónoma de México, 2000.

Quitt, Ricardo Pérez. *Historia del teatro en puebla (siglos XVI a XX).* Mexico City: Benemerita Universidad Autónoma de Puebla, 1999.

Rabasa, José. *Writing Violence on the Northern Frontier.* Durham: Duke University Press, 2000.

Ralli, Teresa. "Fragments of Memory." Trans. Margaret Carson. In *Holy Terrors: Latin*

American Women Perform, ed. Diana Taylor and Roselyn Costantino. Durham: Duke University Press, 2003.

Rama, Angel. *The Lettered City*. Trans. John Charles Chasteen. Durham, NC: Duke University Press, 1996.

———. *Transculturación narrativa en América Latina*. Mexico City: Siglo XXI, 1982.

Ramiréz, Ignacio. *Discursos y artículos*. Mexico City: Imprenta Victoria, 1915.

Ramos Smith, Maya. *El actor, en el siglo XVIII*. Mexico City: Colección Escenología, 1994.

———. *La danza en México durante la época colonial*. Mexico City: Alianza Editorial Mexicana, 1990.

Ramos Smith, Maya, Tito Vasconcelos, Luis Armando Lamadrid, and Xabier Lizarraga Cruchaga, eds. *Censura y teatro novohispano (1539–1822): Ensayos y antología de documentos*. Mexico City: Conaculta, INBA, Citru, 1998.

Renan, Ernest. "What Is a Nation?" In *Nation and Narration*, ed. Homi Bhabha. London: Routledge, 1990.

Reyes de la Maza, Luis. *El teatro en México durante el segundo imperio (1862–1867)*. Mexico City: Imprenta Universitaria, 1959.

———. *El teatro en México en la época de Juarez (1868–1872)*. Mexico City: Imprenta Universitaria, 1961.

Ridley, Matt. *Genome*. New York: Harper Collins, 1999.

Roach, Joseph. *Cities of the Dead: Circum-Atlantic Performance*. New York: Columbia University Press, 1996.

Robelo, Cecilio A. *Diccionario de mitologia náhuatl*. 2 vols. Mexico City: Editorial Innovación, 1980.

Rodríguez Cuadros, Evangelina. *La técnica del actor español en el barroco hipotesis y documentos*. Madrid: Editorial Castalia, 1998.

Rogers, Mark. "Spectacular Bodies: Folklorization and the Politics of Identity in Ecuadorian Beauty Pageants." *Journal of Latin American Anthropology: Performance, Identity, and Historical Consciousness in the Andes* 3, no.2 (1998):54–85.

Rony, Fatimah Tobing. *The Third Eye: Race, Cinema, and Ethnographic Spectacle*. Durham: Duke University Press, 1996.

Rosaldo, Michele. "The Things We Do with Words." In *Language and Society*. 11 (1982): 203–35.

Rowe, William, and Vivian Schelling. *Memory and Modernity: Popular Culture in Latin America*. London: Verso, 1991.

Rubio, Miguel. "Encuentro con el hombre andino." In *Grupo Cultural Yuyachkani, Allpa Rayku: Una experencia de teatro popular*. 2d ed. Lima: Edición del Grupo Cultural Yuyachkani y Escuelas Campesinas de la CCP, 1985.

Ruíz de Alarcón, Hernando. *Treatise on the Heathen Superstitions*. Trans. J. Richard Andrews and Ross Hassig. Norman: University of Oklahoma Press, 1984.

Sahagún, Bernardino de. *Florentine Codex*. Ed. and trans. Arthur J. O. Anderson and Charles E. Dibble. Books 1–12. Santa Fe, NM: School of American Research and University of Utah, 1982.

——. *Historia general de las cosas de Nueva España*. 4 vols. Mexico City: Editorial Porrúa, 1956.

Salazar del Alcazar, Hugo. "Los músicos ambulantes." La escena latinoamericana, no. 2 (August 1989): 23.

Sassen, Saskia. *The Global City*. Princeton: Princeton University Press. 1991.

Saussure, Ferdinand de. *Course in General Linguistics*. New York: Philosophical Library, 1959.

Schechner, Richard. *Between Theater and Anthropology*. Philadelphia: University of Pennsylvania Press, 1985.

——. *The Future of Ritual: Writings on Culture and Performance*. London: Routledge, 1993.

——. *Performance Studies: An Introduction*. London: Routledge, 2002.

Schechner, Richard, and Willa Appel, eds. *By Means of Performance: Intercultural Studies of Theatre and Ritual*. New York: Cambridge University Press, 1990.

Scheffler, Lilian, Regina Reynoso, and Victor Inzua C. *El Juego de Pelota Prehispanico*. Mexico City: Ediciones Coyoacan, 1998.

Schilling, Hildburg. *Teatro profano en la Nueva España: Fines del siglo XVI a mediados del XVIII*. Mexico City: Imprenta Universitaria, 1958.

Schneider, Rebecca. "Archives Performance Remains." *Performance Research* 6, no. 2 (2001): 100–108.

Schroeder, Susan, Stephanie Wood, and Robert Haskett, eds. *Indian Women of Early Mexico*. Norman: University of Oklahoma Press, 1997.

Scott, James C. *Domination and the Arts of Resistance: Hidden Transcripts*. New Haven: Yale University Press, 1990.

Searle, John. "What Is a Speech Act?" In *Philosophy in America*, ed. Max Black. Ithaca: Cornell University Press, 1965.

Seed, Patricia. *Ceremonies of Possession in Europe's Conquest of the New World, 1492–1640*. New York: Cambridge University Press, 1995.

——. *To Love, Honor, and Obey in Colonial Mexico*. Stanford: Stanford University Press, 1988.

Segala, Amos. *Literatura náhuatl*. Mexico City: Grijalbo, 1990.

Sekula, Allan. "The Body and the Archive." *October* 39 (1987): 3–64.

Sepúlveda, Juan Ginés de. *Demócrates segundo, o de las justas causas de la guerra contra los indios*. Madrid: Consejo Superior de Investigaciones Científicas, 1951.

Shohat, Ella, and Robert Stam. *Unthinking Eurocentrism: Multiculturalism and the Media*. New York: Routledge, 1994.

Silver, Brian L. *The Ascent of Science*. New York: Oxford University Press, 1998.

Siméon, Rémi. *Diccionario de la lengua náhuatl o mexicana*. Mexico City: Siglo Veintiuno, 1977.

Skeat, Walter W. *A Concise Etymological Dictionary of the English Language*. New York: Perigree Books, 1980.

Smith, Michael E. *The Aztecs*. Oxford: Blackwell, 1996.

Solis, Antonia de. *Historia de la conquista de México.* Mexico City: Porrúa, 1978.

Sommer, Doris. *Foundational Fictions: The National Romances of Latin America.* Berkeley: University of California Press, 1991.

———. *Proceed with Caution.* Cambridge, MA: Harvard University Press, 1999.

Sontag, Susan. "Notes on Camp." *Against Interpretation.* New York: Dell, 1966.

Sousa, Lisa, Stafford Poole, and James Lockhart, eds. *The Story of Guadalupe: Luis Laso de la Vega's Huei tlamahuicoltica of 1649.* Stanford: Stanford University Press and UCLA Latin American Center Publications, 1998.

Soustelle, Jacques. *Daily Life of the Aztecs: On the Eve of the Spanish Conquest.* Stanford: Stanford University Press, 1961.

Spitta, Silvia. *Between Two Waters: Narratives of Transculturation in Latin America.* Houston: Rice University Press.

Spivak, Gayatri. "Can the Subaltern Speak?" In *Marxism and the Interpretation of Culture,* ed. Cary Nelson and Lawrence Grossberg. Urbana: University of Illinois Press, 1988.

Stam, Robert. "Specificities: From Hybridity to the Aesthetics of Garbage." *Social Identities* 3,.no. 2 (1997): 275–90.

Stannard, David E. *American Holocaust: The Conquest of the New World.* New York: Oxford University Press, 1992.

Sten, María. *Los codices de México.* Mexico City: Joaquin Mortiz, 1972.

———. *El teatro franciscano en la Nueva España.* Mexico City: Conaculta, 2000.

Stoklos, Denise. *The Essential Theatre.* São Paulo: Denise Stoklos Productions, 1992.

———. *500 Anos: Um Fax de Denise Stoklos para Cristóvão Colombo.* São Paulo: Denise Stoklos Productions, 1992.

Suárez-Orozco, Marcelo. "The Heritage of Enduring a 'Dirty War': Psychosocial Aspects of Terror in Argentina, 1976–1983." *Journal of Psychohistory* 18, no. 4 (1991): 469–505.

Taussig, Michael. *Mimesis and Alterity.* New York: Routledge, 1993.

Taylor, Diana. *Disappearing Acts: Spectacles of Gender and Nationality in Argentina's Dirty War.* Durham: Duke University Press, 1997.

———. "Opening Remarks." In *Negotiating Performance: Gender, Sexuality and Theatricality in Latin America,* ed. Diana Taylor and Juan Villegas. Durham: Duke University Press, 1994.

———. *Theatre of Crisis: Drama and Politics in Latin/o America.* Lexington: University of Kentucky Press, 1990.

———. "Transculturating Transculturation." *Performance Arts Journal* 13, no. 2 (1989): 90–104.

Taylor, Diana, and Roselyn Costantino, eds. *Holy Terrors: Latin American Women Perform.* Durham: Duke University Press, 2003.

Taylor, William B. *Drinking, Homicide, and Rebellion in Colonial Mexican Villages.* Stanford: Stanford University Press, 1979.

Thoreau, Henry David. *Walden and Civil Disobedience.* New York: Penguin Classics, 1986.

Todorov, Tzvetan. *The Conquest of America.* Trans. Richard Howard. New York: HarperPerennial, 1982.

Torgovnick, Marianna. *Gone Primitive: Savage Intellects, Modern Lives.* Chicago: University of Chicago Press, 1990.

Townsend, Richard F. *The Aztecs.* London: Thames and Hudson, 1992.

Trexler, Richard C. *Sex and Conquest.* New York: Cornell University Press, 1995.

———. "We Think, They Act: Clerical Readings of Missionary Theatre in Sixteenth-Century New Spain." In *Understanding Popular Culture: Europe from the Middle Ages to the Nineteenth Century,* ed. Steven L. Kaplan. Berlin: Mouton, 1984.

Turner, Victor. *The Anthropology of Performance.* New York: PAJ Publications, 1986.

———. *Dramas, Fields, and Metaphors: Symbolic Action in Human Society.* Ithaca: Cornell University Press, 1974.

———. *From Ritual to Theatre: The Human Seriousness of Play.* New York: Performing Arts Journal Publications, 1982.

Turrent, Lourdes. *La conquista musical de México.* Mexico City: Fondo de Cultura Económica, 1996.

Urías Horcasitas, Beatriz. *Indigena y criminal.* Mexico City: Conaculta, 2000.

Usigli, Rodolfo. *Mexico in the Theater.* Trans. Wilder P. Scott. University, MS: Romance Monographs, 1976.

Valdéz, Luis. *The Shrunken Head of Pancho Villa.* In *Necessary Theater,* ed. Jorge Huerta. Houston: Arte Público Press, 1989.

Vasconcelos, José. *The Cosmic Race/La raza cósmica.* Trans. Didier T. Jaén. Baltimore: Johns Hopkins University Press, 1997.

Vespucci, Amerigo. *Letters from a New World.* Trans. David Jacobson. New York: Marsilio, 1992.

Vetancourt, Agustin de. *Teatro mexicano: Crónica de la provincia del Santo Evangelio de México.* Mexico City: Porrúa, 1982.

Vidal, Hernan. *Socio-historia de la literatura colonial Hispanoamérica: Tres lecturas orgánicas.* Minneapolis: Institute for the Study of Ideologies and Literature, 1985.

Villanes, Carlos, and Isabel Cordova. *Literaturas de la América precolombina.* Madrid: Ediciones Istmo, 1990.

Villaseñor y Sánchez, Joseph Antonio. *Teatro americano.* Mexico City: Trillas, 1992.

Virilio, Paul. *Speed and Politics.* Trans. Mark Polizzotti. New York: Foreign Agents, 1977.

Wa Thiong'o, Ngugi. *Penpoints, Gunpoints and Dreams.* Oxford: Clarendon Press, 1998.

Wardy, Robert. *The Birth of Rhetoric: Gorgias, Plato, and Their Successors.* New York: Routledge, 1996.

Watanabe, José. *Antígona.* Lima: Yuyachkani/Comisión de Derechos Humanos, 2000.

———. *Antígona.* Trans. Margaret Carson. In *Holy Terrors: Latin American Women Perform,* ed. Diana Taylor and Roselyn Costantino. Durham: Duke University Press, 2003.

Weber, Carl. "AC/TC: Currents of Theatrical Exchange." *Performing Arts Journal,* nos. 33–34 (1989): 11–21.

Weber, Max. "Domination and Stratification." In *Sociological Writings*, ed. Wolf Heydebrand. New York: Continuum, 1994.

Webster, Susan Verdi. *Art and Ritual in Golden-Age Spain*. Princeton: Princeton University Press, 1998.

Williams, Eric. *From Columbus to Castro: The History of the Caribbean*. New York: Vintage Books, 1970.

Wolf, Eric. *Sons of Shaking Earth*. Chicago: University of Chicago Press, 1959.

Woodyard, George, ed. *The Modern Stage in Latin America: Six Plays*. New York: Dutton, 1971.

Yañez, Augustín. *Crónicas de la conquista*. Mexico City: Universidad Nacional Autónoma de México, 1993.

Ybarra-Frausto, Tomás. "Rasquachismo: A Chicano Sensibility." In *Chicano Art: Resistance and Affirmation, 1965–1985*, ed. Teresa McKenna, Yvonne Yarbro-Bejarano, and Richard Griswold del Castillo. Los Angeles: UCLA Wight Art Gallery, 1991.

Young, Robert J. C. *Colonial Desire: Hybridity in Theory, Culture and Race*. London: Routledge, 1995.

Zantop, Susanne. *Colonial Fantasies*. Durham: Duke University Press, 1997.

Zavala, Silvio. *La filosofía política en la conquista de América*. Mexico City: Tierra Firme, 1947.

Zevallos, Ortíz de. *El Perú en los albores del siglo*. Lima: Ediciones del Congreso del Perú, 1998.

Zorita, Alonso de. *Relación de la Nueva España*. Vols 1–2. Mexico City: Conaculta, 1999.

INDEX

Abercrombie, Thomas, 36
Abuelas de Plaza de Mayo, 165, 168, 169,
170, 173, 175, 178, 180, 188, 274; *Memoria
gráfica de Abuelas de Plaza de Mayo*
(exhibit), 178–80
Acosta, José de, 35
Acts of transfer, 1, 2, 46, 50, 54, 57, 69, 113,
120, 165
Adorno, Theodor, 204, 211
Aesthetics: of everyday life, 3, 15
African Americans. *See* Race
AIDS, 135, 152, 154
Alarcón, Norma, 99
Altar, 46, 109, 155, 252–55
Althusser, Louis, 234
Androgyny, 212, 231–32
Anzaldúa, Gloria, 99–100
Appadurai, Arjun, 236
Appropriation, 194–95, 209–10, 221
Arawack, 61
Archive, 29, 34, 36, 52, 55, 58, 62, 82, 89,
113, 114, 120, 123, 154, 171, 176, 178, 185,
186, 192–93, 195, 201, 206, 211, 241, 267,
268; definition of, 19–23

Areitos, 15, 35, 42
Arguedas, José María, 200–201
Aristotle, 4, 8–9, 15, 148–49, 236, 261–62
Artaud, Antonin, xiv, 4, 10, 23, 77, 105–7
Ashcroft, John, 260, 277
Astiz, Alfredo, 182
Atahualpa, 31
Austin, J. L., 5, 7, 125
Avila, Fray Francisco de, 34, 36
Aymara, 14, 192
Aztecs. *See* Mexica

Bakhtin, Mikhail, 22
Barthes, Roland, 25, 28, 177, 182
Barta, Roger, 93
Bauch, Pina, 214, 232
Baudrillard, Jean, 131
Bellevue Hospital, 245, 249
Benjamin, Walter, 147
Bhabha, Homi, 71, 102–3, 153
Blair, Tony, 151
Boal, Augusto, 197, 211, 227, 234
Botánica, 114–19
Bourdieu, Pierre, 31

Brecht, Bertolt, 10, 12, 32, 67, 105–8, 194, 197, 214, 223

Bronfen, Elisabeth, 145

Browning, Barbara, xvi

Buenaventura, Enrique, 196, 227

Bush, George W., 234, 244, 262, 276

Butler, Judith, 5, 121, 148

Calmecac, 18, 35

Camp, 113, 125, 126–30

Cantares, 35

Capitalism, 198, 228, 276

Carballido, Emilio, 79–86, 103–8; *Yo también hablo de la rosa*, 79–80, 83–86, 103–9

Carruthers, Mary, 24

Case, Sue-Ellen, 68

Catholic Church, 1, 28, 39, 44–50, 63, 112, 114, 120, 153, 175, 228

Census 2000, 122

Cervantes, Miguel de, 73

Charles, A., 135, 157

Chico, 135, 155–60, 255

CIA, 161, 182, 188

Cisneros, Sandra, 99–100

Citizenship, 3, 130–31, 252

Class, 114–20, 121, 122–23, 125–28, 269

Coatlicue, 50, 220

Codices, 17, 34

Colonialism, 33–43, 67, 73–75, 130, 134, 153, 155, 194, 209, 210, 211, 227–28, 232, 271; and postcolonialism, 155, 271; and racial formation, 87–109

Columbus, Christopher, 21, 45, 55–64, 68, 69, 76, 93, 223

Connerton, Paul, 54, 82

Conquergood, Dwight, 27

Conquest, xviii, 13, 17–18, 125, 193, 228, 273; scenarios of, 29–33, 55–64, 70

Cope, Douglas R., 88

Corpus Christi, 10, 49

Cortés, Hernán, 31, 46

Coyolxauhqui, 91

Curandero, 114, 124

Cursi, 125–26

Dawkins, Richard, 173, 188

Debord, Guy, 13, 135, 145, 228, 233

de Bry, Theodoro, 56, 61–62

de Certeau, Michel, 13, 19, 22, 24, 29

Decipherability, 131, 212, 227; and indecipherability, xiv, 37, 60, 97, 229, 271

De la Vega, El Inca Garcilaso, 95

Derrida, Jacques, 5–6, 25, 142, 247

Díaz del Castillo, Bernal, 91

Digital technologies, xix, 4–5, 16, 22, 154

Dirty War: in Argentina, 169–71, 273, 274; in Brazil, 217, 228; in Peru, 202

Disappearance, 8, 16, 20, 22, 34, 39, 41, 143, 151, 153, 193, 204–5, 247, 276; children of the disappeared, 169, 183–86; the disappeared, 160, 168–70, 177–89, 252. *See also* H.I.J.O.S.

DNA, 25, 176–77

Durán, Fray Diego, 33–34, 45

Edict, 43

Ephemeral, 5, 9, 19, 36, 38–39, 193, 211

Episodic structure, 105–6, 274–78

Escrache, 14, 161–83; definition, 180–82

Ethnicity, 86–93

Ethnography, 75–78

Eugenics, 98

Evita. *See* Perón, Eva

Feminism, 152

Fetish, 37–38, 67, 144, 154

Florentine Codex. See Sahagún, Fray Bernardino de

Flores, Richard, 20

Florescano, Enrique, 17

Fox, Vicente, 1

Freire, Paulo, 214, 236

Freud, Sigmund, 25, 121

Memes, 4, 173–74

Memorial walls, 135, 146, 157

Memory, 8, 16, 19, 21, 24–25, 35, 80, 82, 118, 178–79, 185, 210; as act, 82–83; archival, 22; circuits of, 195; communal, 193, 211; cultural, 82–83, 86–93; custodian of, 89; ethnic, 21; lieux de mémoire, 21–22; living, 35; milieux de mémoire, 21–22; paths, 36, 210; as political practice, 179–80; traumatic, 169, 180, 187, 209

Mercado, Walter, 110–21, 125–32

Mestizaje, 79, 93–103, 119, 192

Mexica, 14, 17, 22, 33–43, 80–81, 83, 113–14, 142

Migra, 130, 147

Migration, 49, 201, 217, 232–33, 262, 271, 276, 277–78

Mimesis, 14, 30, 32, 38, 45, 60, 106, 134; and colonial mimicry, 102–3, 221

Missionary theatre, 45. See also Moors and Christians

Mitchell, W. J. T., 60

Modernity, xviii, 119

Molloy, Sylvia, 231

Moors and Christians, 20, 30–31, 277

Moraga, Cherríe, 99–100, 123

Mothers of the Plaza de Mayo. See Madres de Plaza de Mayo

Mother Teresa, 135, 138, 145, 152–53, 155

Motolinía, Fray Toribio, 10

Murals, 135, 155–60, 232–33

Museums, 66, 178; Museum of Natural History, 267, 269, 272; Whitney Museum, 65, 68

NAFTA, xv, xviii

Nahuas. See Mexica

Náhuatl, 14, 38, 88, 92

Neoliberalism, 182, 275–76

Nepantla, 96–97, 100, 102–3, 153

Nora, Pierre, 21–22

Novak, Lorie, 243, 249

Olin, 14

Oñate, Don Juan de, 31

Ong, Walter, 105–8

Orality, 105–8

Oral literature, 26

Originality, 221

Ortiz, Fernando, 94, 104–9

Pantoja, Julio, 183–87

Pastorela, 20, 277

Patriot Act, 276

Pavis, Patrice, 11

Paz, Octavio, 92–96

Percepticide, 28, 244, 275

Performance, xvi, 1; as claim, 175–76; definitions of, 3–6; and disappearance, 205, 211; as episteme, 3, 67; and ethnography, 75–78; hauntology of, 73, 142–46; indigenous, 44–50, 199, 210; multicoded, 44, 50, 228–29; popular, 196–97, 210; pre-Conquest, 33–50, 203; as protest, 161–65, 168–70, 177–82, 188; and September 11, 255–58; solo, 217, 226–32; translating "performance," 12–15; and trauma, 165–68, 203–11

Performance studies, xvi–ix, 2, 10, 26–27, 34, 125, 193, 266, 278; and ahistoricity, 10, 12; and anthropology, 6–9; overview of field, 6–12; and theatre studies, 6, 9–12; and trauma studies, 165–68, 173

Performatic (performático), 6, 12, 16, 118

Performative, 5–6, 125, 130; "happy," 125

Performativity, 5–6

Perón, Eva, 109, 135, 141, 143–46, 152–53

Phelan, Peggy, xvi, 5, 142–43

Photographs, 192–93, 205, 209, 239–44, 250–58; as evidence, 175–77, 255; as identification, 176, 183–85, 187; as performance, 177–87

Pinochet, Augusto, 187

Pizarro, Francisco, 31, 206

Previously published versions or portions of chapters in this volume include the following: *chapter 1*: "Translating Performance," *Profession 2002* (MLA): 44–50; *chapter 2*: "A Savage Performance: Guillermo Gómez-Peña and Coco Fusco's Couple in the Cage," *TDR* 4, no. 2 (1998); *chapter 5*: "Diana: A Study in Hauntology," in *Mourning Diana: Nation, Culture, and the Performance of Grief*, ed. Adrian Kear and Deborah Lynn Steinberg (London: Routledge, 1999), and "Dancing with Diana: A Study in Hauntology," *TDR* 43, no. 1 (1999): 59–78; *chapter 6*: "'You Are Here': The DNA of Performance," *TDR* 46, no. 1 (2002): 149–69; *chapter 7*: "Staging Social Memory: Yuyachkani," in *Psychoanalysis and Performance*, ed. Patrick Campbell and Adrian Kear (London: Routledge, 2001), "Staging Social Memory," in *The Color of Theater: Race, Ethnicity and Contemporary Performance*, ed. Roberta Uno (London: Athlone, 2001), and "Yuyachkani: Remembering Community," in *Performing Democracy: International Perspectives on Urban Community-based Performance*, ed. Susan Chandler Haedicke and Tobin Nellhaus (Ann Arbor: University of Michigan Press, 2001); *chapter 8*: "The Politics of Indecipherability: Denise Stoklos' 'Civil Disobedience,'" *TDR* 44 (2000); *chapter 9*: "A Different Kind of Tragedy," *Theatre Journal* 54, no. 1 (2002): 95–96.

Diana Taylor is Professor of Performance Studies and Spanish at New York University. She is the author of *Theatre of Crisis: Drama and Politics in Latin America* (1991), which won the Best Book Award from the New England Council on Latin American Studies and honorable mention in the Joe E. Callaway Prize for the Best Book on Drama; and *Disappearing Acts: Spectacles of Gender and Nationalism in Argentina's Dirty War* (Duke University Press, 1997). She is editor of *Stages of Conflict: A Reader of Latin American Theatre and Performance* (forthcoming), and coeditor of *Holy Terrors: Latin American Women Perform* (Duke University Press, 2003), *Defiant Acts/Actos Desafiantes: Four Plays by Diana Raznovich* (2002), *Negotiating Performance in Latin/o America: Gender, Sexuality, and Theatricality* (Duke University Press, 1994), and *The Politics of Motherhood: Activists from Left to Right* (1997), among other books. She is founding director of the Hemispheric Institute of Performance and Politics, funded by the Ford Foundation and the Rockefeller Foundation.

Library of Congress Cataloging-in-Publication Data
Taylor, Diana. The archive and the repertoire : cultural memory and
performance in the Americas / Diana Taylor.
p. cm. — (A John Hope Franklin Center book)
Includes bibliographical references and index.
ISBN 0-8223-3136-5 (alk. paper)
ISBN 0-8223-3123-3 (pbk. : alk. paper)
1. America—Civilization. 2. Memory—Social aspects—America.
3. Performance art—Political aspects—America. 4. Performing
arts—Political aspects—America. 5. America—Ethnic relations.
6. North and south. 7. Postcolonialism—America. 8. Postcolonialism
and the arts—America. 9. Ethnicity—America. 10. Minorities—America—Social
conditions. I. Title. II. John Hope Franklin Center Book (Series)
E20.T39 2003   306.4'84—dc21   2003006808